THE RISE AND FALL OF THE WOMAN OF LETTERS

NORMA CLARKE

PIMLICO

Published by Pimlico 2004

2 4 6 8 10 9 7 5 3 1

Copyright © Norma Clarke 2004

Norma Clarke has asserted her right
under the Copyright, Designs and Patents Act 1988
to be identified as the author of this work

First published in Great Britain by Pimlico 2004

Pimlico
Random House, 20 Vauxhall Bridge Road,
London SW1V 2SA

Random House Australia (Pty) Limited
20 Alfred Street, Milsons Point, Sydney
New South Wales 2061, Australia

Random House New Zealand Limited
18 Poland Road, Glenfield
Auckland 10, New Zealand

Random House South Africa (Pty) Limited
Endulini, 5A Jubilee Road, Parktown 2193, South Africa

Random House UK Limited Reg. No 954009

A CIP catalogue record for this book
is available from the British Library.

ISBN 0-7126-6467-X

Papers used by Random House UK Limited are natural,
recyclable products made from wood grown in sustainable forests.
The manufacturing processes conform to the environmental
regulations of the country of origin.

Typeset by Deltatype Ltd, Birkenhead, Wirral
Printed and bound in Great Britain by
Mackays of Chatham

PIMLICO

647

THE RISE AND FALL OF THE WOMAN OF LETTERS

Educated at the Universities of Lancaster, London and Kent, Norma Clarke is a Senior Lecturer in the English Department, Kingston University. She is the author of five novels for children, numerous articles and several books, including *Ambitious Heights* (1990), and *Dr Johnson's Women* (2000).

Contents

Acknowledgements

The research for this book has been accumulated over many years and in scattered locations, some of which I have undoubtedly forgotten. It is easy to remember the pleasures of a week in Lichfield, crossing the Cathedral Close each morning to walk to the Johnson Birthplace Muscum where Anna Seward's manuscripts were made available to me in a comfortable room at the top of the house. My thanks to the curators, and to the staff at the Lichfield Record Office and Library; the National Library of Scotland, Edinburgh; the Fitzwilliam Library, Cambridge; the Bodleian Library, Oxford; the British Library and the London Library.

I am grateful to the English department at Kingston University which gave me a semester's leave in 2001–2, and the AHRB which, through its research leave scheme, awarded me a matching second semester. It would not have been possible to write the book otherwise. Special thanks to my referees, Catherine Hall, Cora Kaplan and Jenny Uglow, for their support. Funding from the UCLA Center for Seventeenth- and Eighteenth-Century Studies and the William Andrews Clark Memorial Library made it possible for me to travel to California where I participated in the 'Genealogies of Feminism' conference at the Clark Library in October 2001. It is a pleasure to thank Anne Mellor, Felicity Nussbaum, Lynn Hunt and Margaret Jacobs for their hospitality; likewise Carla Hesse and Tom Laqueur who invited me to speak at Berkeley during the same trip. Faculty funding from Kingston University covered accommodation costs for a research trip to the Huntington Library. The award of a stipendiary visiting fellowship at the Institute of Advanced Study, University of Indiana, in September 2002 enabled me to meet and exchange ideas with scholars at Bloomington, especially the Eighteenth Century study group. I thank Sarah Knott and Dror Wahrman for the original invitation, Mary Favret and Deirdre Lynch for sponsoring me, and the scholarly community there for their warm welcome. Staff at the Institute of Advanced Study were unfailingly helpful. Thanks also to the Erasmus Darwin Centre in Lichfield which invited me to speak, and the Johnson Society in London; both provided formidably learned audiences, as did the Centre for Eighteenth-Century Studies at the University of York. Cora Kaplan invited me to give a talk at the University of Southampton and also at Chawton House – an exciting new library and research centre for students of women's writing before 1800. A collective thanks to the many colleagues and friends who have listened and talked, formally and informally, especially fellow researchers on the 'Feminism and Enlightenment' project (1998–2001), directed by Barbara Taylor; and particular thanks to Cora Kaplan, Alison Light and Barbara Taylor who not only read the entire manuscript in its first draft but took the time to go through it carefully with me. I didn't always take their advice but I rewrote a great deal and heeded the appeal for sub-headings, especially when it was echoed by Ellah Allfrey, my editor at Random House, whose close reading and suggestions have been invaluable. It has been a pleasure to work with Will Sulkin, who commissioned the book as a Pimlico Original, and I am grateful to Jenny Uglow at Chatto who recommended it to him. The enthusiasm and effectiveness of my agent, Michal Shavit, of the Wylie Agency has been a delight; and I should also like to mention here my thanks to her predecessor, Rose Gaete, who first approached me after reading *Dr Johnson's Women*. My sons, Nick and William Tosh, continue to keep a sharp eye on developments (and grammar). The book is dedicated to them.

Introduction

Asked to name a female author of the eighteenth century, most people would have to stop and think. Jane Austen wrote *Pride and Prejudice*, *Sense and Sensibility* and *Northanger Abbey* in the 1790s but none of her novels appeared in print until 1811. Mary Wollstonecraft might be known, especially for her ground-breaking feminist polemic, *A Vindication of the Rights of Woman* (1792), and Fanny Burney for the sensationally successful *Evelina* (1778) which Jane Austen enjoyed, and which, along with the later novels, *Cecilia* (1782) and *Camilla* (1796), secured Burney's place in English literary history. So far so good – and I have tried the experiment a number of times. The difficulty begins when we reach back into the mid and early eighteenth century. Someone might mention Sarah Fielding, sister of Henry; or Frances Sheridan, mother of Richard Brinsley; but usually the next name produced will be Aphra Behn.

Aphra Behn, hailed by Virginia Woolf as the first woman writer to earn a living by her pen, died before the eighteenth century began. She was active as a poet, novelist and dramatist in the 1670s and 1680s, a hundred years before *Evelina*. If Aphra Behn was the first (which may or may not be true), who was the second? What happened between Aphra Behn and Fanny Burney? Were there no women writers worthy of being remembered? Of course not. Was literary life so unwelcoming to women that they chose not to be part of it? Not at all. For though their names may not be as well known to us as the great nineteenth-century novelists the Brontë sisters and George Eliot, or the poets Elizabeth Barrett Browning and Christina Rossetti, the simple fact is that they were there. Less simple is why we don't know about them.

The Rise and Fall of the Woman of Letters investigates female authorship in the eighteenth century and it makes available writers who were once well known, women who were admired for their writings, even if, as was sometimes the case, what the public admired was their insistence on privacy. However, as the title suggests, the book aims to do more than bring a number of fascinating individuals into the light of our own day. It also tries to explain why they became obscure, exploring the mechanisms by which some writers enter literary history and others do not, how some become 'lost' and some 'found', some are enabled to 'rise' while others have to 'fall'. These concerns have guided the organisation of the material which unfolds backwards, from the late eighteenth to the late seventeenth century.

I have used the term 'woman of letters' for several reasons. 'Letters', the humanist term for literature and scholarship, incorporates all kinds of literary work and few eighteenth-century writers confined themselves to a single genre. The woman of letters might be a poet and a novelist, a historian and a critic; she might busy herself with translation or religious meditations; she might write for the theatre, edit a magazine, be a ferocious polemicist, or a sage and coolly reasoning philosopher. Typically, she engaged in a variety of bookish pursuits – reading, writing, circulating ideas, keeping up with current debate in the full consciousness that to do so was a way of contributing to the improving cultural stock of the nation. For the most part, her activities were intensely and inescapably political, for politics permeated cultural and scholarly life.

To be a woman of letters was to be a public figure, and this is the second reason for using the term. From the restoration of monarchy in England after 1660 and through to the collapse of prerogative symbolised by the American and French revolutions in the 1770s and 1780s there was, broadly speaking, cultural affirmation for the woman of letters. The 'ingenious' woman, the witty woman, the woman who wrote poems or translated Hebrew and understood theological debates, was admired as an ornament and exception to her sex. If she was a young prodigy like Elizabeth Singer (later Rowe) in the 1690s or Elizabeth Carter in the 1730s, both country girls (one born in Somerset, the other in Kent), her fame might spread to the metropolis and beyond. If she was a bold philosophical thinker, like Mary Astell or Catharine Trotter (later Cockburn) in the 1690s, philosophical men were happy to correspond with her. If she wrote plays, like Susannah Centlivre, theatre managers were pleased to produce them. If she wrote novelistic prose of any kind, publishers were eager to promote it: Delarivier Manley, Elizabeth Thomas, Jane Barker and Eliza Haywood were among those who had no difficulty finding an audience for their work in the early decades of the eighteenth century.

That the rise of the woman of letters should begin with the return of monarchy is no accident; nor that her fall should coincide with the beginnings of democracy and the undermining of a system based on deference. Monarchical rule provided the model for the celebration of female literary power, just as it offered the only form in which women were accorded political power. Kings and queens perched at the apex of a hierarchical system that invested them with divine attributes; they were admired as much (or more) for the rank they occupied as for the qualities they brought to the task of leadership. Similarly, the praise lavished on writers like Katherine Philips, 'the matchless Orinda', and Aphra Behn, 'the divine Astraea', situated them as objects of worship above the rank of ordinary mortals. Philips and Behn may be considered the originating figures in a distinctively female tradition; they were by no means the first women to write seriously, but they were the first to acquire iconic significance. As women they represented the female sex and showed what it was capable of; their example set the standard for other women to emulate. As geniuses they were seen as exceptions to the sex, vessels of the muses, who in their divinity and matchlessness could only be adored not imitated. When Elizabeth Montagu, the wealthy and powerful bluestocking (the name by which intellectual women came to be known in the mid eighteenth century), was dubbed 'queen of the blues', it was in acknowledgement of her will to rule over a literary system conceived on monarchical lines. In this fantasy, built on the socio-historical fact that literature emerged from courtly and aristocratic milieux, those who were admitted were raised by the association and were expected to behave accordingly.

By the end of the eighteenth century, national prosperity, improved educational facilities, a vastly expanded commercial press and the reading and buying public that sustained it, had produced women writers in abundance. Prodigious and ingenious women were everywhere. The mythology of divinity so bound up with aristocratic ideology was largely exploded. What had once been 'high' in a social order based on absolute distinctions of rank might be 'middling' or 'low'. What was 'low' might be 'high', or at least in the process of striving to be so. The eighteenth century witnessed the slow decline of patrician culture which can be traced, among its other manifestations, in the shift of literary power from the country houses of the great to the offices of the major booksellers. In the 1720s, when the publisher Edmund Curll (the so-called 'unspeakable Curll') took writers into his household and into his pay, practising a commercial version of the old aristocratic habit of giving houseroom to estimable writers, this was 'low' compared to the 'high' honour of patronage from, say, the Earl of Dorset who plucked Matthew Prior from a tavern, or the Duke of Weymouth at Longleat whose protégée was the young Elizabeth Singer. By the 1780s, when Mary Wollstonecraft sought out Joseph Johnson in St Paul's Churchyard, she understood that his interest in her signified the possibility of honorable independence: her talents in writing meant she could support herself 'in a comfortable way'. Johnson was a successful publisher well aware (like Edmund Curll earlier) of the commercial value of female authors: he had recently brought out the poems of two 'lisping Sapphos' of seventeen and fourteen. Wollstonecraft readily assented to his proposition that she stay with him for a few weeks and then move into a house that he would find for her. Putting herself under Johnson's protection was not a 'low' move; by contrast, her time as a governess in the aristocratic household of the Kingsborough family had felt to her like servitude.

It was not only lisping Sapphos who were of interest to the public Mary Wollstonecraft aimed to reach. Classicists, historians and literary scholars acknowledged the extraordinary fact that women, disadvantaged by their sex, were producing heavyweight intellectual work. Scholarly bluestocking Elizabeth Carter's translation from ancient

Greek of *All the Works of Epictetus* came out in 1758 and was widely acclaimed; so was Catherine Macaulay's massive *History of England* which ran to eight volumes and was published over a twenty-year span (1763–83). Elizabeth Montagu's *An Essay on the Writings and Genius of Shakespeare* which appeared in 1769 earned her celebrity in both England and France. (The essay was a rebuttal of Voltaire's criticism of Shakespeare.) Montagu's title, which echoed Joseph Warton's *Essay on the Writings and Genius of Pope* (1756), an important early work of literary criticism, as well as her choice of subject, made clear her ambition to position herself at the head of this emerging genre. Clara Reeve, in an 'Address to the Reader' in her *Original Poems on Several Occasions* (1769), explained that there was nothing blameable in recognising and using one's God-given talents. Indeed, it was a duty 'to cultivate, to improve and to communicate'. She went on to describe her own journey to this understanding:

> I formerly believed that I ought not to let myself be known for a scribbler, that my sex was an insuperable objection, that mankind in general were prejudiced against its pretensions to literary merit; but I am now convinced of the mistake, by daily examples to the contrary. I see many female writers favourably received, admitted into the rank of authors, and amply rewarded by the public; I have been encouraged by their success, to offer myself as a candidate for the same advantages.

Being known as 'a scribbler' might be problematic, but by 1769 a woman could make use of more dignified formulations: she could be 'admitted into the rank of authors'.

English literature as we understand it came into being in this period in the shift from the classics to the vernacular and in the development of textual scholarship, literary history and literary criticism, along with new genres like the novel, literary biography and memoir. The move away from the classics opened a space for women and they began making the novel their own: the astonishingly prolific Eliza Haywood dominated for almost four decades after *Love in Excess* (1719), so much so that in the 1730s Henry Fielding put her in a play as 'Mrs Novel'. But the status of the novel as a literary form was equivocal. Unlike poetry and drama, it had no classical antecedents; it offered no means by which authors could feel themselves enrolled in a lineage that reached back to antiquity and might reach forward into posterity. In the hierarchy of genres poetry was high, the novel low. Poetic and dramatic criticism, by contrast, could share in the high status of the works and writers discussed and be rooted in a classical past by references to Aristotle, Longinus and others.

For many women, the novel was a form to be avoided, especially because of its association with tales of illicit love. Apart from Eliza Haywood, only three of the early eighteenth-century writers discussed in this book – Jane Barker, Delarivier Manley and Mary Davys – were novelists, and none of them exclusively so. Jane Barker was a poet and autobiographer; Delarivier Manley a poet, dramatist, political propagandist and autobiographer; and Mary Davys a dramatist. Of the others, Elizabeth Elstob was an Anglo-Saxon scholar; Elizabeth Thomas a literary critic and poet; Anne Finch a poet; Catharine Trotter Cockburn a dramatist and philosopher; Elizabeth Singer Rowe a poet who later published short prose fictions; Martha Fowke Sansom a poet and autobiographer; Lady Mary Wortley Montagu a poet and letter writer; and Anna Seward a poet, literary critic and letter writer. The many women who *did* write novels in the middle and later decades of the eighteenth century, such as Sarah Fielding, Sarah Scott, Charlotte Lennox, Frances Sheridan and others, often took pains to distinguish themselves from 'low' practitioners like Eliza Haywood, a habit of rejection that earned a famous rebuke from Jane Austen in *Northanger Abbey*.[1]

Some readers will be uneasy about a chronology which locates a 'rise' for the woman of letters in the late seventeenth century and a 'fall' in the late eighteenth. Was it not at the end of the eighteenth century that, in the words of Virginia Woolf, 'the middle class woman began to write'? The answer is both yes and no. Woolf herself acknowledged that there was a longer history when she added:

> masterpieces are not single and solitary births; they are the outcome of many years of thinking in common, of thinking by the body of the people, so that the experience of the mass is behind the single voice. Jane Austen should

have laid a wreath upon the grave of Fanny Burney, and George Eliot done homage to the robust shade of Eliza Carter.[2]

In fact, Jane Austen did pay her dues to Fanny Burney, naming her in *Northanger Abbey* as being among the novelists whose knowledge of human nature and whose wit and humour 'conveyed to the world in the best chosen language' were slighted by those who preferred to be seen reading the *Spectator*. But the general point, which both Austen and Woolf understood, remains an important one: the middle-class woman writer already had a history when she 'began' to write at the end of the eighteenth century. The problem was that she was not supposed to know about it, and perhaps genuinely didn't. Fanny Burney should have laid a wreath on the grave of Jane Barker or Delarivier Manley. That she did not do so and was never likely to is an important fact in itself.

The generation of women who came of age as writers in the 1770s and 1780s entered on a mixed inheritance. The bluestockings had made high achievement praiseworthy, but the duty to cultivate talent which Clara Reeve pointed to was by no means straightforward. In the classical texts which were the foundation of male education at the time, learning and lewdness in women came together. Juvenal warned that women who read a great deal and conversed freely with men upon learned topics became correspondingly bold in their sexual behaviour, and – worse – then used their wit to justify libidinous ways. This model permeated eighteenth-century thinking. It identified the pleasures of study and the delight of unfettered enquiry with a general loosening of restraints. Independence of mind in women signalled the likelihood of disreputable freedoms with the body.

Women believed this too, if not about themselves then certainly about other women. The conduct of female writers in the past supposedly illustrated it. Thus, if talent were to be developed in a woman who seemed capable of producing work of literary merit, the consciousness of that talent had best be free from 'pride, impudence and self-conceit'. She had to show that she was virtuous. Virtue was identifiable by modest behaviour, not just sexual modesty but modesty about having talent. John Duncombe in *The Feminiad* (1754) explained that women who 'prize / Their own high talents . . . deserv'd contempt'. So-called 'conceit' of this sort was among the vices: vice was 'bold', noisy and 'unblushing'. Those identified as 'vice's friends' in the past were to be passed over in silence and veiled from sight. Duncombe made brief mention of Delarivier Manley, Aphra Behn and Susannah Centlivre, all of whom had been 'admitted into the rank of authors' in earlier eras, but only to say that they could not be included in his poem. Female authors from the first half of the eighteenth century who came into the category of the vicious included those who noisily and unblushingly laid claim to authorial personae, such as Eliza Haywood and Laetitia Pilkington.

Duncombe's *The Feminiad* was one of a number of texts which promoted elevated images of the woman writer, putting into verse the bluestocking agenda which dominated English letters for much of the middle and later eighteenth century. The bluestocking movement succeeded in uncoupling the Juvenalian link between learning and lewdness. (In its place emerged an alternative stereotype of the intellectual woman as a mannish, sexless creature.) Led by upper-class women imbued with a vision of the English past in which 'great ladies' in their country houses had engaged in literary projects as a function of sociability and rank, the early bluestockings reached out of their own sphere to the bright and educated daughters and sons of clergy, doctors, lawyers and the like, and sometimes – though this tended to be more fraught – to milkwomen, shoemakers and laundresses, aiming to create constituencies that were modelled on country-house coteries. Leisure was a sign of social elevation. Learning and literature – letters – properly deployed, showed that leisure had been well used; it added virtue to privilege. Approved knowledge was not to be hoarded, it was to be shared. The vision was of mixed-sex gatherings where minds mingled and words were valued as products of the mind. The appetitive body and its desires, be it for sex or food, ribbons or jewels (the milkwoman poet Ann Yearsley's purchase of ribbons upset her bluestocking patron Hannah More), was not valued.

The bluestockings opened up the conversation of the leisured classes to carefully selected individuals from lower down the social scale who showed their willingness to be improved and governed. If there was no room in this for the body, nor could commerce be asserted as a value: the 'scribbler' who wrote for pay was a lower order of life, a Grub Street hack, or in Virginia Woolf's disdainful image of Eliza Haywood, 'a domestic house fly'.[3] The bluestockings were uncomfortable about bodies (and often uncomfortable *in* them) and about payment, even though numbers of them, including Elizabeth Carter, Clara Reeve and Hester Chapone, badly needed the money. Propaganda against 'scribblers' was intense, much of it emanating from scribbling types themselves, those who were dependent on the commercial press whilst seeking approval from the aristocracy.

Richard Samuel's portrait, *The Nine Living Muses of Great Britain*, of 1778, depicting nine prominent women of arts and letters, marked a high point in the celebration of virtuous female talent as a social good. These women, whose activities spanned all kinds of writing (Montagu, Carter and Macaulay, along with Anna Barbauld, Elizabeth Griffith, Hannah More and Charlotte Lennox) as well as the performance of vocal music (Elizabeth Linley) and painting (Angelica Kauffman), were to be admired to the point of worship – the setting was the Temple of Apollo and they were, after all, 'muses' – and emulated. The painter made no attempt at creating individual likeness but that was not the point. In its printed version as an engraving in *Johnson's Ladies New and Polite Pocket Memorandum for 1778*, the painting had wide circulation and symbolic meaning. The women were icons of Englishness rather than individuals. Elizabeth Montagu wrote to Elizabeth Carter with a bravura amusement that betrayed just a little unease: 'it is charming to think how our praises will ride about the world in everybody's pocket. Unless we could be put into a popular ballad, set to a favourite old English tune, I do not see how we could become more universally celebrated.'[4]

This universal celebration was not to last. The bluestocking ideal did not survive the combined impact of political upheaval and commercial expansion. ('Bluestocking' became a pejorative expression well before the century was out.) Its values lingered on, however, not least in the critical division between 'high' or 'literary' and 'low' or 'popular' writings. In the transformations of the Romantic movement, writings categorised as 'high' and 'canonical' became gendered as male, 'low' and 'popular' as female. In this sense the Romantic period marks an end, or 'fall', for the woman of letters as the eighteenth century knew her.

As for her rise, the extent of women's involvement in literary activity in the late seventeenth and early eighteenth centuries is only now beginning to be understood. By focusing on some key figures –

9

Elizabeth Singer Rowe, Jane Barker, Delarivier Manley, Elizabeth Elstob, Catharine Trotter Cockburn and Elizabeth Thomas in particular – I have tried to make available for a general readership some of the exciting developments in scholarship of the period.

As well as reflecting the chronology I have outlined, the title, *The Rise and Fall of the Woman of Letters*, is also intended to capture the characteristic movement of individuals who came to public attention and fell into obscurity again – a repeated pattern within the period. This is a fact of literary life but it has particular relevance for those of us who write about women writers of the past, given the widespread assumption until very recently that women were denied a place in culture and were never famous except when 'fame' rhymed with 'shame'.

That Anna Seward became obscure is readily understood; that she was famous – as a poet, a critic and as 'Britain's Muse' – is much harder to convey.[5] This book begins with Seward because she was a characteristic product of the bluestocking era: a provincial clergyman's daughter able to imagine herself high within a literary system based on rank. Growing up in the 1740s and 1750s when liberal progressives like her own father were well disposed towards intellectuality in women (in 1748 Thomas Seward published his poem, 'The Female Right to Literature'), she imbibed a sense of entitlement that remained with her to her death in 1809. 'Miss Seward' was a figure of national repute whose pronouncements were attended to, whether she was discussing the relative merits of Dryden and Pope in the *Gentleman's Magazine*, or insisting on Dr Johnson's limitations as a literary critic. English literature, especially poetry (or, as she would say, 'the poetic science'), was her passion. At a time when criticism was still in its infancy, she constructed an authoritative role for herself, espousing the absolute value of a literary canon based on correct critical principles, defended by self-selected elites – readers and writers like herself who were independent of booksellers and patrons, and whose judgements were arrived at after diligent study and thought. Key to her project was the decision to enshrine her views in a literary correspondence conducted for most of her adult life, which she intended would be published after her death.[6]

There were numerous provincial circles such as the one Anna Seward presided over at Lichfield, full of men and women of 'taste' who took seriously their duty to form and monitor the nation's culture. Not infrequently, the central figure in such circles was a woman of exceptional abilities. Her renown brought lustre to the local community, and it might bring celebrated visitors. William Hayley, 'the Bard of Eartham', was the most famous poet of the day when in 1781 he wrote and invited himself along to meet Miss Seward, 'the Swan of Lichfield'. He stayed two weeks in her home. The following summer she travelled to Sussex to stay with Hayley, his wife and the painter George Romney. There was no hint that the unmarried poetess's freedom might betoken sexual impropriety, though Hayley had an illegitimate son, Tom, whose mother was the daughter of his housekeeper, and Romney had abandoned his wife twenty years earlier. Bringing her literary passions, 'the sprightly charms of her social character, and ... the graces of a majestic person' as Hayley put it, Miss Seward settled for six weeks, thrilled by Hayley's conversation and Romney's talent. Hayley and Seward's ecstatic delight in each other as king and queen of the national literature became public knowledge since they each published poems on the subject. They were mocked for authorial vanity, but not for other putative sins.[7]

Hayley saw in his exciting new friend a physical resemblance to Elizabeth I. The virgin queen was a suggestive role model for the bluestockings, partly because her reign was so rich in enduring literary works, and partly because she was a scholar and writer herself. Elizabeth's use of the idea of virginity was an important element in the representation of her power. The deference that was paid to leading bluestockings and the cultural authority invested in them did not require them to be virgins as such but it was complicated by sex and marriage, if not always in practice then certainly symbolically, because of the absolute requirement (enshrined in the marriage vows) that a woman obey her husband. By 1781, Seward had already struggled with this dilemma and reached her own solution. She had decided that she would probably never marry. Committed to what she called her 'celibaic spinsterhood', she was, however, established in a relationship with the man whom she loved above all others. He, unfortunately, was already married.

There is little doubt that Seward's reputation as an exceptional woman and the bluestocking insistence on women's entitlement to sociable interchange with like-minded men made it possible for her to live openly (though not co-habiting) as the companion of John Saville, the vicar-choral of Lichfield Cathedral. Her triumph was that she refused to give him up. She forced the world to accept the relationship on her terms, as a union of soulmates tragically denied full expression. It was a union that extended across forty-three years – longer than most marriages – until Saville's death in 1803. Some scandal did, of course, attach itself to her name as a consequence, but what is more remarkable is her ability to ride that scandal. She neither left the country, as Helen Maria Williams did, nor was she forced to endure the obloquy poured on Mary Wollstonecraft after William Godwin published a memoir of his wife's life and spoke openly about her former lovers.

Anna Seward's ambitions were directed towards posterity: she believed her genius and application had earned her a place in English literary history. Men cared about posterity too (it was one of the commonplaces of eighteenth-century literature that posterity ranked higher than present company) but an alert eighteenth-century woman had cause to take special measures to ensure her survival. Seward had followed the fortunes, in life and death, of numerous female authors. She was anxious that *her* version of her story should survive in as complete a form as possible, and she edited and re-edited her papers with this in mind throughout her life. The letters were key to this project, for they displayed her critical acumen and critical authority in a form which incorporated other people's acknowledgement of the significance of her views. Seward hoped to bequeath to posterity her status as well as her opinions. But posterity did not remember that eighteenth-century culture had celebrated the woman of letters; and quite soon it ceased even to know that a girl born in 1742 could grow up and imagine a future for herself in the annals of the nation's literature.

Chapter One

ANNA SEWARD, BLUESTOCKING

Prior tells us, that every man of ability should, either by compass, the
pencil, the pen, or the sword, leave his name in life's visit.

Anna Seward[1]

Leaving a name in life's visit

In 1784 Anna Seward (pronounced See-ward), a provincial clergyman's
daughter, began transcribing her letters. The laborious copying out was
no light undertaking since she had an extensive network of correspondents, but she had decided that the letters should be published after her
death as a record of her life and opinions. The transcripts, which were
to grow into thirteen thick volumes (though these represented less than
a twelfth of those she actually wrote), were frequently returned to in the
years that followed: they were read over, edited, rewritten – often more
than once. In 1807, in poor health and knowing that she was unlikely to
live much longer, she prepared them for the press. She spent much time
planning how her posthumous works should be put before the public,
deciding that she would bequeath the letters to Constable on condition
that he brought out the volumes at the rate of two per year. Meanwhile,
she also began negotiations for a complete collection of her poetry and
prose, published and unpublished. She had arranged these and
estimated that they would run to six or possibly eight volumes of verse
and four of miscellaneous prose in addition to the thirteen volumes of
letters. Walter Scott, who had agreed to be her literary executor,
conducted negotiations for her. She set a high price on her works: she

wanted one thousand guineas plus fifty copies to give out as presents – that is, fifty complete sets of the ten or twelve volumes.

Anna Seward was a poet. By 1784, when she took the decision to preserve copies of selected letters, she had already established for herself a national reputation. Her published output was relatively small, a fact which neither inhibited acclaim nor diminished her own sense of herself as an important writer. There was the 'Elegy on Captain Cook', published in 1779, and the 'Monody on the Death of Major Andre' (1780), two substantial poems which extended what had until then been a local reputation in Lichfield and Bath, where she had won the prizes at Lady Miller's Batheaston poetry contests. Most importantly, there was her novel-poem, *Louisa*, which was a great success, going into four editions on its appearance in 1784. James Boswell reviewed *Louisa* favourably, as did William Hayley. One purpose of the correspondence was to circulate information of this sort, promoting an image of herself in the minds of individuals who would then pass it around their own circles. 'You will be kindly gratified to hear,' she wrote to her correspondent the Revd Thomas Whalley, author of the well-received poem, *Edwy and Edilda*, and a wealthy Bath socialite, 'that I receive the highest encomiums upon my poem, *Louisa*, by the first literary characters of the age. I enclose the beautiful eulogium with which it has been honored by Mr Hayley. This eulogium has appeared in several of the public prints.'[2]

Constable declined to pay a thousand guineas and there was never to be a twenty-five-volume edition of Seward's complete works. Nor, when it came to it, did he issue the thirteen volumes of letters as instructed. After Seward's death in 1809, he published a selection in six volumes, bringing them out all at once in 1811. (It is not known where the originals are or if they survive.) Robert Southey thought she had been 'ill-used' and that the publisher had 'no other thought than how to make the most immediate profit by the bequest'.[3]

Walter Scott published in full the posthumous letter he received from Seward, giving him directions about what he was to do. This explained that he had exclusive copyright to all the published and unpublished verse, four sermons and a critical dissertation, and a collection of 'juvenile' letters from 1762 to 1768. Everything had been made ready for the press and there were 'specified directions to the printer through their whole course'. What Scott was explicitly *not* bequeathed were the transcribed letters from 1784. He was not trusted with these treasured materials, apparently, because they included strongly expressed political views with which she knew he did not agree. Scott was a Tory while Seward was a Whig and passionately opposed to what she called the 'sanguinary' war policy of William Pitt's government.

> To Mr Constable, rather than to yourself, have they been bequeathed, on account of the political principles which, during many past years, they breathed. Fervent indeed, and uniform, was my abhorrence of the dreadful system in our cabinet, which has reduced the continent to utter vassalage, and endangered the independence of Great Britain. Yet I know these opinions are too hostile to your friendships and connections with the belligerent party, for the possibility of it being agreeable to you to become the editor of those twelve epistolary volumes.[4]

The literary correspondence of a provincial spinster poet might seem an unlikely location for incendiary political opinions. This seems to have been Scott's view. He claimed that he had wanted nothing to do with editing the letters, assuming that they were full of scandal and tittle-tattle, and having, as he put it to his friend Joanna Baillie, 'a particular aversion at perpetuating that sort of gossip'.[5] Nor did he much enjoy what he *had* agreed to do, which was to edit the poetry (or rather, proofread, since Seward had already edited them heavily herself) and provide a biographical essay.

Unfortunately, Scott had a low opinion of the poetry, telling Baillie he thought it 'execrable'; and though he had been charmed by Seward when they met and 'really liked her' – indeed, he allowed himself to be persuaded to stay two nights when he had planned only a brief call: 'such visits', his hostess crowed, were 'the most high-prized honours which my writings have procured for me' – the charm did not survive the arrival of the manuscripts. He doubted what he called 'the general reception' her poems were likely to meet. He decided to reduce the complete works down from a potential twelve volumes to three, suppressing an unfinished epic, *Telemachus*, which Seward considered her life's major work in poetry, and removing the poems by her father which she had wanted to include.

Scott found the job wearisome (he called it his 'penance'). In his biographical essay he drew attention to the public nature of Seward's fame, a fact which in itself justified the memorialising of her life: 'The name of Anna Seward,' he began, 'has for many years held a high rank in the annals of British literature; and the public has a right to claim, upon the present occasion, some brief memorials of her by whom it was distinguished.' The essay as a whole offered a measured, affectionate and shrewd assessment of a woman who represented for him a bygone era, but there was no disguising his own feelings: a barrage of urbane double negatives unconsciously stressed the 'uniform', 'idle', 'tedious', and 'uninstructive' aspects of his task: 'As the tenor of her life was retired, though not secluded, and uniform, though not idle, the task of detailing its events can neither be tedious nor uninstructive.'

Robert Southey, another young man of letters who, like Scott, was flattered by and, in professional terms, understood the value of Anna Seward's approbation, seems to have been jealous that Seward chose Scott as her literary executor. In Southey, Seward had recognised one of the 'rising stars' of the new generation (along with Coleridge whom she also admired), considering Southey's *Joan of Arc* to approach 'in genius, nearer the *Paradise Lost* than any other epic attempt in our language'. Of *Thalaba* she had some criticisms, but by *Madoc* she was enraptured. Southey's name was ever on her lips and in her letters. He began a correspondence in 1807, and in the summer of 1808 made a visit, accompanied by a friend, Miss Barker, a young woman who had 'a quick sense of the ludicrous'. On this first meeting, the young people were shown up to find the sexagenarian Miss Seward at her writing desk, copying out some verses of her own in Southey's praise. Southey noted her beautiful eyes, the hair in unexpectedly youthful ringlets, her 'warmth', 'liveliness' and 'cordiality' – though all a little too youthful, too spirited – and then described the 'tragi-comic or comico-tragic' scene that followed:

> After a greeting so complimentary that I would gladly have insinuated myself into a nut-shell, to have been hidden from it, she told me that she had that minute finished transcribing some verses upon one of my poems – she would read them to me, and entreated me to point out anything that might be amended in them. I took my seat, and, by favour of a blessed table,

placed my elbow so that I could hide my face by leaning it upon my hand, and have the help of that hand to keep down the risible muscles, while I listened to my own praise and glory set forth, in sonorous rhymes, and declared by one who read them with theatrical effect. Opposite to me sat my friend Miss Barker, towards whom I dared not raise an eye, and who was in as much fear of a glance from me as I was of one from her.[6]

The giggling pair stayed two days and no doubt had other occasions to 'keep down the risible muscles' since reading aloud in a theatrical manner was Anna Seward's forte. The future Poet Laureate's difficulty in keeping a straight face didn't stop him regretting, after her death, that she had not left him some memento in her will: 'She might have left me a set of her works, or some piece of her plate, and I should have shown such a token with pleasure.' She was a collectable and her name carried a charge.

Young men like Walter Scott and Robert Southey were the coming generation and they paid homage to the leading lights of the generation that had gone before, a number of whom were bluestocking women. The books that were important to them as literary men, such as Boswell's *Life of Samuel Johnson*, which had appeared in 1791, evoked a world Seward had been part of. Whether her own poetry was good or not was a secondary consideration; what attracted them was her celebrity. She had made herself into a powerful figure whose opinions influenced other people's ideas about poetry. One contributor to the *Gentleman's Magazine* declared that it would be hard to produce any female writer who equalled her.

In style and content, however, Anna Seward had become old-fashioned. The degree of control she sought to exercise over posthumous publication was one sign of this; another was her unembarrassed self-regard. She expected her considered thoughts to be received as something akin to laws. As a critic, she trusted her own judgement not only about others but also about herself. She did not think she was a great poet, but she did think she was a great (and perhaps the nation's best) critic. She summed up her view of her own abilities in these words:

Many excel me in the power of writing verse; perhaps scarcely one in the vivid and strong sensibility of its excellence, or in the ability to estimate its claims – ability arising from a fifty years sedulous and discriminating study of the best English poets, and of the best translations from the Greek, Roman, and Italian.[7]

There might be merit or mediocrity in her own sonnets and elegies, her verse epistles and paraphrases from Horace, and in any case, like all poetry, they would be subject to the vagaries of fashion and critical opinion. Her real achievement was in reading and evaluation. For fifty years she had brought her 'vivid and strong sensibility' – her enthusiasm – to the study of poetry. Anything which sent her scurrying through the volumes of poetry on the library shelves was a joy to her. She could spend pages arguing the merits of the dropped 'e' in words ending '-ed', citing example after example to prove her point, or discussing the merits and demerits of the Petrarchan sonnet over the Miltonic. Poring over Thomas Warton's edition of Milton's juvenilia she was in ecstasies over the notes. They were 'some of the most exquisite writing I ever beheld', and she read them 'with the same thrill of delight that the poetry on which they comment inspires'. Poetry was a 'science' which could be understood by hard study; poetic criticism could be exquisite and exciting. Purposefully reading and writing, she had made herself into a woman of letters and gained a proud public reputation. This reputation, though it built on the success of her poems, rested most securely on her powers as a literary critic.

It was for her public, both present and future, that Seward began copying and assembling her correspondence (not the letters she received, only those she wrote) in 1784. Scott was wrong in imagining a collection of letters full of 'gossip'. The purpose of the correspondence was to put in place something magisterial and permanent, not a record of the trivial and everyday. It was not about personalities – except her own – but about issues; it was less about actions – except the act of reading – than about thoughts.

Seward dramatised herself as a sedulous and discriminating reader of English literature. She believed she had lived through a time of tremendous achievement in poetry and the arts, one in which the English vernacular tradition had flourished. The achievements of the poets she most admired – Milton, Mason, Collins, Gray, Hayley,

Cowper – were insufficiently appreciated, in her view, because the vernacular tradition was not yet treated with critical seriousness. One of the qualities that distinguished her from others, she claimed, was her capacity to recognise and give credit to contemporary genius. A gentleman's education was an education in the classics. Having no languages (unusually, she did not even read French), Seward made a virtue of her necessities in concentrating on English poetry and working from prose translations of the classics. (Some prose translations, especially the Odes of Horace, were supplied by gentlemen friends for her to paraphrase into English verse which was then published in the *Gentleman's Magazine*.) As a critic, she went further and gave a gendered dimension to the stance she took. 'A masculine education,' she wrote, 'cannot spare from professional study, and the necessary acquisition of languages, the time and attention which I have bestowed on the compositions of my countrymen.'[8]

If the vernacular tradition was in the early stages of formation, so too the institutions of criticism were newly coming into being. There were no departments of English in the universities producing cohorts of scholars of English literature. Professional literary criticism was practised by anonymous reviewers in the *Monthly Review* and the *Critical Review* (founded respectively in 1749 and 1758), some of whom were sensitive and serious in their critical writing, many of whom were hacks. Seward characterised them all as the enemies of originality – 'ingenious composition' – and, because anonymous, as inclined to be motivated by 'spleen'. The history of the reception of English poetry demonstrated, she argued, that the public needed proper guidance: even the 'immortal' Milton's early poems, including *Lycidas* and the sonnets, had 'remained in oblivion full twenty years after the *Paradise Lost* had emerged'. This proved 'the absolute incompetence of the public to discern and estimate the claims of genius, till, by the slow accumulation of the suffrage of kindred talents, it is taught their value'.[9]

For the task of teaching the public she considered herself well qualified. This involved more than polite exchanges about the merits of Milton's juvenilia. Cultural activity carried a responsibility. The forming of taste, arbitrating between this manifestation or that (this poem, that play), the shaping of the imaginary and its expression, was a job of work. It was forming a national literature. It was forming national types, constructing selves around particular values, hence the importance of the vernacular tradition. Seward saw herself as one of the ruling classes – the 'kindred talents' – of English culture, establishing by democratic discussion – 'the slow accumulation of the suffrage' – the bases of English poetry for future generations. Poetry was important to a large public and it was no accident that she was dubbed by an admirer, 'Our British Muse', 'th'immortal Muse of Britain', for her concerns were essentially political, and to be celebrated as the personification of national identity was wholly appropriate.[10]

There was another dimension to her thinking on these matters which perhaps explains why it was in 1784 that she began to select and assemble her correspondence. In December of that year, Samuel Johnson died. He had spent much of the summer in his home town of Lichfield and Seward had seen him frequently, though they were not friends. ('Johnson hated me' was her candid assessment.) Johnson had dominated English letters from the mid eighteenth century. His engagement with literary history and the English language did a great deal to raise the status of literary activity in general, and especially of literary criticism. There was an authority attached to knowledge and judgement which lent a prestige to the activity in which, paradoxical as it may seem, the creation of literature itself, even poetry but especially fiction, did not share. As a young writer, Seward had studied him closely, compared him with Addison, whose *Spectator* essays were required reading for all young women, and rated him far above the earlier writer. In this opinion she deliberately confounded stereotypical expectations: supposedly, 'the delicacy of female taste' preferred Addison. She showed by an analytic comparison of the two men that Johnson's style was superior, at the same time demonstrating her own superiority to what she identified as 'prejudices' about female taste.

Modelling herself on Johnson, Seward became increasingly critical of his methods. What she admired in Johnson was the 'truth and daylight' of his reasoning; what she disliked were the passages where 'passion and prejudice' warped his judgement. This she considered most evident in his *Lives of the Poets* (1779–81) which infuriated her because of the slighting treatment of some of her favourites, especially Thomas Gray, 'the greatest lyric poet the world ever produced', whose *Elegy* was 'one of the most perfect poems ever written'. But she found Johnson in general 'a very indifferent reader of verse', inclined to rely on dogmatic assertions that drew on memory rather than regular rereading. 'He had not patience to examine and compare; yet, on all subjects, had the temerity to decide, without scruple, against the opinions of persons of great ability, who had examined and compared. I believe he seldom looked into the poetry he was criticizing, but pronounced judgement from the recollection of his juvenile impressions.' Milton's *Lycidas* was the test: 'To read it without pleasure – to have read it without frequent recurrence, argues a morbid deficiency in the judgement and the affections.' Johnson 'reprobated' Milton's *Lycidas*, a sign, she believed, that the passion of envy had overwhelmed his reason. Johnson was 'the imperious and gloomy Intolerant'; his influence was 'despotic' and, after *The Lives of the Poets*, malign.[11]

An important object of the correspondence was to keep in place a sustained alternative model of criticism, one based on a fervent (some would say pedantic) close reading. Many of Seward's letters were extended literary essays, defending her favourites or attacking those whom meretricious reviewers had overpraised. Meanwhile, her poems, too, were often driven in quite explicit ways by her reading of established male writers, so that they also functioned as criticism. She began *Louisa*, a sentimental novel-poem in four epistles, after reading Pope and Prior. The poem was inspired by 'an idea of its being possible to unite the impassioned fondness of Pope's Eloisa, with the chaster tenderness of Prior's Emma; avoiding the voluptuousness of the first, and the too-conceding softness of the second'. The 'Epistle to Cornelia' attacked Pope's representations of women, dismissing him as 'the spleenful Bard', 'tetchy' and frustrated, who 'sore with disappointment's galling pain / Hated the sex, to which he sued in vain'. Hogarth's series of pictures, *The Rake's Progress*, was a more truthful version of 'the heart of Woman and the vice of Man!'. In 'Verses to the Rev. William Mason', poetry and criticism came together in chastisement of Mason for not coming to the defence of 'the injured muse' of his friend Thomas Gray. Johnson's account of Gray in *The Lives of the Poets* had been motivated, she insisted, by envy: having wanted in his early days to shine as a poet, Johnson hated those who had acquired more fame as poets than he and had taken on the task of writing their lives to gratify

'that dark passion'. Readers, meanwhile, were also gratified by disparagement of the famous, hence the appeal of such writings. Mason's
silence under the circumstances was shameful. He was ordered to

> Blush, Loiterer, blush, that from thine able arm
> Truth's victor pebbles were not slung ere now,
> The Giant's vaunting prowess to disarm,
> And sink, deep buried in his haughty brow![12]

Johnson's death in 1784, coming hard on the success of *Louisa* – 'the
best and ablest of my productions' – may have prompted Seward to
make a bid for the throne of literary criticism. The 'unqualified praise'
that was showered on Johnson's tomb obscured his 'real' character,
which her privileged place as a Lichfieldian whose grandfather had been
Johnson's schoolmaster enabled her to know.

Boswell's *Tour of the Hebrides* (1786), which she admired, lent
strength to the growing mythic Johnson whose style of literary criticism
was inevitably being emulated. Boswell's account of travelling through
Scotland with Johnson was the immediate provocation for a campaign
which Seward waged from February 1786 until December 1793, mostly
via letters to the *Gentleman's Magazine*, the columns of which she
already considered her home base. The first of these was sent from
Wellesbourne, the country home of new high-ranking friends the
Granvilles, who, along with Court Dewes, another literary correspondent ('a refined gentleman and an excellent scholar'), were related to
Mary Delaney, the celebrated first-generation bluestocking. Thus
protected, Seward went public with views she had already made known
in her own circles.

She was on good terms with Boswell at the time: in the summer of
1784 he had stayed with her. There had even been some sort of
flirtation. Boswell left a sealed note marked 'Read this when alone'
which declared: 'I have been in a flutter ever since we parted ... Write
to me without delay, and as a token enclose me a lock of that charming
auburn hair I admired so much the delicious morning I was last with
you.'[13] Writing to the *Gentleman's Magazine* and signing herself
'Benvolio', Seward praised Boswell for an 'infinitely-entertaining work'
which faithfully reproduced the Johnson she had known, a man full of

'malice and irascibility'. The *Tour of the Hebrides* displayed Johnson's religious intolerance, his bad manners towards the Scots, his meanness to friends like David Garrick, whose role in popularising Shakespeare Johnson refused to credit, and his contemptuous dismissal of rival contemporaries such as Elizabeth Montagu whose *Essay on Shakespeare* he abused. She questioned Boswell's decision to include such matters ('Ought Mr Boswell to have recorded Dr Johnson's unjust contempt of Mrs Montagu's able and beautiful Treatise on Shakespeare in the lifetime of that lady . . . ? An assault upon a reputation so established must startle the public'), but her letter was not an attack on Boswell.

Nor was her second letter, which followed a few months later and which addressed 'the historians of Dr Johnson's life and conversation', an attack on Mrs Piozzi, whose *Anecdotes of the late Samuel Johnson* had also appeared. Seward's point was simple. These 'historians' gave accurate accounts of Johnson: he was 'the late stupendous but frail Dr Johnson', a mixture of 'genius and absurdity, wisdom and folly, penetration and prejudice, devotion and superstition, compassion and malevolence, friendship and envy, truth and sophistry'. And yet they were setting him up as an idol to be worshipped. Johnson had been part of Mrs Piozzi's household for many years, but her intimate memoirs revealed him as a 'human hornet'. Still, Mrs Piozzi opined, 'he was great beyond human comprehension, and good beyond the imitation of perishable beings'.

At the heart of the matter was the question of truth, not the truth of the biographers – both of whom, as Seward observed, followed the precepts laid down by Johnson in his 1750 *Rambler* essay on biography and showed their subject with all his faults – but the truthfulness of the subject. If he was not truthful, could he be good? And if he was not good should he be emulated? The test of his truthfulness was, among other things, those literary opinions which were driven by envy: 'the praise of another was ever a caustic on the mind of Dr Johnson, beneath the smart of which truth and justice were too generally disregarded'.

Seward found in the writings of Boswell and Piozzi a Johnson she recognised, but she drew different conclusions from the stories they told. She was not prepared to put him on 'a noble pedestal'. She castigated Johnson on Piozzi's behalf for his treatment of her. She argued that a man who 'delighted to destroy the self esteem of almost all who approached him by the wounding force of witty and bitter sarcasm' could not be good. His 'inhumanity' made him not only a bad model but a dangerous one. The 'deep stain of malignity' in Johnson revealed by anecdotal evidence and in his *Lives of the Poets*, his 'reviling and tyrannous spirit', the 'internal bitterness' and lack of generosity to the feelings and writings of others, set an alarming precedent for the future of literary criticism and literary biography. It was her 'zeal for the honour of my century, and the reputation of those whose talents are its glory' that animated Seward's campaign. It was in the defence of Milton ('calumniated' by Johnson), Prior, Gray and others that she addressed the reading public and found herself doing battle with Johnson's 'worshippers' and 'enemies' alike.[14]

When Anna Seward read in her beloved Matthew Prior that every man of ability should leave his name in life's visit, she included herself in the designation. She responded eagerly to a culture which made literary knowledge available and which praised those – men and women alike – who cultivated it to a high standard. The leading figure in a provincial coterie, she was able to imagine herself forming national opinion. In her own mind she was more than the equal of the giant Samuel Johnson. Prior's 'finely observed' lines were taken to heart:

> That the distinguished part of men
> By pencil, compass, sword, or pen,
> Should in life's visit leave their name,
> In characters which may proclaim
> That they with ardour strove to raise
> At once their art, and country's praise.[15]

Those blessed with talent had a duty to improve it. This was a widely shared view and it was the basis of the bluestocking agenda.

Becoming a writer

Growing up in Lichfield, where she lived all her life in the Bishop's Palace in the Cathedral Close, Anna Seward had more opportunities than most girls to acquire the self confidence of a bluestocking. Lichfield was a centre of enlightened scientific and literary enquiry. It was the home of Erasmus Darwin, grandfather of the more famous Charles, doctor, botanist, inventor and poet, and a significant early influence on young Anna's development. Her father, Thomas Seward, was canon-residentiary of the cathedral; her mother, Elizabeth Hunter, was the daughter of John Hunter who had been headmaster of the school Samuel Johnson attended. If the Bishop's Palace was, as Richard Edgeworth later wrote, 'the resort of every person in that neighbourhood, who had any taste for letters', it was also the operational base from which an ardent and assertive writer projected the figure of Miss Seward, a woman of feeling and imagination, of judgement, knowledge and opinion, on to the national stage.[16]

Lichfield society had acknowledged her pre-eminence and her identity as a woman of letters even before she published anything: Miss Seward was a 'reigning personage' in their gatherings. She was an intellectual and she made one subject – English literature – and one branch of it – poetry – peculiarly her own. In her spacious rooms in the palace or on the terrace overlooking Stow Vale which she loved, with access to her father's excellent library, she read and wrote. She had no interest in secret or merely 'private' writing, and every interest in being received as a superior woman whose life was dedicated to a serious purpose. There was nothing shy or retiring or self-subduing in her disposition; rather, she had a domineering nature and all the instincts of a pugilist. With her particularly good speaking and reading voice she was in demand for reading aloud, and would recite her own verses, so it is said, with 'a fiery vivacity'; but she also read Shakespeare and Milton, Pope and Gray. Going to spend Christmas 1785 with the Granville and Dewes families at Wellesbourne, she took with her for reading aloud *The Task* by William Cowper, 'the first very distinguished fire of a star lately arisen in our poetic hemisphere', and William Hayley's *Essay on Epic Poetry*, to read from and comment on, interspersing the whole with titbits displaying her personal acquaintance with Hayley. The statuesque figure and general presence – she was a beauty, with brilliant eyes and flowing auburn hair – as well as her dramatic powers, led people to compare her to the actress Sarah Siddons. Seward took the comparison as her due, though she could make fun of her appearance: Erasmus Darwin and herself, two poets walking along together, looked, she said, like the butcher and the fat cook's maid.

Habits of performance began early. By the age of nine, Anna Seward could recite the first three books of Milton's epic *Paradise Lost* and she did so to admiring visitors in the Lichfield drawing room. Educating his daughters himself, her father read Shakespeare and Milton to her when she was barely three. The Revd Seward, at that time editing the plays of Beaumont and Fletcher, was one of a number of scholarly men making the English literary past available to eighteenth-century readers, many of whom, like his own daughters, would have no Latin or Greek. Naturally, he kept up with current publications. Periodicals like the *Gentleman's Magazine* and Johnson's *Rambler* were a feature of life at the Bishop's Palace, as were important new publications like William Warburton's edition of Pope (1751) and Joseph Warton's *An Essay on the Writings and Genius of Pope* (1756). These joined what was a substantial library of English poetry and drama, history, essays and sermons, as well as fiction and miscellanea through which young Nancy had permission to range at will. She was to become a notably well-read woman with a fund of quotation ever at hand.

Her father's pride in her preciosity and his encouragement of her literary enthusiasms were not unusual for the time, though most fathers did not do as Thomas Seward did and put their opinions into verse. In Thomas Seward's 'The Female Right to Literature, in a Letter to a Young Lady from Florence', which appeared in *Dodsley's Collection* (1748), the poet expressed the view that young women's minds should be fed with every kind of knowledge and that they were capable of reaching the topmost heights. A young lady named Athenia, symbolising wisdom, was exhorted:

> Proceed, Athenia, let thy growing mind
> Take every knowledge in of every kind;
> Still on perfection fix thy steady eye,
> Be ever rising, rise thou ne'er so high.[17]

Steeped in literature, she was ambitious to excel. The house she grew up in was associated with gentlemanly learning, having been the home of Gilbert Walmesley, lawyer and scholar, whose patronage had been important to Samuel Johnson, and Lichfield's other famous son, David Garrick. It was 'classic ground' on which 'rising genius' (poor, but male) had been given the 'nutriment of attention and praise'. Palatial in scale (in later years, if it was too icy to go out, Seward could take her daily two-mile walk along the corridors), in size and name alone the Bishop's Palace conferred social elevation. The local literati continued to gather there, card parties and concerts were held, and conversation flowed.

Johnson and Garrick – contemporaries of her father, but poor boys – had left Lichfield for London in 1737 where eventually, after much struggle and poverty, both achieved fame. How was the clergyman's daughter to imagine her literary future? She was not poor; she did not occupy 'an inferior station'. Nor was she male, and without the attention of a Gilbert Walmesley to nurture her 'uncommon talents', to be for her like the sun that ripened the grain, she could not see her way forward. The best families in Lichfield knew her as a precocious child and teenage genius; they showed no inclination to earn immortality for themselves by raising her name from provincial obscurity. At twenty, Seward complained that the lack of such a patron was holding her back: 'Had it been my lot to have been animated by the smiles, and sustained and encouraged in my studies, and in my little sallies of poetic invention, by the applause of a Walmesley, I might perhaps have ventured myself among the candidates for the literary palms.'[18]

Perhaps Lichfield was 'inauspicious soil'. Seward contemplated leaving for London, but without relations living there it is unlikely that she viewed it as a serious option. And, as she acknowledged, life at home had its satisfactions. She and her younger sister, Sarah, had their own apartment, a suite of rooms on the second floor where they read, worked and received guests, often having three or four evenings a week to themselves for 'books, pens, talk'. This freedom was appreciated: 'left so much to ourselves, and perfectly aware of the value of time, how interesting have been our employments, how animated our pleasures!' Under these easy circumstances much could be tolerated, even irritating parents: 'some violence of temper, and vapourish despondency, from causes provokingly trivial, on my mother's part, some absurdities on my father's'. There was an adoptive sister, Honora, to teach:

My father and mother are gone out to a card-party. The curtains are dropt, and the chill white world shut out . . . Little Honora draws her chair to the table as I write, Hawksworth's *Almoran and Hamet* open in her hand. What a beautiful story! – How sublime its moral! Honora looks at me, her eyes sparkling with intellectual avidity – The young mind must not be deprived of its evening nutriment.[19]

Honora was delicate and adored. Sarah was loving and docile: 'Without possessing much of that faculty called genius, my sister has a very intelligent mind.' Anna was the genius in the family, a role she took seriously from an early age. The two younger girls looked up to her. She recorded her sister's remark, 'Ah! Nancy, you lively nymphs, with all the fire and energy of your imaginations, are less competent than we gentler creatures to the fatigues of patient and steady *self-resistance*.' Self-resistance was not part of Anna's agenda, but being a creature of 'fire' and 'energy' brought its own difficulties. Convinced of her own superiority, hot-tempered and outspoken, she clashed with her parents and others. She admitted, 'I cannot always command my resentments.'

People who were unwilling to credit her with genius, such as the Lichfield folk who demurred when Erasmus Darwin, at a crowded party, used the word to describe her, roused such resentments. In her view they merely displayed spite, unwilling to acknowledge in her 'an atom more *mind* than the generality of Misses'.[20] Darwin's approbation was important; he was, after all, a serious poet as well as a man of science and invention.

By comparison with what we know of other women writers, Anna Seward did not lack for support. She had the applause of a Darwin as well as that of her father, even if neither were quite satisfactory – Darwin's sarcasm often wounded her sensibilities, and she claimed that her father had become envious of her poetry after Darwin told him she was the better poet. She rated her father 'a scholar, tho perhaps not a deep one', and little more than a 'tolerable poet'. (Her mother she described as having 'no literary curiosity'.) When Richard Edgeworth came to Lichfield seeking out Erasmus Darwin, he was charmed by the Seward household. Later, he was to marry Honora and earn Anna Seward's lifelong hatred – she blamed him for Honora's early death – but for some years he was one among the many who 'comprehended and tasted those powers of mind which take the *higher* range of intellect' and could recognise and welcome it in the brilliant conversation of the canon's daughter.

It was a commonplace of the time that reason should temper passion. Women, especially, were exhorted to cultivate their reason and beware the force of passion, a message Anna Seward took to heart when she became of marriageable age. Woken one night by thoughts of love, she went to her writing table and wrote as to a female friend:

> How much a more powerful stimulus to awakened attention are the interests of the *heart*, than those of the *understanding*! But may we always strive to encourage and cultivate the *latter*, lest the former, by their monopolizing tendency, confine us to the merely selfish circle; and so depress the dignity, and narrow the extent of minds which nature has, I trust, cast in a superior mould to those of the smart misses who can think and talk of nothing but their gowns, their caps, their laces and their lovers![21]

Passion was more immediately compelling than the cultivation of the mind, but for a young woman imagining a future for herself in literature it represented narrowed options. Anxious to distinguish herself from the 'smart misses', but not uninterested in lovers, Seward's claim to be treated differently from other females rested on the evidence that she *was* different and the ordinary rules did not apply. There was a value attached to being able to talk about Shakespeare and Milton rather than gowns, caps, laces and lovers (and we should remember that this was an era when the 'value' of a marriageable young woman, the exact amount she was worth, was openly discussed and might be printed in the newspapers). Having a 'superior' mind gave her status, it entitled her to some autonomy and self-expression, and allowed her to imagine extending her sphere of action beyond the immediate circle. But these advantages could be attacked from within as well as without: the dismaying 'fact' that pleasurable feeling (desire) was stronger than thought (the will) – 'Alas! How perpetually sensation baffles our free agency!' – had serious implications.

Free agency for a woman, as Seward understood it, was an objective that could be aspired to and it was located in the mind, or will, or understanding. It required hard work and self-discipline. Head represented the higher sphere and heart the lower; if heart, which more or less defined femininity, was allowed to flow unchecked it would overwhelm head. Following the impulses of the heart led women away from free agency, towards a narrowing of their lives and a lessening of their dignity, because the heart had a 'monopolizing tendency'. Heart, or love and sexual feeling, led to marriage; marriage might mean confinement to 'the merely selfish circle'.

Seward's struggle in the years during which she made herself into a writer was to balance her own impulses – the mixture of head and heart – in a way which did not deny desire, but which also did not narrow her intellectual, imaginative and social life. Desire was an essential function of genius and hence the integrity of the desiring self had to be protected. Autonomy was vital, especially in the matter of choosing her own society: the writing life was understood as a social affair, it was not solitary, it depended on the stimulus of like minds. A young man forming himself for a future as a poet or critic might choose to marry but he would not expect to sacrifice his literary ambitions for it. If a young woman of talent married, everything depended on her husband's goodwill since custom and law denied free agency to women once they married. In England, a wife became legally subject to her husband. Once married, a woman ceased to exist as far as English law was concerned. A pamphlet of 1735, *The Hardship of the English Laws in Relation to Wives*, usually ascribed to Sarah Chapone, declared the legal status of married women 'deplorable'; they were put 'in a worse condition than slavery itself'. Slaves had some rights of redress but wives, since they had no existence in law, had none. Marriage was 'irrevocable', and divorce effectively out of the question.

The challenge was to ensure that reason entered into the choice of a husband: head not heart should make the crucial decision. Dignity need not be depressed and happiness was possible so long as the man had similar intellectual abilities. Anna Seward's 'petition to the ruling star of my destiny' was to be granted 'an *interesting* caro sposo', by which she meant one whose interest in literature matched her own. A 'marriage of mental inequality' was a dreadful prospect, to avoid which it was imperative that she use her mind to control desire.[22]

The terms in which Seward thought about these matters derived as much from her poetic and literary studies as from daily life in Lichfield. She was immersed in Shakespeare and Milton, Matthew Prior and Alexander Pope, Samuel Richardson and Jean-Jacques Rousseau. No ardent reader of these eighteenth-century favourites could fail to notice that questions about female virtue and female agency were central to their works. Even more explicitly, a number of the most widely read and discussed texts of the time engaged directly with the very issue that concerned herself, dramatising the dilemmas that faced not just young women but *superior* women of marriageable age.

As a young writer, Seward wrote and thought about her own life by taking up characters and themes from male writers. She responded to conversations begun in poems from the early eighteenth century, especially Prior's 'Henry and Emma' and Pope's 'Eloisa to Abelard' and *The Rape of the Lock*; and she read, rewrote and imaginatively lived the characters and situations in Richardson's *Clarissa, or The History of a Young Lady* and Rousseau's *Julie, ou la Nouvelle Héloïse*, the two most influential novels of the mid century.[23] Young women were by no means the only readers of these texts: fathers and mothers, brothers and cousins, aunts and uncles, bluestockings and 'smart misses', aristocrats and commoners, men of science like Erasmus Darwin and clergymen like Canon Seward all read and formed some of their views of life, and female choices – especially with regard to men and marriage – from them. Nevertheless, for a young woman who was also an aspiring writer, there was an additional appeal.

Richardson's heroines in *Pamela* and *Clarissa* were, like Rousseau's Julie in *La Nouvelle Héloïse*, women with pens in their hands. Like Pope's Eloisa in 'Eloisa to Abelard', they were at once 'natural' and involuntary authors, writing 'to the moment', and telling their stories in epistolary form to a correspondent. The issue at the heart of *Clarissa* concerned female autonomy and agency. Daughters should obey fathers and fathers were entitled to require obedience from their daughters; wives had to obey husbands; but Clarissa, a virtuous, high-minded, ardent and intelligent young woman, was betrayed by the men who should have protected her. The behaviour of the men in this novel, told across eight volumes and over a million words – cold and greedy father and brother, hopeful or scheming lovers – served only to destroy a woman of integrity who had committed no fault except, perhaps, the fault of pride in thinking she could 'rescue' the rake Lovelace from his wicked ways.

Heartlessly tricked by Lovelace into lodging in a brothel, and subsequently drugged and raped, Clarissa's sexual fall was not a consequence of her sexual desire. Rousseau's *La Nouvelle Héloïse*, first translated into English in 1761, offered a heroine who gave in – once – to sexual passion. Anna Seward was an early reader and admirer, advising her friends about the novel the following year, unsure whether she thought it was safe or not. She wanted men to read it so that they would become more sensitive but she had doubts about its 'softening' tendency where women readers were concerned. *La Nouvelle Héloïse* swept young women off their feet. (Men too.) In France, it went through almost seventy editions before the century was out. Julie was the 'new' Héloïse because the story was based, like Pope's 'Eloisa to Abelard', on the well-known tale of the twelfth-century monk, Abelard, and his brilliant pupil, Héloïse, whose letters survived and had been re-worked by numerous writers. Abelard and Héloïse, 'two of the most distinguished persons of their age in learning and beauty' as Pope put it, fell in love and had an affair which ended tragically. Héloïse (a canon's daughter) had tried to reconcile the desires of the heart with the superior understanding of the head: she was a scholar but also a passionate woman. Her letters, which Pope drew on more closely for his poem, 'Eloisa to Abelard', than Rousseau did for his novel, revealed 'the struggles of grace and nature, virtue and passion'.

All over Europe, young women of passion and intellect adopted the name Julie, or Julia, as a sign of their identification with Rousseau's compelling version of the legendary figure. Novelists, including Helen Maria Williams, named their heroines after her. Anna Seward became 'Julia'. It was inevitable. The persona reflected her preoccupations as a young writer. Already familiar with Pope's version, which vividly endorsed Eloisa's sexuality and the desire of lovers for that 'happy state! when souls each other draw / When love is liberty, and nature, law', what she took from Rousseau (who had in turn drawn much of his inspiration from Richardson's *Clarissa*) had far-reaching implications for the way she figured herself as a writer.

Pope's Eloisa, like the original, was a nun, depicted in her convent having renounced the world. Rousseau, however, presented scenes which eroticised the pupil/teacher relationship within gentry house-holds. He dramatised a common experience: the passion that flowed between teacher and taught in the private experience of shared reading. And he established a powerful sentimental paradigm: the tragedy of *La*

Nouvelle Héloïse lay in the fact that the tutor's social rank was lower than that of his employers, while his intellectual and spiritual capacities (as well as his sexual charms) were greater. Technically, too, *La Nouvelle Héloïse* was innovative. Written, like *Clarissa*, in a series of letters and as if the action were happening at the moment of writing, this novel – which Rousseau claimed was not a novel – introduced new ways of reading. The boundaries between self and other, real and fictional, were blurred. Rousseau offered his readers and invited from them a form of reading that allowed for self-creation. Through imaginative identification with the characters, the reader's own life was transformed by the act of reading, accomplished through external signs of emotional affect: readers sobbed, sighed and wept their way through the pages. Some of them went further and ran off with their tutors. The important message Rousseau conveyed – following Richardson – was that the reader helped produce the meaning of the text. St Preux, the tutor, tells Julie that her 'active mind makes another and sometimes better book of the book you read'. It was a powerful message for young female writers, endorsing both their active minds and the importance of what they felt and wrote.

To feel oneself to be Julie, or to make Julie up in one's own likeness, was to be a most admired figure. Julie was heroic. That her heroism was a heroism of renunciation made her all the more noble. For the heroine of sensibility, giving up a passion represented gain rather than a loss; her character was amplified by it. In stark contrast, the prospect of becoming a wife (giving in to passion) had nothing obviously heroic about it. Indeed, it suggested a diminution of character, a sinking down to the level of the 'smart misses' whose conversation was all gowns, laces and lovers. The worst fate, but also the most likely for a superior woman, was to be a Julie and end up married to a man who was intellectually inferior.

Resisting matrimony

Much of our information about Anna Seward's early development comes from the series of fictionalised letters to 'Emma' written between 1762 and 1765, beginning just before she was twenty, which she bequeathed to Walter Scott.[24] Scott published a selection in the first volume of his edition of her *Poetical Works* (1810) under the heading, 'Extracts from Miss Seward's Literary Correspondence'. The letters provide glimpses of her social, intellectual and family life at the time. They were Miss Seward's 'literary correspondence' not in the sense that they were letters to other writers but in the sense that they concerned themselves with literature and with the creation and presentation of a literary self. Like the later correspondence that she began to transcribe and arrange in 1784, they were a version of autobiography.

Marriage and its pressures, along with literature and the self-conscious presentation of the heroine author, provided the subject matter. Pursuing the theme of genius and virtue, the 'only human distinctions' she considered worth striving for in herself as well as seeking in others, Seward projected herself in these letters as a writer resisting matrimony in favour of spinsterhood and a quietly domestic literary life. Hence, although she had suitors, like the healthy fox-hunting army major who courted her and to whom she was attracted and whose lively company she enjoyed, their charms were resisted. She took due note of what the major's sister said 'with earnestness, though gaily, about my having transformed the soldier, the sportsman, and the justice, into a character not *native* to him'. The major had no interest in literature, and while she was 'soothed', 'comforted' and 'grateful', her heart 'was not *deeply* impressed'. She wondered what the winter evenings would be like if nobody came in to relieve them from each other's company. There was a 'Mr V.', a great kisser of hands who unfortunately had a wart on the end of his nose, who stayed in Lichfield for the pleasure of Miss Seward's conversation. Erasmus Darwin having told her that listening well was 'a much more captivating accomplishment than talking well', she listened and was bored: 'but I hemmed away my yawnings; forced a laugh every minute at his frothy gaiety to keep myself awake; – kept clear of books and abstract ideas; talked little and heard well . . . Doubtless Mr V. tells you that I am very agreeable.'

Romance was fine but marriage would interrupt the progress of a writing life. Reading, writing, walking and talking already filled the day. Money mattered: she wanted 'love and a competency, not love and a cottage' if she was to marry at all, but mostly her thoughts were set on financial independence. It was important to have enough money to provide 'a steady anchor on which to lean in the harbour of celibacy, should the bark of love be blown back by the storms of disappointment'. Life as a single woman 'exempted from the fatigues of domestic economy' suited her. The prospect of lifelong celibacy and of becoming an old maid was less alarming, in the end, than the hazards of marriage: 'O! dearest Emma, that word "irrevocable"! – Well! However plentiful the *numbers*, I wonder there are not yet *more* old maids, ambling and bridling over the dim, unvaried plains of celibacy.'

In 1764, the perils of matrimony were forcefully dramatised in the unfolding tragedy of Seward's younger sister Sarah's engagement to Joseph Porter, a merchant based in Italy whom she had never met. Porter was a son of Johnson's wife, Tetty, and the engagement had been arranged by Thomas Seward and Porter's sister, Lucy, who lived in Lichfield. The plan was that Sarah would go to live in Italy for at least two years and Anna would accompany the happy pair. Anna looked forward to seeing with her own eyes the land her father had told her about from his years as tutor to the son of the Duke of Grafton on his Grand Tour. But Joseph Porter's first visit to claim his bride, which happened to coincide with a card party at the Bishop's Palace, fell short of romantic imaginings. He was old and unprepossessing. Anna Seward thought he looked like a mountebank: 'a thin, pale personage, somewhat below the middle height, with rather too much stoop in the shoulders, and a little more withered, by Italian suns, than are our English sober bachelors, after an elapse of only forty years.' Nor, on closer acquaintance, did she warm to his personality which she judged peevish and dictatorial. Sarah, young, impressionable, already once disappointed in love, seemed to be throwing herself away on a 'fretful and despotic' man. In Anna's account, rendered with all the immediacy of fiction, Porter approximated to the revolting Solmes in *Clarissa*, whom Clarissa's parents insisted on her marrying. The Sewards, however, did not behave like the Harlowes: Sarah was invited to change her mind about the wedding. Sarah refused, but before the marriage could take place she became ill with typhoid fever and within a few weeks she was dead.

Marriage did not kill Sarah Seward, but anguish about whether the decision was the right one, Porter's desire to hurry the marriage on and his presence throughout her illness ('his sensations seem more like vexation than grief'), combined with Anna's conviction that her sister's strength had been undermined by the effort of forcing herself to believe she could love an unattractive stranger, made it seem that it was indeed plans for marriage rather than typhoid that precipitated calamity. Anna recorded the sequence of events as they happened in a diary letter beginning 2 June 1764, the morning after the night in which Sarah had woken her at 3 a.m. to say that she was 'very ill' and a week before the wedding was due to take place. The letter has a present-tense urgency. It tells of relapses and revivals. It displays its Richardsonian act of writing 'to the moment': 'I leave you, that I may refresh myself by combing my dishevelled hair.' And it vividly conveys the drama, as in the arrival of a Worcestershire clergyman with a local reputation for successfully administering James's powders 'in very dangerous cases', to whom a chaise and four had been sent begging him to come.

> Sunday. – Mr Bayley is come; he arrived at tea this morning. The instant he came into the room, my mother rushed to him, and, falling on her knees, clasped her arms wildly around him, exclaiming, in the piercing accent of anguish, – 'Dear angel-man, save my child!' He burst into floods of humane tears, as he raised her from the ground.

But by the Wednesday following there was no hope. 'I have hardly strength to tell you . . . she cannot survive this night.' In the letters Sarah's actual death was not described, but if she did indeed not survive the night then she died on the day fixed for her wedding. After a lapse of several weeks, Anna's next letter began: 'I have sat almost an hour at the writing-table, my hands crossed upon this paper, unable to take up the pen; that pen which I used to seize with such glad alacrity . . .' Grief-stricken and torn, what she described after recording the difficulty of beginning to write was her sister's funeral; and in doing so she inevitably evoked the wedding: 'thus cold is the bridal-bed of my dear sister!' Still, death figured as Sarah's escape from a worse fate: 'O heavy, heavy loss! Yet bow thy stubborn grief, O my spirit! And remember the reason thou hadst to fear for her happiness in that union, from which she was so awfully snatched away.'[25] There was much cause to fear for happiness in marriage even when the husband-to-be was more personable than Joseph Porter. For Anna Seward, there was never to be a man for whom she did not prefer the idea of a *distant* to that of a *near* union.

By the mid eighteenth century, intellectual English women writers were disposed to be wary of the feeling heart. The heart was the lower organ and in literary terms, for women, it was associated with productions that had lower status. Men could write about love and sex, including love and sex from the woman's point of view: Pope's 'Eloisa to Abelard' is a sensitive and empathetic portrayal of female sexual desire. But even though the story of Héloïse had a powerful resonance for women, as the success of Rousseau's novel demonstrated, it was Julie's voice and example that was adopted – the voice of reasoned renunciation of once-tried passion – not the sexual fantasies, the 'raptures, of unholy joy' of Pope's Eloisa. Pope's contemporaries – Elizabeth Singer Rowe, Jane Barker, Anne Finch and Delarivier Manley (all writing before Richardson and Rousseau) – did, as we shall see, write about female desire, and his friend Judith Madan wrote an answer to 'Eloisa to Abelard' from Abelard's point of view, but women on the whole were not drawn to offer their version of the story and by the mid century were most unlikely to delineate sexual ecstasy.

Anna Seward wrote a sequence of epistles and elegies between two lovers, Evander and Emillia, which was partly based on 'Eloisa to Abelard'.[26] The note to the poems explained that the 'Love Elegies and Epistles' were not 'entirely imaginary'. It went on to claim that the author had been 'entrusted with the perusal of a prose correspondence between that unhappy pair [Evander and Emillia] which bore the same sort of relation to the ensuing poems, as the real letters between Abelard and Eloisa bear to Pope's Love-Epistle, "Eloisa to Abelard" '. The purportedly 'real-life' story was of an attachment between 'a lady of birth, rank, beauty, and talents' and a 'gentleman much her inferior in family and station, without fortune, and her equal only in intellect, merit and affection'. Out of a supposed bundle of letters, Seward composed a sequence of verse epistles. Most (thirteen out of fifteen) were in Evander's voice, addressed to Emillia. Emillia's sexual feelings were not explored. Rather, the emphasis was on whether Evander was worthy of her. Emillia doubts his love and Evander is required to protest the truth of his commitment to her 'bright self', until in the final epistle ("'Tis o'er!') they lock hands across the grave of her mother and offer each other their vows. Father remains a tyrant to the end, full of 'proud disdain' and baffling the mother's dying attempt to provide for her daughter.

In Emillia and Evander we can find heightened versions of Anna Seward and her own lifelong love, John Saville, drawn according to the model offered by Rousseau in *La Nouvelle Héloïse*. John Saville, like Rousseau's St Preux, was of a lower social class. He was vicar-choral of the cathedral, a passionate Handelian with a fine tenor voice. As well as being responsible for choral music in the cathedral, he was the tutor in the household (Anna took harpsichord lessons from him). Like Julie, Anna had beauty and talents and if not born high she certainly felt herself to have rank in Lichfield.

To follow the logic of 'Love Elegies and Epistles' it helps, in addition, to be familiar with Prior's 'Henry and Emma' as well as Pope's 'Eloisa to Abelard', for both were in a sense being rewritten.[27] In a similar way, Pope's and Prior's heroines were taken up and taken over in Seward's *Louisa, A Poetical Novel in Four Epistles*, which had as its stated aim the desire to improve these representations of womanhood, offering a less voluptuous Eloisa and a less compliant Emma. Prior's Emma was the prototype for Seward's Emillia in 'Love Elegies and Epistles', evoked in the eighth epistle when Evander replies to a presumed epistle from Emillia, 'Yes, my Emillia, I can say with truth, / Had Emma's Henry really stain'd his youth / With those dark crimes his jealousy assumed, / By murder branded, and to exile doom'd . . .' and goes on to agree that the trial Henry put Emma through (telling her lies about himself to test her) was 'needless and severe'.

Seward's poems responded to Prior's by restoring a dignity to Prior's Emma which his poem had undermined. In 'Henry and Emma', Henry puts Emma through a series of tests of her virtue – in imagination, not in practice. (Richardson, in *Pamela* and *Clarissa*, dramatised the tests of virtue his characters were put through as 'real' events happening to 'real' people.) Henry pretends he has killed a man and must run away. He gets Emma to agree to go with him and tests how far she would go. Would she slum it with outlaws and prostitutes in the woods? Would she look on when he took a younger mistress? How far would her love-derived desire to serve him take her? And if it took her all the way, what did that reveal about her virtue? Could a virtuous woman agree to do such things?

Like Rousseau's Julie, Prior's Emma combined high birth with all the noble qualities. She was courageous, truthful, faithful and undaunted. The poem claimed to have a didactic purpose, explained in the 'real-life' prologue address 'To Cloe' in the poet's voice: Cloe, the poet's lover, was invited to listen and be pleased at the revival of a medieval tale, 'the Nut-brown Maid', which refuted traditional views about women's fickleness and inconstancy. The poet, and Cloe his lover, were the modern-day equivalents of Henry and Emma. Cloe was entreated: 'O let the story with thy life agree; / Let men once more the bright example see; / What Emma was to him, be thou to me.'

The 'bright example' Prior's Emma offered was of a woman who put true love above social censure, who was prepared to lose her reputation but would not 'yield' her virtue; but Cloe, the real-life 'bright example' was, as every reader of Prior knew, his lover who had indeed yielded her virtue. In the fiction of the poem, Emma agreed to follow Henry into the woods, the haunt of outlaws and fallen women, in pursuit of right loving and until Henry's name was cleared. Society might judge her fallen; she would know she was not. She had confidence that her capacities and integrity were equal to any challenge she might meet; and that she was motivated by high-minded considerations not low lusts.

The bad faith in Prior's poem taken as a whole meant Emma's 'trial' was severe in more ways than one and, like a number of intelligent female readers (Sarah Fielding and Lady Mary Wortley Montagu among them), Anna Seward was uncomfortable with the resolution. For, in Prior's version, Henry's tests revealed that a woman's heroism could take her nowhere except down: *she* might be constant but Henry admits he would tire of her and want a younger woman: 'Each man is man; and all our sex is one, / False are our words; and fickle is our mind.' (He does not say that he would actually want a woman who *would* yield her virtue, though this is the unspoken point.) The poem, remaining true to cultural sanctions in insisting that for a woman outward reputation (what people thought) mattered more than inner virtue (what she actually did), and complacently contrasting it with men's freedom to be vicious, offered her no future but the grave. In

Seward's version Evander is not that kind of man and there is no vulgar mention of sexual fickleness. Emillia's heroism enables love to triumph. Faithful love protects them like a 'robe of pure asbestos' from persecution's fires. Clasped in each other's arms they care nothing for wealth, censure or pride; they live together unmolested by reproach and undismayed by penury.

The relationship with John Saville began in the mid 1750s when Anna Seward was a girl of thirteen and Saville a young man of nineteen, newly arrived in the Cathedral Close. He became a regular visitor at the Bishop's Palace and an important figure at the musical and literary parties held in and around Lichfield. He sang professionally, organised concerts, conducted oratorios around the country and was under contract to Covent Garden. By the time Anna was in her mid-twenties, Saville had a wife and two children but preferred to spend his time with the canon's daughter. They were together every day, reading, studying, playing music, walking, gardening, alone with each other or out and about in Lichfield society. She called him 'Giovanni', or 'Il Penseroso Saville', in appreciation of his rendering of Handel's setting of Milton's poem. (His wife, meanwhile, was described as 'unamiable', 'shrewish' and 'vulgar'.)

John Saville's cultural enthusiasms ensured him a place in Miss Seward's coterie, which by 1770 included Richard Lovell Edgeworth and Thomas Day along with Erasmus Darwin.[28] If Saville was not quite on a par with 'the lively, the sentimental, the accomplished, the scientific, the gallant, the learned, the celebrated, Mr Edgeworth', he was nevertheless 'a man of strong imagination and benevolent sensibility, with a considerable fund of classic and scientific knowledge'. In any case, his role was to sing. The learned and literary friends assembled at the Bishop's Palace were rarely without Il Penseroso Saville, 'sighing and singing to us, sharing or imparting our enthusiasms'. 'Our rambles up on the terrace,' Seward exulted, 'have been *very* animated these last evenings.'[29]

These pleasures were threatened in the summer of 1771 when Mrs Saville decided enough was enough and raised her voice in protest (or, in Anna's words, 'the breath of censure threatened to blast our tranquillity'). The injured wife refused any longer to receive the magnetic poetess – a public statement of how *she* understood the relationship. Mrs Saville took her complaint to Canon Seward, who tried to get his daughter to end the intimacy. She also went to the Dean since it was his job to 'correct any irregularities'. Parents and cathedral authorities came down heavily. Anna Seward was ordered not to see John Saville. This she refused to do.

Tranquillity in the Cathedral Close was blasted for a number of years, and perhaps Seward never got over her rage at the clergy. She was furious at her parents, too. She took the moral high ground. By siding with the Church authorities her parents had betrayed her, declaring to the world that they believed her guilty, thereby allowing 'low' interpretations of her actions. She insisted on her innocence. The Dean and his family decided they could no longer visit her. All Lichfield was up in arms. What had been 'an Edenic scene' between 1766 and 1771 became a place of turmoil and gloom.

An additional reason for gloom was the marriage of Anna's adoptive sister and pupil, Honora Sneyd, to Richard Edgeworth. Canon Seward performed the ceremony in the Ladies' Choir of the Cathedral. 'The good old man,' according to Edgeworth, 'shed tears of joy.' For Anna there were tears of grief and abandonment. A number of sonnets written at the time record a painful estrangement: 'Chilled by unkind Honora's altered eye', 'Affection is repaid by causeless hate!' and 'Ingratitude, how deadly is thy smart / Proceeding from the form we fondly love!'[30] Earlier poems help account for these feelings, although they do not provide an explanation for the accusations of ingratitude and unkindness. Honora was loved for her personal qualities; she was also idealised as the symbol of a happy past. In 'The Anniversary', a poem carefully dated 'written June 1769', which commemorated the anniversary of Honora's arrival in the household as a little girl of five, Seward wrote: 'Why fled ye all so fast, ye happy hours, / That saw Honora's eyes adorn these bowers?' and admonished her fourteen-year-old self for not realising how much of a 'thrice happy day!' it had been.

Honora was 'Born to console me'. When Sarah died, 'My friend, my sister . . . Sickning and sinking on her bridal morn', it was Honora, now grown into a heroine of sensibility, who took her place. She was the friend who always put the other first:

Dear Sensibility! How soon thy glow
Dyed that fair cheek, and gleam'd from that young brow!
How early, Generosity, you taught
The warm disdain of every grov'ling thought,
Round sweet Honora, e'en in infant youth,
Shed the majestic light of spotless truth;
Bid her for other's sorrow pour the tear,
For other's safety feel th'instinctive fear;
But for herself, scorning the impulse weak,
Meet every danger with unaltering cheek

Honora's departure for a month's residence in Shropshire was like a death
– Seward wrote an elegy marking the occasion: 'Honora fled, I seek her
favourite scene . . .'[31] The many poems to 'dear Honora' suggest not just a
deep level of affection but Honora's role as a poetic muse.

In 1773 she 'lost' Honora to marriage. She would not give up Saville.
Meanwhile, Saville's marriage had evidently broken down and he left
his wife, moving into a small house next door. Exasperated, the Dean
tried to buy him off, offering him his full salary for life if he would only
leave Lichfield. Anna Seward declared that she could not live without
him, and that misery 'probably for life' would be inflicted on her if he
left. He stayed. The scandal rumbled on. She marked 1773–6 as years of
depression, when the 'established habits of my life were broken, and the
native gaiety of my spirit eternally eclipsed . . . No sprightly parties did I
promote, or when I could help it, join.'[32]

By the mid 1770s, Seward was well into her thirties, in 'middle-age'
in the parlance of the time. She was old enough to value her 'established
habits' and to know something of her own nature; also old enough to
give proper weight to her future and her own scope in shaping it. Iron
undoubtedly entered the soul, but that her gaiety of spirit was 'eternally
eclipsed' is an exaggeration. She returned to the social pleasures by
which she was always 'very seducible', loving animated conversation,
music parties, evening entertainments among small groups and large,
flirtatious excitements, visits and house parties and, not least, the letter-
writing that cemented it all. Brilliant, well informed, self-assured, with
an active, questing intellect, hers was a large presence that took on extra
lustre in the limelight.

Though she was to struggle for the rest of her life 'in the indissoluble toils of my affection', Seward insisted that she had done nothing wrong. She declared that she was fully entitled to live in the closest degree of friendship with a man whom she could not have as a husband, since he was bound to another woman by vows she respected, but with whom everything short of married relations was allowable and decent. That she loved Saville there can be no doubt: he was the person in her life she could not imagine being without. That they were lovers in the full physical meaning of the word is unlikely, given Seward's insistence on her 'stale maidenhood' and 'celebaic spinsterhood' combined with the stress she laid on absolute truth-telling. If sexual congress was a part of their closeness, then her public persona was based on a lie. What is more plausible and more interesting is that she told the truth about the relationship. Telling the truth and requiring others to live with it was fundamental to the self she presented to the world. Like the high-born, the high-minded could avail themselves of a combination of self-assertion and privilege.

Lichfield didn't like the relationship but it was required to put up with it. Anna Seward defied parents, Church and community. Republican, even revolutionary, sentiments leapt to her lips. The crisis, she said, was an instance of 'the frequent cruelty and injustice of arbitrary power, exerted in private families'. She inveighed against an authority 'so barbarously exerted upon people advanced to the middle of life, who surely, if they are not fools, have, at such an age, a right to think, judge, and act for themselves'. To a close friend she explained:

There is *no* evil can happen to me so heavy and insupportable as the knowledge that in all human probability I should never behold him more. I have thought deeply upon this subject and can never be persuaded that it is either my duty to renounce the sight of him and those little transient conversations we sometimes have or that there would be any virtue in doing it – therefore I could never expect the reward you mention of Heaven for bringing so much and such insupportable torture upon myself, even if I believed that providence made all worthy people happy here which that it does not every days experience evinces . . .

As to my parents after having made me miserable to the utmost extent of their power after their deaf and inexorable cruelty to me last summer the part they took with my worst foes the stigma they fixed upon me by the prohibition so disgraceful to my character they have very little right to expect

43

that I should inflict upon myself the additional torture to which their power does not extend. If they attempt further persecutions the consequences will be more desperate. I loved Saville for his virtues. He is entangled in a connection with the vilest of women and the most brutally despicable. He cannot be my husband but no law of earth or heaven forbids that he should be my friend or debars us the liberty of conversing together while that conversation is innocent. The world has no right to suppose it otherwise – if it will be so unjust we cannot help it – all its severest censures we should both look upon as a less misfortune than that of seeing each other no more.[33]

This was the trenchant position she held for the next thirty years, until Saville's death in 1803 brought about the insupportable evil of separation. Grief-stricken, she could not leave her house for four months; 'my soul's dearest comforts', she wrote, were buried in the grave with him.[34]

Anna Seward had built a family life of sorts on the relationship, accepting some responsibility – especially financial – for Saville's dependants. She was not rich but she was better off than the music master and her social status was certainly higher. Unable to be wife and unwilling to be mistress, she had to some extent been (and been considered) John Saville's patron. When his daughter Elizabeth showed musical talent, she encouraged her to accept professional and semi-professional engagements. The trio had made country-house visits where Saville and Elizabeth sang to the company, Elizabeth's presence helpfully reinforcing an emphasis on being geniuses together with a shared passion for the arts, while at the same time serving as a sign of respectability.

In literature the loving couple might care nothing for wealth, but Seward understood its importance in life. Her 'pure and disinterested attachment' to Saville's 'unblemished worth' was made possible by her secure finances. This, as she understood, was what enabled her to cling to her 'soul's chosen friend'.

Nothing but a considerable independent fortune can enable an amiable female to look down, without misery, upon the censures of the many; and even in that situation, their arrows have power to wound, if not to destroy peace. Surely no woman with a nice sense of honour, – and what is she worth who has it not? – would voluntarily expose herself to their aim, except she has unwarily slid into a situation where the affections, making silent and unperceived progress, have rendered it a less evil to endure the consciousness of a dubious fame, provided there is no real guilt, than to renounce the society of him without whom creation seems a blank.[35]

Prior's Emma, Richardson's Clarissa, Rousseau's Julie were all amiable females exposed to the censures of the many, both within the pages of the fictions that produced them and in the polite circles of readers who discovered themselves and their friends and relations depicted there. Female life, especially young female life, went on in a glare of publicity. Money was a key factor in determining whether a woman's fame was 'dubious' or honorable, not only because it could buy privacy and therefore dignity but because money ensured high status. A 'considerable independent fortune' enabled a woman to look down on the censurers shooting their arrows up at her. Had she run out of money, Seward's fame would have taken on a different character.

Over the years, John Saville became increasingly at home in the Bishop's Palace, especially after Mrs Seward's death in 1780 and Canon Seward's stroke shortly afterwards. He remained separated from his wife though he continued to maintain her. The writer Mary Martha Sherwood, visiting Lichfield as a girl with her mother, recalled much debate about whether it was proper to accept a dinner invitation from Miss Seward, and having decided it was worth the risk discovered Mr Saville doing the honours of the table. 'He had been putting out the wine, we remarked, like a man in his own home, and on some particular wine being wanted, he directed the servant where to find it.' He was 'a handsome, gentlemanlike man' but a grave presence and, Mary Martha Sherwood thought, sad. In contrast, Anna Seward was 'tall and majestic, and was unrivalled in the power of expressing herself . . . [I]n a little while [she] made us forget every person but herself . . . She was the first female, and perhaps I may almost say the last, who ever gave me the idea of overpowering fascination . . . independent of either youth or beauty.'[36]

The Swan of Lichfield

Anna Seward stood up to everybody on the subject of what Bishop Percy, far away in Ireland, called her 'very improper attachment to

45

Saville, one of the singing men of Lichfield Cathedral'. She was an unmarried woman of thirty-something whose parents were still living, and she insisted on her 'right' to 'think, judge, and act' for herself in such a matter. And, furthermore, she broadcasted the fact publicly. If we ask what enabled her to do so, some obvious answers may be found in her personality: she was strong-willed, confident and combative. But the episode invites us to move beyond the particulars of place and personality, especially if we reframe the question and pose it less in the terms suggested by Bishop Percy – that she refused to break free from an 'improper attachment' – and more in the terms that Anna Seward herself insisted on. For her, a child of the bluestocking era, it was an issue of female autonomy. More precisely, it was an issue about the scope of female genius.

Seward believed that 'nature' had cast her 'in a superior mould' and she felt her superiority in point of merit. Being more gifted than others entitled her to make her own judgements and even required her to do so by conferring some responsibility of leadership – a leadership which her father and the men of the Church signally failed, in her view, to demonstrate. She prided herself on her powers of reason and judgement and she was convinced that her love of justice rendered her arguments objective.

She was high-minded and unyielding. Other people's reflections might be 'unworthy' but she knew that her relationship with Saville was a 'pure and disinterested attachment'. She described him to Thomas Whalley as 'an injured man', whose virtues the world at large failed to recognise because of its own frivolity and snobbery. 'Were he prosperous,' she told Whalley, 'his virtues would ensure him your esteem.' She lived to congratulate herself on her resolution. 'No prospect of worldly disadvantage – and I was threatened with the highest – could induce me to renounce the blessing of a tried and faithful friend; but by ill-advised and mistaken authority, most of its sweetest comforts were mercilessly lopped away.' And again (for this was a subject her pen was more than happy to dwell on):

The most diabolical machinations of spite and envy, the pleas of interest, and the interposition of misled authority were exerted in vain. The wishes of a noble heart, the affection of a most ingenuous sensibility, conscientious

46

piety, with an awakened taste for every elegant science, these qualities constituted the counterpoising blessing. I preserved it at every hazard, and am rewarded with the entire approbation of my own mind on the subject, besides the delight I take in the virtues of my friend.[37]

Having 'the entire approbation of my own mind' was sufficient. Still, for all that, Anna Seward did not need James Boswell to remind her, as he did in the course of their acrimonious correspondence on the pages of the *Gentleman's Magazine*, that 'poetesses . . . have too often been not of the most exemplary lives'. If sex was bad and adultery worse for a woman's reputation, a dalliance of whatever sort with a mere musician compounded the crime. The widow Hester Thrale's love for the unmarried musician Gabriel Piozzi caused uproar in polite circles.

Of course, whether the man was a musician or not was a minor detail; the sexual slur itself was sufficient. Men like Boswell could conduct their sexual lives in whatever way they pleased without it detracting from their literary reputations. But women who put themselves in the public eye as poets, novelists, dramatists, historians, learned women − all the kinds of writing encompassed in the phrase 'the woman of letters' − were fair game for gutter journalism. Seward's response to the difficulty she found herself in owed much to her unique personality; it also owed something to the particular historical moment in which she came of age as a woman and a writer. She believed she was entitled to find her own solution to the problem − which she did. Furthermore, she felt entitled to require the world to accept that so long as *her* conscience was clear *it* had no further business with the matter. What she claimed, essentially, were rhetorical equal rights: she gave her word as a gentlewoman, and as a woman of letters whose concern was with truth, and she expected her word to be enough. She was 'innocent'.

In 1784, when Seward took the decision to begin keeping copies of her literary correspondence, it was partly in acknowledgement that the world did accept her on her own terms: her fame as a writer was at its height. She was 'the Swan of Lichfield', a soubriquet we might hear as mocking and belittling but which she accepted as apt and appropriate, putting her in the tradition of Pope, 'the sweet Swan of Twickenham', and Shakespeare, 'the Swan of Avon'. The letters were the major task of her maturity. They vindicated her judgements in life and literature, including the relationship with John Saville. They displayed her at her life's work and they were a record of that work. They revealed her personality, gave details about her family and friends, and recorded important experiences. Where additional information might be needed, it was provided in a footnote.

From her correspondence, future generations would glean an unrivalled impression of the lived life of a dedicated woman of letters. Following her about in imagination, they would understand the values that underpinned that life. Reading her exchanges with different individuals, they would take the measure of the profound importance attached to opinion, and be instructed by the many clear statements of *her* opinion on contentious issues, especially those to do with literary value. From her letters, posterity would know that Anna Seward was at the centre of admiring circles. Though scandal had brushed her name, it had not tarnished her reputation.

She was a Rousseau-ite enthusiast and wherever her sincere enthusiasm led her she felt entitled to go. She travelled about the country a certain amount, staying with families and individuals who were part of her correspondence network, forming ideal little communities of taste: reading, walking, discussing and playing music together. The sociable sharing of art, literature, music and feeling was the *raison d'être*. 'Friendship' was a key concept, built upon the circulation of conversation and books – those they wrote as well as those they read – and of letters that would be read aloud to the group. Musical instruments, including the human voice, were played at evening gatherings; landscape – domesticated and rugged – was explored, enjoyed, enthused over, described. The feelings that were sought – what the eighteenth century labelled 'sensibility' – combined head and heart to produce lively sensation. Writing to one of her friends who was about to set off on a tour of Spain, Seward imagined some of what she expected him to feel, namely, 'that thrill, which from the operation of enthusiasm upon associated ideas, brings water into the eyes ... Few sensations are so pleasant. Of these thrills of sensibility, I hope you will have many as you journey onward, to reward the fatigues and inconveniences of the expedition.' She herself was reluctant to pass up good opportunities for thrills of sensibility. At Scarborough, when the sea was running high and lashing the rocks of the promontory, she went, at night, alone except for a strong servant – 'nobody but myself being inclined to venture' – along the beach and up the steps to the parapet of the fort, with the waves crashing 'scarce three yards from me' and the spray wetting her through. Thunderous, noisy, dark and stormy, it was 'a scene congenial to my taste for the terrible graces' and 'sufficiently gratified my rage for the terrific'. Her maid had refused to accompany her, and we do not know what the servant of her host, Court Dewes, thought about it all. 'I stood at least half an hour on the wild promontory's top, almost totally encircled by the dark and furious main.'[38]

Fusing life, criticism and creativity, the correspondence was an attempt to rewrite the endings of the epistolary novels of Richardson and Rousseau much as she re-wrote Prior's 'Henry and Emma'. The high-minded heroism of Clarissa, Julie and Emma was turned to better purposes in her life and work than Richardson, Rousseau and Prior had allowed. Neither rakish and libertine men nor gentlemanly scholars were allowed to overcome the heroine of these letters. There were no rakes and libertines in her circles and when gentlemen repeatedly disagreed with her views, as George Hardinge did, they were dropped. (He later became the patron of Helen Maria Williams.) As the living counterpart of the fictional Clarissa or Julie, she emerged triumphant from every encounter.

Unapologetic about her passion for John Saville, Anna Seward wrote up his day-to-day presence in her life, figuring it through the lens of the most high-minded interpretation of his character and their friendship. The heroic renunciations implied were modelled, in all but one detail, on those of the lovers in Rousseau's *La Nouvelle Héloïse*: unlike St Preux and Julie, Saville and Anna were not to be considered as having engaged in a sexual act. Rhetorically speaking, Saville's place as the loved object in this correspondence testified not to lust but to the power of judgement and feeling. That he was a performer helped, since he could often be presented in the text through descriptions of his singing: ravishing – nobody sang as Saville sung. Meanwhile, this rhetorical strategy opened up the space for Seward's own performance of self as the authoritative voice of cultivated taste.

The letters spoke to the potentially silencing effect of a possibly scandalous relationship, and their function was to assert, in polemical fashion, her victorious refusal of the terms. As such they may take their place alongside more obviously polemical and political writings of the time that were presented as epistolary utterances: Burke's *Reflections on the Revolution in France* supposedly 'had their origin in a correspondence between the author and a very young gentleman at Paris'; and Paine's uninvited rabble-rousing answer was authorised as an answer to a letter. To some extent, in formal terms, we can see the genre choice as a 'polite' (because supposedly 'private') version of the pamphlet exchanges by means of which literary and political arguments were conducted. Seward's theme was not the French Revolution but female dignity and the revolution in female scope. Given the pressures on this subject – living and representing life as the new Héloïse or the new Clarissa was not easy – it was necessary to lay more than usual emphasis on female dignity and autonomy. Her battles were conceived as public as well as private battles, and her letters, no less than those of Horace or Seneca, Burke or Paine, which also drew on fictions of privacy to make public statements, were instruments of political propaganda.

Her cause was 'the posthumous fame of our English classics', and her own fame – a heroine laying down right rules for literary criticism – was intimately bound up in it. Arguing for impartial standards had a particular meaning for a woman critic in a social order which declared that it was right to be partial in evaluating women's texts on the grounds that partiality towards virtue was the proper first consideration. In attempting this, Seward took upon herself a heroic, high-minded endeavour. What she produced might best be seen as an epic – a finished epic, unlike the unfinished *Telemachus* which Scott chose not to print.

Nowadays, as part of the general recovery of women's writing, there is some interest in Seward's poetry, which is likely to be included in certain anthologies of verse, but little interest in the correspondence. To an extent this reflects the relative accessibility of the short poem over the long series of letters: social and literary historians make use of letters but teachers of literature do not teach them as they teach a poem or a novel. It also reflects assumptions about the value of different genres, and how cultural expectations of writers – what a writer might be and do – have changed over time. In the late eighteenth century, neither poems nor novels were 'taught': their value was located in social sharing rather than educational practice. The ability to read aloud well (poetry, a letter being passed around the social circle) and thereby aid social pleasure was rated more highly than skills in close textual analysis. Similarly, the performance of the authorial self, with its responsibilities and duties, formed part of the expectation of what might be received along with the poem. The poem on the page did not exist in a void: it was attached to the person and place that produced it.

When Anna Seward began transcribing her letters in 1784, it was because she had made a judgement that a carefully constructed collection of literary letters was a better bet for posthumous reputation than the poems for which she was already known. Unlike other letter collections assembled after an author's death, these were written and rewritten with a view to publication, selected and ordered by the writer to provide a portrait of herself and enshrine her views about matters she considered of particular importance. When she rewrote, it was not in the spirit of a letter-writer falsifying documents, but as a professional writer revising her manuscripts.

Seward's subject was herself, her own life and English literature. Her 'great object in life', as the shocked Victorian editor of Thomas Whalley's letters and journals noted in 1863, was 'literary fame'.[39] Fully controlled at source, a deliberate construct, not at all dependent on the accidental preservation of individual items, the correspondence was a manifesto and a monument. It conveyed a message about the meaning of a literary life in the late eighteenth century, showing what a writer born female in 1742 could be and do. The woman of letters as the bluestockings imagined her marched through these volumes, individual, but also representative.

Since authorship did not depend on professional training and was not a professional career, it was open to women in ways that other culturally significant activities were not. Authorial identity was available if the community of readers agreed to confer it – which meant agreeing that certain individuals were to be considered as more than enthusiastic readers and writers, more than amateur and provincial, more than merely female. An author was one whose views carried weight, whose forms of expression warranted attention. Authorship was invested with authority. It was the task of the letters to enshrine this truth about literary life in the late eighteenth century, and Anna Seward's personal achievement in securing a permanent place within it – as an amateur, a provincial and a female.

Chapter Two

THE FEMALE RIGHT TO LITERATURE

I love to rise ere gleams the tardy light,
Winter's pale dawn; – and as warm fires illume,
And cheerful tapers shine around the room,
Thro' misty windows bend my musing sight ...
          ... Then to decree
The grateful thoughts to God, ere they unfold
To Friendship, or the Muse, or seek with glee
Wisdom's rich page: – O, hours! More worth than gold ...

Anna Seward[1]

The female mind

In the 1730s, the Revd Thomas Seward had been private chaplain to the Duke of Grafton. Travelling on the Continent as tutor to Grafton's son, Lord Charles Fitzroy, Seward had imbibed progressive ideas about the relations of the sexes and the intellectual capacities of women. In France and Italy, salon culture took for granted women's active participation in and leadership of discussion. Men of sense enjoyed the company of such women. (Lady Mary Wortley Montagu found court circles in Venice far more amenable to an intellectual woman like herself than court circles in 1730s London.) Thomas Seward's verse epistle, 'The Female Right to Literature, in a Letter to a Young Lady from Florence', was probably composed during his travels, though it was not published until 1748, after he had returned to England and become the father of two daughters.

In urging the female right to literature, Thomas Seward modelled himself on forward-thinking cultivated men who were attempting to institute in Britain attitudes and practices they admired in other European countries. Debates about women's education (of which their entitlement to literature was a part) were understood as signalling the larger debate about women's place in culture, society and politics. These discussions had a long history which could be (and was) recycled. Readers were familiar with it, and as classical texts such as Juvenal's sixth satire were translated, so the terms of the debate reached an even wider audience. Any writer could make use of certain stock themes – that former ages were lewd and libertine, as witnessed by women's public speech; or, by contrast, that former ages were shockingly illiberal in their treatment of women writers; that women were ignorant, or that they were well read and knew too much. In Juvenal, the greatest 'plague' was 'The book-learned wife, in Greek and Latin bold; / The critic-dame, who at her table sits, / Homer and Virgil quotes, and weighs their wits.'[2] This was an image that was endlessly circulated both by those who opposed learning in women and those who supported it. Dryden translated Juvenal in 1692, and in the introduction to the sixth satire he went to great pains to distance himself and his own time and countrywomen from its sentiments. He pointed out that this 'bitter invective against the fair sex' was the source from which 'the moderns' had stolen the best lines, that it was Juvenal's wittiest satire and it needed to be so because 'truly he had need of all his parts to maintain with so much violence so unjust a charge'. Dryden did not think Juvenal would convince the modern reader, and he was anxious that no reader should suppose he himself shared Juvenal's views: 'let me satisfy the world that I am not of his opinion. Whatever his Roman ladies were, the English are free from all his imputations.' Juvenal's satire, he insisted, 'is no way relating to them' and it was only the fact that nobody else was prepared to undertake so 'ungrateful' an employment that had persuaded him to do it.[3]

For Dryden in 1692 it was unfashionable to be misogynist; it showed a lack of polish. Several generations of literary men were to model themselves on Dryden in this regard, Thomas Seward among them. Seward made use of a crusading rhetoric, figuring a new modern world against the dreadful bad old days, when, as his title implied, women were denied the right to literature. 'Why,' the poet asks, revealing his familiarity with Juvenal,

                              does Custom bind
            In chains of ignorance the female mind?
            Why is to them the bright ethereal ray
            Of science veil'd? Why does each pedant say,
            'Shield me, propitious powers, nor clog my life
            With that supreme of plagues *a learned wife.*'

Seward presented himself in heroic mode, a standard bearer writing
lines which 'dare against a world decide / And stem the rage of custom's
rapid tide'.[4] The argument was about 'the female right to literature', but
the ground of contestation was also between classical literature and the
vernacular (as represented by the contributors to *Dodsley's Collection* in
which the poem appeared). By implication, such an argument incorporated women since only in exceptional cases did women have that
grounding in the classics that all young gentlemen received as a matter
of course. Some of the urgency in the poem belonged to the larger
political vision of Britain as the new Greece and Rome, idealised as the
home of liberty. Thomas Seward claimed that what used to be true of
Greece and Rome – that they respected women's minds and did not
reduce them to be the toys of men and slaves of lust – was in his own
time making its last stand in Britain. In Britain, liberty could still be
invoked to prevail over domestic tyranny. The 'sons of Britain' had it in
their power to prefer love, friendship and liberty to all the pleasures of
licentiousness and rule. It was not true that a learned wife was a 'plague':
'Must knowledge give offence? / And are the graces all at war with
sense?' The poem answered in the negative: 'blest truth' was the
'offspring of sense and industry'.

   Thomas Seward's daughter was in a position to take 'The Female
Right to Literature' personally. It gave her permission not merely to
write, but to situate herself in a patrilineal line. Along with *Dodsley's
Collection* as a whole, the poem gave Anna Seward an investment in the
poetry of the early and mid century, and in a larger sense it accounted
for some of the intensity of her commitment to the English poetic
tradition in general and her defence of the vernacular. That tradition as
she understood it was a male tradition: it was Shakespeare, Milton,
Prior and Pope. Reviving or discovering female poets from an earlier era

was not something that concerned her. The female right to literature spoke to the present and the future, not the past.

Progressive men and women of the mid eighteenth century who argued for the female right to literature took for granted that women's development had been stifled. Hence, although Seward insisted on the achievements of women writers in her time – instancing her own writings, especially her *Louisa*, Helen Maria Williams's long poem, *Peru*, the writings of Hannah More, Anna Barbauld and others, all of which testified to female poetic vigour in the later eighteenth century – she offered no comparable praises of important women poets of the past. Whatever merit there was in the English poetic tradition did not reside in female poets and it was not in their works that a national lineage was to be traced.

Nor, in another sense, was it in the experiences of female authors that any encouraging precedent was to be found. The absence of female names in Anna Seward's galaxy of poetic stars might mean an absence of talent but it could equally be interpreted as a lack of care – the failure of the institutions of literature to nurture and preserve such talent as had revealed itself. This was one of the themes of the larger movement her father was part of, a movement which grew in strength from the 1730s onwards, and which took some of its energy from the rhetoric of earlier women writers themselves, especially poets. Thomas Seward's injunction to his daughter to 'Take every knowledge in of every kind', to feed her intellect and resist the customs that would bind her in 'chains of ignorance', to step out boldly as a learned woman and rise to the topmost heights, belonged in a proto-feminist tradition of protest best exemplified by Lady Mary Chudleigh, whose *The Ladies Defence* (1701) identified learning as the key ingredient.

Women were slaves, according to *The Ladies Defence*, and slavery was 'shameful'. The lack of respect paid them by men would be transformed if only women would 'study to be good and wise'. *The Ladies Defence* lamented women's failure to penetrate deeply into 'the labyrinths of learning'. It laid the blame partly on women who took satisfaction from the 'toys' of dress and dance and needlework and fun – 'As if we were for nothing else designed, / But made, like puppets, to divert mankind' – and partly on social conditioning. It acknowledged the unfairness of a social system which blamed women for being 'fools' yet refused them the means to become anything else:

> 'Tis hard we should be by the men despised,
> Yet kept from knowing what would make us prized;
> Debarred from knowledge, banished from the schools,
> And with the utmost industry bred fools.

And it expressed considerable exasperation – 'O that my sex would all such toys despise, / And only study to be good and wise.'[5] The overall message of the poem located the problem as much in 'my sex' as in the men by whom 'we' are despised. It was 'hard' to be despised, but it wasn't surprising. Women *were* fools, they *did* behave like puppets. Only a few women were likely to be able and willing to resist the temptations of a puppet-like life. Those few might rise. Those few would be looked to as an example to raise the rest of the sex, all of whom, as a sex, were in need of raising.

In this rhetorical tradition, which was to help form the bluestocking movement, women were urged to change society by changing themselves. Thomas Seward's 'The Female Right to Literature' imagined an altered future, one which his daughter was encouraged to live out. His poem was one of a number of mid-century productions driven by indignation at how women and the social system had worked together to fail women. All put their faith in the power of example. All were moved to search the past for illustrious women. Exceptional individuals, 'the truly wise, the virtuous, persons eminent for great and good qualities, for their extraordinary accomplishments, and the use they made of them', as the 1739 biographer of Elizabeth Rowe put it, should not be allowed to disappear into oblivion. Their lives and achievements should be recorded for posterity. Their writings should be made available so that other women would be in a position to emulate them.

A crop of publications extolling the virtues of Britain's 'letter'd nymphs' appeared within a few years of each other in the 1750s: George Ballard's *Memoirs of British Ladies who have been celebrated for their writings or skill in the learned languages, arts and sciences* (1752), *The Feminiad* by John Duncombe (1754) and *Memoirs of Several Ladies of Great Britain* by Thomas Amory (1755). Also, there were compilations of works by women, such as Colman and Thornton's *Poems by Eminent Ladies*; sympathetic reviews of women's writings in the periodical press, especially the *Gentleman's Magazine*, along with commemorations of the literary achievements of women of the past; and a willingness to subscribe to *Miscellaneous Verses* or *Poems on Several Occasions* by living women poets of recognised worth but small income, such as Mary Jones whose *Miscellanies in Prose and Verse* in 1750 was supported by 1,400 names headed by the Princess Royal.

These initiatives and publications built on the commonplace view that clever women should have access to all the opportunities for learning that men had, and that having such learning would make women good. The rhetoric that accompanied them rested in varying degrees on the assumption that women in their natural state were not good; without the bracing help of books, they would descend into 'trifling follies' and become slaves to their sensual lower natures. However, by its very nature, the act of recovery demonstrated that some women, though few, *had* studied to be good and wise. Lady Mary Chudleigh's exhortation in *The Ladies Defence*, urging women to fill their minds with 'solid notions', to 'let their reason dictate to their will' and take themselves 'Through all the labyrinths of learning', implied that she at least had followed such a path against the 'ill-natur'd world' and the contempt and 'barbarous usage' of men. *The Ladies Defence* spoke for women like herself, those who 'Instead of novels, histories peruse, / And for their guides the wiser ancients choose', and it was a rallying call for the kind of men who did not want to deride women nor use them barbarously.

Elizabeth Elstob and George Ballard

In 1735, an elderly schoolmistress, who, under an assumed identity, had recently taken charge of the village school at Evesham in Gloucestershire, responded to a letter from a young tailor living in nearby Chipping Campden. The tailor was George Ballard, and his mother was the local midwife who, through her network of clients, knew Sarah Chapone, who ran a boarding school for girls in Stanton. Chapone, a writer and intellectual, was a friend and correspondent of Samuel Richardson and Mary Delaney. Sarah Chapone knew that the Evesham village schoolmistress, known locally as 'Frances Smith', was actually one of the country's leading Anglo-Saxon scholars. Her real name was Elizabeth Elstob and she had disappeared from public view almost two decades earlier.

George Ballard, an amateur historian and numismatist, had a keen interest in Anglo-Saxon and he was teaching himself the language in his spare time. Mrs Chapone guided him to Elizabeth Elstob and thus set in train a meeting of minds and enthusiasms, indignations and aspirations that was to lead, eighteen years later, to Ballard's only published work, the two-volume *Memoirs of British Ladies who have been celebrated for their writings or skill in the learned languages, arts and sciences*.

Elstob, or 'Smith', was lonely and in poor health. The labour of teaching reading to the children of sheep farmers and stocking weavers was wearing her out: 'these long winter evenings to me are very melancholy ones,' she told George Ballard, 'for when my school is done, my little ones leave me incapable of either reading, writing or thinking, for their noise is not out of my head till I fall asleep, which is often too late'.[6]

Having been in hiding for so long, and having suffered a good deal, Elizabeth Elstob was more than happy to have her identity revealed. Sarah Chapone, distressed at finding a scholar of Elstob's 'merit and abilities' living out a miserable old age, with very few possessions and hardly any books, had begun to scheme some sort of rescue. It wasn't just the overwork and poverty that bothered her, but the lowly company Elstob was forced to endure: among the stocking weavers there were none fit to recognise her worth. In a better situation, Chapone hoped Elstob might resume her Saxon studies, or if not that, she would at least have the company of other intelligent and educated people with whom she could converse, 'conversation being the proper entertainment of a thinking person', as Mrs Chapone put it.

Although grateful to Chapone for her interest, Elstob wasn't at all sure that she wanted to leave a school it had taken her seven years of patient waiting and working to obtain and which was small enough for her to manage single-handedly. At Evesham, people had been kind and she had met with 'a great deal of friendship and generosity from the good ladies in this place'. When George Ballard, prompted by Mrs

Chapone, suggested that the school was beneath her, she became indignant: 'As to your objection on the meanness of the scholars I assure you I should think it as glorious an employment to instruct those poor children as to teach the children of the greatest monarch.' This was a woman who in her better days had taught her nine-year-old serving boy Latin and Saxon so that he could help transcribe the ancient manuscripts on which she and her brother worked.

Her life had become 'a life of disappointments' and, in her depressed state, Elstob did not expect it to change. However, the interest Chapone and Ballard took in her had a tonic effect. She enjoyed writing to Ballard. He revived memories of her much loved brother, William, long since dead. She hoped that he would visit, but gave a disparaging picture of herself: 'You will see a poor little contemptible old maid generally vapoured up to the ears, but very cheerful when she meets with an agreeable conversation.'

The prospect of meeting Ballard and discussing Anglo-Saxon matters once more was so exciting that Elizabeth Elstob worried in case the young tailor would find her too talkative. It was twenty years since she had had any such conversation, or been in contact with antiquarians or learned men of any sort. She sent him a small transcript from the Saxon that she had made herself, boasting that it was 'written I believe by the first woman that has studied that language since it was spoke'. Ballard wrote to thank her. They agreed that it was regrettable to note how 'the language of our ancestors' was once again falling into neglect. The expectation that she would resume her studies in a serious way was, however, quickly checked: she no longer had the materials and perhaps she no longer had the heart for it. She assured him he would understand when he knew her story, which she would tell him if he would be 'so good as to visit', for she was willing to speak about the shaming circumstances of her disappearance but she would not write any of it down. He was sworn to secrecy.

George Ballard came, and in due course Elstob also visited him. That outing was a cheerful affair. Feeling 'gay and impertinent', the fifty-five-year-old spinster joked that it was the first time in her life that she had ever 'rid five miles to visit a gentleman'. He was like a doctor; his attentions had 'cured a gentlewoman of a lethargy'. At Chipping Campden she met Ballard's mother and an 'ingenious' sister, Elizabeth, who was a voracious reader, especially of English history, and a coin collector like her brother. The family were well known in antiquarian circles. The Oxford scholar Thomas Hearne was impressed by them, especially Elizabeth, whom he described as 'very curious in coins and physic, she designing to be a midwife by the assistance of her mother . . . [She] reads very much in physic and history, and procures many of the best books that way.' Hearne also noted that Ballard himself, then aged about twenty-four, 'does little or nothing at his trade, but rambles about after coins, and endeavours to make a perfect series of the Roman ones. He lives chiefly upon his mother.'[7]

Thomas Hearne was the second keeper of the Bodleian, a man assured of his place in the Oxford system and with a reputation as one of the greatest medievalists of the century. He could not quite approve of a working man neglecting his trade, no matter how enthusiastic he himself was about coin collecting (he was surely, we can assume, as keen as any other numismatist on getting 'a perfect series' of whatever his current enthusiasm was). On the other hand, no hint of criticism appeared in his account of twenty-six-year-old Elizabeth Ballard. For an unmarried woman to spend her time reading books and collecting coins, to become knowledgeable in a range of antiquarian pursuits, as well as learning the useful skills of midwifery, was wholly admirable.

This was the household into which Elizabeth Elstob was introduced, full of self-educated, hard-working enthusiasts. It was a setting in which she felt quite at home. Mother and sister followed the discussions that went on among the educated and well-to-do men who corresponded with Ballard, historians and collectors of artifacts such as Thomas Rawlins, Richard Graves, William Brome, Browne Willis, James West and Joseph Ames. When Elstob's identity was revealed, these antiquarian friends came to pay homage and talk about Saxon manuscripts. They brought books and small gifts; she was discreetly provided with money. Ballard made her a dress. Some of her energy returned in an atmosphere that recalled the happy and productive years she spent when she lived with her brother, and whose death in 1715 had precipitated catastrophe.

Ballard honoured his promise to Elstob to reveal nothing of what she told him about the years that followed her brother's death over two decades earlier. We know that she was left with neither home nor income, that she had no immediate family willing to take her in, that her possessions may have been seized, and that she probably went into hiding to escape creditors. She seems to have managed to avoid debtors' prison, but where she went and how she survived will probably never be known.

For Ballard and Sarah Chapone and their friends, Elizabeth Elstob was more than just a learned lady who had fallen on hard times. She was the living emblem of the nation's failure to value women who made the effort to improve themselves, women who, in Lady Chudleigh's words, studied 'to be good and wise'. If anybody had penetrated into 'the labyrinths of learning' it was Elizabeth Elstob; she was an exception, and yet her reward appeared to be a miserable and exhausting life teaching elementary reading to the children of the poor. Saving such a woman was an act that had political symbolism. Even more important was the significance of Elstob's published work on the origins of the English language, in which could be found not only her thoughts on Anglo-Saxon but also a powerful argument for literary criticism as the special province of female scholars.

By the time of William's death, when she was in her early thirties, Elstob had published three pioneering books and had an established reputation as one of the leading Anglo-Saxon scholars in the country. The great Saxonist and supporter of learned women, George Hickes, admired her and had given her every encouragement. Cambridge University was happy to trust its manuscripts and books to her. In Oxford she was a familiar figure, working on ancient manuscripts from Bodley's library, recognised as one of the community of Saxon scholars associated with Queen's College. Though not officially a member of the university (as a woman that was impossible), she lived with William and worked with him on a translation of King Alfred's version of Orosius's history. Later, when William became rector of St Swithin's Church, they lived and worked together in London. Ralph Thoresby recorded in his diary that he had visited at Parson Elstob's where the 'Saxon Nymph' showed him 'a large volume of Saxon homilies from the public library at Cambridge, being an antient and noble manuscript upon parchment, which she is now transcribing in a curious character for the press, with her translation from the Latin and the Saxon.'[8] In 1713,

George Hickes praised her to John Montagu for her 'incredible industry' and 'learned and useful notes'.[9]

Elizabeth Elstob's first publication was a translation from the French of Madeleine de Scudery's *Essay on Glory* (1708). This was followed by Aelfric's *An English-Saxon Homily on the Birthday of St Gregory* (1709) and *The Rudiments of Grammar for the English-Saxon Tongue* (1715), both of which carried lengthy scholarly (and polemical) prefaces. On the title page of *The Rudiments of Grammar for the English-Saxon Tongue*, the first Anglo-Saxon grammar, she put a recommendation by George Hickes which drew attention to the special fitness of women for linguistic and literary study: 'Our earthly possessions are truly enough called a patrimony, as derived to us by the industry of our fathers; but the language that we speak is our mother tongue, and who so proper to play the critics in this as the females.' Hickes had written this in a letter, a fact Elstob made public, though she did not actually name him (her own name was clearly given on the title page): under the quotation was written, 'In a letter from a Right Reverend Prelate to the Author.'

Elstob was making a conscious polemical point. The argument for the vernacular tradition over the classical was of obvious use to women. The established institutions of learning, the Church and the universities, excluded women and rooted scholarship in a classical training. By quoting a 'prelate' – a leader of the Church, home of spiritual and textual authority – handing over possession of the native language, 'our mother tongue', to women as their 'proper' concern, Elstob opened up a path for women that was independent of the old forms and practices, and untainted by foreign associations. The Anglo-Saxon grammar was represented in nationalistic terms as an aid to understanding 'our ancient English poets'. Poetry in the vernacular could be freed from the powerful interests of established institutions and function as a vehicle for newly formed modes of working that had no tradition of excluding women.

Elstob was aware that being born female had limited her opportunities. When Ballard persuaded her to write a memoir of her life – a task she found 'unpleasant' and which she only managed to complete by leaving out key details (telling him, 'I thought it unnecessary to stuff it with the particular misfortunes and disappointments I have met with') – she laid special emphasis on a period in her childhood when she had been prevented from pursuing her studies. This followed her mother's death in about 1691, when she was sent to live with relations in Canterbury. Her uncle, Charles Elstob, was a canon at Canterbury Cathedral. Writing about herself in the third person she recalled the crass and unthinking misogyny of this senior churchman who became her guardian, contrasting it with the happy memory of her mother's encouragement of her desire to learn:

From her childhood she was a great lover of books, which being observed by her mother, who was also a great admirer of learning, especially in her own sex, there was nothing wanting in her improvement so long as her mother lived. But being so unfortunate as to lose her when she was about eight years old, and when she had but just gone through her accidence and grammar, there was a stop put to her progress in learning for some years, for her brother being under age when her mother died, she was under the guardianship of a relation who was no friend to women's learning, so that she was not suffered to proceed, notwithstanding her repeated requests that she might, being always put off with that common and vulgar saying that one tongue is enough for a woman. However, this discouragement did not prevent her earnest endeavours to improve her mind in the best manner she was able, not only because she had a natural inclination for books herself but in obedience to her excellent mother's desire. She therefore employed most of her time in reading such English and French books (which last language she with much difficulty obtained leave to learn) as she could meet with, till she went to live with her brother who very joyfully and readily assisted and encouraged her in her studies, with whom she laboured very hard as long as he lived.[10]

William Elstob did not share his uncle's views about women. Like George Ballard, he valued the intellectual companionship of a clever sister. Unmarried and living with her brother, Elizabeth not only participated in his social and intellectual circles but was also able to draw on the benefits of his institutional status as a clergyman. Never well off, they managed to get by and – crucially – Elizabeth's mature scholarship was encouraged and welcomed beyond as well as inside the home. Industrious and with a shared passion for the subject, the brother and sister had spent their days transcribing Saxon manuscripts, referring to one or other of the textbooks that had recently come out –

Thwaites's *Heptateuchus* or Hickes's grammar and *Thesaurus*. Subscriptions were raised for her proposed publications. There were 268 subscribers to *An English-Saxon Homily on the Birthday of St Gregory*, including many scholarly aristocrats, as well as leading antiquarians like Thwaites and Hickes, clergymen and their wives and daughters (altogether, 116 of the subscribers were women), and a substantial representation of the citizens of Newcastle which was the Elstobs' home town. The book was the result of a vigorous communal endeavour, but its author was Elizabeth Elstob and her name appeared on the title page. That she, a mere woman, had produced work of such high achievement was a source of surprise but also of additional praise. There was a willingness among supporters and subscribers to make up to some extent for the failings of social arrangements, particularly the inadequacies of women's education as compared with men's, and rally behind an exceptional, hard-working woman.

An English-Saxon Homily on the Birthday of St Gregory was a translation into modern English of a sermon used in Anglo-Saxon churches to help spread the gospel to those who had no Latin. Gregory was the Pope who had sent Augustine to England to convert a nation of pagans to Christianity. In a sixty-page preface, Elstob explained how she came to undertake the translation and why the book was important. Like many other prefaces and dedications by women, this long essay began with an autobiographical account. Elstob described how she 'accidentally' first read some Saxon, an extract from King Alfred's version of Orosius which her brother – 'a near relation and friend' – was preparing for publication. She found it easy to understand once she had mastered the alphabet. She was intrigued to note how many words seemed familiar to her, particularly because she had grown up in the north of England where the language had retained more of the Saxon influence.

The revival of Saxon studies that began in the 1690s at Queen's College, Oxford, led by George Hickes, which the Elstobs were part of, had a religious as well as scholarly impetus: its aim was to trace the roots of the English Church back to the days before the Norman Conquest, to recover theological traditions from the writings of the primitive fathers of the Saxon Church which had no connection to either present-day Catholicism or Nonconformity and could therefore offer an alternative to the doctrinal antagonisms of the time. Elstob's *English-Saxon Homily*, in Hickes's view 'the most correct I ever saw or read', was a work that he judged would be 'of great advantage to the Church of England against the papists . . . and the credit of our country, to which Mrs Elstob will be counted abroad as great an ornament in her way as Madame Dacier is to France'.[11]

With a formidable display of erudition, Elizabeth Elstob's preface engaged the readers of her 'treatise' on what she anticipated would be contentious points. There was the fact that she was a woman – 'I know it will be said, What has a woman to do with learning?' – and that she was a Saxon scholar – 'Admit a woman may have learning, is there no other kind of learning to employ her time? What is this Saxon? What has she to do with this barbarous antiquated stuff?' To those whom she imagined making such objections, she robustly set out her credentials and convictions, having first made it plain that she viewed them (more in sorrow than in anger) as 'addicted to censure' because of their own inadequacies. Such critics were likely to be men, and men had always believed that learning made women 'impertinent' and led them to 'neglect their household affairs'. Elstob agreed that where this happened it was a fault: 'But it is not the fault of learning, which rather polishes and refines our nature, and teaches us that method and regularity which disposes us to greater readiness and dexterity in all kinds of business.' She added:

> I do not observe it so frequently objected against women's diversions that they take them off from household affairs. Why therefore should those few among us who are lovers of learning, altho' no better account could be given of it than its being a diversion, be denied the benefit and pleasure of it, which is both so innocent and improving. But perhaps most of these persons mean no more than that it makes them neglect the theatre, and long sittings at a play, or tedious dressings, and visiting days, and other diversions which steal away more time than are spent at study.[12]

That men (such as Uncle Charles) should try to deny women learning was no surprise and fully deserved sarcastic comment. In a warm footnote it was pointed out that the usual objections 'gentlemen' made had been fully answered 'in a scholastic way, and in very elegant Latin, by that glory of her sex, Mrs Anna Maria van Schurman'. But women were censurers too: 'I am more surprised, and even ashamed, to find any of the ladies even more violent than they in carrying on the same charge.' Women who objected to women's learning were 'contemptible' and to be pitied because in declaring openly, for example, that 'they hated any woman that knew more than themselves', they revealed their ignorance, envy and folly.

More significant than these 'admirers of ignorance' were those women who had a little learning, who knew how to value it in themselves, who read plays, romances, novels and poems, might 'perhaps entertain themselves a little with history', enjoyed raillery and witty conversation, and who were satisfied with these accomplishments. One reason they were more significant was that these women were to some extent Elstob's target audience. George Hickes himself had urged that Elstob would serve as an example to such 'ladies', who might then turn from foreign 'embellishments' to discover the faith, religion, laws, customs and especially language of their ancestors – the original of their mother tongue.

By publishing the homily, Elstob would promote not just the study of Saxon but the cause of female learning in general by making available a lost tradition: far from being 'barbarous', the primitive fathers were 'very zealous to encourage good learning amongst the ladies' as witnessed by surviving epistles from Saints Jerome, Augustin, Chrysostom and Gregory. Roger Ascham, tutor to Queen Elizabeth, had made a catalogue of the saints' epistles to excellent women. 'I assure you,' Elizabeth Elstob told her readers, 'these are considerations which have afforded me no small encouragement in the prosecution of these studies.'

As the preface made clear, Elstob's studies had been more than superficial. She had read deeply in ecclesiastical history (much of it in Latin) and had strong views about the way the conversion of the Saxons had been 'misrepresented' and even 'perverted' by later historians because of the ignorance of scholars – their 'want of a more perfect acquaintance with the affairs of that time' – or their prejudice – the 'violent prejudice against everything that bore any relation to the name of Rome'. A partisan in more ways than one, she offered a revisionist history which sought to restore Gregory and Augustine to their central place in the most important event in the nation's early history, 'the happy circumstances of our conversion'. She believed that Gregory deserved to be honoured for his saintliness and his status as 'the English Apostle' who first taught the English the Christian faith, motivated by nothing but zeal at a time when the Catholic Church was a sound organisation still in touch with original doctrine. The failure to honour Gregory, along with the misrepresentation of Augustine, struck a chord in the female scholar diligently working for no reward but zeal.

Though Elstob did not draw out the analogies, it is striking that in her account the accusations against Augustine were those that clever women had to negotiate. Augustine had been sent by Gregory to reform a corrupt English Church. The villains were the Romano-British bishops who had no interest in converting the pagan Saxons; and later historians who would go to any lengths to deny Augustine and Gregory the credit. A long discussion of the 'maligners' of Augustine turned to a considerable extent on whether he was arrogant or not: words like 'presumption' and 'vanity' were fixed on Augustine because he had done such a notable thing as convert a whole nation. In painstaking detail, Elstob laid out her grounds for concluding in favour of Augustine's 'humility' and 'the meekness of his conversation', challenging some authorities, endorsing others, and showing her capacity for clear reasoning and command of the sources. She was able to conclude that there was no evidence for 'haughtiness' or 'an assuming disposition'; the accusation depended, as did so many accusations against women, 'as much upon conjecture as some other circumstances of the history which are urged to his disadvantage'.

Elstob drew on the authority of ancient chroniclers such as Bede and Thorn, and the authority of her contemporaries, senior churchmen and learned antiquarians, with some of whom she had personal acquaintance. Comparing accounts of the slaughter of the monks at Bangor, she was able to refer to manuscript evidence provided for her by 'the reverend and learned Dr Smith, Prebendary of Durham, who is preparing a most exact edition of Bede', which corresponded with the views of Mr Wanley, Mr Wharton, Sir Henry Spelman and Mr Collier. Like these scholars she was exact, diligent, and worked with the best evidence available. Having taken her transcript of the homily on St

Gregory from one source, she checked it against another. She was able to examine

that ancient parchment book of homilies in the Bodleian Library amongst Junius's books NE.F.4 being the second of those volumes that had formerly belonged to the Hattonian Library, an account of which we have in that most elaborate catalogue of Saxon manuscripts by Mr Wanley, which makes the second volume of Dr Hickes's *Thesaurus* p. 43. I had access to this book by the singular courtesy of Dr Hudson.[13]

Like Dr Hickes, Dr Hudson was a champion of female learning. Did Elstob go into the Bodleian? Historians have always taken it for granted that women were denied entry but it may be that exceptions were made for exceptional women. Elstob doesn't exactly say that she was there, although her precise referencing gives the impression of a reader finding her way among the stacks. Other men who were part of the close-knit community of antiquarians working with these sources at the Bodleian (and who later formed the Society of Antiquaries) did not object that they were made available to a female scholar. Thomas Hearne was not alone in finding the preface 'judicious, learned and elegant'.

Bringing the preface to a close with the usual thanks and acknowledgements, Elstob paid testimony to her brother – 'always ready to assist and encourage me in my studies' – and picked up an earlier reference to the Saxon Queen Berhta to enumerate a short genealogy of illustrious women alongside whom she, and all those 'ladies ... of the best rank' who were her supporters and subscribers, implicitly took their places. As the first Christian Queen of England, it was Berhta who converted her husband, King Ethelbert, and then the whole of the south of England; and it was their daughter, Edelburga, who took the message to the north, having first converted *her* husband, Edwin. The significance of English female agency is extended further: the conversion of the whole Roman Empire is credited to Helena, mother of Constantine the Great, 'affirmed to have been a native of this island'; and, looking beyond English shores, there was Chlodesuinda, daughter of King Chlotharius, who converted her husband Alboinus, King of the Lombards; and Ingundis, who converted her husband

Hermenegildus. All these women contributed to the advancement of religion, but it was enough to name 'two of the greatest monarchs that the world has known, for wisdom and piety and constant success in their affairs, Queen Elizabeth, and Anne Queen of Great Britain'. Publishing *An English-Saxon Homily on the Birthday of St Gregory* during the reign of Queen Anne was in itself a justification for addressing it to 'the Ladies of Great Britain' since she was 'both an example and encourager of all virtues and laudable qualities in those of her sex'.

The ambition manifest in this and in the later *Rudiments of Grammar* was no less than to reshape the direction of the nation's cultural politics. Elizabeth Elstob played for high stakes. As well as engaging in pioneering scholarly work, she took financial risks, committing herself to expensively produced books she could never underwrite from her own resources since she didn't have any. In the memoir she later wrote for George Ballard she listed a number of large-scale projects she had already begun or had in mind:

> She designed, if ill fortune had not prevented her, to have published all Aelfric's Homilies of which she had made an entire transcript with the various readings from other manuscripts and had translated several of them into English. She likewise took an exact copy of the Textus Rossensiss upon vellum, now in the library of that great and generous encourager of learning, the Right Hon. The Earl of Oxford. And transcribed all the hymns from an ancient manuscript belonging to the Church of Sarum. She had several other designs, but was unhappily hindered by a necessity of getting her bread.

In the British Library there is a twenty-four-page booklet that purports to be 'a letter from the publisher to a doctor of divinity'. The doctor of divinity was Elstob's Uncle Charles, and the publisher was the respected John Bowyer who printed the *English-Saxon Homily*. But the letter, which is really an advertisement for a proposed new book by Elstob, wasn't by Bowyer at all: it is signed and dated – St Swithin's Day, July 1713 – by the doctor of divinity's 'niece'. Probably Charles Elstob had suggested that his niece produce it as a means for him to help drum up subscribers for her.

In presenting these elaborate proposals Elizabeth Elstob also presented herself. She made it clear that the new work which was planned – the complete edition of Aelfric's homilies referred to in the memoir – was likely to be expensive: it was to be beautifully produced and would need 'all manner of assistance, from learned and generous persons', but she pointed out that both the universities were already on side: 'The university of Cambridge, which hath indulged me with the use of the manuscript from which I take my copy, hath been already very liberal in her subscriptions, and promiseth me the favour of farther encouragement', and Oxford was going to print it, a fact which 'cannot but appear with a very good grace in the front of the catalogue I am now to give you'. Testimonies from learned men of the nation's need for the work itself followed. Elstob justified the high production values by reference to the honour of the nation: 'somewhat is to be permitted to the honour of a nation, the politeness whereof is in greater or less esteem accordingly as performances of this kind shall have more or less of elegance and ornament.' There was a fulsome tribute to Queen Anne and a handy compressed description of the project that might be copied on and sent around, plus a reminder to every subscriber to pay up at once because it was going to be a work of 'great labour' and 'great expense' and 'published at the sole charge of the editor' who was not skilled in getting subscriptions and did not expect to make a profit but didn't want to lose by it either. She gave warning that anyone not paying their half of the subscription in advance should not expect to receive the book when it was published.

These proposals in 1713 are evidence of the success of Elizabeth Elstob's 1709 *An English-Saxon Homily on the Birthday of St Gregory*. They indicate that learned men trusted her and that the well-born were willing to reach into their pockets to support her. Those who had subscribed to the *English-Saxon Homily*, with its elegant illustration and Saxon type, needed to do no more than take down their own copies from their library shelves to be reminded that these books were expensive and complicated to print. From the point of view of her printer, producing more Anglo-Saxon texts was a good investment since he had had to make up a special type, drawn according to her specifications, for the books already published. Anything which helped nurture the burgeoning scholarly industry in this area was good news for him. (This Anglo-Saxon type still exists and is in the possession of Oxford University Press.)

William's early death in 1715 was a catastrophe. It left his sister homeless and alone. George Hickes also died in the same year. It is likely that there were debts that Elizabeth, without an income, was unable to pay. Certainly, if she had taken money from subscribers for a book which in the disarray of her life she was unable to produce, that would have counted as debt. If her goods were seized she may have lost property belonging to the university libraries of Cambridge or Oxford. Some valuables – books and manuscripts – left with a friend disappeared after that friend decamped to the West Indies. One way and another a great deal went missing, including manuscripts in progress and copies of her own works.

Elstob seems to have managed to stagger on for some years and may have tried to establish a boarding school in Chelsea where Mary Astell was an active and well-known figure.[14] George Hickes was aware of Astell's work: he recommended her books in the 1707 edition of his translation of Fenelon's treatise on the education of daughters, *Traite de l'education des filles.* Under the auspices of the Society for the Propagation of Christian Knowledge (SPCK), Astell had established a charity school for girls, stipulating that it was 'always to be under the direction of women', and she was still involved with it in 1718. Chelsea was home to a group of wealthy, aristocratic ladies, in particular Lady Catherine Jones, Lady Elizabeth (Betty) Hastings and Lady Ann Coventry, who provided emotional and financial support for Astell. It's likely that Elstob was drawn there by her admiration for Astell, an important role model from the previous generation, and by the hope that like her fellow Northerner (Astell also grew up in Newcastle) she too might benefit from the practical and moral support of a community keen to promote female scholarship. Elstob rented a building for her school and perhaps took out a loan for the purpose. Six months later, her name disappeared from the rent rolls and she herself had fled. Of the miseries of the years between William's death in 1715 and her disappearance in 1718, she told George Ballard in 1748: 'It is at least thirty years since this happened to me, and you may reasonably think it has made me very unhappy ever since, which if my friends were sensible of, I must believe they would avoid all occasions of bringing it to my remembrance.'

Memoirs of British Ladies

Among the projects that Elizabeth Elstob had begun to develop and which she had been forced to abandon in the wreckage of 1718 was one that had nothing apparently to do with Anglo-Saxon and everything to do with exceptional women like herself. She wanted to recover examples from the past and compile a history of intellectual women. She had made a list in a notebook of some forty learned women: queens, aristocratic ladies and nuns for the most part, but also including the poet Katherine Philips, and Samuel Pepys's wife, Elizabeth. The notebook survives, and though the entries are brief it is clear that the plan was an ambitious one.

Given the example of his mother and sister, it is not surprising that George Ballard was sympathetic to a project of this kind. The 'supposed incapacity of the female sex' was, he later wrote, a 'vulgar prejudice'. He already knew about Margaret Roper, the brilliant daughter of Sir Thomas More; and he asked Elstob about Mary Astell and others. Fired by her enthusiasm and inspired by her knowledge, he became indignant about the many 'ingenious women of this nation' who had been famous in their own time but who were 'not only unknown to the public in general, but have been passed by in silence by our greatest biographers'.[15]

Ballard took up Elstob's project. Biographical writing appealed to him. In 1732, he had contemplated writing about the Elizabethan scholar John Dee, one of the most learned men of his time, who 'for all his valuable and wonderful parts, was neglected and necessitated to the last extremity, being forced oftentimes (saith Lilly in his *Life and Times*) to sell one book or other to buy himself a meal'.[16] A year later, Thomas Hearne noted that Ballard was interested in writing a life of the historian John Stow. Now, he began to collect information about exceptional women, asking his friends to send him whatever small details they came across in their antiquarian researches. He pursued his subjects through rare books, parish records, wills and legal documents, manuscripts, the memories of descendents, and even inscriptions on tombstones and monuments.

It was a long and laborious undertaking, but in 1752 Ballard had the satisfaction of seeing the *Memoirs of British Ladies who have been celebrated for their writings or skill in the learned languages, arts and sciences* into print. It was a work which was intended to preserve for the nation all the illustrious women about whom he could find sufficient information. His purpose was to 'set their great excellencies and attainments in a true and proper light', and to inform readers of 'those particulars in their lives and manners' which best deserved imitation. Volume One covered learned ladies in the fifteenth and sixteenth centuries, beginning with two holy women, Julian of Norwich and Margery Kempe, about whom little was known, Ballard noted in a sideswipe that probably reflected Elstob's opinions, because of the 'negligence of the ecclesiastics' whose job it was to transmit 'intelligence of all sorts to posterity' and who had failed to do so in this regard. Volume Two covered the seventeenth and early eighteenth centuries, but included only very selected figures from the recent past. It ended with Mary Astell who by the mid eighteenth century, when the book appeared, was all but forgotten. Astell herself might not have been surprised to know this, given her own observation that history tended to record the exploits of men and to ignore those of women. Ballard's account, drawn largely from what Elizabeth Elstob was able to tell him, has been the most important single source of information about Mary Astell's life.

The *Memoirs of British Ladies* articulated the views that Ballard and Elstob shared. It was driven by a passionate indignation at the way 'custom' had diminished women's opportunities and how a nation had 'forgotten' its learned women. In his preface Ballard pointed out that, in general, 'those who have distinguished themselves in the republic of letters, have seldom been unattended with their memorialists' and yet, although the present age could boast many more biographers than previous eras, they were not producing biographies of 'the very many ingenious women of this nation, who were really possessed of a great share of learning'. Why was this so? Why were women being denied the honours due to them? If 'the preserving from oblivion the memory of illustrious persons' was 'commendable', why were women being allowed to slip out of the historical record? In the march of progress, this was a sign of backwardness: 'learned foreigners' – Italian, French, Spanish, German – were busily commemorating their women, and 'it is pretty certain that England hath produced more women famous for literary accomplishments than any other nation in Europe'.

Ballard's work on the book was a tribute to Elizabeth Elstob. In its inception it had been her project and perhaps she saw it as a tribute to Mary Astell. For Ballard, Elstob was the living representative of all the lost, neglected and poorly rewarded women writers throughout history and in his own time. Life was unfair to them and custom unkind. Though she did not feature as a subject – probably because of her anxiety to ensure secrecy about her lost years – there was one mention of her: Ballard cited 'the learned and ingenious Mrs Elstob' as his authority for saying that Lady Arabella Seymour's papers were in the Harleian and Longleat libraries, not having seen them with his own eyes.

The polemical objective of *Memoirs of British Ladies* was to make scholarship respectable as a female activity. Sarah Chapone and Mary Delaney – who served as a patron and to whom the second volume was dedicated – shared this view. They actively participated in shaping the book. What they sought to promote was as far from the realities of Elizabeth Elstob's bad times as could possibly be imagined. As for Elstob herself, she became an object of charity and her life was transformed. In October 1738, she was persuaded to go to Bath, supposedly for her health but also so that she could be seen and informally interviewed by potential employers. She was still insisting that her school suited her: 'while I can get my bread in a just and honest way I desire no more . . . It is a way of life I must confess I am fond of, if it were not precarious and fatiguing.'

Mrs Chapone and her circle had other ideas. The Duke and Duchess of Portland, a wealthy young couple with three small children, were in need of a governess. Evidently they were satisfied with what they saw of Elstob and at Bath that autumn an agreement was concluded. For £30 per annum the nation's foremost Saxon scholar would become a part of the Portland household, spending winters in Whitehall and summers at Bulstrode, their country mansion in Buckinghamshire. She would teach the little children to read. The arrangement would begin the following summer but payment was to be backdated to the previous year.

In an early letter to George Ballard, Elizabeth Elstob had described herself as one who was 'inured to disappointments', who having 'rubbed thro' most of her life was content with very little. She identified with those who had talent but remained poor, self-educated men (like Ballard) as well as women like herself: 'I often compare myself to poor John Tucker, whose life I read when a girl in Winstanley's *Lives of the Poets*, which affected me so much I cannot forget it yet. He is there described to have been an honest industrious poor man, but notwithstanding his indefatigable industry, as the author writes, no butter would stick on his bread.'[17] Now the butter was about to stick on her bread: 'neither my best friends nor myself could have wished for a more happy and honorable situation for me'. She was yet to discover that her 'charming little ladies' were to be with her all the time; and though she was 'the happiest creature in the world' in her new and comfortable surroundings, she soon realised that there was even less likelihood that she would do any serious scholarly work than when she taught the children of the stocking weavers: 'I have less time than I ever had in my life to command because it is not my own.'

Even so, she busied herself in raising subscriptions for Ballard's book, distributing his proposals and collecting money: in 1750 she had ten guineas to pass on to him from twenty subscribers.[18] (She also took care to name him when the Duchess and her friends admired the brown gown she wore and which Ballard had run up for her.) The experience of collecting subscriptions was not all sweetness and light (perhaps it revived unhappy memories?): the 'ill nature of an ungenerous person' soured her on at least one occasion. 'I am extremely ill,' she told Ballard, 'and can only add that I hate this ill natured world and heartily rejoice to think I cannot continue long in it.'

Elizabeth Elstob's last years were little less obscure than her middle ones. She was an aged retainer in the circles of the elite. Her health was not good and she had to be helped down stairs. There are surprisingly few references to her in the correspondence of other scholarly women, even though the Duchess of Portland and Sarah Chapone were important first-generation bluestockings and Elizabeth Montagu was a protégée of the Duchess. Montagu was often at Whitehall and

Bulstrode during the years that Elizabeth Elstob was a part of the household. The letters that were constantly exchanged within this family and friendship network might have been seen by Elstob and she and Montagu certainly met. Consciously or unconsciously, Elizabeth Montagu's later work on Shakespeare followed the path Elstob had opened up when she quoted George Hickes on the title page of her 1715 Anglo-Saxon grammar: 'the language that we speak is our mother tongue; and who so proper to play the critics in this as the females'. Montagu played the critic, choosing Shakespeare as her subject: Shakespeare's 'small Latin and less Greek' threw the emphasis on his English. He could be presented as a key figure in the evolution of a national language whose origins went back to Anglo-Saxon.

Fittingly, the last surviving letter from Elizabeth Elstob to George Ballard was written to thank him for his book. It was a short letter and – like many written from Bulstrode where there was always much 'hurry' and activity – it apologised for not saying more, but in this case she had a good excuse: 'I think every minute lost that hinders me from the pleasure of reading your book.' Alas, there is no record of what she thought of it.

Chapter Three

MID-CENTURY MODELS: RECOVERY, EULOGY AND SILENCE

The sluggish, the indolent part of mankind, whose life itself differs little from death, being but one degree above the animal, are justly condemned to oblivion . . . But, surely, the truly wise, the virtuous, persons equally eminent for great and good qualities, for their extraordinary accomplishments, and the use they made of them, to the honour of the supreme Being and the benefit of mankind, these ought not to be swept away into forgetfulness with the common rubbish of the species.

Theophilus Rowe, *The Life of Mrs Elizabeth Rowe*[1]

Merit in distress

George Ballard's male friends were surprised that he did not intend to include in his book those women 'of gay imagination', the well-known playwrights, Aphra Behn, Delarivier Manley and Susannah Centlivre. Ballard's answer (in which we might hear the advice of Sarah Chapone and Mary Delaney) was that all women of 'real' learning were good, they did not misapply what they learned, but there were those who carried 'more sail than ballast'. Carrying sail rather than ballast was the intellectual equivalent of wearing make-up and jewellery to cover ravage and disease – it was morally suspect. Thus, to say, as Ballard did, that 'none of that slight sisterhood were ever thought women of learning, or had any pretence to be called women of knowledge' implied a judgement about their morals.[2]

This separating out of good writing women and bad in the name of knowledge and learning became the new orthodoxy. Rhetorically, the lines ran roughly as follows: women who were intellectual (who led with the head not the heart), of high rank or invested in the values of those of high rank, and solvent (engaging in literature and scholarship out of desire for personal moral and spiritual improvement rather than material necessity) were good. Some women who merely entertained were also good, but unlikely to be celebrated as illustrious. Those who did not present as intellectuals, were not associated with the values of rank or appeared to have disgraced their births as Delarivier Manley was accused of doing by John Duncombe in *The Feminiad*, were bad. (Duncombe was grieved to see 'One nobly born disgrace / Her modest sex, and her illustrious race'.)[3]

With rank and power behind it, this orthodoxy was remarkably effective. It produced a version of what the female author looked like that was – perhaps not surprisingly – as severely controlled and as much of a fiction as the versions of everyday ideal womanhood with which the culture abounded. When the Revd Thomas Birch was approached in the 1740s to write a biographical memoir of Delarivier Manley's sometime friend and sister playwright Catharine Trotter Cockburn, he had no hesitation in accepting. Over thirty years had passed since Catharine Trotter, as she then was, had been among the women of 'gay imagination' and even then she had been as well known for her philosophical writings on the work of John Locke as for her plays. Having married a poor clergyman and brought up a family of three children, she had been living for many years in remote Northumberland.

Thomas Birch was a populariser who could turn his hand to more or less anything. In preparing his memoir of Cockburn, he took as his model the recently produced *Life and Works of Mrs Rowe*. He knew it well. His friend Elizabeth Carter had contributed celebratory verses to it and had even arranged its serialisation in the *Gentleman's Magazine* with which Birch was also associated. (Elizabeth Carter and Catherine Talbot, as well as the Duchess of Portland, were among Cockburn's subscribers.) Birch's memoir of Catharine Cockburn followed that of Elizabeth Singer Rowe in presenting Cockburn as a writer who was 'truly wise' and 'virtuous'. The full title emphasised her religious and moral concerns, which the selection of writings reinforced: *The Works of Mrs Catharine Cockburn, theological, moral, dramatic and poetical. Several of them now first printed, revised and published, with an account of the Life of the Author* (1751).

Catharine Cockburn had been revising and assembling her works and networking among the senior clergy of the north for decades in the hope of seeing the collection in print. Alas, she died in 1749 and never had the satisfaction of reading what Birch wrote about her nor of holding the handsome volumes in her hands. Had she done so she would surely have been pleased. In Birch's version, Catharine Cockburn figured as an 'extraordinary' person about whom it was a 'justice due to the public' that her story should be known. This public was conceived as an eternal one, endlessly renewed in future years and never ceasing to be interested in the subjects covered: '[P]osterity at least will be solicitous to know to whom they will owe the most demonstrative and perspicuous reasonings upon subjects of eternal importance.' Among that public, women had a special interest and were to be considered as being specially served by the publication: 'her own sex is entitled to the fullest information about one who has done such honour to them, and raised our ideas of their intellectual powers, by an example of the greatest extent of understanding and correctness of judgement, united to all the vivacity of imagination'.

Birch then went on to praise Cockburn for her achievements in philosophy, making the comparison with ancient times when it was well known there were famous female philosophers:

> Antiquity indeed boasted of its *female philosophers* . . . But our own age and country may, without injustice or vanity, oppose to those illustrious ladies the defender of *Locke* and *Clarke*; who, with a genius equal to the most eminent of them, had the superior advantage of cultivating it in the only effectual method of improvement, the study of a real philosophy, and a theology truly worthy of human nature, and its all-perfect author.[4]

Cockburn's 'superior advantage' was to have been born into a Christian rather than a pagan era. The nation's opportunity was to do better than classical civilisation, hitherto the yardstick for every cultural achievement. Birch accorded a dignity and stateliness to Catharine Cockburn, a monumentality appropriate to her role as figurehead of 'our own age and country'. She was a national treasure.

In choosing to rescue Catharine Cockburn from obscurity as a 'remarkable genius' who had not had her due, Cockburn's supporters played down her own efforts to get herself back in the public eye. They emphasised her virtuous intellectuality and did not dwell on her years as a successful and very well-known playwright between 1696 and 1708. They did not mention any of the vile things Delarivier Manley said about her (see Chapter Seven). The clergymen whom she succeeded in rallying to her cause, and the subscribers who helped bring her work to a new audience, combined views about how wrong it was to deny women education merely on the grounds of sex, with patriotic fervour. National prestige was enhanced by the superior literary talent of British women. Britain's female worthies could be enlisted in a cause patterned on classical precedent: Plutarch's *Mulierum virtutes* ('Virtuous Deeds of Women') and its Renaissance imitators, such as Boccaccio's *De claris mulieribus* ('On Famous Women').[5]

Idealising women was an available posture, an element in the repertoire that appealed to those who were busy constructing a high-minded version of English literary history. Catharine Cockburn was recovered as an icon pointing the way to a more glorious future, a move which was accompanied by denigration not only of other women – those women of 'gay imagination' – but also of what was perceived to be the failure of the national past to revere female worth. When the works of Susannah Centlivre were published in three volumes in 1760-1, they came with a biographical preface which sought to show that the present age was superior to the past by virtue of its celebration of women: 'the custom of the times', the biographer wrote, vaguely and misleadingly referring to the early decades of the eighteenth century, 'discountenanced poetical excellence in a female ... See here the effects of prejudice, a woman who did honour to the nation, suffered because she was a woman. ... Hold! Let my pen stop, and not reproach the present age for the sins of their fathers.'[6]

This rhetorical move – lamenting the blinkered past and claiming that former ages 'discountenanced poetical excellence' in females – was a way of boasting about the present. As it happens, in the case of Susannah Centlivre it is hard to see how her own times 'discountenanced' her: she was an immensely popular playwright whose works had gone on being performed. But the fantasy of 'discountenanced' females has a life of its own which can be discovered at almost any point one pitches into literary history. Literary history itself, from its beginnings, mythologised the idea of the lost or 'discountenanced' woman writer.[7] Like the compilations and celebratory biographies of the mid eighteenth century, medieval and early modern texts produced the woman writer as a 'lost' figure in order to 'discover' her. These opportunities for the enterprising were much imitated.

Catharine Talbot, who was the adopted daughter of the Archbishop of Canterbury and lived at Lambeth Palace when she was not staying with aristocratic friends, read Birch's edition of Cockburn with pleasure. Like Sarah Chapone discovering Elizabeth Elstob grinding out narrowed days among agricultural labourers and stocking weavers, Talbot was shocked by the contrast of high abilities and lowly circumstances. The perplexing combination of genius, obscurity and poverty revealed in Cockburn's life troubled her:

> She was a remarkable genius, and yet how obscure her lot in life! It seems grievous at first, and such straitness of circumstances as perplexes and cramps the mind, is surely a grievance; but on consideration, what signifies distinction and splendour in this very transitory state? . . . But methinks those who knew such merit did not do their duty in letting it remain so obscure.

What were the duties of those who knew someone of merit? Should merit in distress be transplanted into scenes of splendour such as those Elstob no doubt encountered living with the Portlands at Bulstrode? Talbot thought of Elizabeth Carter, in her view Cockburn's 'superior', living obscurely in Kent and tutoring a nephew in classical studies for his university entrance. (The examiners made a special point of congratulating him on the high standard his tutor – known to be a woman – had brought him to.) In 1751, Carter had yet to produce a major work that would establish her reputation and secure her finances. 'Alas,' Talbot wrote, 'will not she live and die perhaps as obscurely, and what alas can I do to prevent it?' Carter might be 'lost' to the nation before she had even been found.[8]

Elizabeth Carter herself, meanwhile, wanted Talbot to exert *her* talents and live less obscurely. She repeatedly urged her friend to edit and arrange the as yet uncollected papers of that other remarkable genius, Elizabeth Singer Rowe. The two-volume *Life and Works of Mrs Rowe* (1739), to which Carter had contributed, had included extracts from Rowe's letters as well as a good sample of her writings, but by no means all. There was much that could be done to make more of Rowe available to a wider readership. Talbot, at that time moving in a higher social sphere than Carter, had access to Rowe's letters through her friendship with Frances, Countess of Hertford. The Countess, though much younger than Rowe, had valued the older woman's letters so much that she had copied them out in her own hand and kept them in a green leather folder, 'the green book', which guests like Talbot were invited to peruse. Carter wrote more than once about what she called her 'favourite point', the green book; it was 'intolerable' that Talbot was letting the opportunity slip when staying with the Countess: 'I hope a few of your leisure hours will be bestowed on that most excellent green book which I so sincerely wish to have the world the better for.' Talbot had the skills: she was one of the inner circle around Samuel Richardson, advising and commenting on his drafts and correcting the entire manuscript of *Sir Charles Grandison*. But she claimed not to have the time, nor quite enough help in essential research from her hosts: 'I attempted once or twice to ask questions about it, but being referred to some other time, that other time has never yet come.' She read the folder through and made notes for how she might arrange the materials but could find 'no order no connection in it. It wants an introduction – so it is returned to the *considering drawer*, with many of its ancestors . . . The other papers, yours and all, lie in the same hopeless condition.'[9]

The 'very respectable' Mrs Elizabeth Rowe

Mrs Rowe's lot in life was far from obscure. By the time of her death in 1737, she had been in the public eye for the best part of five decades: in the 1690s she was the famous 'Philomela' whose poems lit up the *Athenian Mercury*; by the 1720s she was the well-known author of epistolary prose fictions that dwelt on the pleasures of a heavenly afterlife; and in the 1730s her devotional writings, edited by Isaac Watts, found their way into almost every private collection of books in the country.

For the bluestockings, she was a figure from an earlier era whose life and work carried significance for the younger generation, some of whom were to achieve celebrity themselves, although her appeal was by no means universal. Elizabeth Carter seems to have modelled her early moves into the public realm of print on the pattern of Elizabeth Rowe, and certainly in 1737, when she wrote 'On the Death of Mrs Rowe', Carter's avowed intention was to emulate her. On the evidence of that poem alone (in its several different versions), emulating Mrs Rowe in the late 1730s was achieved by refusing other potential exemplars, an example Mrs Rowe herself, supposedly, set. Mrs Rowe's 'sense' (a quality she was 'blessed with' by heaven) had enabled her to distinguish herself by applying her genius well, charming the fancy, amending the heart and withdrawing the reader's mind from 'trifling follies'. Trifling follies did not sully Mrs Rowe's pages, which were dedicated to 'better purposes'. She was, according to Carter, 'our sex's ornament and pride' and her writings were of 'a nobler kind' than those of (unnamed) other 'female wits' whose imaginations had for too long been filled with wanton tales and novels and romances. Mrs Rowe, in other words, represented the new order: 'No lawless freedoms e'er profaned thy lays, / To virtue sacred and thy maker's praise.'[10] She was a woman carrying ballast not sail.

Fifty years later, when bluestocking Clara Reeve included Mrs Rowe in her literary history, *The Progress of Romance* (1785), it was as one of the most well known of modern writers. Mrs Rowe was 'very respectable'; few would fail to recognise her name; her writings breathed 'a true spirit of piety' and her *Letters Moral and Entertaining* were 'very proper for youth'.[11]

That Mrs Rowe was 'very proper' was certainly the message of the *Life and Works of Mrs Rowe*, which was the eighteenth-century prototype of the family-controlled biographies of successful bluestockings that appeared in the early nineteenth century. The 'lives and letters' format which Elizabeth Carter, Elizabeth Montagu and Hester Chapone favoured and for which they saved, shaped and preserved their papers, was modelled in some degree on this exemplary text. Part of what made Mrs Rowe 'proper' was that she was a comfortably-off gentlewoman with powerful aristocratic connections. Though she wrote for commercial markets she did not need to write for gain; and though she lived for a short time in London and kept up connections there, she repeatedly expressed her preference for rural retirement, solitude and privacy.

The *Life and Works of Mrs Rowe* told the story of an author's life about which it was not deemed necessary to be silent, although silence was one of the virtues Mrs Rowe preached. The two volumes came heavily protected into the world: they were written and compiled by devoted friends and family, and, as an additional safeguard, included a memorial to Mrs Rowe's long-dead husband, Thomas Rowe, as well as an assemblage of his poems. If, as George Ballard complained, Anglican clergy had been negligent in transmitting to posterity intelligence about excellent women, the same could not be said of Dissenting circles, at least so far as Mrs Rowe was concerned.

The *Life and Works of Mrs Rowe* was conceived partly in a spirit of evangelism – as a sincere believer, Mrs Rowe's life served as an example to others of how a pious Christian life might be led – and partly as a defence against more vulgar representation. Her death had given Edmund Curll the opportunity to commission what would undoubtedly be a popular title, a *Life of Mrs Rowe*. Partly through the efforts of publishers like Curll, writers' lives, brought out at speed to capitalise on interest provoked by the subjects' deaths, were a burgeoning market. (Pope's friend Arbuthnot described Curll as one of the new terrors of death.) It was supposedly to prevent this that Mrs Rowe's family and friends compiled the collection of her works to which the *Life* served as an introduction.

Elizabeth Rowe, a professional to her fingertips, had of course been putting her papers in order and preparing them for publication well before her death. It was customary for a prefatory life to be appended to any significant edition of the works, and she had been careful to copy many private letters that she was content should be published (and, no doubt, to destroy others). Nor would she have been surprised to discover that Curll had her in his sights: he had already reissued her 1696 volume of *Poems* without asking permission. Perhaps she didn't really need the stimulus of his attention. Mrs Rowe's concern about managing the moment of death, her attention to details such as where it was to take place (in her own home), what mood death should find her in, and her desire that her final messages to friends and public should not be out of date, had led to a high state of preparedness. Multiple 'last letters' survive. Her instructions to her executors were every bit as precise as were those which Anna Seward later left.

Rowe's biographers paid attention to her feelings about death and preparations for it, explaining that her 'ardour' for the afterlife was 'inconceivably great'. Death represented an 'enlargement of mind, and perfection of every faculty'. Entering upon immortality was to 'commence the life of angels'. Sainthood beckoned. The letter left for the Earl of Orrery reminded him that distinctions of rank would no longer matter; in fact, the poor might be better off: 'The immortal mind, perhaps, will quit a cottage with less regret than it would leave the splendour of a palace; and the breathless dust sleep as quietly beneath the grassy turf, as under the parade of a costly monument.' (Gray's *Elegy* was to pick up the theme.) She quoted Pope's 'The Dying Christian' – 'O grave! where is thy victory? / O death! where is thy sting?' – and assured him that her thoughts had 'grown familiar with the solemnity of dying'. Death seemed to advance 'as the peaceful messenger of liberty and happiness'.[12] To be unafraid of it was a sign of serene belief. To advertise it was to lay an emphasis on piety which, in Mrs Rowe's case, did double duty: it promoted her writings, and it reinforced an image of her as a specially virtuous, spiritual writer whose poems were more like hymns of praise and whose prose works were not so much written as received from beyond.

For Elizabeth Rowe, death marked a transition, not a break, between this life and the next. There might not be publishing houses in heaven but there was correspondence, as her own prose fictions bore witness. Her popular titles were epistles from the dead to the living: *Friendship in Death, or, Letters from the Dead to the Living* (1728) and *Letters Moral and Entertaining* (1729–32). Even in life, she used the metaphor of writing her letters as a dead person from 'another world' to convey to friends in town the remoteness of her quiet rural existence. Like life, death included entertainment, speculation, songs, fables and 'transporting fiction'. The physical body died but the soul – which she identified as the source of her writing – found its true home: 'the soul with a noble freedom ascends the celestial heights, in search of the great original, the fountain of its excellence'.[13]

Rowe's writings expressed the continuity between life and the afterlife, dramatising it in story, poem and meditation. At the same time they made their own claims on eternity. Like the soul given form in her pages, Rowe's books aspired to exist not just in her lifetime but in her eternal life, not only now but for ever. Readers understood that her concern was to make herself available to a never-ending posterity through her writings. Posterity and heaven were interchangeable places of permanence. Elizabeth Rowe's often enunciated 'wished for' death was, among other things, a way of locating reputation beyond the grave; praising her for her pious resignation was an encouragement to others to pitch their expectations into the future, it was a way of endorsing activities, like writing, that had a future as well as a present reference.

Receiving this message was undoubtedly part of the pleasure of reading her and it proved successful as a strategy for ensuring reputation, even if of a strictly 'pious' kind. Isaac Watts's edition of her *Devout Exercises of the Heart* went through twenty-four separate editions before the eighteenth century was out, and the *Life of Mrs Rowe* was frequently reprinted as a text in its own right without any accompanying works, or with a selection from *Friendship in Death* and *Letters Moral and Entertaining*. No other life of a female author had such prominence. Her readers were the same readers who read Isaac Watts in such large numbers throughout the eighteenth century and beyond, taking comfort from religious writings that stressed pleasure in this world while reassuringly evoking even more pleasure in the next.

The Feminiad

In *The Feminiad*, his eulogistic long poem to female genius, John Duncombe pictured a smiling Mrs Rowe travelling skywards to meet her Maker and her dead husband and explained in a note that the character of Mrs Elizabeth Rowe and her writings was 'too well known to be dwelt on here'. The apparent paradox that a writer, whose public identity was built on her desire to live in retirement from the world in a state most nearly approximating to the retirement afforded by heaven, should be 'too well known' to need to be described passed without comment. Duncombe's further remark that 'without any previous illness she met at last with that sudden death for which she had always wished' confirmed the impression of a recluse with no interest in the living world whose removal to heaven was the fulfilment of desire: 'Released from earth, with smiles she soars on high / Amidst her kindred spirits of the sky.'[14]

The aspiration to privacy by women with public reputations was like the aspiration to silence by those who wrote books (often the same people): it did not so much claim privacy or silence but was a bid to be allowed to be virtuous. This was not a bid that was on offer to certain other women whose characters and writings were also but 'too well known'. *The Feminiad*, published in 1754 and 1757, and also given wider circulation through anthologies and extracts, followed Ballard's *Memoirs of British Ladies* in refusing a place to celebrated and well-received female authors such as Aphra Behn, Delarivier Manley and Susannah Centlivre, even though Duncombe acknowledged in the verse itself that their work had merit. He depicted them, along with autobiographers Laetitia Pilkington, Constantia Phillips and Lady Frances Vane, as 'vice's friends and virtue's female foes'. Supposedly servants of 'a wanton Muse', these writers were named in order to be cast out. They could not expect 'impartial praise' for their 'genuine wit' and harmonious verse because, as a note explained, they had 'endeavoured to immortalize their shame, by writing and publishing their own memoirs'. The job of the critic was to be partial; to praise virtue's friends and attack the rest.[15]

Following the custom of the times, Duncombe eulogised and demonised, constructing a 'true' literary world inhabited by cultivated and learned angels – 'a blooming, studious band' – who soared on high, and a 'false' or lower region of the excluded. Duncombe's poem did not describe literary achievement as something occurring in a recognisable social world. Like Richard Samuel's later portrait *The Nine Living Muses of Great Britain*, the representational style of *The Feminiad* was pitched at a level of vague idealisation. In characteristic mid-century mode, the tone was either cloyingly sweet or indignant, the Popeian couplets sprinkled with exclamation marks and rhetorical questions. Duncombe's target was 'lordly man' (a phrase only ever used ironically in this period) that 'tyrant of verse, and arbiter of wit', who was not to be allowed to continue to view female genius with 'regardless eye'. 'Justice forbid!' Samuel Richardson was invoked: 'O thou! The sex's friend / And constant patron, Richardson! Attend!' Men who thought of women as mere vessels of sensuality were like 'eastern tyrants'. Such a view belonged in the seraglio. The very idea that British women might be sensual – 'Careless of ought but music, joy and love' – was loathsome and could only be propounded by those who refused to recognise that women had minds and souls. (As for British men enjoying the company of such women – 'Heavens! Could such artful, slavish sounds beguile / The freeborn sons of Britain's polished isle?') In place of this tempting vision of music, joy and love, Duncombe offered the products of British freedom: women who united domestic comforts with mental improvement. Unvoluptuous, these dazzling creatures read philosophy instead of making love or visits.

The 'sister muses' were moral. To earn a place in *The Feminiad* it was necessary to be well bred (best of all, like the Countess of Hertford, was to unite 'The Peeress, Poetess and Christian') and the posture for receiving their works was one of 'reverence'. Everything was modest and proper, and where modesty was lacking – the 'bold unblushing mien / Of modern Manley, Centlivre, and Behn' – only head-shaking sorrow appropriate.[16]

Like Thomas Birch, John Duncombe was a literary all-rounder of some influence in the mid century, friends with Richardson and Johnson, and a regular contributor to the *Gentleman's Magazine* whose book review section he edited. (His father, William, had been a friend of Mrs Rowe.) His poem made available both a canon and an anti-canon of women's writings. Positioning virtue as a key concept in the evaluation of female-authored texts was not new, but the explicit instruction to readers about how they should behave in relation to 'the dangerous sallies' of 'tuneful' but 'wanton' muses had a new urgency at this time. Duncombe's advice that 'The modest muse a veil with pity throws / O'er Vice's friends and Virtue's female foes' only mentioned Manley, Centlivre and Behn because these writers seemed to be revived in their modern counterparts: Phillips, Pilkington and Vane. Historically distanced, Manley, Centlivre and Behn were not particularly potent names for mid-eighteenth-century readers, but Phillips, Pilkington and Vane certainly were, not least in the *Gentleman's Magazine* which ran many pieces about or by them. *The Feminiad* might seem to have been inspired by a pure desire to praise the many charming and meritorious female authors of the day – 'Tell how, adorn'd with every charm they shine, / In mind and person equally divine, / Till man, no more to female merit blind, / Admire the person, but adore the mind' – but, as even those wholesome lines imply, the message needed to be told because other messages were getting through.

The Feminiad was in part a response to the currency given in the mid century to less divine versions of female authorship. Duncombe's anti-canon, his brief note explaining that Phillips, Pilkington and Vane had, in writing their memoirs, immortalised shame, is the pivot on which the poem turns. The huge interest generated by these women's texts – Phillips's *An Apology for the Conduct of Mrs Teresia Constantia Phillips* (1748) and Laetitia Pilkington's *Memoirs* (1748–54) – closed down some of the space being made available for 'modest' writing women. In doing so, they also closed down opportunities for men like Duncombe and Birch, or 'the sex's friend' Samuel Richardson, who were invested in women's participation in literary practice – socially, as correspondents, or in women as subject matter. Constantia Phillips, an avowed courtesan whose ruin at the age of thirteen was so well known that a bookseller offered her a thousand pounds for her story which he then got a ghost writer ('a proper person') to write up, and Laetitia Pilkington who was divorced for adultery by her curate husband, projected themselves as women who were prepared to be witty and entertaining on the subject of their lost reputations.

Had their books and their persons been less popular, it might not have been necessary to do so much to insist, for mid-century readers, on modest veils and rural sainthood as the proper signs of female authorship. But Phillips's *An Apology for the Conduct* and Pilkington's *Memoirs* delighted readers, high and low, male and female. The women's combativeness, their feisty refusal to do as Elizabeth Elstob had done and be silent about shame, met with a response. Their stories dealt with scandal but their claims to public sympathy did not go unanswered. In both cases it was clear that the men involved had behaved badly. The women might not have been innocent virgins (as Pilkington said of herself, she did not 'set up for immaculate chastity') but the men were certainly rakes, libertines, hypocrites, liars and fools.

The title page of Phillips's *An Apology for the Conduct* carried an epigraph from Nicholas Rowe's *The Fair Penitent* which lamented women's tendency to trust men: by choosing fools women became their victims, but they might have chosen 'men of sense' and then they would not have ended up 'betrayed'. The readers of Pilkington and Phillips were the same people who read and discussed Richardson's *Clarissa*, which came out at much the same time, and who bought prints of Hogarth's *The Rake's Progress* to hang in their parlours. Libertines, liars and fools were much in evidence in the mid century. Men of sense needed to distinguish themselves from the rest but the lines were inevitably blurred. Samuel Richardson, for example, who was the pattern to men like Duncombe, was at the heart of a huge network of women with whom he corresponded and on whom it is no exaggeration to say that he depended as a writer. Richardson befriended Pilkington. He acknowledged her for the ambitious poet and literary anecdotalist she was, kept her letters (partly for research purposes) and helped her out with sums of money. He was pleased to receive her comments on *Clarissa*. (She and the actor Colley Cibber cried together over Clarissa's death.) It was Richardson who first seems to have made the parallel between Pilkington, Phillips and Vane, and Haywood, Manley and Behn that writers like Duncombe took up. The modern sexually tarnished women were 'a set of wretches' Richardson declared, who made their predecessors 'look white'. Richardson called on other women, 'the same injured, disgraced, profaned sex', to favour the world with 'the antidote to these women's poison!'[17]

Injury, disgrace and profanity were, as Richardson himself dramatised at such length in his novels, visited on the female sex by men. Richardson may have meant that women like Pilkington and Phillips were 'wretches' who put 'poison' out into the world in the form of self-justifying memoirs, and that by doing so they injured, disgraced and profaned the female sex. But there is an ambiguity. The emphasis of his remark could be seen to fall equally on men. In his own life, Richardson offered a model of how men might behave towards needy literary women in what Laetitia Pilkington averred were his 'boundless and repeated acts of humanity to me and my children'. She was certainly wretched at the time. Pilkington first met Richardson in 1743 when she was told to go to his house off Fleet Street to pick up some money sent to her from Ireland by Patrick Delaney who had been a friend of her father's. She had come out of jail having been briefly imprisoned for debt, had nowhere to live and was destitute. Delaney had sent twelve guineas. Richardson, after 'a very civil reception' (she did not expect a printer to be quite such a gentleman and had been 'extremely surprised when I was directed to a house of a very grand outward appearance') and after giving her first breakfast and then dinner with 'his agreeable wife and children', took her into his study and handed over not just Delaney's twelve guineas but an additional two of his own.

This money was given to her as a token of her merit and in response to her distress. With it and some other funds she was able to open a pamphlet shop. At that point she had not yet published her *Memoirs*, and was viewed as a woman of talent and possible goodness (her husband Matthew's unsavoury reputation serving her well). She was available as an object of compassion. The actor Colley Cibber explained the rules: had she been 'stupid, insensible, or wicked' she would not have been helped, no matter how destitute she was.[18]

The separation of the virtuous and the vile, the admired and traduced, seems to have been subscribed to by more or less everybody. Indeed, it set the terms by which eighteenth-century women writers were received until very recently. Foremost among those who endorsed the practice were women who took up their 'female right to literature' and began writing in the mid eighteenth century. The message they took from the past, as it was made available to them through texts like George Ballard's *Memoirs of British Ladies*, John Duncombe's *The Feminiad*, Thomas Seward's *The Female Right to Literature*, Theophilus Rowe's *Life of Mrs Rowe* and Thomas Birch's *Life of Catharine Cockburn*, was that it was laudable to aim to be an exceptional woman. However, there was little point searching through dusty folios for a critical mass of women's writings from earlier eras since most women in the past had been 'debarred from knowledge' and 'bred fools'. As to those who supposedly brought dishonour to the sex, the words of Theophilus Rowe summed up the general view: 'the kindest thing we can do, is never to speak or think of them more; since, if they are remembered, it must be to their disadvantage, with contempt and infamy affixed to their characters'.[19]

Eliza Haywood

The 'justice' that was due to the public, in Thomas Birch's words about Catharine Cockburn, included silence as well as speech. Posterity was entitled not to know as well as to know. Cockburn was recovered on the grounds that she 'raised our ideas' about women, and in matching fashion those who were deemed to have lowered 'our' ideas were suppressed.

One measure of the effectiveness of the mid-century orthodoxy is how little we know about professional women writers at the time and of the immediately preceding generation, those who were active in the 1720s and 1730s, when Eliza Haywood (still alive and still writing when Ballard's and Birch's books came out) became one of the most widely read authors of the period. The latest estimate of the number of works Haywood published between *Love in Excess* in 1719 and her death in 1756 is seventy-three, many of them multi-volume. It is an astonishing fact that a writer who produced seventy-three works over thirty-seven years of intense literary activity, whose name was a byword for a certain kind of writing, who was embedded in London networks of writers, theatrical companies, booksellers and printers, could later be as obscure as Eliza Haywood.[20] In a related way, the currency of Delarivier Manley's *New Atalantis* (1709), which became emblematic of compulsive female reading – Pope, in *The Rape of the Lock*, refers to the *Atalantis* as a feature of life no less eternal than fish in streams and birds in the air – makes it surprising that it became so little known by the mid century, even bearing in mind the vicissitudes of time and fate. And similarly, much less is known about Charlotte Lennox, who in the 1750s and 1760s pursued a career in London as a successful professional writer, gaining prestigious commissions, operating in the public marketplace, well known and well respected by the trade and by other writers (including Thomas Birch who was a friend of Lennox's good friend Samuel Johnson) and who continued to write until the 1790s, than is known about her contemporaries Elizabeth Carter, Elizabeth Montagu and Hester Chapone (the daughter-in-law of Sarah Chapone), none of whom presented themselves as public or marketplace writers though all wrote for the public. Posterity seemed more amenable to these so-called 'private' writers than to the avowedly public ones.

Perhaps posterity was more amenable to some writers than to others because it responded to those who courted it. Carter, Montagu and Chapone were all carefully memorialised by dutiful relations, after the fashion of *The Life of Mrs Rowe*. Well-ordered caches of papers were left – intended for the purpose. (The relations give laboured explanations in their prefaces justifying the publication of these 'private' papers of supposedly modest and unassuming private ladies.)[21] No grieving member of the family nor any well-intentioned friend wrote lives of Eliza Haywood, Delarivier Manley or Charlotte Lennox. Very few papers survive by which reliable accounts of their lives and experiences as writers might be reconstructed. Their histories have been effectively hidden, partly by natural erosion and the chance occurrences of fate, and partly by the selectivity of commemorative processes, but also, more maliciously, because they did not fit the model that the later eighteenth century chose to valorise.

Clara Reeve defended Eliza Haywood in bluestocking style in *The Progress of Romance* on the grounds that she 'repented of her faults, and employed the latter part of her life in expiating the offences of the former'. Reeve probably read David Erskine Baker, Eliza Haywood's first biographer, who, when he compiled the *Biographica Dramatica* in 1764, explained that Haywood herself had taken steps to prevent information about her life becoming known. Less than a decade after her death, he could learn very little: 'from a supposition of some improper liberties being taken with her character after death . . . she laid a solemn injunction on a person who was well acquainted with all the particulars of it, not to communicate to any one the least circumstance relating to her'.[22]

To express the wish for silence about one's private life (whatever the nature of that life) was in itself a sign of virtue. Shutting the door on public knowledge was proper. It did not necessarily mean there was something to hide. Baker's use of the term 'solemn injunction' to describe Haywood's request that her friends say nothing about her life introduced a prayerful tone that was wholly appropriate: it alerted the reader to the fact that the Eliza Haywood of 1756 was not the same as the Eliza Haywood of the 1720s and 1730s. She had recrafted her image. Her work had become, after the manner of Mrs Rowe, 'moral' as well as 'entertaining'. It was the moral Haywood who reached out from her deathbed to preserve the proprieties, who 'laid a solemn injunction' on her friend. To be figured thus, in the act of desiring silence about her personal life, was half a step to sainthood.

Haywood had been able to take some advantage of the new vogue for celebrating women as hard-working servants of a polite reading public. When she died in February 1756, *The Whitehall Evening Post: or London Intelligencer* carried the news that 'the celebrated authoress of some of the best moral and entertaining pieces that have been published for these many years' had succumbed to a severe illness of three months 'which she bore with great fortitude and resignation'. It went on to predict that her most famous titles would survive: 'those elegant productions the *Female Spectator*, and *Epistles for the Ladies*, together with her histories of Miss Betsy Thoughtless, Jemmy and Jenny Jessamy, her Invisible Spy, and the Fortunate Foundlings, will ever remain as living monuments of her merit'.[23]

In fact, little remained, and Haywood's 'merit' was far from being the keynote in what did. She had a walk-on part in Pope's *The Dunciad* as the prize in a pissing competition between two publishers, a 'Juno of majestic size, / With cow-like udders and with ox-like eyes'. She was known as a novelist of popular amatory fiction and therefore likely to be unsavoury or at least 'low' rather than 'high' (leading with 'heart' not 'head'). Swift's dismissal of her as 'a stupid, infamous, scribbling woman' (to which he added, 'but have not seen any of her productions'), along with her own exceptionally prolific output and Virginia Woolf's bad-tempered judgement that she was 'a writer of no importance', all served to diminish serious interest in her.[24] Ignorance and colourful falsehood were added to obscurity. It used to be thought that she had run away from a clergyman husband. An advertisement in the *Post Boy* in 1721 announced: 'Whereas Elizabeth Haywood, wife of the Reverend Mr Valentine Haywood, eloped from him her husband on Saturday the 26th of November last past, and went away with out his knowledge and consent: this is to give notice to all persons in general, that if any one shall trust her either with money or goods, or if she contract debts of any kind whatsoever, the said Mr Haywood will not pay the same.' Whoever Valentine Haywood's wife was, it was not the Eliza Haywood who, two years earlier, had achieved success with the novel *Love in Excess*, whose play *The Fair Captive* was performed in March 1721, and who by 1724 qualified for a four-volume edition of her works: *The Works of Mrs Eliza Haywood*.

We know that Eliza Haywood had crossed to Ireland and begun working, apparently against her family's wishes, as an actress, appearing at the Smock Alley Theatre in Dublin in *Timon of Athens* in 1714. By 1717 she was back in London and acting at Lincoln's Inn Fields. She was to be associated with the theatre throughout her writing career, but wrote in 1720 that 'the stage not answering my expectation, and the averseness of my relations to it, has made me turn my genius another way'. Her literary talent was at once recognised. She was the 'ingenious Haywood' who, as one enthusiastic reader explained, 'writes like one who knew / The pangs of love and all its raptures too'. In describing such feelings, it was her particular gift to inspire others to write in similar vein – an important element in the writer's role at a time when 'realistic' fictions were beginning to be avidly consumed. This anonymous reader's verse 'Writ on a blank leaf of a lady's *Love in Excess*' went on to announce emulatory intent: 'My passion I so clearly would display, / And to your view my soul so open lay, / Describe in words well chose and apt to move, / The agonizing torments of my love.'

Love in Excess went through at least six editions before being included in *The Works of Mrs Eliza Haywood* in 1724. It was one of the three most popular works of fiction – along with Daniel Defoe's *Robinson Crusoe* (1719) and Jonathan Swift's *Gulliver's Travels* (1726) – before Richardson's *Pamela* in 1740, by which time it had gone through as many editions as Defoe's *Moll Flanders*. Like Defoe and Swift, Eliza Haywood's core readership was middle and upper class. Her booksellers were the respectable William Rufus Chetwood, Daniel Browne Jr and Samuel Chapman, and they produced her books in handy octavo format priced between one and three shillings, or sometimes at a more pricey five shillings (*Letters from a Lady of Quality to a Chevalier*, bound in calf, gilt back). Her friends and possible lovers, all of whom were at any time likely to become enemies when she put them into her scandal fictions, were well-known writers: Richard Steele, Richard Savage, Aaron Hill and Henry Fielding. In the 1730s she returned to acting and was associated with Fielding's various theatrical ventures. Some of her parts drew on her off-stage fame as 'Mrs Novel' (as she was caricatured in Fielding's *The Author's Farce*) or made direct allusions to it as in the playbill for *Arden of Feversham*, in 1736, which lists 'Mrs Haywood, the Author' playing Mrs Arden. To be identified as the original of a stage character was a measure of her success; raffish and gossipy, she was a popular icon, and since she went on working with Fielding it is likely that she did not object to being styled 'Mrs Novel', probably appreciating the free publicity.

Eliza Haywood responded to the popular appetite for political commentary, journalism, self-help manuals with advice on social and romantic conduct, and realistic fictions that spoke out clearly on the challenges young men and women (particularly the large army of domestics) faced going out into the world. In monthly issues of the *Female Spectator*, which ran from 1744–6, and in *The Parrot* which followed (its title page declaring it to be 'by the author of the *Female Spectator*') she drew on her extensive experience of life to address a female readership, having by then fended successfully for herself one way or another for over two decades. In the first issue of *The Parrot*, she advertised her success. Speaking as the parrot, she began, 'Well, I am got upon my swing, the Town are gathering thick about me, and I have liberty to prate (as my publisher flatters himself) to a very crowded audience.' She was 'a bird of parts, and, indeed, I cannot well be otherwise, considering the various scenes of life I have gone through'. The 'scenes of life' instanced were appropriate ones for an exotic bird – being born in Java and given away to a French merchant before being launched on a sequence of picaresque adventures – but as the Town well knew, Haywood's credentials included her own many and various scenes of life which had bestowed on an observing and critical intelligence the authority of experience.

Clara Reeve and *The Progress of Romance*

For posterity, as it began to be constructed in the mid eighteenth century, Haywood's 'liberty to prate' (especially to 'a crowded audience') was exactly the problem. Unregulated speech and the varied, rich experience of life Haywood displayed, did not suggest virtuous femininity, whatever else might be known or known to have been said about her. The 'solemn injunction' laid upon Haywood's friends not to reveal details of her life was one of the signs of her atonement for that life. With no biography in print to remind readers, it was an easier task to throw a covering of virtue over her memory. The bluestocking Clara Reeve blamed Delarivier Manley and Aphra Behn for Haywood's early amorous novels: it was they who 'seduced [her] into the same track', but Haywood 'had the singular good fortune to recover a lost reputation, and the yet greater honour to atone for her errors. She devoted the remainder of her life and labours to the service of virtue.'[25]

Rhetoric of this sort was designed to discourage further enquiry. You do not interrogate devotion and service, and where they are to be found it is proper to 'cast the veil of compassion' over former faults. The characters in Reeve's *The Progress of Romance* who form themselves into a weekly book group to discuss the development of English fiction agree that Mrs Haywood's later works, such as *The History of Miss Betsy Thoughtless* (1751), had 'merit' without managing to 'rise to the highest pitch of excellence'. Her earlier works were not fit to be discussed: 'May her first writings be forgotten.'[26] As for the writings of Delarivier Manley, they were not even fit to be mentioned by name. Manley 'hoarded up all the public and private scandal within her reach, and poured it forth, in a work too well known in the last age, though almost forgotten in the present . . . I forbear the name, and further observations on it, as Mrs Manley's works are sinking gradually into oblivion.' Oblivion was the right place and silence the only virtuous response to a book like the *New Atalantis* and an author who had had such liberty to prate to crowded audiences that her writings were but 'too well known'. Since she was writing a history of fiction, Reeve could not honestly leave Manley's writings out, though she explained that she wished she could: 'I am sorry to say they were once in fashion, which obliges me to mention them, otherwise I had rather be spared the pain of disgracing an author of my own sex . . . Let us pass them over in silence.'[27]

By wishing to pass them over in silence, Clara Reeve, a provincial clergyman's daughter, displayed her own virtue. Little more is known about Reeve than about Haywood, though like the earlier writer she was both successful and prolific and like Haywood she supported herself by her writing. Nobody wrote her life after she died in 1807 and nor has she received much attention since, even though one of her novels, *The Old English Baron* (1778), became a minor classic, constantly reprinted throughout the nineteenth century. The obituary that appeared in the

Gentleman's Magazine occupied less than half a column, and there were apparently insufficient materials for more. One thing we do know about her is that she was poor: a rare and undated letter by Reeve quoted by Anna Barbauld in her preface to *The Old English Baron* in *The British Novelists* series explained: 'I have been all my life in straitened circumstances, and used my pen to support a scanty establishment.'

Clara Reeve was not diffident about her abilities. She incorporated self-promotional information about herself and her works into her texts, not only in addresses to the reader and prefaces, but in the body of the text, as when she advertised her translation of Barclay's *Argenis*, a seventeenth-century romance, in *The Progress of Romance* and fulminated against the publisher.[28] She also made it clear that as an author of socially recognised merit she was embedded in a network of 'friends' who advised and supported her endeavours. Many of these came from the neighbourhood around Ipswich and Colchester where she lived all her life. Like Elizabeth Carter in Kent and Anna Seward in Lichfield, Clara Reeve's success testified to the values of polite provincial circles. There were some six hundred subscribers to her 1769 *Poems on Several Occasions*. Being a writer was not something to hide, but without a separate income her options – including acts of self-promotion aimed at posterity – were limited.

In a more familiar way, too, Reeve's artistic choices were constrained. Her desire to write oratorios and operas had to be suppressed because there was no money in it. She described her love of music in characteristic bluestocking fashion:

> I have a natural affection for music, I say affection rather than passion, because I am not intoxicated by it, but can reduce the pleasure arising from it under the regulation of reason; I am indeed too apt to moralise away all my pleasures, and whilst I enjoy them am always investigating the subject, and endeavouring to find out why I am pleased or displeased. I have read many books on the subject of music, have reflected upon them, and drawn such inferences as reason, and sometimes as fancy have suggested to me; but vocal music has more particularly engaged my attention.

Dismayed by the poor standards of writing in songs that were set to music, she would have liked to develop her interest in the harmony of words and sound but could not do so because she couldn't afford to work without pay.[29]

In *The Progress of Romance*, Reeve presented herself as a critic through the knowledgeable figure of Euphrasia, a woman whose male friend, Hortensius, has been shocked to hear her deride the classics and defend romances. Over a course of twelve Thursday-evening meetings, the friends engage in a Socratic dialogue, with an experienced but naive woman reader, Sophronia, functioning as a chorus (fairly dim, and furnishing mostly anecdotal responses). Euphrasia explains that she will 'trace Romance to its origins' and follow it through to show 'how the modern novel sprung up out of its ruins'. Further, she would 'examine and compare' the merits of both, expounding her view that it was mere prejudice to rate ancient epics over the old romances, and furthermore that the modern novel could be considered superior to both. Euphrasia is eloquent, independent-minded, and planning to publish the results of her meditations and researches 'to all the world'.

For this radical assault on the classical tradition, Euphrasia prepares like any other lecturer by consulting the authorities and coming armed with her arguments and illustrations. Hortensius, having had a gentleman's classical education, cannot patiently allow Homer and Virgil to be 'degraded into writers of romances'. Euphrasia, working from Pope's 'admired translation', claims to venerate both, but she has criticisms. Her 'bold attack', which shocks (and silences) Hortensius, derives from her female freedom from a classical education. Boys who imbibe the classics at an early age, she explains, are loath to part with early instilled prejudices even when they become 'men of sense and learning'. Euphrasia wants Hortensius to learn to think differently. He needs to listen to coherent thoughts and a connected argument drawn from female reading: romances of every kind and classics in translation. He needs to see that imaginative investment in stories is a universal, be they the stories of Homer or those of the *Arabian Nights* such as Sinbad the Sailor, featuring heroes from history or from fiction; and that the distinction between epic (good) and romance (bad), or 'works of high and low estimation', came from 'prejudice only'. Hortensius is asked to submit to the proposition that 'there is a certain degree of respect due to all the works of genius, by whatever name distinguished'. Above all, he needs to acknowledge that many of his assumptions have been based on hearsay: he had formed 'contemptible opinions of books [he] never knew, nor enquired after'.

Euphrasia's critical opinions are rooted in sound historical scholarship. She is a bibliophile. Knowing the publishing histories of the titles she mentions, she is able to give dates and warn about corrupt editions. Her library contains many rare books, some of which Hortensius is invited to borrow. She explains that reading different views about the Elizabethan John Lilly's *Euphues* had made her want to purchase it, which 'by good fortune' she was able to do. Perhaps she found it in one of the bookseller's catalogues mentioned in the discussion about the old romances where, in 1777, an edition of *The Romaunt of the Rose* from 1409 could be had for £11. 11*s*. 6*d*. It is easy to imagine Reeve browsing such catalogues and wishing she could afford a 1409 *Romaunt of the Rose*. As Hortensius observes, the price 'shows its estimation'.

A little gentle ribbing of Hortensius for what his friends might make of his decision to meet weekly with two women to talk about romances barely interrupts the flow of Euphrasia's weighty exegeses. Hortensius periodically declares that Euphrasia 'has carried all her points triumphantly'. Euphrasia has the authority of a published writer, having translated and given to the world a version of one of her favourite romances, the once popular *Argenis* of John Barclay. At this point the fictional Euphrasia and the real Clara Reeve who translated the *Argenis* of John Barclay blend into one: Reeve expresses her anger at the critics of the *Critical Review* and *Monthly Review*, who, less learned or less punctilious than Reeve/Euphrasia, failed to give the book its due. She also lambasts the publisher who exposed her to the charge of plagiarism by insisting on a new title. Sales were badly affected. Clearly, sales and celebrity would have been welcome, but Reeve/Euphrasia can draw strength from the approbation of her own community of readers: 'I have a circle of friends who cannot be biassed by these self elected censors of books.' In that circle, her authority is sustained, tested and supported.

As she approaches modern times, Euphrasia feels the difficulty of judging with truth and candour. The discussion of modern novels takes place in Euphrasia's library so that volumes can be taken down from the shelves at will, as can the issues of the reviews which notice them. Titles and authors proliferate. Women now come into their own. Beginning with Charlotte Lennox – 'one of the distinguished female writers this age has produced' – Euphrasia goes on to discuss Frances Sheridan, Mrs Brooke, Sarah Scott, Mme de Beaumont, Mrs Griffiths and others, in the context of concerns about virtue and the deleterious effects of the Circulating Libraries. With this shift towards female novelists comes a corresponding emphasis on female readers, especially young ones; by the end, *The Progress of Romance* has modulated into a guide to parents on choosing suitable books for daughters. This genre shift probably reflects Clara Reeve's concern for what Hortensius describes as 'the best reward of your labours, fame and profit!'

Translation and the national language: Reeve, Carter, Elstob

The Progress of Romance is a well-informed literary history dealing with what was, at the time, the more or less untheorised subject of fiction and its origins. The book was the first to address the relationship between the old romance and the new novel and to make explicit some commonplace gendered prejudices, to wit: that there was 'literature', which men were having important conversations about, and 'romance', a lower form, traditionally the province of women. Romance was 'popular' while 'literature' belonged to the learned.

The Progress of Romance can also be understood as a meditation on Reeve's own literary choices. The four-volume translation of Barclay's *Argenis* had appeared in 1772, and her most successful novel, *The Old English Baron*, in 1778. The *Argenis* was recovered as part of the English tradition but it had been written, as many literary works then were, in Latin. (Milton wrote Latin sonnets.) The publisher gave it a new title, *The Phoenix*, and though her name was not on the title page, the fact that it was translated 'from the Latin by a Lady' was made explicit. Reeve went further and drew extra attention to herself as a female in the preface. At a time when there was much popular agitation and conflict between the classes ('Wilkes and Liberty' was the slogan of the rioting London crowds) she put in her word for the restoration of traditional hierarchies while at the same time claiming space for women:

> Since England is become a nation of politicians, and men of all ranks and degrees believe themselves capable of investigating the art of government, and since women have written with success upon the subject, the editor has

thought herself at liberty to aim a blow at popular error from behind Barclay.[30]

The 'popular error' was to suppose any but those of high rank should participate in government. Politically, Clara Reeve was no democrat, no believer in 'the idol Equality' as she put it in a later work, the *Memoirs of Sir Roger de Clarendon* (1793), a historical novel set in the fourteenth century. She believed in subordination: 'a true and regular subordination is what makes all orders and degrees of men stand in need of each other'.[31] In this usage, 'men' included women. Women like herself, placed high by merit, were not just at liberty to speak on the arts of government but had a duty to do so. Among the women who had 'written with success' were the Whig historian Catherine Macaulay, who was at the height of her reputation in the early 1770s. In her multi-volume *History of England*, Macaulay attempted to reshape the understanding of the English past by looking back at a key moment – the English Civil War and the execution of the King – when a republic was founded and failed.

A political thinker, Macaulay was inspired by the literature of Greece and Rome. 'From my earliest youth,' she wrote, 'I have read with delight those histories that exhibit liberty in its most exalted state, the annals of the Roman and Greek republics.'[32] No less political, but equally no republican, Clara Reeve wrote as a cultural historian and novelist, and her inspiration was 'Gothic' rather than classical. *The Old English Baron* was subtitled *A Gothic Story* and it took issue with the 'founding' Gothic romance, Horace Walpole's *The Castle of Otranto*.

In the preface to *The Phoenix* Reeve explained that what might seem at first sight a 'low' form, or merely entertaining, was not low at all: under 'the appearance of a novel, a book of real intrinsic value is here offered to the public'. She apologised for giving a new title to what was a translation of a once well-known work: 'a romance, an allegory, and a system of politics'; and describing herself as an 'editor', she outlined some of the principles guiding her translation practice. No apology appeared in *The Old English Baron*, but that, too, was supposedly a translation of a manuscript from 'the old English language'.

One of the ways in which translations of fictional texts fitted the bluestocking ideal of being 'moral' as well as 'entertaining' was through a concern for the national language. Reeve probably knew something of Elizabeth Carter's thoughts on translating from the Greek of Epictetus and it is not impossible that she had some knowledge of Elizabeth Elstob on Anglo-Saxon. Her comments on translating the *Argenis*, or *Phoenix*, have echoes of both. She explained that she had 'endeavoured to reform the language, without destroying the simplicity of the style, and ha[d] aimed at a language suitable to the subject, believing that a medium between the former antiquated one and the present fashionable one, would best answer that purpose'. She thought her 'favourite' hero, Poliarchus, 'would appear to greater advantage in the majestic simplicity of a plain habit, than in the affected garniture of a modern beau; or, in other words, she is of opinion that our language has not gained any advantages by the innovations that have been made in it within the last twenty years; that it has lost more in strength and conciseness than it has gained in sweetness and elegance'. Barclay himself was 'rather prolix in his manner; therefore, instead of practising the modern art of wire-drawing, the chief labour of the editor has been to contract this work into as small a compass as was possible, without injuring the sense of the author'. Former translators having been too literal and therefore flat, and modern methods tending towards too much freedom, she had opted for the middle way.[33]

These observations seem to owe something to Elizabeth Carter's very similar concerns. Carter shared the view of Archbishop Secker that Epictetus, a plain man who spoke plainly, should not be represented by a too polished translation.[34] Like Macaulay, Carter's reputation stood high in the 1770s. Her probity and famous love of privacy represented the public face of bluestocking virtue. John Duncombe gave over thirty lines of praise to her in *The Feminiad*: 'undisturb'd by pride, you calmly tread / Thro' life's perplexing paths, by wisdom led.' There may have been some epistolary contact between Reeve and Carter: 'Mrs Carter of Tunstall' (where Elizabeth Carter's brother-in-law was rector) subscribed to Reeve's poems; and Carter, along with Katherine Philips and Charlotte Lennox, was named as an exceptional woman in Reeve's poem, 'To My Friend, Mrs— on her Holding an Argument in Favour of the Natural equality of Both the Sexes'. In this dialogue poem, Reeve presented herself as having become a believer in 'difference of sexes'. As such she had low expectations of women's productions. Men had the more capacious brains. Women's writings were 'superficial, light and various; / Loose, unconnected, and precarious'; they had life but lacked weight; they did not have 'The strength that fills the manly page, / And bids it live to future age.'[35] Exceptional women, however, like herself and Carter, had more of the masculine in their make-up and were not in the category of the low, loose and light.

A woman with Clara Reeve's views, offering the world a four-volume translation from the Latin, was making a bid to be considered as weighty as any man. It is equally certain that she hoped her page would live to a future age. Of course, we don't know if she knew Elizabeth Elstob's Anglo-Saxon grammar with its title-page quotation from George Hickes explaining that the language we speak 'is our mother tongue', but it is possible; in any case, questions of language use were central to those who engaged in translation work. Clara Reeve translating from Latin, Elizabeth Carter from Greek and Elizabeth Elstob from Anglo-Saxon, were all led by the practical demands of their tasks (combined with the desire to be and be seen as authoritative) into theoretical and critical discussion.

From Elstob through Carter to Reeve we can trace a lineage of sorts. Carter probably was familiar with Elstob's work: there were many subscribers to Elstob in Canterbury which suggests that when Elizabeth Carter was there as a budding young linguist and general prodigy she would have heard of her and had no difficulty getting copies of her books. Certainly in her *Epictetus* Carter followed the principles Elstob had pursued in her Anglo-Saxon translations: she too favoured intelligibility over elegance, and aimed for a plain style rather than anything 'polite and elaborate' because, as she explained in much the way that Elstob had before her, plainness suited the original.

Elstob went further than Carter in asserting that her 'true old Saxon' which had not only been forgotten but was misrepresented by 'the polite men of our age', needed to be recovered for the sake of the nation. Men who dismissed Anglo-Saxon, 'the language of their forefathers', claiming it was 'barren' and 'barbarous', who were guilty of 'ill treatment of our mother tongue', were missing an important component of national honour: 'Pro Patria mori used to be one of the great boasts of Antiquity . . . The justness and propriety of the language of any nation hath been always rightly esteemed a great ornament and test of the good sense of such a nation.' Divesting English of its Saxon origins, dressing it up in a character not its own, was both wrong and foolish.[36]

The defence of the Saxon origins of the English language led Elizabeth Elstob, in her preface to the Anglo-Saxon grammar, into an essay of poetic criticism. Her concern was to stress the importance of the monosyllable (stemming from the 'somewhat antiquated' times of Chaucer and Lydgate) to all good English poetry, and to show that the finest English poets had not disparaged it. She claimed that her Northern ear made available to her some of the 'rude sweetness' that Dryden found in Chaucer. As the mention of Dryden demonstrated, politeness was not incompatible with a vernacular English tradition.

Language use was heavily charged: 'plain', 'ornate', 'smooth', 'polished' were all words that carried ideological freight. Women who spoke up for plain speech took the risk of being considered beyond the sphere of the 'polite', which meant outside the realm of the literary. Style mattered as much as substance because knowing how to speak was a sign of rank, hence the importance attached to harmony. (In critical terms, the key text was Pope's virtuoso *An Essay on Criticism* in which he laid it down as a rule that sound mattered as much as sense.)

Elstob drew on a range of examples to illustrate her point. Pope and Dryden because of their translations were key to her argument, but she worked through a long list of 'numerous instances', offering in some twenty pages of argument and illustration not so much a 'digression' as a progress of English poetry, beginning with 'father' Chaucer and quoting from those, such as the Earl of Surrey, whose 'gentle' muse made him attractive to 'our sex'. She included Drayton, who 'of all our English poets, seems best to have understood the sweet harmonious placing of monosyllables, and has practised it with so great a variety, as discovers in him a peculiar delight, even to fondness; for which however I cannot blame him, notwithstanding this may be reputed the vice of our sex, and in him be thought effeminate'. Then came Spenser, 'the incomparable'; Ben Jonson, Cowley, Waller, Roscommon, Orrery – quoting his poem to Katherine Philips – and other 'witnesses of quality'; Addison; and that darling of the muses, Prior, 'with whom all the poets of ancient and modern times of other nations, or our own, might seem to have intrusted the chief secrets and greatest treasures of their art ... how great a master he is, and how much everything is to be valued which bears the stamp of his approbation'. Prior's 'Poem in answer to Mrs Eliz Singer, on her Poem upon Love and Friendship' was but one of many instances of his verse quoted. Finally, she gave examples 'from some of our female poets': Mrs Philips on the death of the Queen of Bohemia; Mrs Wharton on the lamentations of Jeremiah; and Anne Finch, Countess of Winchilsea.

Whether Elstob had read Finch's preface to her *Poems* of 1713 in which the English monosyllable is also defended she does not say. The preface to the Anglo-Saxon grammar ends with a vindication, not of female poets, translators, linguists and critics, but of antiquarians. Those who were 'employed in refining and ascertaining our English tongue' (polite, literary circles) needed to 'entertain better thoughts both of the Saxon tongue, and of the study of antiquities'. They should stop referring to such studies as 'low'. Antiquarians might be 'studious men of a private character' but that did not mean they lacked 'politeness' or were 'men of low genius'.

Elstob argued aggressively for recognition of her chosen subject: 'if this preface is writ in a style that may be thought somewhat rough and too severe, it is not out of any natural inclination to take up a quarrel, but to do some justice to the study of antiquities, and even of our own language itself, against the severe censurers of both, whose behaviour in this controversy has been such as could not have the treatment it deserved in a more modest or civil manner'. The quarrel had wider ramifications. The complaint about roughness was to some extent a protest against the incursions of outsiders, men like George Ballard who were of humble birth and women like Elstob who were not men. Elstob was responding in particular to Jonathan Swift who in his *Proposal for Correcting, Improving and Ascertaining the English Tongue* (1712) had satirised Anglo-Saxonists.[37] The debate about proper style and correct writing descended, as the century wore on, into the trite (but effective) commonplaces about women being pedantic (antiquarians were 'pedants' rather than 'wits') and not knowing grammar. When Elstob refused the label of a pedant, she did so in the same spirit in which Clara Reeve refused the imputation of 'feminine' triviality to her interest in the old romances.

Elizabeth Elstob, as we have seen, was unable to continue with her Anglo-Saxon work after her brother's death. After 1715, the intellectual passions that animated arguments such as these were denied full expression. She had limited access to books, educated company, writing materials and opportunity. By the time she was rescued from obscurity and poverty, it was too late. What she might have done, thought and written, and the contribution she might have made to eighteenth-century literary culture, can only be imagined.

Clara Reeve, by contrast, was able to be single and self-supporting throughout a long and productive life. In the 1790s she had a cottage in Ipswich and 'a tolerable collection of books'. She published some twenty-four volumes, all of which she saw through the press herself, and wrote much else besides: one novel was lost on the Ipswich to London coach; and there were many 'beginnings' of works, 'many works unfinished' and 'several drawers' full of manuscripts.[38]

Chapter Four

THINKING BACK THROUGH
OUR MOTHERS

Whatever effect discouragement and criticism had upon their writing . . .
that was unimportant compared with the other difficulty which faced
them . . . when they came to set their thoughts on paper − that is that
they had no tradition behind them, or one so short and partial that it was
of little help. For we think back through our mothers if we are women.

Virginia Woolf, *A Room of One's Own*[1]

A Room of One's Own

When literary history began to be written in the seventeenth century as
part of the larger project of constructing national traditions, metaphors
of genealogy traced a male line of influence and inheritance. Ben Jonson
understood this when he encouraged the younger poets who admired
him to call themselves the 'sons of Ben'. Claiming a family relationship
in this way, placing oneself in the direct line of descent, was a way of
establishing authorial identity. It was a powerful myth and it put
women on the periphery: daughters did not inherit.[2]

In the twentieth century, Virginia Woolf, the first woman of letters
to pay detailed attention to literary history and the place of the woman
writer in it, suggested that though literature was in her own time 'open
to everybody' in the sense that there was no bolt that could be set upon
the freedom of the mind, everybody's inheritance was not the same.
Men built on the common literary property that was formed and passed
down to them by other men; but 'we think back through our mothers if
we are women', and the female tradition available to women writers was

both a 'short' and a 'partial' one. It was short because women began writing later than men, and it was partial because they fitted themselves into already established forms which were not necessarily adequate to express women's experiences. Literary genres and even the basic sentence available for use had evolved out of men's needs and desires. 'There is no reason to think that the form of the epic or of the poetic play suit a woman any more than the sentence suits her. But all the older forms of literature were hardened and set by the time she became a writer.'[3]

In *A Room of One's Own*, which began as a lecture series to the women students at Cambridge in 1928, the year the franchise was finally given to all women, Virginia Woolf investigated the conditions of female authorship.[4] In her analysis she contrasted the material, social and cultural support available to her as a modern woman with the limitations with which women had historically struggled. She pondered the psychic effects of men's use of women, and the 'very queer composite being' one encountered in literary sources, especially when moving between what was offered as 'fact' (or history) and 'fiction' (literature):

> Imaginatively she is of the highest importance; practically she is completely insignificant. She pervades poetry from cover to cover; she is all but absent from history. She dominates the lives of kings and conquerors in fiction; in fact she was the slave of any boy whose parents forced a ring upon her finger. Some of the most inspired words, some of the most profound thoughts in literature fall from her lips; in real life she could hardly read, could scarcely spell, and was the property of her husband.[5]

A Room of One's Own mounted a scathing attack on the social construction of femininity. Dramatising the moment of beginning research, Woolf depicted herself looking up the category 'Woman' at the British Museum and discovering, to her horror, 'the most discussed animal in creation'. Searching among this abundance of verbiage, she did not find her own image. The discussion seemed not to be about women at all but about something men – the 'professors' – wanted from the idea of woman. This eagerness of men to write about women she represented as a current (and unhealthy) obsession. By contrast, as she explained to the students at Cambridge, when she tried to establish concrete facts about women in earlier periods she could barely discover anything beyond the fact that men were allowed to beat them.

She asked why men were angry at women, wondered what effects women's rage had on the quality of writing they produced, and contemplated the impact of poverty and repression on female creativity through the ages. If women were to go on writing and if the 'odd monster that one made up by reading the historians first and the poets afterwards' was to become less odd and less monstrous, she declared, women needed independence, meaning money of their own, and freedom of thought, symbolised by a room with a door that could be locked.

Like Woolf's avowed experiments in biography – *Flush, Orlando, Roger Fry* – *A Room of One's Own* had multiple tasks to perform. It had to illuminate for the intelligent and educated young women who were her audience the precariousness and novelty of their own opportunities; and it had to carry some of her own grievance at not having had those opportunities (the Stephen boys went to Cambridge; the girls did not). Using the devices of fiction, it offered a portrait of the working woman writer of the twentieth century, vividly embodied in a Virginia Woolf whose private thoughts and public actions were seamlessly made available. This writer had enough money in her purse to be independent and a room of her own to write in. She could dash to the British Museum, dine at Oxbridge colleges (male and female), talk, read, make notes, observe the world and report on its dealings with her as a writer and as a woman (as a writer she could lecture the students; as a woman she could not walk on the college lawns nor enter the library without a letter of introduction). Above all, she could think. She was thinking all the time. She was thinking about literature and history, about what it meant to be a woman and a writer, about money and tradition and power, and about what helped or hindered her thinking. The presentation of herself in the act of thinking – a mobile activity which took place not at a desk in a room but out on the streets of London and Oxbridge – was far more important than any conclusion she might come to. No nugget of truth is offered at the end of *A Room of One's Own*, for 'when a subject is highly controversial – and any question about sex is that – one cannot hope to tell the truth'.[6]

If one cannot hope to tell the truth, one can at least produce a fiction. The heroine's freedom of movement (except when accosted by college beadles) and freedom of thought fictionalised an ideal that arose from a differently constituted reality. Women in former eras – 'our mothers, our grandmothers, our great-grandmothers' – had lived lives defined by constraint. According to *A Room of One's Own*, everything Woolf had and represented had been grudgingly or fortuitously delivered. Her inheritance in the female line was full of deprivation and denial. Its symbol was prunes with custard, not rich meat, gravy and claret. The light that was lit halfway down the spine, the 'profound, subtle and subterranean glow which is the rich yellow flame of rational intercourse', was not ignited when she dined in utilitarian fashion at the women's college. This was because 'our mothers had mismanaged their affairs very gravely', for they had failed to make money and endow colleges which could offer 'partridges and wine, beadles and turf, books and cigars, libraries and leisure' to women as well as men and give them access to 'the urbanity, the geniality, the dignity which are the offspring of luxury and privacy and space'. Nevertheless – and this highlights one of the fictions of *A Room of One's Own* – Woolf's heroine *had* all the urbanity that libraries and leisure, luxury and privilege could bring. As a thinking writer, she was equally at home in the men's colleges as the women's (and better fed and housed). Woolf's heroine passed in both worlds. Or we could say that the fiction declared she needed her mother; the fact was, she didn't.[7]

The chronology Woolf offered to describe her own existence as a writer followed an evolutionary model in which increasingly complex forms of life emerged not from slime and mud but out of the 'unlit corridors of history'. Committed to the proposition that nothing was known about women before the eighteenth century and that 'the women were dumb' in the sixteenth century when 'literature is exclusively masculine', for Woolf the key moment was the end of the eighteenth century, for it was then that 'the middle-class woman began to write' in significant numbers. What the middle-class woman began to write, according to this view, was prose fiction. The domestic woman and the domestic novel rose together, producing, in the nineteenth century, Jane Austen, the Brontë sisters, Mrs Gaskell and George Eliot. Poetry, apparently, did not count since women 'have not had a dog's chance of writing poetry': 'the highly gifted girl who had tried to use her gift for poetry would have been so thwarted and hindered by other people, so tortured and pulled asunder by her own contrary instincts, that she must have lost her health and sanity to a certainty'.[8]

To convey the impossibility of poetry for women, Woolf invented a sister for William Shakespeare, Judith, whose gift was equal to that of her brother. Judith was deprived of an education, discouraged from writing, beaten by her father, rejected by the professional theatre in London, seduced, impregnated and abandoned. She ends by killing herself.

Woolf's myth of Judith Shakespeare – a vivid narrative device, an only-too-believable fiction – took compelling hold of the imaginations of feminist critics and literary historians. Judith's fate was the universal fate of the gifted woman: denied opportunity, silenced, sneered at, sexually vulnerable and doomed. Conditioned by this socio-historical 'reality', what kind of subjectivity could be expected of the female self? When women writers sat down to continue each other's books and tell the common tale of female life, what did they reveal? Not surprisingly, according to many critics of the mid twentieth century, they revealed frustration and rage. The female self was an oppressed self, thwarted, excluded and dispossessed; she was the madwoman in the attic of the house of fiction.

In the essay 'Professions for Women', Woolf reflected on her own conditioning as a young woman born in 1882 into the upper-middle-class Victorian intelligentsia. In order to become the writer who was the heroine of *A Room of One's Own* she had had to do battle with two 'phantoms' which she identified as the 'Angel in the House' and 'telling the truth about my own experiences as a body'. These phantoms – the force of gender ideology – had assumed crushing power in the era that immediately preceded her own. The 'Angel in the House' was the self-sacrificing, self-denying ideal Victorian woman whose purpose in life was to serve men; and the truth could not be told about the female body because that body was full of 'passions which it was unfitting for her as a woman to say'. If it was 'unfitting' to speak about the body, if female experience was unsuitable for utterance, then the subject position of woman was uninhabitable. To be a writer in the fullest sense of the word as Woolf envisioned it and to be a woman was impossible.[9]

Virginia Woolf understood how her own identity as an author had been shaped by such struggles. To some extent she read them back into earlier periods where 'nothing' was known and much had to be imagined. Woolf the novelist produced brilliant empathetic accounts of women writers – Aphra Behn, Anne Finch, Countess of Winchilsea, Eliza Haywood, Mary Wollstonecraft, Jane Austen – which mythologised her own journey from 'a girl in a bedroom with a pen in her hand' to the grown woman of letters. This tender – or sentimental – image generalised across the centuries was one of a family of images Woolf used to take the sting out of transgression. If she was just a girl in a bedroom, or a girl secretly writing (Jane Austen), or a 'shy girl' with 'the importunity and indiscretion of a child' (Margaret Cavendish), or a 'harmless' woman wandering dreamily around the fields (Countess of Winchilsea), or an emotionally turbulent young woman with a 'girlish creed of independence' (Mary Wollstonecraft), then the enormity of her transgressive desires might be hidden. Nobody would see her murdering the Angel in the House and nobody would hear her speaking about the female body.[10]

The force of these prohibitions suggests that they were not universal but historically specific (hence the need to insist on them), and that Woolf was writing about the social construction of femininity and female authorship at a time when there was considerable pressure for change. This dialectic seems to be characteristic, however, of the longer past, too: there was always pressure on femininity and invariably some answering pressure for change. Throughout the long eighteenth century every 'she' who went into print, the 'she philosophers' and poetesses, the dramatists, novelists, critics, scholars and polemicists, did so as women as well as writers. But what it meant to be a 'woman' and a 'writer' was not the same in 1660 as it was in 1730 or 1790. Nor, indeed, in 1928.

Culturally, throughout the eighteenth century, there was a high degree of consciousness of sex which always needed to be negotiated in some way. How far this social fact translated into a *self*-consciousness of sex varied in individual writers and at different times, as did the uses a woman might make of her sex or of the available rhetoric. How society treated women in general and how women functioned in the literary world were related, but these processes did not necessarily run in parallel and to read one off from the other can be misleading. To assume that 'the women were dumb' or that poetically gifted girls were beaten into silence by their families is to assume that the construction of femininity – society's need to mould women into an agreed form – was always and everywhere a more powerful force than the construction of authorship. This is not self-evidently the case, but what was the case was that the rhetoric of femininity was more powerful than the rhetoric of authorship. (And women themselves, it should be said, contributed far more to the rhetoric about femininity than to the rhetoric about authorship.)

In a society in which they were the subordinate sex, women's opportunities could never equal those of men. We might regret how few women were able to become writers in the eighteenth century, but we should also recognise that an astonishing number of them did so – especially given the fact that women did not customarily receive the education their brothers were likely to have, might not be born into families that encouraged literary pursuits, and, above all, that if they did not already have enough money to live on, let alone to buy partridges and wine, writing books was unlikely to provide them with it.

A Room of One's Own is about the social construction of femininity but it is also a powerful statement about female authorship. It draws on a rich and mixed ambiguous tradition and it situates its heroine in it. It is surely no accident that Virginia Woolf, that most well read of writing women, figured herself in the opening paragraph not in a room but sitting on the banks of a river engrossed in free-floating thoughts about literary history and criticism. Furthermore, that she took the 'liberties and licences of a novelist' (for that was the female tradition, after all) to explore questions about women as historical subjects and to ask questions about inheritance through the female line in the form of a story – the story of her thoughts as she pondered the subject of her lecture – and by means of a fictional character. What she described, she assured her audience and readers, had no existence: ' "I" is only a convenient term for somebody who has no real being.' This 'I' who had no real being told her story 'to the moment', apparently artlessly, as she lived it: sitting on the bank, walking on the grass, hurrying through London streets, coming home alone so late that all human beings under the Oxbridge sky were asleep. Woolf's heroine was confident, enquir-ing; she had duties and responsibilities – her free movements were in search of Truth and her notebook was poised to receive it.

This 'I' had no real being because as well as failing to make money our mothers had 'mismanaged their affairs' in failing to leave a usable history for female authors who came after them. How was the woman writer to present herself to the world? Not even an author as well read as Virginia Woolf could find satisfactory models to turn around in her mind. Even in 1928 she had to be made up, although making her up was exactly the problem which gave rise to the 'odd monster' or queer composite being to be found in literary sources. To make her up Woolf reached back beyond the nineteenth-century novelists, those women 'without more experience of life than could enter the house of a respectable clergyman' (who nevertheless out of their narrow experien-ces wrote great books), and to an earlier period. If we could put a date to the moment in time from which Woolf drew her inspiration for the heroine of *A Room of One's Own*, it would have to be some time before Jane Austen who 'never travelled; she never drove through London in an omnibus or had luncheon in a shop by herself', but also before Richardson's *Clarissa* in the mid eighteenth century. Clarissa is part of the 'queer composite' created in *A Room of One's Own* partly from literary and partly from lived experience.[11] Her presence, though not alluded to, can be strongly felt. Equally strongly felt are the fictional self-projections of female authors writing between 1700 and 1740: Delarivier Manley, Elizabeth Thomas, Jane Barker and Martha Fowke Sansom, and their alter egos: Manley's 'Rivella', Thomas's 'Corinna', Barker's 'Galesia' and Fowke Sansom's 'Clio'.

Female authors from the early eighteenth century offered fictional-ised versions of themselves as women engaged in a busy world of others, including men, including fellow authors. They travelled about alone on stagecoaches if not omnibuses, and had adventures if not luncheon. They did not convey the sense that female life was narrower than male life, nor that it was essentially inward and private and certainly not that it was a state of siege. But around 1740–50, after *Pamela* and *Clarissa*, things changed. The room became the proper place for woman rather than the street. Clarissa had a room of her own with a vengeance; she was marooned in it, writing for her life and at the mercy of Lovelace who made her his prey. Richardson drew on a familiar set of associations: traditionally, the room of one's own had been valued (by those who had such a space) as the place for quiet reflection, retirement from domestic distractions, reading, praying and writing. It symbolised spirituality and goodness; it was not loaded with the task of defending a threatened virginity against encroaching male violence.

Woolf's heroine, her fictional 'I', who is so accustomed to the free movement of body and mind that she is taken by surprise when the beadle accosts her (causing her to lose the thoughts that had begun to form), is both a commentary on and a parodic counterpoint to Richardson's imprisoned and ill-used Clarissa. *A Room of One's Own* forcefully asserts that women of the twentieth century belong on the streets as well as in rooms. The ambiguity of the phrase 'on the streets' matches the ambiguous status of the room. Both needed to be reclaimed: the streets as part of the tradition of free movement we inherit if we think back far enough through our mothers; and the room as the place of autonomy and freedom rather than imprisonment and rape.

Sarah Fielding's *Remarks on Clarissa*

The significance for female authors of Samuel Richardson's 1748 *Clarissa* was immediately evident. Within a year, Sarah Fielding had published a pamphlet essay of literary criticism about *Clarissa*, addressed to Samuel Richardson as a letter. The successful author of *The Adventures of David Simple* (1744) and *The Governess* (1749), sister of Henry, and a classical scholar whose later translations of Xenophon were to remain standard texts well into the twentieth century, Fielding was on friendly terms with Richardson who had praised *David Simple*. Her fifty-six-page shilling pamphlet went out with no name on the title page and it was not recognised as being by Fielding until the late twentieth century. The full title linked Clarissa to Prior's Emma in what was to become for women critics a standard association: *Remarks on Clarissa, addressed to the author. Occasioned by some critical conversations on the characters and conduct of that work, with some reflections on the character and behaviour of Prior's Emma.*

The essay began: 'Sir, Perhaps an address of this nature may appear very unaccountable, and whimsical, when I assure you my design is fairly to lay before you all the criticisms, as far as I can remember them, that I have heard on your history of Clarissa.' The 'unaccountable' and 'whimsical' project was in fact a carefully composed, many-layered examination of controversial issues, showing Fielding at work as a critic, listening, thinking, making notes and then ordering her materials, and, like Woolf, mixing fiction and fact. In 1749, every thinking and reading person was thinking about *Clarissa*. In the *Remarks on Clarissa*, Fielding seems to have resolved, as Woolf did later, to represent the female authorial persona in a state of free movement. Fielding described herself going about to the houses of friends like a gossip or a spy on the author's behalf to listen to their conversations and report back. This servicing role raises her to a level with the author, conveying the impression that their communion extended beyond the text.

In 1749, there was no model for how intelligent criticism of fiction should be written, nor any established understanding of who it was for or by whom it should be practised. Fielding was one of the first in the field with an original text that dramatised and commented on her own and Richardson's practices. The epistolary form gave them both considerable freedom: Fielding has one of her characters observe that 'many liberties' were allowable in familiar letters, which might otherwise be 'condemned' for incorrectness.[12] Fielding's liberties included questioning the social construction of femininity in the 'real' world of the social groups she supposedly reported on, as well as in the pages of fiction – although, of course, the whole point about the new ('novel') form of the novel was its liberty-taking with subject matter and form. Henry Fielding, for example, in *Joseph Andrews* (1742) has two men discuss drama while kidnapping the heroine, styling it 'A discourse between the poet and the player; of no other use in this history but to divert the reader'.[13]

Fielding conveyed the controversy aroused by *Clarissa* – 'In the first conversation I heard on this subject, the whole book was unanimously condemned' – and also her own partiality: she couldn't wait to get away from that particular social circle and move on to spend an evening 'with a family in whose conversation I am always agreeably entertained'.[14] Like the female adventurer who falls into conversations with people in lodging houses and in coaches, common in fictions from the late seventeenth century onwards, Fielding's persona is open to whatever she hears in polite social circles whose composition reflects the society depicted in *Clarissa*: there are obedient daughters and selfish fathers; thoughtful mothers and assertive, witty, intellectual women; civilised gentlemen and rakes. Distinguished above the rest is Miss Gibson. Miss Gibson is our guide whenever an important moral is to be drawn. It is Miss Gibson, 'with her usual penetration', who devastatingly explains that representations of women cannot be trusted to bear any relation to fact: 'A prude cannot, by an observing eye, be taken for a coquet, nor a coquet for a prude, but a good woman may be called either, or both, according to the dispositions of her resolved censurers.'[15]

Miss Gibson's comments are apropos some accusations made against Clarissa – that she was both a prude and a coquet – 'in a printed paper'. Sarah Fielding's pamphlet thus takes its place as a contribution to public discussion; in producing it she was engaging in a current debate by pretending to write a letter to Samuel Richardson. The mode was private and real but it was at the same time public and fictional. Fielding the writer was more like Richardson the writer than she was like the Miss Gibsons and Bellarios whose spoken comments she recorded or invented.

Hester Mulso, later the Mrs Chapone who wrote *Letters on the Improvement of the Mind addressed to a young lady* (1773), also addressed literary criticism to Richardson in letters about *Clarissa* which were subsequently published as *Letters on Filial Obedience* (1807). Like Fielding, Mulso used the letter of introduction as a way of introducing herself into the company of readers and writers whose friendship and society she sought as one of their own kind and whose reception of her gave her the status of a woman of letters.

The character of an author

In the early decades of the eighteenth century there was no significant discursive opposition to the idea that women might be writers, and little ideological weight behind the suggestion that to be known as a certain kind of writer was compromising for 'the sex'. Other and connected things might be compromising, such as mixing in theatrical circles and being friends with actresses who were known to be kept women, but even then, if we take the case of Susannah Centlivre, it was never the basis for arguing against the writing of the comedies for which Centlivre was praised. (Centlivre was married to a cook in the royal household, an association with rank that did her no harm.) On the other hand, there were few positive versions of female authorial lives for succeeding generations to take up and use in the way that, from the mid century onwards, male authorial lives were made available. By the 1760s and 1770s, the idea of emulating earlier writers – Addison, especially – figured as an important element in the formation of young male authors. James Boswell liked to imagine himself back in the era of Queen Anne when Addison and Steele were publishing their *Spectator* essays and Pope was a brilliant young man, perhaps because this was when the authorial persona first became a significant factor in cultural life. Mid-century works of criticism and biography, such as Joseph Warton's *Essay on the Writings and Genius of Pope* as well as his critical edition of Pope's works, and Samuel Johnson's *Life of Richard Savage* (1744), his life of Milton and the later *Lives of the English Poets* (1779–81), made 'the English poets', all of whom were male, available.

Several women who were active as writers in the first half of the century, most notably Jane Barker and Delarivier Manley, but also Elizabeth Thomas and Martha Fowke Sansom, published autobiographical or semi-autobiographical representations of female authorship. Jane Barker's *Love Intrigues* (1713) and her *A Patch-Work Screen for the Ladies* (1723) and *The Lining of the Patch-Work Screen* (1725) introduced a persona, Galesia, who was first and foremost a writer, responsibly collecting and disseminating stories and reflecting for her readers on her own experiences and on the world around her. Delarivier Manley's *The Adventures of Rivella; or, the History of the Author of the Atalantis* (1714) was a self-told life story by, as the title emphasised, a famously successful author, and it had as one of its objects the desire to parade that success. Elizabeth Thomas's autobiographical *The Life of Corinna*, written after she was imprisoned for debt in 1727, pleaded her case by demonstrating that she was an exceptional woman who had been received as a poet and critic by persons of distinction in polite society. Martha Fowke Sansom's *Clio* was written in response to praise of her poetry and notice from Aaron Hill. It took the form of a letter to Hill in which she expressed her adoration of him, but the narrative itself was not about her love for Hill or any relationship with him, but rather about her poetic formation. Written in 1723 when a female poet could express fervour – and even sexual passion as Mrs Rowe did in her 1715 poem 'On the Death of Mr Thomas Rowe' – it was not published until 1753. By that time the language of love and gallantry was associated with female ruin and commercial writing. When *Clio* came into the world it was presented as a 'secret history' and associated with that 'set of wretches' – Behn, Manley, Haywood, Pilkington, Phillips and Vane – against whose 'poison' good women like Mrs Rowe existed to provide the antidote.

These explorations and dramatisations of the social role of female authorship, all (except *Clio*) published by Edmund Curll and all predating *Clarissa*, were experimental in form. Perhaps this is one reason that they were not received as accounts of writers' lives. (Perhaps another is that they were published by Curll.) There seems to have been little interest in the construct of the woman writer as an identity to be acknowledged, defended, justified or opposed. There were, of course, a number of ways in which the experiences of authorship might be conveyed indirectly, such as in letters and notes to the reader or prefatory material in plays and books, some of which could be quite detailed and lengthy. Also, there were familiar and well-rehearsed rhetorical positions deriving from debates about the nature of women, but the fact of authorship did not drive those debates. All writers made use of the modesty topos, so no special weight need be attached to women's use of it in a general way.

The *Life of Mrs Rowe* gave an impetus to Catharine Cockburn and encouraged her to begin collecting support for her own *Life and Works*, but as we have seen, biographies of women writers were not an established genre. Nor were there critical studies, or editions of their works which made them available for future generations. There was no *Essay on the Writings and Genius of Delarivier Manley* to match Joseph Warton's book on Pope, nor a *Life of Jane Barker* that preserved an account of her adventures in the world (and glamorised it) as Johnson's *Life of Savage* did for Richard Savage.

Much of Johnson's *Life of Savage* was based on oral testimony – conversations with Savage himself as the two men walked the London streets, conversations with other writers whose memories stretched back into the last century. In his *Lives of the English Poets*, Johnson laid stress on the importance of personal knowledge. Writing about Addison, he observed: 'History may be formed from permanent monuments and records; but Lives can only be written from personal knowledge, which is growing every day less, and in a short time is lost for ever . . . The delicate features of the mind, the nice discriminations of character, and the minute peculiarities of conduct, are soon obliterated.'[16]

Being remembered in itself defined authorship. Johnson explored the way each of his subjects effected the transformation from writer to author, how poets like Milton and Pope were able to 'realise' their 'genius' in the writing they produced, achieving in the process that 'timeless' quality that conferred the status of an author within the tradition. Johnson's *Lives of the English Poets* contained no female authors (a stark witness to how personal knowledge could be lost altogether) even though he was personally a helpful supporter of them, drawing up proposals and collecting subscriptions for Anna Williams, for example. His emphasis on the conversations of literary men as the source of literary biography and literary history was not an eccentric view at the time and it had obvious implications for the way the 'mind', 'character' and 'conduct' of a female author was likely to be transmitted. So long as the literary record depended on men's memories and conversation, the space it accorded to female authors would always be small and probably equivocal.

Many evolving conventions and practices were built on the model of criticism as a conversation between literary men. In 1751, William Warburton, Pope's literary executor, published his 'elegant' nine-volume edition of the poet's works. Five years later, Joseph Warton declared that with Pope's entire corpus now properly available, the task of determining where Pope should be 'placed' could be undertaken. In *An Essay on the Writings and Genius of Pope* Warton set out to do this. His purpose was to offer a critical assessment of Pope's achievement in relation to the whole of English literature. This large and ambitious project was described in casual terms as 'a few reflections' and introduced as a conversation between himself and Dr Young. The *Essay* was addressed to Dr Young in an introductory letter, so that Young was included in the exercise as the implied recipient, marshalled as a 'character' and employed to lend it some of his own dignity. Warton's *Essay* began:

> Dear Sir, Permit me to break into your retirement, the residence of virtue and literature, and to trouble you with a few reflections on the merits and real character of an admired author and on other collateral subjects of criticism that will naturally arise in the course of such an inquiry.

The motif of breaking into the author's 'retirement' was taken straight from Pope – especially the 'Epistle to Dr Arbuthnot' – which, since it so happened that Warton was to go on to question how far Pope was a 'true' poet, lends a certain irony. The letter form made the *Essay* seem less of a public statement and more like private remarks: not so much a book for the general public as an extension of a familiar conversation or correspondence between two men of letters. Warton and Young were both poets, and that they should exchange ideas about the most 'admired' poet of their time and attempt to rank him, which is what Warton explains that he set out to do, is wholly appropriate. The literary friend has permission to break in on the residence of virtue and literature. The conversation is between insiders; the reader is invited to overhear it. Though it is not at all hard to imagine a female reader contributing her views to the discussion – Sarah Fielding, say, or Joseph Warton's clever sister Jenny (also a writer) – it *is* hard to imagine a female subject as the object of such a conversation – as the 'true' poet whose rank needed to be settled.

When men discussed women it was likely to be like the gentlemen in Fielding's *Remarks on Clarissa* who, in discussing heroines like Clarissa and 'the lovely Emma', can only do so by imagining themselves as their lovers. (Miss Gibson wishes Prior's poem had been 'long ago buried in oblivion' and invites the gentlemen to think about Emma not as a mistress but as if she were a daughter.)[17] Women critics, meanwhile, were not breaking in upon each other's retirement, the residences of virtue and literature, to reflect on the merits of admired female authors. When women presented themselves as critics, the authors they discussed were men – Shakespeare, Milton, Prior, Richardson, Pope – and the heroines these men created.

Perhaps it was to underline her status as a famous author – a real heroine – that Delarivier Manley structured her version of her life as a conversation between two men. In *Rivella*, two fictional cavaliers meet so that the one who knows Rivella's story can communicate it to the other. The 'character' exchanged between the men is the character of 'an admired author'. Rivella is no beauty, being both fat and scarred with smallpox; but she is immensely fascinating, her fascination lying in her intellect, conversational charm and sociability. In fact, as we shall see (in Chapter Seven), two men *had* been planning to tell Delarivier Manley's story: Edmund Curll and Charles Gildon. It is most unlikely that they would have eulogised Manley as her own fictional cavaliers were depicted as doing. One of the fictions of *Rivella*, knowingly elaborated by a shrewd and sophisticated worldly woman author, was that men left to themselves spoke politely and admiringly about 'admired' women.

When Delarivier Manley died in 1724, the Historical Register recorded the loss of 'a person of a polite genius, and uncommon capacity' whose writings were 'naturally delicate and easy' and whose conversation was 'agreeably entertaining'.[18] That she was a superior woman was taken for granted, but 'polite genius' and 'uncommon capacity' were not gendered, and nor were natural delicacy and ease; they were signifiers of rank. Authorship was subsumed in 'polite' behaviour. Manley's father, Sir Roger Manley, had been highly placed at court and Manley herself, after an early, bigamous marriage to her cousin, John Manley, had spent time in the household of Charles II's former mistress, Barbara Villiers, Duchess of Cleveland. In *Rivella*, Manley characterised herself in personal and professional terms, stressing her good breeding and liberal education. She had lost her looks but 'considering that disadvantage [had] ... the most easy air'. Her conversation fascinated and her company was never wearisome. She displayed her 'polite genius' by not displaying it: she never spoke of her own writings except when properly and professionally asking the judgement of friends. She was 'haughty' and 'impatient of contradiction', signs both of genius and rank. A believer in the privileges of sex and birth; benevolent towards the afflicted; loving expense 'even to being extravagant, which in a woman of fortune might more justly have been termed generosity' (extravagance by those who could afford it was a virtue), she was pleased with her own 'perfections' but not boastful about praise, and an utter stranger to hatred and revenge except in the case of Richard Steele 'whose notorious ingratitude and breach of friendship affected her too far'.[19]

Authorship as a social role, which women as well as men engaged in, was newly defined in the early decades of the eighteenth century and came under new pressures, chiefly the pressure of publicity. Steele's ingratitude and breach of friendship were 'notorious' because Manley lost no opportunity of attacking him in her works. Their feud, apparently originating in Steele's refusal to lend her money after her separation from her lover, John Tilly, also reflected political and class differences: Steele was a Whig and 'a wretched common trooper' (Manley and Steele had conducted a literary correspondence when Steele was a soldier stationed on the Isle of Wight), Manley a Tory of high birth. Under the pseudonym Isaac Bickerstaff, Steele attacked Manley in the *Tatler* in 1709 and Manley responded in her *Memoirs of Europe* the following year by revealing Steele's identity in a sardonic dedication and publishing his private letter to her. (In the dedication to her play, *Lucius, the First Christian King of Britain* in 1717, she apologised; by that time they had become reconciled.)[20]

Publishing private letters was a regular means of conducting literary wars. Scraps of correspondence known or supposed to have come from the hands of a prominent writer, anecdotes about lives and relationships, gossip and innuendo, outright lies and defamation, all acquired commercial value. Commerce was 'low' and literature 'high', except that literature was understood to be permeated by envy and interest, which commerce could exploit; and commerce provided funds which writers like Steele, Manley and Pope badly needed. All traded on the fictive possibilities print made available, hiding or revealing or inventing identities and voices according to requirements.

Elizabeth Thomas

Smaller fry caught up in the violent exchanges that characterised literary life in the early eighteenth century ran the risk of damage. Had Elizabeth Thomas died in 1722, after the publication of her first volume of poems and before she sold letters in her possession written by Pope, Lady Mary Chudleigh and John Norris, she might have been remembered as a harmless gentlewoman who haunted the bookshops of literary London.

The evidence suggests that until 1718 or so Elizabeth Thomas, a spinster living with her widowed mother in lodgings in Great Russell Street, was able to function as a known woman of letters in a literary coterie which appreciated her writings, shared some of her views, and gave her a sense of value. From at least 1699, when Thomas wrote to Dryden, sending him a sample of her poems, she had lived the life of a dedicated poet. Dryden gave her the name 'Corinna'. Pope visited her. She was friendly with Pope's friend Henry Cromwell. She engaged in correspondence with men and women of similar interests and literary ambition. In that position she did not need to go into print. Poems to her patron, the Right Honourable the Lady Dowager De La Warr, such as 'On her saying I hid my candle under a bushel', appear to respond to pressure from others to go public and reach out through print to a larger audience. Whatever her views on the subject, the poems refused this. They staged the poet in Horatian mode as one withdrawn from the vices of 'the Town', preferring 'quiet and obscurity' in order to get on with her 'rural lays' (mostly in Great Russell Street). She claimed that her dull muse was not sprightly enough, that she hated flattery and 'pert obsceneness', could not suck up to patrons, and was in the happy position of being able to resist the temptations of 'sordid gain' or 'popular applause'. The poet's job was to reform the age – an impossible task that would be rendered even more difficult by publication. The worst thing about going into print was that 'every would-be writer' would feel entitled to criticise, heaping censure not praise. Coteries protected and praised, but in the uncontrolled world of print the writer was likely to be 'mauled'.

Thomas offered a picture of herself as a true poet in the classical tradition, and she consciously evoked the Milton of *Lycidas*: 'Alas! what boots it with uncessant care / To tend the homely slighted Shepherds trade, / And strictly meditate the thankless Muse?' She was no mere 'would-be writer' but a chosen one whose muse would not allow her to rest. Her muse 'Commands me from my bed to rise, / And follow her where'er she flies'.

Thomas wrote stinging poems in the female protest tradition, condemning the double standard which gave men and women 'different licences' in marriage – 'The man may range from his unhappy wife, / But woman's made a property for life' – but she did not protest about double standards in the opportunities available to or the reception of male and female writers except when satirising the folly of those who would prevent women improving themselves by reading serious books. 'On Sir J— S— saying in a Sarcastic Manner, my Books would Make me Mad. An Ode' is a wonderfully vigorous riposte against those who prated that women should confine themselves to needlework and chat 'Or such like exercise as that / But still denied th'improvement of our mind!' Its scathing tone assumed reader agreement. It mocked Sir John and his ilk as antediluvian, making such men the fools at fault in the poem, not the woman poet.[21]

The Horatian persona was used in a similar way by Mary Jones who offered herself in her verses as poet friend to the great; one who, having only a modest income and an inferior status generally, appreciated the luxuries afforded by friends like Martha Lovelace, who was a maid of honour at court, and Lady Bowyer, with whom Jones stayed at Windsor Castle. Jones protested her determination to be contented with little. Fortune hadn't served her well (she was a clergyman's dependent sister) but she could extol the Horatian simplicity of her life – 'the cottage, the mutton, and the feather-bed' – and acknowledge that her friends were her good fortune which she had earned by her merit and talents.

For this relation of poet to a circle of highly ranked supporters and patrons, Pope was the important living model. Mary Jones cast herself as a Popeian recluse from the court where many of her friends spent much of their time. Reading Pope's *Letters* with 'inexpressible pleasure' in 1735, she explained: 'I have always admired the author, but now I love the man.' She admired his spirit of benevolence, his tenderness (looking after his elderly mother) and affectionate friendships. She copied Pope in publishing her letters along with her poems (Elizabeth Carter specially liked the letters). Far from hiding her relative poverty and inferiority of status, she made much of it, throwing the emphasis on her role as poet: high-ranking people had her to stay on their landed estates not because she had any right by birth to be there but because of what she was able to offer as a poet. Emulating Pope gave her what she wanted: a literary life, reputation and financial independence. Having achieved this, as witnessed by the successful subscription for her volume of poems in 1750, she ceased publishing. Like Elizabeth Carter, the clergyman's daughter whose *Epictetus* enabled her to buy a house at Deal, Mary Jones probably secured her future finances with this one publication. Further print publishing might have worked against the position she had achieved. As commercial print grew in influence and power, aristocratic networks and practices weakened, so the decision not to print was a statement of allegiance to a threatened way of life. (It was rarely a sign of modesty or temerity, and the idea that it required special bravery to allow one's work to appear in print is not supported by strong evidence.) In the 1740s, Edward Cave, the publisher of the *Gentleman's Magazine*, repeatedly urged Elizabeth Carter to write for him as she had done in the 1730s, but when set against all the advantages of notice by the highly ranked, the more arduous life of the professional writer did not appeal and was evidently not necessary. Elizabeth Carter preferred the social round in St James's to anything Grub Street had to offer.

Mary Jones also copied Pope in figuring herself in her verses as someone superior to the contrivances and servilities of literary life. In 'An Epistle to Lady Bowyer' she modestly put herself second to Pope (the 'genius' who rose once in an age) and made fun of authorial vanity in the name of higher virtues: honesty, independence and private worth rather than public place and the flattery required to obtain and keep it: 'the joy to see my works in print! / Myself too pictured in a mezzotint! / The preface done, the dedication framed, / With lies enough to make a lord asham'd! / Thus I step forth, an Auth'ress in some sort . . . ' Jones set herself to explain the true grossness of literary life to her patron:

> And yet you'd have me write! – For what? For whom?
> To curl a favourite in a dressing-room?
> To mend a candle when the snuff's too short?
> Or save rappee for chamber-maids at court?
> Glorious ambition! Noble thirst of fame! –
> No, but you'd have me write – to get a name.
> Alas! I'd live unknown, unenvied too;
> 'Tis more than Pope with all his wit can do . . .

To have a soul that rose above all this was to be the true poet (serving none but the Muses), an achievement not even 'lofty Pope' could boast.

Mary Jones, who lived until 1778, became a well-known and well-respected figure in Oxford literary circles. She had enough money to support a genteel existence which enabled her to figure at parties given by, for example, Thomas Warton, the Oxford Professor of Poetry and brother of Joseph Warton, where she was considered 'a very ingenious poetess', and where she met visiting luminaries like Samuel Johnson. Writing and publishing gave her credit and status. She might represent herself as 'a fool with too much reading' (spilling tea as she read Swift) and as one who had never 'shown / One steady purpose of my own', but she may have been even more successful than we know. One source reported that at her death she was 'Post-mistress of Oxford', possibly a sinecure given to her after her brother's death in 1775. If she had managed, through her contacts and her writings, to gain a scarce government post then she certainly put her ingenuity to good purpose.[22]

The contrast with Elizabeth Elstob and Elizabeth Thomas a generation or two earlier could not be more pointed. For Thomas, like Elstob, catastrophe followed the death of a significant other: though well established in her literary community, she could not find the means of existence after her mother died. Elstob went into hiding and seems to have managed to avoid arrest; Elizabeth Thomas was less fortunate: she ended up in jail.

For sixteen years, from about 1700, Thomas had maintained a literary correspondence with a lawyer, Richard Gwinnet, whose family did not consider her wealthy enough to be his wife. It was an engagement of sorts, though they met only once or twice a year since Gwinnet lived in Gloucestershire and Thomas in London. For most of that time she nursed her mother, who had cancer, maintaining them both by selling off their valuables bit by bit, one year a damask bed or a gold watch, another some jewels of a chest of fine linen, and last of all her books which she had been collecting all her life and which had been valued at £150 (a very large sum) but for which, when she sold them, she only realised £50. The pair sank slowly into debt, so that by the time of her mother's death in January 1719, 'when she lay dead by me', Thomas owed £333. Plunged, as she put it, into 'unforeseen and unavoidable ruin', forced to go into hiding to escape creditors, she left

Great Russell Street, 'retreated from the world, and . . . buried myself in a dismal place, where I knew none nor none knew me'. She never emerged from debt and the rest of her life was 'a lingering death' dogged by misery.[23]

Six months earlier, Gwinnet had offered to marry her. Thomas had refused on the grounds that her mother's condition, so near to death, made it impossible. Shortly afterwards, Gwinnet, who was consumptive, also died, leaving Thomas a legacy of £600 (an amount that would have secured her comfort for life) which his family refused to pay. And 'sorrow', she wrote in *The Life of Corinna* which prefaced the posthumous collection of her writings, *Pylades and Corinna*, 'has been my food ever since'.[24] Exposed to 'the insults of poverty', she claimed that she was 'barbarously used' by his family, and that Gwinnet's brother went so far as to offer £1,000 to anyone to blacken her character. The tricks of the lawyers meant she lost still more: 'The gentlemen of the long robe had made me sign an instrument that they should receive the money and pay themselves.' She claimed she received almost nothing and was compelled to 'abscond' from her creditors, 'and starve in a corner till last winter; when, betrayed by a false friend, I was hurried to a jail; where, unless it shall please our gracious sovereign and the parliament to grant an act of insolvency, I must end my days'.[25]

As if that were not bad enough, her posthumous fate was to be even worse. It was in the attempt to pay off her debts that Elizabeth Thomas sold Edmund Curll autograph letters she had in her possession, 'letters of my dead or absent friends', some by Pope (very much not dead), and others by Dryden, John Norris and Lady Mary Chudleigh. The letters were a financial resource, though not very effective. Curll published them in 1727, the year Thomas was confined to the Fleet prison for debt. She was there for three years in spite of having the support of senior clergy like the Bishop of Durham who paid her chamber rent. She died, destitute, not long after her release. Pope put her in *The Dunciad* as 'Curll's Corinna', one of the two prominent female dunces (Eliza Haywood was the other), and, like Haywood, associated with the sewer. Pope depicted Edmund Curll sliding about in a lake of piss and shit deposited by Thomas, 'obscene with filth . . . Fallen in the plash his wickedness had laid'.[26]

If anybody fell in filth it was Elizabeth Thomas. In one of his facetious notes to *The Dunciad*, Pope apologised for the 'low and base' nature of the incident, claimed that he only mentioned it because Thomas had sold his letters which were full of immature judgements and levities, and argued that any more 'delicate' satire would have been lost on the objects who were, like piss and shit in the streets, vile 'common nuisances'. He concluded that 'the politest men are sometimes obliged to swear, when they happen to have to do with porters and oyster-wenches'.

Lack of money exposed Elizabeth Thomas to insult. If, from a chamber in debtors' prison, it was difficult enough to maintain the ordinary dignities of respectable female life, assuming the airs and graces of a superior woman was impossible. Nobody commemorated Thomas nor Elstob and neither of them features in traditional literary histories; nor has much space been found for them in histories of women's writing. But both are important. Elizabeth Thomas, born in 1675, and Elizabeth Elstob, born 1683, were pioneers: Thomas in living among and writing about an urban literary milieu and Elstob in her Anglo-Saxon work and the scholarly polemical prefaces to her books. Mrs Rowe, available for construction as the nearest thing to a saint the literary world could boast, and Catharine Cockburn, in her role as a precise philosopher, could be recovered for posterity in the mid century; Aphra Behn, Delarivier Manley and Eliza Haywood, all 'sinners', and Elstob and Thomas among the shamed, could not. They could not be allowed to mix with the 'blooming studious band' whose arts engaged the reverence of polished people in a polished land. As John Duncombe put it, 'Some turn the tuneful, some the moral page' and some 'led by contemplation, soar on high, / And range the Heavens with philosophic eye'. Rhetorically speaking, those lofty heights were the preferred location for the woman of letters by the time Duncombe wrote *The Feminiad* in 1754.

Martha Fowke Sansom's *Clio*

Unsurprisingly, Martha Fowke Sansom, whose *Clio* was issued in 1752 as a 'secret history' – a sort of composite association with early eighteenth-century secret histories, such as Delarivier Manley's *The New Atalantis*, and contemporary memoirs, such as those by Constantia

Phillips and Laetitia Pilkington in the late 1740s – also joined the ranks of the excluded. Posterity showed little interest in Martha Fowke Sansom and it was not until *Clio* was edited and reprinted in 1997 that she became available to any but the most determined researcher. This is unfortunate because, like the lives and writings of Elstob and Thomas, *Clio* warrants close attention from literary historians. It is one of the few self-told 'lives' of a successful female author from the early period (drawing on the example of Manley's *Rivella*); but more than that, it is a remarkably innovative piece of writing. Martha Fowke Sansom attempted to reverse the convention whereby the adored female serves as poetic muse to the male poet. In *Clio*, the female poet is the active lover and the male object of her love serves as the inspiration for her poetry. Aaron Hill – the 'divine Hillarius' – was the 'Guide of my life, inspirer of my muse' as well as 'Sweet patron of my lays', and his function in the text was to 'guard my fame'.[27] Just as Virginia Woolf fictionalised herself in *A Room of One's Own*, her 'I' being 'only a convenient term ... call me Mary Beton, Mary Seton, Mary Carmichael or by any name you please', so Martha Fowke Sansom was not 'I' but 'Clio', and she too might have said, along with Virginia Woolf, 'Lies will flow from my lips, but there may perhaps be some truth mixed up with them.'[28]

It was probably the publication in 1731 of Elizabeth Thomas's *Pylades and Corinna* that inspired the reissue under an altered title of a correspondence between Martha Fowke Sansom and William Bond which had first appeared in 1720. The verse *Epistles of Clio and Strephon* appeared in a third edition in 1732 with the title *The Platonic Lovers, consisting of Original Letters that passed between an English Lady and an English Gentleman in France*. This edition included a glowing critical essay by John Porter, praising Fowke Sansom's wit, humour and delicacy.

Martha Fowke Sansom (generally referred to as Martha Fowke) was a poet and a wit, well known in literary circles from at least 1711 when she began publishing under her own name in periodicals and miscellanies. Richard Steele esteemed her 'extraordinary wit' and Giles Jacob, in his *Poetical Register* of 1720, described her as 'an accomplished young lady' who had a 'genius that would let her be Britain's Dacier'.

Preferring to take up the equally frequent comparison to Sappho, Fowke adopted the poetic name 'Clio' – Sappho's daughter – and made clear her wish for fame: her verses expressed the hope that she might 'touch the reader's heart' as Shakespeare, Donne, Sappho, Philips and Behn had all succeeded in doing, and like them rise 'on the wings of verse'. Sending her his own book, Jacob prefixed a poem, 'To Mrs Fowke, with the second volume of My Lives of the Poets', addressing her as 'thou Sappho of this Isle in fame' and putting her in a line of succession that ran from Milton and Spenser to Pope and Granville. For others she was 'the immortal Clio', an English lady who 'infinitely surpassed' the Greek Sappho and the Roman Tibullus.[29]

Like Elizabeth Thomas, Martha Fowke was a known figure in an active literary circle, but the persona she projected and her modus operandi differed strikingly from those of Thomas. Of higher birth and with aristocratic connections, her writings asserted her quality. In 1723, when she wrote *Clio*, she was in her early thirties and at the height of her fame. The narrative of *Clio* began with her birth into a well-established royalist family whose estates had been lost in the civil wars and whose prosperity in the next generation was not improved by the Revolution Settlement of 1689. Her father refusing to 'submit to the tyranny of oaths', they retired to the country where her mother's money amply supported them. Fowke described her parents' marriage as a loveless one: her mother had been a rich widow and her father a man in search of a fortune. Her mother was 'lovely', an 'excellent manager', and devout; and if 'she could not pray herself into his affections' she nevertheless 'found all things in the Heaven she addressed, and though not fondly, they lived civilly together'. As for her father, he was a man of wit, charm and beauty:

> He was tall, graceful and well made. His complexion was the darkest brown, but something so sweetly commanding shone through that gloom, I have often thought it like some lovely evening, which charms beyond the day. Till he was thirty he had the finest shining dark hair in the world, long and flowing in large curls. He had large dark eyes full of love and fire. His lips and teeth were beyond description, and had something enchanting in them; his hands were equally fine. Thus was his form adorned by Nature, and his soul worthy of it. He was good-natured to excess, and the most amorous of

all mortals. Heaven had designed him for a lover rather than a husband. The chains of marriage pressed him to death.[30]

The chains of marriage did not press so hard that he was unable to have affairs. When his adored and adoring only daughter (there was a younger son who was less favoured) showed, at the age of nine or ten, her remarkable facility in writing, she was 'called the wit of the family' and 'made secretary to my father and mother' which, along with writing answers to 'letters of compliment', also included composing missives for her father's mistresses: 'I often dictated his love letters for him, and that in such a tender manner, he had too much success with them.' The little girl was her father's 'confidant' and pupil in the amorous arts, as witnessed in her description of him which itemises the body parts – stature, complexion, eyes, hair, lips, teeth, hands – customary in descriptions of female beauty. In writing about her own life (and perhaps to some extent in living it), Martha Fowke deployed the conventions she learned at her father's knee. Hence, her 'autobiography' was written as a love letter and addressed to her 'lover'/muse.

Martha Fowke's poetry was admired by Aaron Hill, whose periodical, *The Plain Dealer*, was written in conjunction with William Bond, Fowke's 'Strephon' in the *Epistles of Clio and Strephon*. Hill was an enthusiast for women's writing (his two daughters were named Astraea and Minerva), especially the rapturous kind that 'kindles body into soul'. Platonic love doctrines licensed amorous exchanges that might or might not include sexual intent. Hill was apparently happily married, but he maintained literary correspondences with women in which his appreciation of them was expressed in the language of love. To Fowke he wrote,

save me from this growth of your attraction – condemn me never to behold you more; or let me never be deprived of seeing you. All repetitions of such pleasures as my heart is filled with, when I sit and listen to your sweetness are succeeded by new pains, which you can never rightly judge of because there is no man as worthy of your esteem as you are of mankind's in general. I carry with me from your gentle conversation a thousand inexpressible remembrances of words, looks, movements, softnesses and graces – which, compared with the gay female world make all things tasteless in it, but the image of that single loveliness, where all those excellencies centre.[31]

As the 'divine Hillarius', Aaron Hill was the 'inspirer of my soul, but sweet disturber of it' and the recipient of the love letter which told the story of Clio's life. Whether the choice of a love letter as the form and Hill as the particular love object had any more profound erotic meaning for Fowke than Aaron Hill's use of the language of love to elevate his friendships to that higher plane where bodies became souls is not known; most of what we know about Martha Fowke is drawn from her own writings. But there is some evidence that through the form of the love letter and the partial representation of herself as an anguished, unsatisfied lover/writer, Fowke addressed a wider public and a larger theme. Apparently written for the 'for-ever-lovely Hillarius' and designed to re-engage a flagging attention, Fowke's story was not necessarily inspired by actual disappointment in love nor can we say how much of it was 'true'. The voice of the abandoned woman which dominates the final page as she swoons and thinks of the comforts of death – 'Friday night, the last night of my life or happiness, disappointed in seeing you ... your absence kills me' – is a sudden transition in both tone and situation. The framing of the text as a whole positions Hillarius at beginning and end as addressee and sole recipient: his reception is key, he is the reader for whom the account is written. But what he reads is for the most part a vigorous commentary on the experiences of a woman of talent committed to living the life of a Restoration gallant, in which it is not the absence but the presence of her lovers that threatens to kill her – not through the denial of love but through boredom and loss of liberty.

Fowke's narrative traces Clio's career through many varieties of love and lovers (taking the word in its eighteenth-century sense meaning anything from friendship to sexual intimacy), a gallery of female friends and acquaintances, adventures in fashionable parts of London such as St James's, and spells of reading erupting into affairs in the quiet back gardens of Fulham and Windsor. Married or single, sooner or later every man falls in love with Clio. Or, we could equally say, Clio's function in the narrative is to be the object of unattainable desire while she herself desires the unattainable Hillarius. Desire is the linking device between 'adventures' – mostly relationships – that strain credibility if read realistically and taken as a whole. By the age of fourteen, Clio's conquests already included a Hugenot who was teaching her French and who ran mad with love, and a rich but sickly relation who wanted to marry her, was refused and died. Thereafter, we are introduced to a never-ending supply of vividly characterised men in solidly realised social settings: a handsome Irish nobleman falls in love with her at church; two men in a boat on the river capsize before her eyes and a serious courtship with one of them follows; a cousin comes home from sea and at once 'retired from his friends and business to give himself up entirely to love'; another cousin replaced him; the husband of a neighbour, in whose head 'there was room for twenty Cupids', begged her to run away with him; a blind gentleman aroused her pity and tenderness until, 'as blind as he', she 'began to love in earnest' so that when he urged her to share a house with him she agreed, only to discover that 'love had led me wrong' and the lover had turned into a jealous tyrant; during an interlude at Bath with a lady friend and 'agreeable company . . . wit and music and continual entertainment', a young gentleman tried to rape her – 'in spite of my resistance he threw me on the bed, and I him on the floor' – and a gentler man offered to marry her; back in London, an old roué serenaded and tried to seduce her; one of the cousins returned, hot for love; the Duke of Beaufort 'grew a lover' and 'we had many laughing hours together' but his desire to instruct her in 'platonic love' she found 'coarse' and 'dull' – he 'sought the body more than the soul'; a stranger tricked her into his carriage after a dance and off to his lodgings in Pall Mall, keeping her there all night and offering to settle an income on her and make their children his heirs; there was a fop at Fulham, followed by a doleful whiner – 'he threatened to destroy himself very often' – and two young men meant for other women; the cousin again; a married painter; another relation – old this time; a friend of her brother's; a friend of the friend; a friend of her landlord – and so on.

Clio is a girl about town. She is constantly on the move – changing her lodgings, going to stay with friends or friends of friends, enjoying jaunts on the river, meeting new people and all the time entering into new relationships. Her object is to be free to enjoy herself and avoid dullness. One friend she spent time with, 'an agreeable but dangerous acquaintance', was a 'coquet' full of charm in person but who 'lashed her dearest friends in absence, even me, whom she courted as a goddess'; still, 'her wit was amusing and released me from the duller world'.

Another friend at Parsons Green was the mother of the Duchess of Bolton, 'a woman of gallantry' and wit who 'used to entertain me with all the past gallantries of the age she had shone in; she had read very much, and was a very accomplished woman'. The son of the house adds himself to the list of Clio's admirers.

Thus blessed with 'youth, freedom, and friends', Clio's account of her adventures maintains an energy and humour that belies the broken heart.[32] As the narrative proceeds, the lovers come thick and fast. It's not impossible that the episodes are drawn from memory, but the heaping of incident and increase of narrative pace towards the double climax – marriage to Mr Sansom (a mistake) and the joy, rapidly followed by disappointment, of receiving admiring letters from Aaron Hill ('I looked upon you as a miracle above my hopes, and designed rather to be wondered at than possessed') – is artfully controlled. Two kinds of loss are mourned: the loss of freedom in marriage and the loss of 'the gay prospect of life' which Hill's 'adorable letters' seemed to offer. Though admitting she felt a tender regard for Sansom, she lamented his chief failing, which was that he was not highly born and 'the polite part of the world had not fallen in the compass of his view. His days had been sacrificed to the morose god of business, and his nights to the wanton god of unrefined pleasure, which had not given his mind that delicacy of taste as I wish.' Acknowledging she owed him 'a thousand obligations', she nevertheless complained, 'but I would receive them as marks of his tender affection, not as badges of slavery to bind me down to mean servitude, as he expects'. Politeness, delicacy of taste and refined pleasures operate as opposites to 'mean servitude'. Freedom is high; like generosity, it is what distinguishes the unmorose and unenslaved nobly born. Freedom includes the freedom to exchange stories and keep clear of the 'duller' world. Like the romances she read as a girl ('My mother had a closet finely furnished with the best authors, but *Cassandra* and *Cleopatra* were my favourites. I read there with pleasure the empire of women'), freedom enhanced 'exalted notions'.

Clio's free movement through the text that supposedly records her life is itself a symbol of her worth. Living well incorporates 'the park, the play, and every idle amusement'. Experience feeds judgement and can lead to virtue. Where men were concerned, it required 'little virtue to refuse the half of mankind. 'Tis a justice to ourselves, 'tis a love for ourselves makes us justly unkind to them.' Virtue consisted in loving what was virtuous and 'truly noble. I look down with contempt on the mean mortals who confine virtue to the narrow compass of the body.' Virtue was 'seated in the soul'. Clio's charms are manifestly irresistible, yet these charms are not the charms of body but of the soul, and they consist in her capacity to respond. Nothing depends on what her lovers make of Clio; everything depends on what she makes of them – which is generally not very much. All the lovers are measured against the 'divine' Hillarius, the well-known writer, and all bar one are found wanting. That one is 'divine Shakespeare'. Shakespeare was 'transporting': 'I was so enchanted with this old, yet for ever new lover, that I used to carry him all day in my arms, and at night he was my entertainment. He inspired my dreams, and first made me sigh after immortality.'[33]

Clio combines a swaggering worldliness with yearning for a distant and unattainable ideal. Scattered through the prose narrative of her life are numerous poems to which she occasionally refers, as in explaining that she had written a poem to the Duke of Beaufort for which he came to thank her, thus becoming 'a lover' after first being 'a patron'. It is in these poems that the language of poetic ambition and the claim on poetic identity is made most explicit. In the verse portrait (often reprinted) that prefaced the whole work, 'Clio's Picture', she explained that her large forehead gave 'room enough for all the Muses there', and that her stature was of sufficient height to be 'Worthy the Muses and a generous mind'. Meanwhile, in a song sequence that brings the narrative to a close with images of Clio's bodily death, Hillarius, like Shakespeare, represents immortality. He is all soul, and therefore love for him is the highest love: 'My friends, my lyre, thy empire shall confess, / And all things weep with Clio's tenderness. / The God of love shall to his favourite tell / None ever loved so long, none loved so well.' Loving well leads to the best poetry. No lover could charm or be charmed as she and her 'heavenly charmer', so in loving him she aspires to produce poems such as none had ever produced before: 'Poor bankrupt heart, canst thou do nothing more, / To show thy flame, than others have before? / . . . Let me for love, sweet Heaven, do something more, / Than ever any mortal did before.' And that something is to live on in the memory of the love object. Handing him her words – 'Take this fond offering of my flowing eyes, / And read with reverence what my soul has writ' – Hillarius represents posterity: 'To thy sweet memory my joys I give, / The tender hours when I did more than live. / Let them not from thy gentle memory go, / By other objects, or time's restless flow.'[34]

The little girl who collected and copied 'the most tender parts' from the poems of Cowley and Ovid and addressed them to her delighted father (who showed them to all his friends and boasted about 'his dear child') and who had a 'greater fondness' for writing than for anything else, grew into a woman who turned these formative influences to account. Both her mother and a local Catholic priest tried to reclaim her from 'profane and loose poets'. Her mother 'locked up her books, my pens were burned, and I bound down a prisoner to my needle ... Never did romantic lady deplore her self more than Miss Patty. I looked upon this as the highest affront ... I secretly mourned the loss of my dear pen and ink as if I had lamented a lover.'[35] The loss and possession of 'my dear pen and ink' were inextricably bound up with the loss and possession of lovers. For poets, pen and ink existed to tell the tale of love. The true lover is the true poet. Those, like her mother, who could only see profanity and looseness, lacked soul. But Clio's passion was for the pure poetry of her imagination, not the profane lovers who filled her life, and the 'romantic lady' did not mourn pen and ink for long. Her passion was satisfied by the right lover, an idealised literary man capable of giving her the imprimatur of recognition as a poet: Aaron Hill.

The love of dear pen and ink

Richard Steele in the *Tatler* and Joseph Addison in the *Spectator* frequently took as subjects for their 'lucubrations' questions that concerned the female sex or 'the fair sex'. As we shall see, in doing this they followed a practice established in what is generally considered the first literary magazine, the *Athenian Mercury*, which began in 1691 and in which a group of gentlemen figured themselves as 'the Athenians' in order to lead discussion on mostly literary and social matters from their base in a London coffee house. Steele and Addison were copied in their turn by any number of journalists, pamphleteers and essayists. In one pro-government newspaper of the 1730s, which covered political issues such as the taxation of gin, the woollen trade, and whether the poor were not in fact happier than the rich – 'the real drudgery of the world is not performed by the artisans and labourers but the unhappy men who loll in coaches and six with more uneasiness than their footmen ride behind them' – a writer offered some common observations in passing:

> I have always been an humble admirer of the fair sex, nay, I believe I think of them with more tenderness than any man in the world. I do not only look upon them as objects of pleasure, but I compassionate the many hardships both nature and custom has subjected them to. I never expose the foibles to which education has inclined them; and (contrary to all other authors) I see with a favourable eye the little vanities with which they amuse them-selves . . .[36]

The generous-minded 'man' expressing these sentiments and think-ing about the fair sex as objects of pleasure was Lady Mary Wortley Montagu, cousin to Sarah Fielding. Her observations appeared in a short-lived weekly newspaper, *The Nonsense of Common-Sense*, nine numbers of which she wrote between December 1737 and March 1738 in support of the government of Sir Robert Walpole and against the Opposition paper, *Common-Sense*. If we go on to include the final part of her sentence and read the whole passage with a knowledge of its authorship, the impact, even the meaning, is altered: 'I see with a favourable eye the little vanities with which they amuse themselves and am glad they can find in the imaginary empire of beauty, a consolation for being excluded every part of government in the state.'

Lady Mary Wortley Montagu's decision to enter the conversation of politics as a gentleman was one solution to the problem of being excluded. Her persona – 'the character I have assumed' – was that of 'a moralist'. Men's views of women, especially those expressed by Lord Chesterfield in *Common-Sense*, were among her targets. In her guise of male anonymity, adopting the fictional 'I' of a male journalist, she both reproduced and attacked those views. In a larger sense, the question of what character to assume and how to enter the conversation of literature was the question all women writers faced, not because there were controls in place to exclude them but because forms and practices were in their infancy. The tradition was 'short and partial', as Virginia Woolf described it, but it was so for men as well as women as far as criticism of contemporary culture and vernacular writings was concerned.

Born in 1689, Lady Mary Wortley Montagu was of the previous generation to her Fielding cousin, as well as being much better off. She was an example of a serious female intellectual, a 'mother' through whom Sarah Fielding might have thought back: Fielding's studies in Latin and Greek followed a path Lady Mary set out for herself when she translated Epictetus as a young woman and sent the manuscript to Bishop Burnet for his comments. If the tradition was short and partial when Sarah Fielding was writing, it was even more so in the 1690s and early 1700s when Lady Mary grew up. In 1710, she married Edward Wortley Montagu, and sometime shortly after that she wrote a fragment of autobiography. In this piece of autobiographical writing, in which she claimed that the facts were true though the names were false, Lady Mary created a picture of herself as a young woman ardent for scholarship and passionate about literature. No obstacles stop her pursuing her appetite for learning – she has books, there is no frowning father nor disapproving mother telling her to put down her pen and pick up her needle. Furthermore, the tale ends with the traditional happy-ever-after conclusion of an enraptured lover who determines to marry her, so charmed is he by her mental charms, her love of dear pen and ink. But the story is not a happy one. The life she tells, she warns us at the outset, is the life of an 'unfortunate lady'.[37]

The fragment begins: 'I am going to write a history so uncommon that in how plain a manner so ever I relate it, it will have the air of a romance.' Laetitia, the heroine of this 'life' or 'history' or 'romance', is a young noble woman who, as a child, had a voracious appetite for reading and knowledge. Growing up, as Lady Mary herself did, the daughter of a man of literary interests, she has the good fortune to be able to feed herself in the way she chooses. (One of Lady Mary's favourite stories about her childhood was of being taken by her father to be the toast of the Kit-Kat Club and being handed about from knee to knee of the famous authors and politicians there.)

[Laetitia,] finding in her father's house a well furnished library, instead of the usual diversions of children, [she] made that the seat of her pleasures, and had very soon run through the English part of it. Her appetite for knowledge increasing with her years, without considering the toilsome task she undertook she begun to learn herself the Latin grammar, and with the help of an uncommon memory and indefatigable labour, made herself so far mistress of that language as to be able to understand almost any author. This extraordinary attachment to study became the theme of public discourse.

Opportunity and genius, combined with the willingness to give up childish play for the 'toilsome' acquisition of knowledge, produces public interest: Laetitia became 'the theme of public discourse'. Whether being the theme of public discourse was for good or ill we are not told, but the implication of this 'plain' but 'romantic' relation of the story is that Lady Mary as a young woman earned praise and admiration for her acquirements. Her father, a pleasure-loving man of quality, was proud of his daughter's reputation as a scholar. (In a number of ways, the characterisation of Lady Mary's father resembles that of Martha Fowke Sansom's father: both were men of wit and parts in the Restoration mould.) Through her 'indefatigable labour', Laetitia had so much knowledge of all aspects of literature that she was able to impress Sebastian, 'a thorough scholar' and suitor to 'Mlle' – 'a bragging friend of Laetitia's'. ('Mlle', the original object of Sebastian's affections, is not identified by any fuller name.)

On his first acquaintance with Laetitia, Sebastian is thunderstruck. Tea having been served and a new play mentioned, Laetitia the critic holds forth on its virtues 'in a manner so just and so knowing, he was as much amazed as if he had heard a piece of waxwork talk on the subject'. On poetry, the next subject of her discourse, 'he was still more astonished to find her not only well read in the moderns, but that there was hardly any beautiful passage in the Classics she did not remember'. Laetitia's knowledge and ability to converse on literary and scholarly themes absorbs all Sebastian's attention: 'The conversation grew so eager on both sides, neither cards nor Mlle were thought upon.' Mlle has to call Sebastian several times before she can get his attention and even though he goes over to her 'it was only to continue his discourse with Laetitia'. Laetitia has 'the full pleasure of triumphing over Mlle, who was forced to be silent while they talked what she could not understand'.

Laetitia's well-stocked mind conquers Sebastian's heart. Ordinary female charms such as those that Mlle boasts are as nothing where intellectual conversation may also be had. But (the pleasure of triumphing over Mlle apart) Laetitia is not impressed. The love that follows is all on Sebastian's side, because

> [Laetitia] had a way of thinking very different from that of other girls, and instead of looking on a husband as the ultimate aim of her wishes she never thought of marriage but as a bond that was to subject her to a Master, and she dreaded an engagement of that sort. The little plan she had formed to herself was retirement and study, and if she found any pleasure in Sebastian's company it was only when he directed her in the choice of her books or explained some passages to her in Virgil and Horace.

Laetitia wanted a life of retirement and study apart from men and sex or she wanted a literary friendship. She wanted, perhaps, what Virginia Woolf evoked in *A Room of One's Own*, the freedom to range freely through books and thoughts, uninterrupted by constraints (the beadles, the turf) or demands (subjection to a husband's will), and able instead to be among her own kind, feeling the light in the seat of the soul which was rational intercourse.

What Laetitia wanted, however, did not determine what happened, and Laetitia's feelings and desires did not provide the working out of the story. Because Sebastian was 'transported' by her charms, a courtship of winter conversations and summer correspondence followed and led 'poor Laetitia' to be disposed of in marriage ('the lawyers were appointed to meet on both sides') to 'a man she never had a tender thought for'.

In life, Lady Mary took the 'romantic' decision to elope with Montagu when he and her father failed to agree terms for the marriage settlement: her father had stipulated a large jointure for her and money tied up for the male heir. The components of the tale she wrote about 'Laetitia' resembled those in the romances of Mme de Scudery and others, many volumes of which were to be found in the magnificent library in Lady Mary's father's house and of which (though she told different stories about it) she had free run from her earliest years: a noble family, a library full of books, an ardent young man, a rivalrous (and defeated) female and a heroine who preferred 'esteem' to declarations of love (Sebastian tells her she writes 'as good English as his friend Mr Addison'). The refusal of 'tender' feelings to an apparent story of love introduces a paradox, however, suggesting that true romance lay for her in the lost life alluded to in that phrase, the 'little plan she had formed to herself', which was a plan for a future life of reading and writing that was as untroubled as her girlish immersion in the books of her father's library. Love and marriage were imagined as inimical to reading and writing.

The tradition 'our mothers' were able to draw on in the early eighteenth century was short and partial both in terms of literary genres and practices, and in offering models for how a bookish young woman might live a life that combined bookish desires with tender feelings. The myth that marriage and literature were an antagonistic combination for women was established early and had something to do with the association of celibacy and learning that derived from the fact that monasteries and nunneries had been the traditional homes of scholarship. In reality, many of the best-known women of letters were married, and to men who fully supported their literary endeavours.

Lady Mary Wortley Montagu's separatist vision probably derived from her reading of Mary Astell, one of whose tracts, *A Serious Proposal to the Ladies for the Advancement of the True and Greatest Interest*, argued that women's mental improvement was best served by all-female colleges modelled on nunneries. This tract 'burst upon London in 1694 and was read and talked of from Pall Mall to Grub Street'.[38] With its energy, originality, eloquence and wit, it created Astell's reputation overnight; and like the other literary men who made up the Kit-Kat Club, Lady Mary Wortley Montagu's father would certainly have been one of those talking about it. Later, as we shall see, the two Marys became friends.

The argument of Astell's *Serious Proposal* convinced men and women alike, few of whom seemed troubled by its assumption that women might desire to be seriously intellectual. Daniel Defoe borrowed the theme for his 'Academy for Women' in his *Essay Upon Projects* (1697) and Richard Steele copied more than a hundred pages and passed it off as his own in *The Ladies Library* (1714). Ralph Thoresby, who had noted in his diary his meeting with Elizabeth Elstob, was also pleased to meet 'the celebrated Mrs Astell'. (Astell never married – the 'Mrs' was a courtesy title.) Samuel Richardson was a boy in London during the years of Mary Astell's great fame. Forty years later, in his last important novel, *Sir Charles Grandison,* Richardson gave two whole pages to Sir Charles outlining a scheme for 'a Protestant nunnery'. Even more significantly, Astell has been suggested as Richardson's model for the 'pious and articulate' Clarissa. It would indeed be 'fitting', and might even be true, that 'the independent, passionately rational tones of Mary Astell helped Richardson imagine the first real heroine of English fiction'[39], so long as we bear in mind that, crucially, *Clarissa* marked an end as well as a beginning. Clarissa's rape and death signalled the end of free movement as Mary Astell knew it – the freedom to have her words 'read and talked of from Pall Mall to Grub Street' without becoming in her person an object of sexual pursuit, sexual slander, and sexual, social and personal ruin.

Chapter Five

'PHILOMELA', 'ORINDA' AND OTHERS

But what I find deplorable, I continued, looking about the bookshelves again, is that nothing is known about women before the eighteenth century. I have no model in my mind to turn about this way and that.

Virginia Woolf, *A Room of One's Own*[1]

'Philomela' and the *Athenian Mercury*: the past life of Mrs Rowe

In May 1691, the *Athenian Mercury* published the following question, 'whether it be proper for women to be learned?'[2] Women being 'learned' in 1691 might mean their having basic knowledge of reading, enough to puzzle out a pamphlet or a page of the Bible; it might mean being able to write; or, at the other extreme, being proficient in Latin and Greek and sufficiently well read in such subjects as philosophy and theology to discourse with learned men.

The *Athenian Mercury* was a Whig periodical edited by John Dunton, assisted by the Cambridge Platonist philosopher, John Norris, and Samuel Wesley (father of a numerous brood, including John and Charles, Methodist hymn writers and preachers). It ran from 1691 to 1697, and in a later manifestation as the *Athenian Oracle* or *Athenian Spy* until 1710 – a very long life by the standards of the time. It has been described as the first literary magazine. Using a question-and-answer format, supposedly drawing on real questions sent in by readers, the Athenians canvassed matters of popular debate.

In its answer to the question about whether it was proper for women to be learned, the *Athenian Mercury* adopted a common-sense tone to deliver a progressive point of view. It began, 'All grant that they may have some learning, but the question is of what sort, and to what degree?' Peremptorily dismissing from consideration those who *didn't* grant this much (characterising them as the witless who thought it was enough if women could 'distinguish between their husband's breeches and another man's'), it listed some popular responses to the issue. There were those who thought women should be allowed to read but not to write; some who thought they should do neither. Some thought it acceptable for women to read plays, novels and romances, and perhaps history, but not if they went on to 'meddle with the edge-tools of philosophy'. The Athenians explained the embargo on philosophy sardonically: it was 'for these wise reasons, because forsooth it takes 'em off from their domestic affairs, and because it generally fills 'em too full of themselves, and makes 'em apt to despise others'. This was not the view of the Athenians. Addressing the original question, they made a distinction on the basis of class. Most women would not have the time or means to acquire learning since they had to get their livings or were fully engaged in taking care of a family. But for those 'whose births and fortunes exempt 'em from such circumstances' there was no reason why they should not be learned. If there was a danger that they might become conceited, it was no more so than for men: ''tis a weakness common to our own sex as well as theirs'. The Athenians concluded:

> On the whole, since they have as noble souls as we, a finer genius, and generally quicker apprehensions, we see no reason why women should not be learned now, as well as Madam Philips, Van Shurman and others have formerly been. For if we have seen one Lady gone mad with learning – we mean a late famous Countess – there are a hundred men could be named whom the same course has rendered fit for Bedlam.

Praise of women and denigration of men came together. True to its journalistic purpose, the answer offered less than it at first seemed to promise, sliding away from the issues in favour of a populist deployment of celebrity names: the poet Katherine Philips; the learned Anna Maria van Schurman, the title of whose dissertation, *The Learned Maid, or Whether a Maid may be a Scholar* (published in Latin in 1641 and translated into English in 1659), can be heard in the question which the

Athenians posed; and Margaret Cavendish, Duchess of Newcastle, the 'late famous Countess' whose omnivorous intellectual curiosity, literary gifts, rank and wealth had led her to publish many books and who was popularly known as 'mad Madge'. The casually allusive manner in which these names were introduced suggests their likely currency with readers of the *Athenian Mercury*, whether the periodical was encountered in metropolitan coffee houses or on country estates.

Although the propriety of women's learning was posed as a question, it is clear that as far as the Athenians were concerned there was no real debate: it was already happening and it had support. For a commercial newspaper like the *Athenian Mercury*, women in general and celebrity women in particular were good copy. 'Madam Philips', Anna Maria van Schurman and Margaret Cavendish stood for a host of lesser women all over the country who saw no reason why they should not acquire whatever learning was available to them; and 'learning' incorporated many kinds of reading and writing. Brothers, husbands, fathers and uncles were sharing their knowledge. Jane Barker, in Lincolnshire in the 1660s, learned medicine from her brother; Mary Astell, growing up in Newcastle in the 1670s, was taught Latin by her uncle; Elizabeth Elstob's Latin came via her mother and her Anglo-Saxon from her brother; Elizabeth Singer, in Somerset, studied general literature in the 1680s under the guidance of her father (her sister, meanwhile, studied medicine). Readers were likely to be interested in these facts, and in the writing that such women produced.

The *Athenian Mercury* was distributed by itinerant street hawkers (many of them women) who cried its merits in the streets; it could also be obtained at pamphlet shops such as those of Elizabeth Nutt and Anne Dodd, at the Royal Exchange and Temple Bar which operated as wholesale outlets.[3] Its core readership and editorial base were in the coffee houses – in London alone there were said to be over two thousand coffee houses by 1698. They were mostly frequented by men who, as well as drinking coffee, or sometimes chocolate, tea, wine or ale, went there to pick up the latest news and gossip, engage in political and other discussion, possibly received their personal mail and read the current pamphlets.

Fierce – and fiercely partisan – political, religious and literary debate was commonplace in the coffee houses. In the 1690s, the *Athenian*

Mercury worked whatever was topical to catch attention. It explicitly addressed itself to women, who were invited to send in questions and participate in the new venture. In his autobiography, *The Life and Errors of John Dunton,* Dunton described how upon launching the *Athenian Mercury* the editors were 'immediately overloaded with letters ... Sometimes I have found several hundreds for me at Mr Smith's coffee house in Stocks Market, where we usually met to consult matters.'[4] A newly efficient postal service made the *Athenian Mercury* possible, both by distributing it to outlying parts of the country and carrying back replies. The exchange was anonymous on both sides. Dunton's account conveys the excitement that was felt at the London end – an excitement and romance about postal communication and print that can be felt in the titles of such periodicals as *The Postman* and in the rash of books such as Delarivier Manley's *Letters Written on a Stage-Coach Journey to Exeter* (1696).

When a young woman living in rural Somerset sent in some poems, including a patriotic effusion about King William's triumphs in Ireland, 'Upon King William's Passing the Boyne', the editors were overjoyed. She was young (barely seventeen), female, a poet and a Williamite in full support of the 1688 revolution which had brought the Protestant William of Orange to be King of England in place of the Stuart James. They took her up as a sort of mascot, printing a poem addressed to her as their response, urging her to continue writing in the same vein: 'Great William claims thy lyre, and claims thy voice.' She was exhorted to

> . . . sing, bright maid!
> Thus and yet louder sing
> Thy God and King!
> Cherish that noble flame which warms thy breast,
> And be by future worlds admired and bless'd.

From these beginnings, Elizabeth Singer became one of the main contributors to the *Athenian Mercury.*[5] Through her involvement with it, she launched the literary career that was to see her become a celebrity who – under her married name of Mrs Rowe – was to be the acceptable face of female authorship. Famous for her conduct as well as for her writings (as we have seen, according to *The Feminiad*, her character was too well known to be dwelt on), Rowe was one of the first women writers of prose fictions whose life story, offered as an example to be celebrated and emulated, was made available for consumption by a popular readership. This alone makes her an important figure in the early history of female authorship.

Compared with other women writers of the time, we have reasonably full information to help form a general picture of Elizabeth Singer Rowe's career, including the early relationship with John Dunton and the *Athenian Mercury* about which the writers of *The Life of Mrs Rowe* maintained a discreet silence. As a prominent figure, first as Elizabeth Singer and then, after her marriage in 1709, as Mrs Rowe, she steered her course through many changes in literary fashion. There are clear continuities in her writings and self-presentation, as well as disjunctions, blanks, embarrassments and disavowals; and an insistent and quite self-conscious construction of her (by herself and her supporters) as a particular kind of author: the exemplary pious and virtuous female, living in rural solitude with her books, far from the corruptions of the town. (Rural retreat equated to virtue: it represented the wise choice of a slower, more stable and disinterested mode of life, under the shade of elm and oak, in the vicinity of stately homes and in the company of classic authors.) Elizabeth Singer to some extent, and Mrs Rowe entirely, figured in the public mind as the epitome of authorship as a nun-like retreat from the world.

Nuns, however, as the famous *Lettres portugaises*, translated in 1678 as *Five love-letters from a nun to a cavalier* demonstrated, could signal eroticism. In literature, religion and sex were strongly associated. The poems Elizabeth Singer sent to the *Athenian Mercury* pulsated with sexual energy. She sang her God and King in exuberant verse. As well as the impassioned martial heroics of 'Upon King William's Passing the Boyne', she wrote rapturously about God and the soul, drawing on mystic conventions of divine love to evoke the soul's relationship with the Lord. Carnal passion was scorned – 'Oh son of Venus, mourn thy baffled arts, / For I defy the proudest of thy darts' – nevertheless Cupid and his darts, along with other impedimenta of profane love, often featured; and when she paraphrased the Bible (a popular poetic task at the time) she chose the exotic and erotic Song of Solomon. In

Solomon's 'Canticle of Canticles', a female lover gives voice to the adoration she feels for her man. The poem depicts a relationship between the soul and the Lord. But as in other poems, for example 'The Rapture', 'flesh' was as present as 'soul' if only in the expressed desire to be free of it:

> How then, beneath its load of flesh
> Would the vexed soul complain!
> And how the friendly hand she'd bless
> Would break her hated chain!

Singer's verse ardently urged that mortals who were capable of feeling love should neither control it nor be ashamed. 'Why should I blush to indulge the noble flame?' Love among the angels was a 'holy fire'. Love was the route to higher things. Human love was a homage to the divine kind, as she explained in 'Platonic Love':

> Nor is this greatness of my love to thee
> A sacriledge unto the deity,
> Can I th'enticing stream almost adore
> And not respect its lovely fountain more?

It is no wonder that she so captivated the editors of the *Athenian Mercury*. The same animation invigorated her political and pastoral verse. Being a poet was an exciting thing to be, especially a poet like herself brimful of 'great ideas'. In 'Upon King William's Passing the Boyne', the excitement bubbled over:

> What mighty genius thus excites my breast
> With flames too great to manage or resist . . .
> Oh were the potent inspiration less!
> I might find words its rapture to express;
> But now I neither can its force control,
> Nor paint the great ideas of my soul.

Other early poems, including the cheerful, 'To one that persuades me to leave the Muses', in which she explained that she was 'so scurvily inclined to rhyming / That undesigned my thoughts burst out a chiming', similarly convey the impression of a great natural force that had to be given utterance or burst. The 'flames' of her 'mighty genius' were too great to manage or resist. She was swept by 'potent inspiration'. Driven by irrepressible creative energy, Elizabeth Singer's happy task was to shape, paint, find words to express the feeling.[6]

The editors of the *Athenian Mercury* gave their exciting new contributor different bylines. She was at first the 'Dear Unknown' whose verses charmed, and later the 'Poetical Lady', or 'Pindarical Lady in the West', or – most lastingly – 'Philomela', a poetic signature evoking the nightingale singing its natural song unbidden from the woods. She was praised and coyly flirted with. The whole of Volume Fifteen in 1694 was dedicated to her. Volume Seventeen printed five of her poems with this comment from the editors: 'We thought we could not more oblige our readers than by printing all together in one *Mercury* the following poems, they being all written by the ingenious Pindarick Lady, and printed verbatim as we received 'em from her.'

In their many messages about and to her in the *Mercury*, it was made plain that Singer's contributions were considered superior to all others; she was the gold that shone 'so much the brighter for having so many heaps of dross lying all about it'. Her identity was not known to the editors at this stage, even when negotiations began for her poems to be published in a separate volume. A letter was inserted to her, making the following request: 'That ingenious Pindarick Lady who formerly sent many poetical questions to the Athenian Society is desired to send all those poems she formerly mentioned directed to our bookseller at the Raven in Jewen Street.' In another issue it was noted that these had been safely received and she was asked to send details about how a letter might be directed to her. Evidently Elizabeth Singer responded, because in 1696 the Athenian poems appeared in a volume: *Poems written on several very remarkable occasions, written by Philomela, the most ingenious Pindarick Lady*. It was priced at two shillings, bound and printed for John Dunton.

The book was a commercial venture on Dunton's part. Through everybody's combined efforts, 'Philomela' had a following. Dunton was a skilled publisher: three years earlier he had put out into the world a deathbed narrative, supposedly authentic, of Francis Spira, whose memoir had gone through thirteen editions. The fact that Dunton's publication, *A Second Spira*, was probably fiction, didn't stop him selling 30,000 copies in six weeks.[7]

Sex, death and celebrity were saleable commodities. Poetry in itself was not; indeed, Dunton lamented the way 'poverty and disappointment' seemed 'entailed upon poets': 'alas! . . . when I see an ingenious man set up for a mere poet, and steer his course through life towards that point of the compass, I give him up as one pricked down by Fate for misery and misfortune'. As a businessman, Dunton had no confidence in poetry as 'the very trade of life' but he saw its possibilities as 'a little pretty divertisement'.[8] Like learning, it was for those whose births and fortunes allowed them pleasurable diversion, who had time and leisure: the young, the unemployed, and females without family responsibility. A likely young man setting up for a 'mere poet' might sadden Dunton, but a 'bright maid' like 'Philomela' excited him.

The 'matchless Orinda': model female poet

When John Dunton dubbed Elizabeth Singer 'the Pindarical Lady', he placed her squarely in a line of descent from Abraham Cowley, perhaps the most famous poet of the time, whose *Pindaric Odes* of 1656 had largely invented the genre as it was deployed in England in the seventeenth century, and, by association, with Katherine Philips, the most famous woman poet, who was linked with Cowley through their mutual admiration and her experiments with the Pindaric form. The Pindaric was the recognised ground on which sex-war rhetoric could be raised, pro- and anti-women's entitlements to learning and poetry. In Cowley's terms, verse had been a weapon in man's armoury of love. But during his lifetime, he had seen it seized by a woman whose superiority was acknowledged by all: Katherine Philips, 'Madam Philips' as the *Athenian Mercury* would have it, or the 'matchless Orinda' as she was more widely known. Cowley's poem, 'Upon Mrs K. Philips her Poems', begins as follows:

> We allow'd you beauty, and we did submit
> To all the tyrannies of it.
> Ah cruel Sex! will you depose us too in Wit?
> Orinda does in that too reign,
> Does man behind her in proud triumph draw,

And cancel great Apollo's Salick Law.
We our old title plead in vain:
Man may be head, but Woman's now the Brain.

And in a poem on her death he reiterated the theme:

Now shame and blushes on us all
Who our own Sex superior call;
Orinda does our boasting sex out-do.

Philips's *Poems* were published in 1664 (unofficially) and in 1667. No woman poet before Philips had been so celebrated and elevated. The official 1667 edition, *POEMS by the most deservedly Admired Mrs Katherine Philips The matchless ORINDA*, issued by her friend 'Poliarchus', came complete with seven laudatory poems, six of them by male admirers (two by Cowley) and one by a female. All of these admirers observed the obvious point that Katherine Philips was a woman succeeding in what had hitherto been considered a male preserve, and they all agreed that her genius entitled her to the highest position: 'If Apollo should design / A Woman Laureat to make / Without dispute he would Orinda take.' The Earl of Orrery took the compliment further, assuming that poetry was now demonstrably the rightful province of women more than men, and assuring his readers that he didn't mind this at all: 'In me it does not the least trouble breed, / That your fair Sex does Ours in Verse exceed.'[9]

Whatever elements of flattery or ambivalence we might find in these pronouncements, it is important to register the significance of the chorus of male approval of Philips's achievement. To women poets who came later, Philips's much promoted 'matchlessness' stood as an unassailable male-endorsed example. (Most women writers presented in the first instance as poets: even Mary Astell began her writing career with a collection of poems in 1689.) The confidence of Philips's writing – which included highly acclaimed translations – and the laudatory praises heaped on it announced a triumphant welcome to the voice of female genius. This was no small matter. Every repetition of Orinda's greatness helped keep in place an image of what a successful woman poet looked like. For succeeding generations the picture was composed from the elements offered in the volumes available; and the volumes of Philips's poetry didn't just offer a woman and her poems, they made available a woman poet in a dramatised relationship to a social world.

Philips presented herself as the central figure in a chosen circle. As the reigning personage in her Society of Friendship, she received homage from admirers such as John Davies of Kidwelly, who dedicated part of his translation of La Calprenede's *Cleopatre* to 'the most excellently accomplish'd lady, the Lady Katherine Philips', describing her as 'a person so much above your sex'. Her poems displayed her rule and evoked the comings and goings of the society: births, deaths, loves, partings, meetings and misunderstandings. Philips courted, as a male courtier might, those she wanted for her society. Members adopted pastoral nicknames, a French fashion that came to the English court of Charles I in the 1630s under the influence of Queen Henrietta Maria, an intellectual who promoted the idea of friendship as a Platonic 'science'. *To the Excellent Mrs Anne Owen, upon her receiving the name of Lucasia, and Adoption into our Society, December 28, 1651* conveys the formality of the fiction. Other members were given names such as Antenor, Rosania, Regina, Poliarchus, Ardelia and Celimena.

Through this select and cultivated society moved the confident voice and figure of Orinda, sharing thoughts, feelings and opinions with the reader and implicitly widening the social circle to let the reader in.

The print publication of the poems, which Philips claimed had in the first instance been against her own wishes, introduced an ambiguity in the relation of poet and readers. The Society of Friendship was an intimate, chosen group; readers could be anyone. It was partly to counter the implications of this that the story of the printing of the poems – in which Philips was shown as the victim of an unscrupulous bookseller – was made much of by her supporters. In 1664 a small volume, *Poems by the incomparable Mrs K.P.*, was issued by Richard Marriot. Philips said the manuscripts had been stolen, though in fact her poems had been circulating and contributing to her great fame since the early 1650s. The 'false' edition was suppressed but not before many copies had been sold, such was the demand. Philips died of smallpox later that year, having left a letter for 'Poliarchus', Sir Charles Cotterell, giving permission for a 'true' edition of her works, properly edited and introduced, to be prepared. Cotterell set out to be comprehensive and definitive: 'all industry has been used to make this collection as full and as perfect as might be . . .' Orinda deserved no less.

The 'true' edition was magnificently produced. In his introduction, Cotterell represented Philips as someone whose goods had been seized and damaged, 'deformed' by a speculator who knew their value sufficiently to know he could make a profit from them. Her manuscripts – circulated among the chosen coterie, spoken about by others, given additional lustre by the celebrity Philips acquired on the publication of her translation of Corneille's *Pompey* in 1663 (which had also been successfully staged) – had become objects of desire. The reader holding the posthumous 1667 edition of Philips's works 'restor'd to their native shape and beauty' by her 'particular' friend, who was careful to publish the letter of permission Philips had written, was at once aware of how desirable the contents were and how perilously close she had come to being denied access. Or worse: how close the nation had come to losing a national treasure in its uncorrupted form.

Holders of the 'false' edition were 'false' readers. The 'true' edition offered a place to 'true' readers who were invited in to everything the volume had to offer, the competition between the two editions giving such readers an important role to play: their job was to show their support. The poems could not 'fail of a welcome reception now, since they wanted it not before, when they appeared in that strange disguise'. The legitimacy thus bestowed on the reader spoke to many possible identificatory positions. Saving women poets from unscrupulous book-sellers was one. Being an unscrupulous bookseller another. Collecting, preserving, editing, shaping and giving to the world the 'perfect' version of the works of a 'most deservedly admired' woman poet was yet another. All readers could figure themselves imaginatively inside Philips's Society of Friendship and might give their own meaning to the final couplet of the poem, 'Lucasia': 'No pen Lucasia's glories can relate. / But they admire best who dare imitate.' Imitating Orinda or Lucasia would include expressing an aversion to being in print. This was among the important legacies of the story of the publication of Philips's poems. In her letter, Orinda claimed she had 'never writ any line in my life with the intention to have it printed'. She was anxious that 'the world' should believe her innocent of this desire and of any 'connivance': there had been no 'wretched artifice of a secret consent (of which I am, I fear, suspected)'. She would not go into print at all, not even with corrected copies, if her friends did not persuade her; only their pressure could make her 'yield to it' and then 'with the same reluctancy as I would cut off a limb to save my life':

> I am so far from expecting applause for anything I scribble, that I can hardly expect pardon; and sometimes I think that employment so far above my reach, and unfit for my sex, that I am going to resolve against it for ever; and could I have recovered those fugitive papers that have escaped my hands, I had long since made a sacrifice of them all. The truth is, I have an incorrigible inclination to that folly of rhyming, and intending the effects of that humour only for my own amusement in a retired life I did not so much resist it as a wiser woman would have done; but some of my dearest friends having found my ballads (for they deserve no better name) they made me so much believe they did not dislike them, that I was betrayed to permit some copies for their divertisement; but this with so little concern for them, that I have lost most of the originals, and that I suppose to be the cause of my present misfortune; for some infernal spirits or other have catch'd those rags of paper, and what the careless blotted writing kept them from understanding, they have supplied by conjecture, till they put them into the shape wherein you saw them, or else I know not which way it is possible for them to be collected, or so abominably transcrib'd as I hear they are.[10]

Philips hadn't seen the 'false' edition, but she had a number of concerns about it among which the printing of poems that had been privately circulating was probably the least. Her husband was involved in political 'embarrassments and difficulties' which she had been negotiating on his behalf. The social nature of her poems meant that other people's names had been 'exposed' along with her own. Altogether, the 'torment' had made her sick and led to the writing of many other letters besides this one to Cotterell. Cotterell, however, explained her anxiety in terms of literary reputation: her response showed 'how little she desired the fame of being in print, and how much she was troubled by it'. Troubled or not, he took for granted that not only the poems but her letters and essays too should be printed, assuring the reader that they would 'make a volume much larger than this, and no less worth the reading'.

By printing the whole of Philips's letter to him, Cotterell set up a dialogue in the preface. Against his voice of witness and judgement – he explained some of her working methods, emphasising her 'diligence', and judged her poems to be a 'monument which she erected for her self', which would 'for ever make her to be honoured as the honour of her sex, the emulation of ours, and the admiration of both' – was counterposed her voice of modest denial. Philips did not talk of monuments nor honour. In her vocabulary, writing was a 'scribble', manuscripts were 'rags of papers' and the whole was 'careless' and 'blotted'; poetry was 'that folly of rhyming' and its function no more than 'divertisement', 'amusement in a retired life', for the 'entertainment of friends' whose 'persuasion' was the only possible reason it might go out to a wider public. These terms were to do much service in the centuries that followed. Some of her poems, Cotterell explained,

> would be no disgrace to the name of any man that amongst us is most esteemed for his excellency in this kind, and there are none that may not pass with favour when it is remembered that they fell hastily from the pen but of a woman. We might well have called her the English Sappho, she of all the female poets of former ages being for her verses and her virtues both the most highly to be valued; but she has called herself Orinda, a name that deserves to be added to the number of the Muses.

Only pedants and antiquarians laboured over their writing: true wit came naturally. To say of Philips that her verses 'fell hastily from the pen but of a woman' was high praise. That she was a woman, and therefore by nature and education inferior, threw her genius into higher relief. That she worked quickly was a sign that her gift was divine not earthly. That she was known by a poetic signature raised her to the level of the immortals.

This convention of the two voices – a man praising and ushering the woman forward into the limelight, a woman modestly demurring – became a standard routine. Orinda's was the acceptable face of female poetry. She was a cloth merchant's daughter but to Charles Cotterell, Master of Ceremonies to Charles II, she was a queen. Poets who came after (male and female) were able to celebrate Philips as the original voice in a female tradition because this public persona marked a genuine shift. Its literariness or fictionality was key, offering as it did much scope for invention.[11]

Other models: Margaret Cavendish and Aphra Behn

We can compare the impact on posterity of Katherine Philips with the two other most significant female poets of the seventeenth century, Margaret Cavendish, the Duchess of Newcastle, and Aphra Behn, neither of whom could be said to lack ability in stage-managing their public selves. The authorial voice these women adopted was a proud autonomous voice. They did not address the public through any male intermediary and nor, it should be said, did they die before their works went out into the world. Assertive about themselves as writers, each laid claim to privilege rather than asking pardon: for Cavendish, cultivating a public persona based partly on queenly modes in the 1650s when the monarchy was under attack, this was monarchical privilege; for Behn, an active and hard-working professional writer in the 1670s and 1680s, it was the privilege her male associates had, to write with freedom about the full range of subjects including sexuality.[12]

A maid of honour at the court of Henrietta Maria during the reign of Charles I, Margaret Cavendish went into exile with the Queen in 1643. Not only was she heavily influenced by the Platonic love doctrines so fashionable at court, she also identified with the Queen's situation – her unpopularity and her eventual retreat to a convent. Cavendish wrote compulsively and her texts memorialised the values of Henrietta Maria's court. She also imitated the Queen in her personal manner by adopting formal and artificial modes of speech. Cavendish sometimes dressed herself as a female cavalier (the queen had marched at the head of troops) or in fantastic and original garments that led people to stare at her in the streets (the Queen's enthusiasm for dress verged on the theatrical). Preoccupied as a philosopher with issues to do with subjectivity and mind, Cavendish viewed the authorial role as analogous to monarchical rule: her authority in relation to the worlds within her head matched the monarch's authority over the kingdom. In her utopian fantasy, *The Description of a New Blazing World* (1666), Cavendish produced no fewer than four powerful titles applicable to herself: monarch, princess, duchess and empress. The fantasy features a woman who becomes Empress of an unknown world, with absolute control over it. The title page tells us the book was written by 'the thrice noble, illustrious, and excellent princess, the Duchess of Newcastle', she herself enters the story as a character called the Duchess of Newcastle, and in the preface she explains:

> I am . . . as ambitious as ever any of my sex was, is, or can be; which makes, that though I cannot be Henry the Fifth, or Charles the Second, yet I endeavour to be Margaret the First. And although I have neither power, time nor occasion to conquer the world as Alexander and Caesar did; yet rather than not to be Mistress of one, since Fortune and the Fates would give me none, I have made a World of my own: for which nobody, I hope, will blame me, since it is in everyone's power to do the like.[13]

The invitation to everyone to follow her example and crown themselves rulers of a subjective world was not largely taken up in the eighteenth century. Cavendish did not function as a major example to women writers, although publications like the handsome 1679 edition of poems by Mary Villiers, *Female Poems on Several Occasions, written by Ephelia*, with its Cavendish-like dedication may owe something to her. The dedication is self-addressed to Mary Villiers, 'The Most Excellent Princess MARY, Duchess of Richmond and Lennox', and signed by her with her pseudonym, 'Ephelia'. (Mary Villiers was cousin to Barbara Villiers, Lady Castlemaine, mistress of Charles II, who later provided Delarivier Manley with a fund of scandal which she put to good use in her writings, especially in the *New Atalantis*.) Margaret Cavendish's works remained available: she figures in the catalogues of circulating libraries such as Bathoe's of 1757.[14] But her reputation for unsociable eccentricity combined with her prideful monarchism made her a figure of fun in an age that, after the Revolution Settlement of 1689, liked to think it had put such old-fashioned ways behind it. She evoked the absolutist era of the early Stuarts and the egotism of a court that had put pleasure before its responsibilities to the nation.

Poets writing in the 1680s – Elizabeth Singer, Mary Astell, Jane Barker, Anne Killigrew, Anne Wharton among a host of others named and anonymous – benefited from the celebrity of Aphra Behn, whose many plays, poems, songs, novels and translations brought unprecedented visibility and acclaim for a female writer. Behn was one of the most prolific of Restoration dramatists and poets. The theatre was the most directly commercial literary genre – playwrights took receipts on the third night – and it brought the writer into immediate contact with her audience. In a number of assertive prefaces, Behn demanded the same freedoms male writers had. She insisted she did not want to be limited to what was considered appropriate for women. She expressed her frustration at the inadequacies of her 'female' education: she had no grounding in the classics at a time when there were few translations available (Dryden and Pope with their translations of Virgil and Homer came after) and thus she had no access to 'The godlike Virgil and great Homer's muse', nor to the status attached to familiarity with these works. She wanted to 'tread in those successful paths my predecessors have so long thrived in, to take those measures that both the ancient and modern writers have set me'.

To fulfil such a writerly ambition, Behn required the 'privilege' which, in her preface to *The Lucky Chance*, she defined as 'my masculine part the poet in me.' This preface addressed 'the witty sparks and poets of the town' who had (maliciously, in her view) censured her comedy on the grounds of indecency. Denying the charge, she claimed she allowed herself only what 'others of this age' allowed and that she should not be judged differently on the grounds of sex. As a writer she was entitled to the privileges of masculinity, and without those privileges she might as well give up writing: 'If I must not, because of my sex, have this freedom, but that you will usurp all in yourselves, I lay down my quill.'[15]

Among the 'measures' ancient and modern writers set was sexual licence, or, at the very least, sexual explicitness. Love and sex were among Behn's chosen themes; her poetry was lyrical, pastoral and erotic, and she translated and adapted amorous French works. The commerciality of the stage and the high visibility of Aphra Behn as a writer for it, along with the still relatively novel introduction of women as actresses (beginning with the reopening of the theatres in 1660 after the restoration of Charles II to the throne), linked literature, trade and the female body. Behn's defence of her use of bawdy language in the 1678 comedy *Sir Patient Fancy* on the grounds that she was 'forced to write for bread and not ashamed to own it' drew attention, whether she intended it or not, to the similarities between writing and prostitution.

Aphra Behn was not ashamed to admit that she needed to be paid for her writing, but it is not clear that the trading aspect particularly pleased her, nor that women who came after were enticed by her example to aspire to be 'professional' or 'independent'. Like Philips and Cavendish, Behn was a loyal supporter of the Stuarts, looking to the court for support (she had been a spy for Charles II in the Netherlands in the 1660s). She was spiritually at home inside a royalist tradition of educated ladies, sexual openness, and the political power of wives, mistresses and mothers. She represented herself as seeking literary fame rather than riches, the proper motive in seventeenth-century terms for any heroic action: 'I am not content to write for a third day only. I value fame as much as if I had been born a hero.'[16]

Poetry was neither 'a little pretty divertisment' nor a mere means of filling the belly. Literary immortality was the true reward. Modelling her public image on male writers in a licentious age like that of the Restoration had obvious disadvantages: female 'fame' tended to rhyme with 'shame'. There was no Sir Charles Cotterell to manage Aphra Behn's posthumous reputation, nor could there be given her insistence on her right to share the privileges of masculinity. To some extent Behn became the free-floating signifier of licentious womanhood. As the mere repetition of 'chaste' and 'matchless' constructed Orinda for audiences who knew nothing of her poetry, so it was not necessary to know anything about Aphra Behn's life (about which we still know very little) to know that she signified sexual availability.

It was not Aphra Behn's insistence on autonomous freedom, nor the need to write for bread, but the model of the writer as an admired figure in a self-selected group – the chosen few – devoted to literature, learning, friendship and retirement (themes Katherine Philips made vividly her own) that had the strongest impact on succeeding generations of women writers, especially on the mid-century bluestockings. Meanwhile, literary men learned a number of new positions in relation to the woman of genius: variously, they could praise or condemn, obstruct or assist, and derive profit thereby. The emerging bookseller classes were quick to grasp this and it is no accident that every notable woman writer of the late seventeenth and early eighteenth centuries attracted the attentions of these energetic individuals. Richard Marriot provoked Katherine Philips's wrath; his 'false' edition was the 'pitiful design of a knave to get a groat'. John Dunton, deploying the Platonic love conventions Philips and Cavendish had helped put into circulation, had more success.

The liberties of freeborn Englishwomen

By 1696, a publisher such as John Dunton, obliging his readers with a volume of poems by a young woman like 'Philomela', could draw for commercial advantage on ideas about the rights of Englishwomen that were more explicit than the question about whether it was proper for women to be learned that the *Athenian Mercury* canvassed in 1691. Dunton arranged a preface to Elizabeth Singer's collection of *Poems on Several Occasions*, which was written and signed by Elizabeth Johnson, and which struck a heated note. Johnson's tone was militant:

> Our sex has some excuse for a little vanity when they have so much good reason for it, and such a champion among themselves as not many of the other can boast of. We are not unwilling to allow mankind the brute advantages of strength, they are superior to ours in force, they have custom on their side, and have ruled, and are like to do so; and may freely do it without disturbance or envy; at least they should have none from us, if they could keep quiet among themselves. But when they would monopolize sense too, when neither that, nor learning, nor so much as wit must be allowed us, but all over-ruled by the tyranny of the prouder sex; nay, when some of them will not let us say our souls are our own, but would persuade us we are no more reasonable creatures than themselves, or their fellow animals, we then must ask their pardons if we are not yet so completely passive as to bear all without a murmur. We complain, and we think with reason, that our fundamental constitutions are destroyed; that here is a plain and open design to render us mere slaves, perfect Turkish wives, without properties, or sense, or souls; and we are forced to protest against it, and appeal to all the world, whether these are not notorious violations on the liberties of freeborn Englishwomen? This makes the meekest worm amongst us all ready to turn again when we are thus trampled on; but alas! what can we do to right ourselves? Stingless and harmless as we are, we can only kiss the foot that hurts us.[17]

By 1696, sex-war rhetoric was fashionable. Mary Astell's *A Serious Proposal to the Ladies for the Advancement of their True and Greatest Interest*, which argued for an all-female college, had appeared in 1694 and by 1696 was in its third edition. The author's name was well known, though the text appeared as 'By a Lover of her Sex'. Elizabeth Johnson's sarcasm echoed the acerbic tone struck by Mary Astell. Her references to the constitution and liberties of the freeborn English-woman evoked the language of the Whig settlement of 1689, vividly contrasting it to the treatment of women in less enlightened lands. Men who didn't accept that women were included in the new vision were like slave owners or Turks, denying women their properties, sense and souls – imagery and examples that were used by men and women alike. The collusiveness of the engagement is suggested by the complaisance of Johnson's closing gesture: the worm turns in order to kiss the foot that tramples it.

In its eroticism, this was not an inappropriate preparation for the poems that followed, characterised as they were by an uninhibited rhapsodic expression of love. For the most part Elizabeth Singer's 'transports' expressed love of God or nation in these early poems, but like all mystics – for example St Teresa, to whom she and (rather startlingly) Mary Astell were both likened – she used the language of human desire to produce a sensually charged poetry sanctioned by Scripture. Passionate verse that spoke of love and polemics about the liberties of freeborn Englishwomen made a thrilling combination which Dunton exploited.

Nor need we suppose that the devout Elizabeth Singer was shocked to find her verses introduced in this way. The proto-feminist debate which erupted in the 1690s was a by-product of mainstream debates of the time: philosophical, political and theological. It did not arise from feminist activism, nor from a realm of female thought separate from that of men, although writings like those of Anna Maria van Schurman had inspired at least one learned Englishwoman to write about the need for improvement in elite women's education: Bathsua Makin in her *An Essay to Revive the Ancient Education of Gentlewomen* (1673). Rather, it opened up as a space within men's debates that had a particular resonance for women and to which women could rightfully contribute. At its heart was the question that had agitated the country and produced the terrible upheavals of the seventeenth century: how was the state to be governed, who should have dominion over whom, what were the rights and responsibilities of power? On the national stage, these questions had resulted in the execution of a king, Charles 1, in 1649, and a bloody civil war. Stability and order had been overthrown, families rent apart, and men's and women's deepest passions engaged in trying to understand what it all meant for individuals who believed God shaped them to His purposes. If it was agreed that women had souls, then they were answerable to God for the state of those souls at the day of judgement. Liberty was an essential requirement. Vehemence of expression and animated intensity suited the mood, whether mystical yearnings after God or the need for inner freedom and a life organised according to one's own wishes.

To John Dunton, Mary Astell was the 'divine Astell'. To John Norris, Dunton's collaborator, she was even better known. In 1694, having read Norris's *Discourses*, in which he criticised John Locke, Astell, at that time living alone and unknown in London, engaged him in a correspondence. In doing so, and in approaching him boldly as an intellectual equal with criticisms of his reasoning, she followed a precedent set by Princess Elizabeth of Bohemia, who began such a correspondence with Descartes, Lady Anne Conway with Henry More, and Damaris Masham with Norris himself. Such letters were complimentary – they took care to demonstrate familiarity with the writings of the chosen philosopher – and they were self-promotional: their object was to display the writer's talent in hopes of a gain or advancement of some kind. The exchange of letters between philosophers was a genre understood as potentially leading to publication: Norris's correspondence with Henry More had been published in 1688.

Mary Astell looked to Norris as a mentor, explaining that she had had little formal guidance in her intellectual life: 'Hitherto I have courted truth with a kind of romantic passion, in spite of all difficulties and discouragements; for knowledge is thought so unnecessary an accomplishment for a woman, that few will give themselves the trouble to assist them in the attainment of it.'[18] This appeal, with its discreet sexual metaphor for the pursuit of truth, worked wonders, and Astell and Norris conducted a lively exchange of ideas (mostly about Norris's intellectual preoccupations) for ten months, at the end of which, *A*

Serious Proposal to the Ladies having been successfully published, Norris proposed the publication of their correspondence. The *Letters Concerning the Love of God*, 'between the author of *Proposal to the Ladies* and Mr John Norris', appeared in 1695.

In agreeing to the correspondence with Astell, Norris admitted the special pleasure it gave him. He was, he said, 'not only willing to enter into a correspondence with you, but even to congratulate myself [on] the opportunity of so uncommon a happiness'. Far from discouraging the approaches of such women, men like Dunton and Norris sought them out. The 'fair sex' provided a good part of the subject matter of literary expression by the end of the seventeenth century, at all levels of production from high art to low, and they were recognised as writers and readers as well as working in the trade as booksellers and printers, with considerable overlap in all these roles. John Dunton's wife Elizabeth Annesley, for example, who managed the business side of his affairs and whose death in 1697 marked his collapse into 'errors' and financial problems, was 'Iris' to his 'Philaret' in their courtship letters which he later published. Such names echoed those of the lovers Philander and Sylvia in that well-known work of amatory fiction, Aphra Behn's *Love Letters Between a Nobleman and His Sister* (1684–7), a second edition of which had come out in 1693. Expressed in an exchange of letters between a man and a woman, the intellectual enthusiasms of Astell and Norris (courting truth with a 'romantic passion') existed along a continuum that drew them towards a definition set by Behn's *Love Letters*, or the even more influential *Lettres portugaises*, the *Five love-letters from a nun to a cavalier*. (Supposedly the expression of a nun's erotic feelings for a cavalier, they were written by a man.)

Jane Barker

Male–female literary correspondence carried a sexual charge which might be played up or down according to circumstances. A young bookseller named Benjamin Crayle understood this when he assembled a collection of poems, *Poetical Recreations*, in 1687. This came in two parts: the first part consisted of poems 'Occasionally written by Mrs Jane Barker', while the second, and much longer part, was written by

'Several Gentlemen of the Universities, and Others' including Crayle himself. Crayle's advertisement for the book and the title page for Part One featured Jane Barker's name, a sign that he was alert to the current fashion for women's verse. (In 1685, Damaris Masham observed that women's verse was 'much the fashion of late'.) In his amatory poems written to her or about her and telling of his love, Barker was given the name 'Cosmelia'; but she was also addressed by her own name in poems which foregrounded their relationship as bookseller and poet, as in 'To my ingenious friend, Mrs Jane Barker, on my publishing her romance of Scipina'. That they were friends is clear: they were part of a circle of poets mostly based in Cambridge with whom Barker had been exchanging manuscript copies of her verse. One of her poems, 'To my friends', expressed her gratitude to the 'band of gallant youths' who had encouraged her to write and had praised her work:

> This band of gallant youths, bear me along,
> Who teach me how to sing, then praise my song,
> Such wreaths and branches, they've bestow'd on me,
> I look like Daphne turn'd into a tree,
> Whilst these young sons of Phoebus dance around
> And sing the praise of her themselves have crown'd.[19]

For Barker, they were the 'gayest, sweetest, gentlest, youths on earth'. They sang her praises in commendatory poems that claimed her as the new Orinda. Hailed in the title-page epigraph from Virgil as 'a most glorious virgin' advancing in youth over a great crowd, her authority as a poet was compared to the authority of the great Virgin Queen: the throne of poetry might, like the throne of England, have a male or female monarch.

It's possible that Barker played no part in the publication of *Poetical Recreations*. Some time after 1701, she copied a selection of her contributions into a manuscript compilation of her verses with the note that they had been printed in 1688 'without her consent' and were 'now corrected by her own hand'.[20] Perhaps she was leaving evidence that helped confirm her as the new Orinda. She was an active member of the coterie: her poems were addressed to many different individuals (almost all of them male) and if she minded the fact that her poems had been printed she did not actually say so. It may be that her principal concern was about accuracy: she had not had the chance to proofread and correct the press. Or perhaps she wanted to distance herself from a form of publication she no longer wanted to be associated with: having her praises sung by a band of 'gallant youths'.

Jane Barker's poems displayed a range of tones and postures: playful, intellectual, allusive, often sharp and scornful, always intensely engaged – stylistic characteristics that were to be her hallmark when she emerged as a novelist many decades later. Absent from the representations of herself and others is anything suggestive of sensuality, and nothing that could be called erotic. The image of herself as Daphne turned into a tree is appropriate somehow: free-standing, single and unyielding.

In the 1680s and thereafter, Barker seems to have been able to play a full part in a literary community of her own choosing without developing or being identified with those conventions of female writing that tended towards the 'melting', 'tender', 'warm', and 'soft' end of the spectrum. Her authorial identity did not lend itself to suggestive heterosexual depiction. In 'A Virgin Life' she invoked the muses to protect her from men's 'almost omnipotent amours' and offered a picture of the single life as a valid alternative to marriage: orderly, attractive, productive, virtuous and happy. The old maid was not some 'foul deformity' but closer to the angels, her beauty 'pure, celestial' and her thoughts and words 'divine', 'angelical'. The spinster's life was meaningful, embedded in a network of social, religious and political obligations: she cared for the poor, was a loyal and patriotic subject, attended church, was sociable, and loved nothing better than to be in her closet which was both library and chapel to her: 'She drives her whole life's business to these ends / To serve her God, enjoy her books and friends.'

This virgin life was also a writer's life. Jane Barker was a Catholic convert and a fervent divine-right monarchist opposed to the Revolution Settlement. In 1689, for reasons that are not known but which most likely reflect religious and political principle, she left England, choosing to go into exile with James and his court at St Germain in Paris. There, among the increasingly shabby and quarrelsome Jacobites who Matthew Prior, diplomat as well as poet, described as 'the starving English and Irish at St Germain' whose 'equipages are all very ragged and contemptible', she made herself into the poet of the cause, an unofficial and self-appointed Poet Laureate bent on living out and giving expression to the exile experience. She probably supported herself by practising as a physician, making diagnoses and prescribing medication, since it is known that she had learned medicine from her brother who had studied at Oxford, Paris and Leiden and who taught her Latin, botany, herbal medicine and anatomy.

In her writings, Barker identified love and sexual feeling as the source of women's woes and advised women like herself, those 'Bright Shes' who sought a glorious name for their works and words rather than their beauty and bodies, to freeze their sexual feelings, scorn licentious men and avoid becoming the victimised subjects of men's lust. In literary terms she had no patience with representations of abject womanhood. The literature of female complaint was a genre which had been given a boost in the 1680s in the Dryden–Tonson collaboration on *Ovid's Epistles*, a collection of monologues spoken by abandoned women (contributed to by Aphra Behn) which offered the spectacle of female grief, suffering, rage and despair. For Barker, victimised womanhood was not a dignified version of femininity. She addressed a poem in *Poetical Recreations* directly to the female speakers of the *Epistles*, advising them that had they been only 'warmed' not 'melted' in the flames of love, none of their subsequent problems would have arisen and they would have offered a better example to those, like herself, who came later. Women, through self-control, had the chance of being more powerful than men. What they needed was the 'armour' of 'scorn' and a sadistic ability to laugh as men were consumed in the fires of unsatisfied lust raised in them when they contemplated women:

> Bright Shes, what glories had your names acquired,
> Had you consumed those whom your beauties fired,
> Had laughed to see them burn, and so retired:
>
> Then they could ne'er have gloried in their shames,
> Either to Roman, or to English dames,
> Had you but warmed, not melted in their flames.

You'd not been wracked then on despair's rough coast,
Nor yet by storms of perjuries been tossed,
Had you but fixed your flowing love with frost.

Had you put on the armour of your scorn,
(That gem which does our beauties most adorn)
What hardy hero durst have been forsworn.

But since they found such lenity in you,
Their crime so epidemical does grow,
That all have, or do, or would be doing so.[21]

Scorn was the 'gem' that most adorned women's beauty. Not to be scornful was to be without the defensive armour necessary and proper in a state of war. The reward for regulating sexual passion was power over the self and others, leading (as elaborated in other poems) to a more self-sufficient and satisfying life as well as future fame. The punishment for not regulating passion was catastrophic: shipwreck 'on despair's rough coast'.

Men's desire for sexual conquest was the problem, and the logical solution to this 'crime so epidemical' was to avoid men. It's probable that Barker benefited from the companionship of communities of nuns during her time in France in the 1690s, especially the convents of the Benedictines who were closely associated with the Stuart court. Convents were institutions with obvious appeal for serious-minded women. Mary Astell's all-female college modelled on a convent aimed 'to stock the kingdom with pious and prudent ladies'. This was the 'true and greatest interest' that the full title to *A Serious Proposal to the Ladies for the Advancement of their True and Greatest Interest* proclaimed: a pious life lived self-sufficiently among pious women and books and apart from men. Unfortunately for Astell and her supporters, at a time when religious controversy was still only too real, the likeness of the college to the nunneries smacked of Rome and, though there was interest in it, it never took off as a project.

Barker's description in 'A Virgin Life' could comfortably serve as an idealised image of Mary Astell. The complex of associations summed up by Astell's piety, prudence, separatism, celibacy and the central place she gave to education — the virgin in her closet serving God and enjoying her books and friends, to use Barker's image, or the life of lettered exchange Lady Mary Wortley Montagu lamented as a 'romance' in her fragment of autobiography – was to be an influential element in eighteenth-century versions of the ideal woman of letters. Those who advocated some version of Barker's and Astell's separatism – laughing at the men and retiring – might stress the virtues of female support and female community, but they did not necessarily have a high opinion of women in general. Scorn, perhaps, cuts all ways. Their own learning was less likely to be offered up as a model for others than as a sign of exceptionality. Jane Barker distanced herself from debates about women's education: 'let the world confine or enlarge learning as they please, I care not; I do not regret the time I bestowed in its company, it having been my good friend ... tho I am not so generous, by way of return, to pass my word for its good behaviour in our sex, always, and in all persons'.[22]

Mary Astell was scathing about the 'frivolity' of women. She constructed a figure of woman as one enslaved to sense impressions and in need of rescue for higher things. She wanted to 'persuade them to leave their insignificant pursuits for employments worthy of them', meaning, essentially, that they should do the kinds of things that she did: prayer, good works, and an engagement with serious books. Not all women could be virgins or writers, but these were the activities that might save their souls for eternity. The shallow pleasures of this world (insignificant pursuits) were set against the lasting delights of heaven. Men's sexual interest in women drew them into frivolity and triviality in the first instance, and wrecked them on despair's rough coast in the next.

Ascetic in her day-to-day life, Astell's vehement love of God was rooted in a joyful renunciation, including renunciation of intimate relations between the sexes other than those of the mind. Her intellectual and spiritual passions were in the service of God. Through the contemplation of God, earthly sensation was transcended: God was pure idea, absolute and abstract goodness. By passionately fixing the thought on God, the mind was drawn away from sense impressions of a material nature; and passion, in its earthly sense, was properly moderated. The highest expression of love was the love of God, the philosophy that Norris and Astell developed in their *Letters Concerning the Love of God.*

Elizabeth Singer: early development of a poet

Dryden's Pindaric ode, 'To the Pious Memory of the Accomplished Young Lady, Mrs Anne Killigrew', which prefaced Killigrew's posthumous *Poems* in 1686, provided some simple guidelines for how men might imagine their relationships to female poets and how female poets of warm and ardent tempers might imagine themselves. Dryden represented Killigrew in heavenly terms as a pure inhabitant of the celestial regions, no longer body (and therefore liable to the corruptions of the flesh) but all soul. The dead young poetess was in a position to redeem poetry, the divine art, that gift of God that a 'lubric and adulterate age' had defiled:

> Let this thy vestal, heaven, atone for all:
> Her Arethusian stream remains unsoiled,
> Unmixed with foreign filth, and undefiled;
> Her wit was more than man, her innocence a child.

A 'vestal' and a 'stream', she was both 'more than man' and less. In the final flourish of the poem, Dryden imagined the dead rising from their tombs on the Day of Judgement, the 'sacred poets' with Killigrew at their head bounding towards heaven, having heard the trumpets before everybody else:

> When in mid-air the golden trump shall sound,
>   To raise the nations under ground;
>   When in the valley of Jehosaphat,
> The judging God shall close the book of fate,
>   And there the last assizes keep,
>   For those who wake, and those who sleep;
>   When rattling bones together fly,
> From the four corners of the sky;
> When sinews o'er the skeletons are spread,
> Those clothed with flesh, and life inspires the dead;

The sacred poets first shall hear the sound,
   And foremost from the tomb shall bound,
For they are covered with the lightest ground;
And straight, with inborn vigour, on the wing,
Like mounting larks, to the new morning sing,
There thou, sweet saint, before the choir shalt go,
As harbinger of heaven, the way to show,
The way which thou so well hast learned below.

Elizabeth Singer ('Philomela') was an enthusiastic reader of Dryden – 'Dryden! A name I ne'er could yet rehearse, / But straight my thoughts were all transformed to verse' – and it is inconceivable that she did not know this poem. She probably had it by heart. Like Anne Killigrew, she was also gifted in 'the two sister-arts' of poetry and painting, having begun practising her skills early: 'music, poetry and painting were her three beauties and delights'. As an infant, so we are told, when her supplies ran short she would 'squeeze out the juices of herbs to serve her instead of colours'. She drew constantly and painted the local landscape which she loved, under the guidance of a tutor brought in specially for the purpose. Looking back from the late 1730s, her biographer and brother-in-law, Theophilus Rowe, identified poetry as the essential gift from which all other talents flowed:

Poetry indeed was her favourite employment, in youth, her most distinguishing excellence. So prevalent was her genius this way, that her very prose hath all the charms of verse without the fetters, the same fire and elevation, the same bright images, bold figures, rich and flowing diction. She could hardly write a familiar letter but it bore the stamp of the poet.[23]

Lively and precocious, this daughter of a prosperous clothier and Dissenting preacher of Frome, Somerset, was recognised as 'extraordinary' – she had 'an unusual sprightliness in her temper' – and was loved for it from her earliest days. She was talented, charming and good. The family was comfortably situated, both materially and socially, and her life was one of 'ease and plenty' though not without its sorrows: her mother, Elizabeth Portnell, and one sister had died while Elizabeth was still a child. She and her remaining sister had a close and affectionate relationship with their father Walter, a bookish, religious and benevolent man: the girl Elizabeth 'would rather have died than ever displeased her father'.[24]

Through her father's friendship with Lord Weymouth, she had acquired aristocratic patronage early. Walter Singer circulated a little collection of Elizabeth's youthful poetry, verses she had written at the age of twelve, among the company at nearby Longleat, producing what was no doubt the desired effect: an interest in his gifted daughter. In 1694, Elizabeth visited at Longleat, beginning what was to be a lifelong association with one of the country's premier families, whose grand house was 'the stranger's wonder and the nation's boast' and who had a tradition of being patrons of the arts.

At Longleat, the household included Bishop Thomas Ken, the most famous of the nonjuror bishops who refused to recognise James's abdication and William's accession. A man of conscience who had spent time in the Tower and lost his position because of his views, Bishop Ken was also a scholar and a poet. He was an important influence on Elizabeth's development. His own interests included Italian, French and Spanish literature, of which he had a large collection among his library of books. She studied Italian under the guidance of Henry Thynne, Lord Weymouth's son, and translated Tasso, Ariosto and Guarini into blank verse or heroic couplets. (These exercises in modern translation were to some extent the female version of young men's studies in Greek and Latin.) Bishop Ken took the view that poetry was a gift from heaven, 'designed / To hallow and adorn the mind', and that impious human poets had desecrated it. He favoured serious religious poetry over amorous pastorals, although he didn't exclude the latter, since Guarini's pastoral drama *Il pastor fido* was one of the texts Elizabeth struggled to translate:

> How many unsuccessful attempts I shall make in translating *Pastor Fido* is yet uncertain. I condemn in one moment what I admired just before: I write five or six verses, and think them perfectly fine and harmonious, worthy of Apollo himself, and never to be excelled. I read them with approbation and rapture, and do myself the highest justice; till on a more deliberate view, I sink from my elevations, and grow exceedingly humble, to find every line dull and impertinent.[25]

The self-mocking tone and shrewd understanding of the psychology of writing were characteristics that stayed with her. Bishop Ken suggested she paraphrase the thirty-eighth chapter of the Book of Job, which she did with rather more ease. The resulting production 'gained her a great deal of reputation'.

Elizabeth's literary knowledge was extensive, even before her introduction into the cultivated circles at Longleat. In her family there was no dispute about 'whether it be proper for women to be learned'. She described how, with her younger sister, she would study far into the night. Her sister would read medical books while Elizabeth read poets and general literature. Both took their writing seriously: 'We often retired by consent, each to her chamber, to compose and then to compare what we wrote. She always exceeded me in the number of lines, but mine I think were more correct. She exceeded me much in the fondness of love, but never in the truth and strength of it.' The relationship was not without its tensions: Elizabeth's sister 'desired ever to be with me, and I wanted to be more by myself'; nor was it without sibling rivalry: 'My father in his widowhood took great delight in us, cherished our love to God and one another, but like good Jacob, was fondest of the youngest, admiring all that she said or did.' Elizabeth, the less-favoured eldest (or at least, as the one who thought she was less favoured), was the only surviving child after her sister died at the age of twenty. In pious, Nonconformist households, too much repining suggested a refusal to accept the will of God and, what was worse, an overvaluation of the mortal world against the life to come, but Walter Singer was grief-stricken. Elizabeth's understated comment makes this clear: 'in her death', she wrote, 'he was to be tried.'[26]

In his poem, Dryden placed Anne Killigrew alongside Katherine Philips, 'the matchless Orinda', both having died young from smallpox: 'As equal were their souls, so equal were their fate.' His poem made available the idea of a special role for the sacred poet as sweet female saint. Elizabeth Singer's later writings, the prose fictions she produced in the 1720s under her married name of Mrs Rowe, were to build on this role in a rather literal way. In *Friendship in Death, or, Letters from the Dead to the Living*, her narrators were, like Killigrew at the beginning of Dryden's poem, already in heaven. Writers, those sweet saints, were distinguished from ordinary mortals because their existence was poised halfway between earth and heaven: even when dead they were only lightly covered. The writer travelled between the two states, half earthly and half heavenly, until fully transported.

In maintaining a role of this sort – as 'harbinger of heaven' – it was important not to be too associated with worldly matters, especially if, like Elizabeth Singer Rowe, you did not die young but lived a relatively long healthy life. It was easier to work up associations of sainthood around a celebrated solitary rural existence than for any woman whose life was passed in the town. To live in the country rather than the town was in any case, in popular parlance, to opt for death over life; it was like being immured, 'covered with the lightest ground'. Elizabeth Singer Rowe's achievement was to combine the heavenly associations of rural removal – 'happy in the absence of all that people call amusement and diversion' – with an unabashed celebration of sensuous earthly life including sexual feeling.

In the address to the reader which prefaced Singer's 1696 *Poems* published by Dunton, Elizabeth Johnson praised her as a genius whose gifts were heaven-sent – 'sometimes it pleases heaven to raise up some brighter genius than ordinary' – and located her in the by now standard lineage of female excellence: she was the latest arrival after the 'Sapphos and Behns, and Schurmans and Orindas, who have humbled the most haughty of our antagonists, and made 'em do homage to our wit as well as our beauty'. These products of heaven were angels by virtue of their poetic genius, and it was well known some angels had fallen: 'Angels love, but they love virtuously and reasonably, and neither err in the object, nor the manner; and if all our poetesses had done the same, I wonder what our enemies could have found out to have objected against us.' In any case, Johnson insisted, when women 'fell' it was because they had chosen the wrong men (they erred in the object) and these men had corrupted them. The pleasing prospect her preface held out to readers was of a collection of poems 'writ by a young lady' which were full of 'vivacity' and 'purity', but also had a 'softness and delicacy in the love part' (the evocation of Aphra Behn guaranteed that). Such poems must appeal to the 'pious and ingenious reader'. They combined virtue and 'warmth' – a term introduced and then qualified by immediate reference to the Bible: it was a 'warmth of devotion in the Canticles and other religious pieces'.

A commendatory poem followed in which a male poet described the physical effects of reading 'Philomela's' verses:

> We read, and sigh, and love, and are undone:
> Circean charms and female arts we prove,
> Transported all to some New World of love.

The 'we' who were 'undone' and transported to a 'New World' were not wrecked on despair's rough coast. The undoing was pleasurable when the reader was male. Reading the poems 'writ by a young lady' produced the following symptoms in the writer of these lines: tingling ears, thick drawn breath, a panting heart, pounding blood, swimming eyes, trembling nerves and unsteady feet. In the world of the love poem, the reader became a captive of sensation – 'Tyrannous Charmer hold!' – but fortunately the love so vividly depicted was the love of angels.

The transported poet was Richard Gwinnet, soon to begin a correspondence with his own charming poetess, Elizabeth Thomas. Similarly, Isaac Watts represented himself as a celestial shepherd tuning his harp on the banks of the Thames when 'Sudden from Albion's Western coast / Harmonious notes came gliding by'. In his pastoral/heavenly idyll, Londoners nearby – the 'neighbouring shepherds' – recognised the voice by its 'silver sound': "Tis Philomela's voice,' they cry, while Watts is struck dumb. Enchanted and enraptured by her obvious superiority to him as a poet, he loses all power of volition:

> At once my strings all silent lie,
> At once my fainting muse was lost,
> In the superior sweetness drown'd.
> In vain I bid my tuneful pow'rs unite;
> My soul retir'd, and left my tongue,
> I was all ear, and PHILOMELA'S song
> Was all divine delight.[27]

This poem, 'To Mrs Singer, on the sight of some of her divine poems never printed', suggests the intimacy of a band of poets, showing each other their verses which the public have yet to see (at the same time helping arouse public interest in these 'divine poems never printed'); and it conveys the spread of her reputation, borne on the breezes from rural Somerset to London.

Dunton ensured that Singer's *Poems on Several Occasions* took as dialogic a form as the *Athenian Mercury* and, more pertinently, as dialogic a form as editions of women poets' work in general. The debate about human and earthly love was elaborated by a number of different male voices within its pages, some or all of whom might have been the versatile Athenians. A 'country Gentleman' offered a salacious response to 'Platonick Love' in which he urged copulation as a divine instruction: human love was more than merely bodily sensation, but religion, he explained, required us to increase and multiply. Other voices pronounced Philomela's superiority, dramatising themselves in the act of admiration and providing an applauding audience. Different locations were integrated into the text: Singer's pastoral scenes contrasted with the metropolitan surroundings of her commentators. Poems singing the praises of the nation were interspersed with poems about being overwhelmed by love or managing to give it up. 'The Reply to Mr——' denying any susceptibility to 'wild Fantastick Extasy', claimed 'calmer Reason now Triumphant reigns', but gave in passing an extended description of the 'soft sensations of delight'. The 'young lady', as she was constantly referred to, depicted herself smiling, blushing, gazing, sighing and thinking herself 'undone'. The final poem, 'A Farewell to Love' kept love and the young lady powerfully in view as she three times declared that she wanted to 'hear no more of Hymen, or of Love'.

It was hard to escape love altogether since among the responses that could be expected from the reading experience of poetry in the early eighteenth century were physical sensations that resembled sexual arousal. The preface to a 1704 edition of Singer's poems, in a collection entitled *Philomela, Divine Hymns*, explained:

The great business of poetry . . . is to paint agreeable pictures on the imagination, to actuate the spirits, and give the passions a noble pitch. All its daring metaphors, surprising turns, melting accents, lofty flights and lively descriptions, serve for this end: while we read we feel a strange warmth boiling within, the blood dances through the veins, joy lightens in the countenance, and we are insensibly led into a pleasing captivity.

As 'the richest genius of her sex', whose name signified pure song and pure morals, 'Philomela' went on being of use to Dunton. Some of his schemes were highly dubious. He engaged Singer in a correspondence about a new miscellany, the *Secret Oracle*, which was to 'answer the nicer questions that relate to carnal and spiritual copulation, and which were privately sent to the Athenian Society by the masked ladies and town sparks'. Her name could be casually introduced or explicitly wheeled in for authorisation. Plans for *The Secret Letters of Platonick Courtship*, between the Athenian Society and 'the most ingenious ladies in the three kingdoms, with the form of solemnizing platonick matrimony, invented by the Athenian Society, to which is added their amorous quarrels on the disputable points relating to love and wedlock ... published to direct the bachelor and virgin in their whole amour', came with the assurance that 'Madam Singer (one of the ladies privy to this correspondence) [was] fully satisfied there was nothing but innocence (or a platonick courtship) designed'.[28] The 'pure and virtuous friendship ... between Philomela and Philaret', which it is given to Dunton's wife to testify to in his *Life and Errors*, offered a model to others of 'pure and virtuous' friendship between men and women in which copulation ('carnal and spiritual') and related matters might be discussed.

By 1705, the tone had been sufficiently lowered to make defensive apologies necessary. In publishing a volume of letters from Katherine Philips to Sir Charles Cotterell, the bookseller Bernard Lintot first insisted on their authenticity, and then explained that the letters from Orinda were

the effect of an happy intimacy between herself and the late famous Poliarchus, and are an admirable pattern for the pleasing correspondence of a virtuous friendship: they will sufficiently instruct us how an intercourse of writing, between persons of different sexes, ought to be managed, with delight and innocence; and teach the world not to load such a commerce with censure and detraction.[29]

The world needed to be taught not to load such a commerce with

179

'censure and detraction' because it would be sure to do so; the letters, in other words, had commercial appeal because of the possibility that they might contain material deserving of censure but which could be received in virtuously didactic mode.

Platonic love was love as preached by philosophers, sung by poets and practised by the angels. Mary Astell and John Norris discussed it at length. Susannah Centlivre made fun of it in her play, *The Platonick Lady*, Act Two of which opens with a discussion between Lucinda, who is agitatedly waiting in the park for her lover, Belvil, and her maid, Betty:

LUCINDA: How calm my hours were before I knew this man!
BETTY: I thought Platonick Love never disturbed the mind, Madam.
LUCINDA: Yes, when the friendship is nice and particular.
BETTY: Nay, nay, I never knew friendship in different sexes but came to particulars at last . . .

In the dialogue between Belvil and Lucinda which follows, Lucinda insists that Belvil adhere to the rules of platonic love, which Belvil repeats to show he has understood them: 'I must take pains to make the world understand that our conversation is only friendship, and tho nobody will believe me – swear I admire the beauties of your mind – without regarding those of your person – protest I have no desire to kiss those rosy lips – press that soft white hand – and sigh my soul out in your bosom – '30

As well as mocking this kind of cant, Susannah Centlivre made fun of the (proto-feminist) rhetoric associated with Mary Astell, Lady Mary Chudleigh and other writers of the 1690s and early 1700s who railed against 'tyrant men'. 'Our sex are too apt to credit the appearances of truth from the protesting tyrants,' declares Lucinda, who also delivers a little rant about the double standard – 'Good heavens, who would be a woman?' – which is bombastic and full of clichés: 'What libertine e'er lost a friend for being so; nor stands he less in fame for perjur'd vows that has betrayed a thousand trusting maids, whilst we for every trifling fault condemned become the subject of licentious tongues.' (The elevation of conversational prose to the rhythms of iambic pentameter here is wonderfully histrionic.) Claiming 'an indifference to your whole sex' and urging Belvil to agree to the proposition that friendship is 'the noblest aim of human kind', Lucinda does not convince. Belvil replies, 'Madam, I am of Cowley's mind, when I am all soul, I shall keep your rules.'

Being 'all soul' and no body – being dead – was the only truly effective way to resist the temptations of the flesh. But the idea of death and heaven, the mingling of souls not bodies, could be mobilised to extend the range of female expressiveness, not to mock women's attempts to live lives that included mental and physical association with men but to explore it. Elizabeth Rowe was to be promoted as an icon of propriety by mid-century bluestockings. As 'the pious Mrs Rowe' who supposedly cared only for heavenly virtues, sex did not sully her pages; she was dull and worthy. Like the apparently obvious distinction between private and public, this distinction between pious (no sex) and impious (lots of sex) is less clear upon closer examination. In her own time, sex was an important part of Elizabeth Singer Rowe's appeal. As we have seen, it was not until the mid century that it became axiomatic that a woman writer who wished to avoid scandal had to avoid the subject of sex.

Chapter Six

MARRIAGE AND LOVE

Wilt thou deny the bounty of a kiss,
And see me languish for the melting bliss?
Elizabeth Singer Rowe[1]

Elizabeth Singer and Matthew Prior

At Longleat, in the autumn of 1703, twenty-nine-year-old Elizabeth
Singer met the forty-year-old poet Matthew Prior. Both were protégées
of the Thynne family. They met as professionals. They read each other's
verses: he suggested some improvements to her translation of a passage
from Tasso's *Jerusalem Delivered* which had already been accepted by
Jacob Tonson for the fifth volume of *Poetical Miscellanies*. Tonson's
Miscellanies were prime locations for publication at this time. When
Prior left to return to London, Singer gave him the manuscript of
another passage of translation from Tasso which she hoped Tonson
would publish. She relied on Prior to represent her interests in a general
way, but Prior's enthusiasm for this 'poetical commission' did not
survive their separation. A correspondence ensued, extending over the
next twelve months, and although only Prior's letters remain it is
possible to glean, very faintly, some indication of the ways Singer tried
to use him and how he baffled her.[2]

Many decades later, Hester Thrale, reading the manuscript of Joseph
Spence's *Anecdotes*, observed in *Thraliana* that Prior was 'quite a
scoundrel I see; an apostate in politics, a debauchee in practice, and that
of the lowest kind'.[3] In his letters to Elizabeth Singer, Prior emerges as
a man driven by work commitments and anxious about his prospects.

Keeping well connected and maintaining his place while pursuing a reputation as a poet was stressful: he was 'in such a confusion of business, hopes, disappointments, fears and vexations, that I am even sick to death of ambition, and all the ills that attend it'. Singer's situation as a 'downright country girl' protected from these strains was enviable. He claimed that her letters left him unsure what tone to adopt towards her and he settled on a facetiousness that barely concealed underlying hostility:

> I have received a letter from you full of real wit and affected anger. I would answer it if I knew what style would be agreeable to you, but to the different key in which you sing it is impossible I should keep consort ... So not knowing the mind of my Goddess, I may mistake in the way of my admiration, and whilst in one letter we are to speak as plain as if we lived in the Golden Age, and in another we are to dissemble with each other and talk of stars and destinies, you must give me leave (with all the respect I have for you) to remember that I am writing to a woman.

He admitted he had the 'spleen' and accused her of both causing it in him and displaying it herself. In his vivid, aggressive way, Prior constructed the relationship on romantic lines, chiding himself for supposedly falling in love: 'Fie Mr Prior, a poet to admire one of his own calling, and a philosopher to be in love? A traveller to lose his heart in Hampshire, no, no, Somersetshire, and a man of business to hold correspondence with a country lady.' Often Prior sounds drunk and this letter is no exception, even drawing attention to his drinking:

> You chid me once for drinking from 7 till 12, and to show you how fast I mend, I drank last night from 5 till 2 in the morning. Hang Tonson how could you throw away 4 or 5 lines upon him. When this Miscellany comes out I will send it to you. Hark ye, take my advice get into company and don't play with edge tools. Love's darts may cut your finger and his flames burn 'em.

As a romantic attachment it failed to ignite. Not only was she a country lady (who probably didn't appreciate his remark about remembering he was 'writing to a woman') but she omitted to praise his verses. As a professional relationship it was unprofitable. Prior's difficulty in settling on a tone was symptomatic of the larger difficulties that combined the personal, the professional and the political (Prior was becoming increasingly identified with the Tories). Without Singer's letters it is impossible to make a judgement about her tone: did she present herself to him as a 'goddess' to be admired, as a coquette 'full of real wit and affected anger', as a 'country girl', or as an ambitious poet like himself? We don't know, nor do we know if Prior did anything on her behalf, only that both appeared in Tonson's fifth *Miscellany*, that 'choicest collection' which featured all the 'poets of the hour'.

Anne Finch, Countess of Winchilsea

Prior's reference to 'spleen' owed something to the writings of another regular visitor at Longleat, Anne Finch, Countess of Winchilsea, who was related by marriage to the Thynne family. In 1701, Finch, using the pen name 'Ardelia', published an ambitious long poem, *The Spleen*, which explored the physical and psychological manifestations of what she called the 'black jaundice'. Finch gave the poem a strongly autobiographical turn by linking her own struggle with depressive feelings with the desire to write. She described the depressed state of mind in which writing was felt to be 'An useless folly, or presumptuous fault' and contrasted it with happy and productive creativity:

> Whilst in the Muse's path I stray,
> Whilst in their groves, and by their secret springs
> My hand delights to trace unusual things,
> And deviates from the known, and common way.

Anne Finch's correspondence appears not to have survived and we know nothing about her views on 'Philomela', nor whether two such serious poets, delighting in their work and striking out paths of their own, walked and talked in the groves of Longleat. We know that Prior was important to both. Finch claimed to be indebted to him, calling him 'the master-singer' and casting herself as the imitative bird doing its best to produce the same ravishing song, but Prior's characteristic dash and relish, his bacchanalian excesses – ''Tis the mistress, the friend, and the bottle, old boy!' – seem no more propitious for Anne Finch than they were for Elizabeth Singer.

Anne Finch famously apostrophised Longleat in verse, 'Longleat that justly has all praise engrossed / The stranger's wonder and the nation's boast.' Practices at Longleat imitated those at other country houses, such as Penshurst, associated with Ben Jonson, and Wilton House, where the Countess of Pembroke had been the patron of Spenser, Donne and Nashe. The Countess of Pembroke had collaborated with her brother Sir Philip Sidney on a translation of the Psalms, which she continued after his early death, and had inspired the writing of Sidney's *Arcadia*. There was mythical force behind the idea that the national literature was the possession of the great national families, all the more so after 1688 and the end of what was regarded as divinely ordained Stuart rule. Patronage, promotion, literary and artistic production and display were part of country-house ethos. In these years, Longleat boasted the two most important women poets of the era, the one a clothier's daughter and a Whig, the other a countess, a Tory and a Jacobite.

Longleat provided connections which reached out to the metropolis and beyond. If it added status to a merchant's daughter, it was no less significant to a propertyless countess, as Finch's carefully titled poems – for example, 'To the Hon the Lady Worsley at Longleat, who had most obligingly desired my corresponding with her by letters' – clearly show. As 'country ladies', Finch and Singer carried their association with Longleat like a testimonial and it helped them garner metropolitan reputations for work which was recognised as profoundly serious, the product of sustained labour, systematic study and the highest ambition. Both women spent periods in London: Finch became closely associated with Jonathan Swift, through whom she met and befriended the young Alexander Pope; Singer, after her marriage in 1709 to Thomas Rowe, lived in Hampstead till his death in 1715, mixing in Dissenting circles populated by literary clergymen like Isaac Watts.

Anne Finch had been a maid of honour at the court of Mary of Modena in the 1680s where, along with Anne Killigrew and other literary women, she had imbibed an atmosphere of intellectual and spiritual aspiration. She was to refer slightingly to this period in her life when she later explained that she would never let any of her poems be seen because 'everyone would have made their remarks upon a versifying maid of honour, and far the greater number with prejudice if not contempt', a remark which, according to how you hear it, might suggest either timidity or aggression. (She had no compunction about publishing her poems in 1701, when a number of them, including *The Spleen*, occupied some thirty pages of Charles Gildon's *New Collection of Poems*.) James II's flight in 1688 was a disaster for Finch. She alluded to these events in 'The Petition for an Absolute Retreat', describing herself as 'sad Ardelia . . . / Blasted by a storm of fate, / Felt through all the British state'. Retreat was to become her key trope, as it was also for Elizabeth Singer Rowe, each of them working variations on the public understanding of retreat as a source of political, religious and poetic identity.[4]

An early marriage to a poetry-loving husband, and a forced removal to 'the solitude and security of the country', gave Finch the conditions for cultivating her art. Far from court and 'interest', the couple lived the virtuous retired life, devoted to books, antiquarian study and nature. In this privacy, the beauty of the mansion and estate in which they lived – Heneage Finch's nephew's property, Eastwell Park in Kent – offered itself as subject matter within an established poetic tradition. Anne Finch saw Eastwell Park as a setting that could be mythologised in literary terms in much the same way that John Denham – the 'mighty' Denham – had mythologised Cooper's Hill (and as Pope was to mythologise Windsor Forest):

> methinks my hand
> Might bid the landscape in strong numbers stand
> Fix all its charms with a poetic skill
> And raise its fame above his Cooper's Hill –

By raising 'its' fame, she would, of course, also raise her own. Anne Finch's eagerness to put herself 'in the service of the Muses' knew no bounds. She claimed to have an 'irresistible impulse' to write. As a woman, she expected to be accused of vanity and attention-seeking, presumption and carelessness, some of which she feared might be justified: 'aiming to be admired' she might well be defective in capacity and care. But she still laid claim to 'poetic skill' and believed herself capable of 'strong numbers'. She reassured herself that since the translations of Dryden and Dacier and others there was no excuse for women wilfully to transgress the laws of poetry: she could work hard and achieve correctness. Her model in this was 'our most virtuous Orinda'. Like Katherine Philips, she wanted to write but not 'give scandal' nor be censured, hence she chose 'inoffensive' subjects, avoiding satire and lampoons (though not completely) and steering clear of obvious political references. Her models more generally, as the reference to Denham's 'Cooper's Hill' suggests, were the leading male poets: Milton, Marvell, Dryden. The subject of love she did not choose to avoid, noting with some defiance (and an echo of Aphra Behn): 'I know not why it should be more faulty to treat of that passion than of any other violent excursion or transport of the mind.'[5]

Through her friendship with Swift, Finch arranged for a handsome volume of her poems to be printed in 1713 by John Barber. Although she presented herself as a country lady rather diffident about claiming the identity of author, Finch chose the town's leading printer who was associated with its most prominent woman writer: Delarivier Manley. The following year, Manley and her sister began living with Barber in his house on Ludgate Hill, possibly when Manley and Barber became lovers. Manley was notorious at the time for her secret histories, the *New Atalantis* of 1709 and the *Memoirs of Europe* of 1710. She had become a campaigning Tory journalist, working with Swift on the *Examiner* and succeeding him as editor in 1711. It is tempting to imagine the Countess and the writer of scandalous fictions meeting at Ludgate Hill – which may have happened if, as was customary, Anne Finch went to the printing house to supervise progress on her volume.

The *Miscellany Poems, on Several Occasions* appeared as 'Written by a Lady'. But John Barber inserted a note to the reader on the verso of the title page, making clear who the 'Lady' was: 'The Town having already done justice to the Ode on the Spleen and some few pieces in this volume when scattered in other miscellanies I think it will be sufficient (now that permission is at last obtained for the printing this collection) to acquaint the reader that they are of the same hand; which I doubt not will render this miscellany an acceptable present to the public.'

The following year Pope made use of the town's familiarity with the 'Ode on the Spleen' and its enthusiastic reception of *Miscellany Poems* in his *Rape of the Lock*, which Anne Finch read in manuscript, when he matter-of-factly linked depression with female creativity. The 'spleen' according to Pope was:

> Parent of vapours and of female wit,
> Who give th'hysteric or poetic fit,
> On various tempers act by various ways,
> Make some take physic, others scribble plays.

Finch objected to the trivialising of what had been in her poem a serious exploration of the effects of depression on all people, not just writers, and not only women. Pope's particular use of 'spleen' drew on the association in the public mind of her person with her writings. She reproved him on behalf of women writers in general. The reproof doesn't survive; we know about it because of an exchange of poems which followed. Pope responded with an extravagant compliment in verse, his 'Impromptu to Lady Winchilsea, Occasioned by four satirical verses on Women-Wits, in the Rape of the Lock'. He compared her greatness to Queen Anne and pointed out that she should not concern herself about the 'poetic dames of yore' because her brilliance eclipsed them all. This 'genteel' impromptu 'disarmed' her.

In a long preface to her *Miscellany Poems, on Several Occasions*, Anne Finch presented herself as a woman within a poetic tradition mostly defined by men but in which women had a place. She referred no fewer than three times to Katherine Philips: once for her 'great reservedness' on the subject of love, which others commended and Finch queried; once as authorising precedent for playwriting; and most importantly, as the significant figure whose example occupied the aspiring poet's imagination. Katherine Philips set the impossibly high standard, both in what she wrote and in how she was received. Finch quoted from her own earliest verses to show how important Philips had been to her as she became aware of her own desire to write. She recalled and quoted 'some of the first lines I ever writt' in which she depicted Apollo, the god of poetry, directly refusing her request for poetic inspiration:

> I grant thee no pretence to bays,
> Nor in bold print do thou appear;

Nor shalt thou reach Orinda's praise,
Tho all thy aim be fixed on her.

These lines encapsulate some of Anne Finch's lifelong preoccupations as a poet. In a series of negatives, they tell us what she wanted, what she was anxious about, and where her 'aim' was 'fixed'. Questions that were central to her verse are implicit here: what value should she put on her poetic gifts, should she go into print, how should she situate herself as a woman within the tradition, and how reconcile the delight of poetry with critical judgement? We can interpret the impulse to display Apollo refusing to grant the laurel bays as an attempt to disarm modern-day critics. She was quick to agree that her poetry was unlikely to be correct, since 'from a female hand it came', but explained that it was because friends encouraged her so much that her output had grown 'to the formidable appearance of a volume'. Friends, such as the Countess of Hertford, daughter of Lord Weymouth of Longleat, whose copy of *Miscellany Poems, on Several Occasions* carried the injunction to 'look with favour on Ardelia's muse, / And what your father cherished, still excuse', were depicted as urging her to print. She, the cherished poet, nurtured within a court and country-house ethos, had dutifully responded to the claims of friends; but now, venturing beyond them into the wider realm, she feared the critics.

The dilemma was laid out in the preface, thus ensuring that when she did go into print her verses came accompanied with a strong impression of a particular authorial persona both in and out of the verse, debating issues to do with writing and reflecting on her own responses. Anne Finch was interested in the psychology of writing. She might claim to write because she couldn't help it, like the man in the desert who had to drink when he found water, or because it was too much fun not to – 'We own (who in the Muse delight) / 'Tis for our selves, not them, we write' – but her examples, like that man in the desert borrowed from Beaumont and Fletcher, helped to root her in the literary tradition. Buttressed by references to Dryden, Roscommon, Aristotle, Horace, Rapin, Despreaux, Denham and Waller, she might debate the merits and demerits of printing but there was no doubt that as a writer she pitched for the highest achievement and widest audience her 'Muse' made possible.

The friends whose encouragement she advertised were the friends of literature. Drawing some inspiration from Philips's Society of Friendship, Finch represented herself engaged with her (mostly titled) friends in a shared endeavour in which books, houses, land and responsible leadership all came together. Even 'The Petition for an Absolute Retreat' which petitions for a place 'silent, as a midnight thought. / Where the world may ne'er invade' was sociably addressed and inscribed to 'Armida', the Countess of Thanet. In retreat, this woman poet's chief friend was her husband, 'A partner suited to my mind, / Solitary, pleased and kind ... Slighting, by my humble side, / Fame and splendour, wealth and pride,' who, as Dafnis or Flavio according to the conventions of pastoral verse, featured in poems praising married love.[6]

Finch's poems declared that, *pace* the wisdom of the world, she had found that husbands could be lovers, and such lover-husbands could be delighted to have wives who were poets. She incorporated her husband as a friend of her verses in a number of poems, for example, 'To Mr F. now Earl of W. Who going abroad, had desired Ardelia to write some verses upon whatever subject she thought fit, against his return in the evening', a title which did a great deal of work, especially if we include the additional information supplied, that it was 'written in the year 1689'. In humorous, light-verse mode, the poem makes intimate private life public at the same time as it allegorises loyalty to a particular social order. The mixture is already evident in the title: it is a matter of some importance that 'Mr F.', to whom the poem is addressed, is 'now Earl of W.'. He has rank, though in a poem 'written in 1689' his power might be equivocal. Nevertheless, he can bid his household poet to write for him, as aristocratic patrons in classical times were depicted as doing. 'Ardelia' is both poet and wife. As a poet, the Muses on Parnassus are her special friends. (On the Eastwell estate, there was a hill that they named 'Parnassus'.) When Ardelia appeals to them for help, the Muses drop everything and respond at once because there's 'no female's voice below / They sooner would obey'. The subject Ardelia has chosen to write on is her happy marriage and domestic life; the poem depicts the Muses' surprise that it is a husband Ardelia wants to praise. The Muses have never heard of such a thing – a husband who indulges her verse and who now 'required her rhymes'. Indeed, they do not approve, even though Ardelia is their special friend. They refuse and send excuses: Pegasus is exhausted from writing panegyrics, the tragic Muse will only write about war, and the comic Muse has been bought by theatre management and audience and 'durst not for her life' write in praise of a husband. Urania advises Ardelia that what comes from the heart does not need the aid of the Muses. Ardelia looks within, finds tender thoughts, and takes herself off at the end of the day to meet Flavio returning. There, in a grove, she can offer him the true poem, herself, privately speaking 'the sounds of love' that the poem reports, as she and he together perform 'Hymen's endearments and its ties' in 'stolen secrecy'.[7]

An explicit scene of marital sex brings to a close a poem which is also about politics and literary practices. The poem demands that we ask who it is for: is it a coterie poem with – in this case – a special meaning for a group of displaced Jacobites forced to reinvent their lives? a shared joke for the couple to laugh over at dinner or in bed? Is it a comment on other poets (all those panegyrics in 1689) and the corruption of poetry in a politically partisan literary climate? Is it specially about women writers? At the very least, the light tone and flamboyantly private subject matter – a husband's desires, a poet's perplexities – are not innocent. Nor, in the broadest sense, is the poem modest. Finch authorises her writing and asserts her specialness and superiority – her right to deviate from 'known and common' ways – at two levels: she represents herself endorsed as a poet by her husband and by the gods, without being ruled by either. With protection from friends like these, the status of her fears about the critics must be called into question.

Generous sentiments and elegant desires

In 1709, at Bath, Elizabeth Singer met Thomas Rowe. The encounter was manifestly a love match on both sides, described in extreme terms by one commentator: 'the feeling of each for the other was not a passion, it was a frenzy of love'.[8] She was thirty-six and celebrated; he was much younger – only twenty-three, fresh back from his studies in the Netherlands, an omnivorous reader (he brought a vast library of books back to England), ambitious writer, follower of poetry and a great admirer of her verses in particular. To him, Elizabeth Singer was without question the natural successor to Philips and Behn; she was the darling of the muses who barely even needed the muses' help, being 'sufficient to herself alone'. In his poem 'To Daphnis, An Epistle', Thomas Rowe praised her:

> How smooth her strains! How easy flow her lines!
> Throughout the whole how vast a genius shines!
> Whate'er she writes, in ev'ry part we see
> Astraea's fire, Orinda's purity.[9]

Combining Astraea's 'fire' and Orinda's 'purity' was not an easy task.

By 1709, to write of Aphra Behn in warm appreciative terms was to run counter to the prevailing trend. Thomas Rowe did exactly that: some conventional criticism of Behn's morals was appended to twenty lines of ecstatic praise for her poetic evocation of the feelings inspired by love:

> On ev'ry subject she her art could prove,
> Well on each subject sung, but best of love;
> At once she sung, and felt the pleasing smart,
> Love in her numbers reign'd, and lorded in her heart.
> With what amazing force the charmer writes
> Of the dear passion, and its fierce delights!

That Aphra Behn should have felt the 'fierce delights' of the 'dear passion' and conveyed them in beautiful verse was not a problem for Thomas Rowe, though he wished she had been more inclined to 'permitted pleasures' and 'chaste transports'. His poem was a love letter to the woman he declared was purer than Orinda and fiercer than Astraea. In her poems, too, love 'reign'd'. The following year he and Elizabeth Singer were married. A Latin epigram by a friend eulogised them as Britain's answer to France's famous learned pair, Le Fevre and Madame Dacier. The couple moved to London. Conjugal delights pleased them both. In a poem written after the marriage, 'Ode to Delia', Thomas Rowe admitted:

> I find temptations ev'n in thee:
> Dissolved in bliss, and melting in thy arms,
> I lose the relish of celestial charms;
> On thee alone my wandering thoughts employ,
> And lost in thee, forget superior joy.

She, meanwhile, later wrote:

> Whate'er excess the fondest passion knew,
> I felt for thee, dear youth; my joy, my care . . .

Love was Elizabeth Singer's 'darling theme': 'I think I'll talk of love now, for that's my darling theme.' Rapture, flames, ardour, passion and love – "tis love, O charming youth! Inspires my muse' – were the keynotes of her verse. Love was the 'moving principle' in her life as well as being the quintessential, definitive poetic subject. Her earlier poems had celebrated a personal relationship with God sensuously and physically experienced. Married love, that gift to be celebrated and indulged, came from God: 'For sure the charming passion has a divine original, for God himself is love; by him the sacred flame was kindled, and fills the soul with generous sentiments and elegant desires.' Love was not a force to be resisted: 'with gratitude I acknowledge the power and bless the divinity of love'.

Love and marriage did not mean an end to writing. The couple settled down to serious literary work. Thomas Rowe had started an ambitious historical project, writing the lives of 'illustrious persons' left out by Plutarch in his famous *Lives*. One manuscript already prepared for the press had been given to Richard Steele, who duly lost it. Politically impassioned, a lover of liberty ('The love of liberty had been always one of Mr Rowe's most darling passions. 'Twas a kind of ideal mistress . . .' his brother later wrote) and a fervent Protestant who hated 'ecclesiastical tyranny', Thomas Rowe was a stimulating companion who drew company round them: 'For he could talk– 'twas ecstasy to hear, / 'Twas joy, 'twas harmony to every ear.' Vivid and brilliant, he could also be impatient and quick-tempered. These tendencies were exacerbated by ill health. Within a few years the symptoms of consumption showed themselves and quickly worsened. Thomas Rowe lived long enough to welcome the accession of the Hanoverians in 1714. (Elizabeth wrote a quatrain, 'On the picture of King George 1' in which she insisted that there was so much goodness and sanctity in George's face that it was 'impious' to suggest – the simple truth – that he hadn't succeeded by divine right.) But in 1715 Thomas Rowe died. The happy marriage with its 'generous sentiments and elegant desires' was over. In her grief,

Elizabeth Rowe responded with a poem, *On the Death of Mr Thomas Rowe*, that was unusually intimate in its portrayal of sexual feeling. She was to make a point of commemorating his deathday in the years that followed, often by writing a poem.

On the Death of Mr Thomas Rowe mourned the lover as well as the 'tender husband'. In the conventions of pastoral verse, Rowe was given the name Alexis: 'In what soft language shall my thoughts get free, / My dear Alexis, when I talk of thee?' The poem memorialised him as a man of merit and virtue, valued by his friends; but it was not the public man Elizabeth Rowe publicly celebrated. She wrote from the position of a wife: 'softer ties, my endless sorrows claim; / Lost in despair, distracted and forlorn, / The lover, I, and tender husband mourn.' Becoming a husband, Rowe had remained a lover. The feelings he aroused had nothing 'cold or formal' about them; they were the warm feelings of love not the cold feelings of duty. He was a 'charming youth', and he was 'formed to move':

> Eternal music dwelt upon his tongue,
> Soft and transporting as the muse's song.
> Listening to him, my cares were charmed to rest,
> And love and silent rapture filled my breast;
> Unheeded the gay moments took their flight,
> And time was only measured by delight.
> I hear the loved, the melting accent still,
> And still the warm, the tender transport feel:
> Again I see the sprightly passions rise,
> And life and pleasure kindle in his eyes.

On the Death of Mr Thomas Rowe was much reprinted.[10] It is a rare example from the period of a poem by a woman celebrating socially sanctioned sexual pleasure. However, it is also a poem about death and renunciation. If the love of God, who had no material being, permitted the expression of erotic feeling, so too the death of a husband enlarged the scope of expressive intimacy and made it available for public consumption. The poem contrasts a vividly realised physical relationship with an abstract one: it ends with the consecration of the speaker to her dead love. Like God, he was now beyond. No longer material, he was all idea. What his existence-in-death seemed to require – 'the softest vows that ever love can make' – was renunciation of pleasure on earth:

> For thee all thoughts of pleasure I forego,
> For thee my tears shall never cease to flow;
> For thee at once I from the world retire,
> To feed in silent shades a hopeless fire.
> My bosom all thy image shall retain,
> The full impression there shall still remain.
> As thou hast taught my tender heart to prove
> The noblest height and elegance of love,
> That sacred passion I to thee confine,
> My spotless faith shall be for ever thine.

The fervour of her passion poured itself into active renunciation. Just as Elizabeth Rowe accepted 'excess' in her love for her husband, and celebrated it, so in grief her 'constancy to the charming youth' was the pride and glory of her life. She was haunted by his image: '[He] appears forever in my sight, and I half deceive myself with imaginary joys; but when I recover from the soft delusion, I grow perfectly wild and savage, and fly humankind, because I can see nothing that resembles him; and am disgusted at every sound I hear, because it does not imitate his voice.'[11]

Elizabeth Rowe gained her eighteenth-century reputation not for the bulk of her poems and hymns but for prose works which fictionalised the relationship between the dead and the living, *Friendship in Death, or Letters from the Dead to the Living* (1728) and *Letters Moral and Entertaining* (1729–32). The reception of those works was heavily influenced by the popularity of *On the Death of Mr Thomas Rowe* and the known facts of Rowe's short married life and self-consecration to her dead husband in widowhood. Soon after Thomas Rowe's death, Elizabeth Rowe left London and returned to Somerset. In the years that followed she resisted most invitations to return to the metropolis, though she was courted by those in the highest social circles. Lady Hertford, the Countess of Somerset, was a lady of the Bedchamber and part of Walpole's inner circle (the Queen's favourite and 'a most insinuating woman' as far as Swift was concerned). Urged to join these friends in what she called their 'constant hurry of company', Rowe sent polite refusals and condolences, explaining her 'inducement to retire-ment', not as a cautionary move against being identified with certain factions at court, nor as 'spleen' or melancholy or affectation, but as 'the greatest improvement of my reason and morals, and the best method I can find to be happy . . . one may think in a crowd, and make some imperfect reflections; but 'tis *alone* that you form your most exact and impartial notions'.[12]

The classical ideal of Horatian retreat, where judgement, free will, reason and reflection could be cultivated far from the corruptions of town, combined with virtuous widowhood and a life of service in the community – looking after the local poor, supporting the charity school for girls, taking a keen interest in a colonial settlement in the New World – ensured a reputation for unblemished piety.[13] This choice of a private life which became public knowledge enabled (and to some extent helped construct) an absolute distinction between Mrs Rowe, the purveyor of 'pious' fictions, and the many other women who in the course of her lifetime did as she was doing, which was: bringing a range of fictional and semi-fictional goods to market. That a woman's life and writings could be read off from each other (to the detriment of both) was a commonplace of the times. It was generally used to attack rivals, which is the way Rowe's friend Penelope Aubin used it in her preface to *The Life of Charlotta du Pont* (1723) when she explained that she declined to write in the 'unchristian' 'loose' manner of the times, and was leaving that to 'the other female authors, my contemporaries, whose lives and writings have, I fear, too great a resemblance'. Aubin did not need to name the most famous female authors to whom she was alluding: her contemporaries Eliza Haywood, who swept all before her in the 1720s, and Delarivier Manley, whose books had been the talk of London during the years that Elizabeth Rowe lived there with her husband.

We don't know why Rowe decided in the late 1720s to publish prose fictions, but we can note that there was by then a developed market for it, which she was able, very effectively, to reach. She was never inattentive to issues concerning literary fame. It has largely been for *Friendship in Death, or Letters from the Dead to the Living* and *Letters Moral and Entertaining* that the 'pious' Mrs Rowe has been (unenthu-siastically) included in historical and critical accounts of the literature of the period, figuring as the precursor of the bluestockings and the antithesis of those 'scandalous' autobiographers and popular fiction writers Eliza Haywood, Delarivier Manley and Laetitia Pilkington. Along with Jane Barker and Penelope Aubin, Rowe exemplified 'moral respectability' in female fiction.

Given her reputation as a widow living in an almost religious seclusion, and because they deal in death, it would be easy to assume that *Friendship in Death* and *Letters Moral and Entertaining* lacked the erotic content which lends so much charm to Rowe's verse. Their popularity with eighteenth-century readers, however (both were much reprinted and often presented together in one volume), owes something to that very quality. They feature many familiar ingredients of sensation and romance: there are pirates and sea battles; Turks with harems and Christian ladies at risk of being inveigled into them; imperiled virtue and perilous heroics. Episodes of incest, rape and seduction provide the storylines in letters which, one after the other, offer a glimpse of a relationship ended by death. In each case, the dead person comes back to speak to the living and to demonstrate that an honourable death (typically, in defence of chastity) is worth enduring because the afterlife is a wonderful reward. There is nothing dull about the afterlife. The emphasis is on pleasure and delight. All those who have been transported to 'the mansions of life and bliss' beyond the spacious entrance of the 'crystal gates' find it a vast improvement on earthly life. And this is so in one particular especially: in the home of eternal love, sexual pleasure is 'guiltless' and 'unmolested'.

The afterlife is the stuff of erotic fantasy. A young nun in a convent writing to the English lord she loved is made unhappy by the force of her unrequited desires; once in heaven, the conflict between passion and virtue is at an end and sexual pleasure can be freely taken: 'That unhappy passion which was my torment and crime, is now my glory and my boast: nothing selfish or irregular, nothing that needs restraint or disguise, mingles with the noble ardour.' A man who died at Constantinople writing to his friend in England describes his lost love, Almeria, appearing to him as he dies, welcoming him to the bowers of ethereal bliss:

how dazzling! How divinely fair! Exstasy was in her eyes, and inexpressible pleasure in every smile! Her mien and aspect more soft and propitious than ever was feigned by poets of their goddess of beauty and love. What was airy fiction *there*, was *here* all transporting reality. With an inimitable grace she received me into her ethereal chariot, which was sparkling sapphire studded with gold; it rolled with a spontaneous motion along the heavenly plains, and stopped at the morning star, our destined habitation. But how shall I describe this fair, this fragrant, this enchanting land of love! the delectable vales and flowery lawns, the myrtle shades and rosy bowers; the bright cascades and crystal rivulets rolling over orient pearls and sands of gold! Here they spread their silent waves into broad transparent lakes, smooth as the face of Heaven; and there they break with rapid force through arching rocks of diamond and purple amethist. Plants of immortal verdure creep up the sparkling cliffs, and adorn the prospect with unspeakable variety.

Oh my Beville could I lead you through the luxurious bowers and soft recesses where pleasure keeps its eternal festivals, and revels with guiltless and unmolested freedom! Whatever can raise desire, whatever can give delight, whatever can satisfy the soul in all the boundless capacities of joy is found here! Every wish is replenished with full draughts of vital pleasure such as elevate angelick minds, and gratify the noblest faculties of immortal spirits. Oh Beville, my Almeria is as much superior to her former self here as I thought her superior to the rest of her sex upon earth.[14]

Almeria is a superior woman. Meeting her lover and taking him in her chariot to the land of love with its 'soft recesses where pleasure keeps its eternal festivals', she is a character who could have stepped out of the pages of Delarivier Manley's the *New Atalantis* or *Rivella*, or out of Eliza Haywood's *Love in Excess*.

Reading these books it is hard to uphold the distinction between the supposedly 'loose' purveyors of amatory fictions and the exemplars of moral respectability. Furthermore, any simple distinction is complicated by the uses the women themselves made of it. In reading women's texts, we imbibe along with them the fierce ideological and commercial battles of which they were part. In 1720, when Delarivier Manley produced *The Power of Love in Seven Novels* (mostly adaptations from French and Italian novels in Elizabethan translations), she offered them not as political scandal or even erotic delight but as ancient history, factual and true, the recovery of which was implicitly moral in itself. 'These novels,' she explained in the dedication, 'have truth for their foundation; several of the facts are to be found in ancient history, to which, adding divers new incidents, I have attempted in modern English to draw them out of obscurity.'

Manley and Haywood, no less than Aubin and Rowe, claimed that their tales were 'moral' as well as 'entertaining'. In practice, the distinction might depend less on the nature of the texts produced than on fantasies about the lives lived by their authors, some of which were carefully encouraged by those texts. It is likely that Elizabeth Rowe's awareness of the potential for inconvenient comparisons lent force to her insistence on the charms of rural solitude. For women writers, 'moral' and 'immoral' could easily be reduced to place of residence: the open innocent spaces of a country estate versus the close, confined, hectic rush of the town where speed and luxury and 'interest' and clamour signified moral confusion. In everyday speech, a woman of the town was a prostitute. Prostitution was a resource for vast numbers of women. The slippage of language between being on the town with a body for sale and on the town with books for sale was inevitable as the commercial market for women writers opened up.

Mrs Rowe's *Devout Exercises of the Heart*

Managing relationships with men who might be readers, writers, relations, close friends, lovers, editors, fellow scholars or booksellers was an important element in the life of a woman of letters. The married Katherine Philips's 'happy intimacy' and 'virtuous friendship' with Sir Charles Cotterell was an example of one that was successfully managed, both at the time and subsequently when it was available for use as an example to others. We don't know how Elizabeth Singer viewed her relationship with Matthew Prior, nor with John Dunton. We can only speculate about what she wanted from her poems and the way Dunton and others presented them. But we do know that she was keen to be published and welcomed the recognition that followed, and that Dunton was not the only bookseller she dealt with, nor Prior the only male writer.

Isaac Watts met Elizabeth Singer when she was already celebrated. She may have been in London in the early years of the century and met him there, or he may have met her in Bath. Like Prior, he was a fellow poet; unlike Prior, he became a trusted friend and, later, the editor of a posthumous collection of her manuscripts, the *Devout Exercises of the Heart* (1737), which was to be a popular devotional manual throughout the eighteenth century. Watts did much to keep Elizabeth Singer Rowe in the public eye, taking over from John Dunton in some ways and championing her as a poet who could help reform a national literature that had drifted away from its Christian origins.

In his preface to *Devout Exercises of the Heart*, Watts admitted that he had sometimes toned down her verses: 'Here and there a too venturous flight is a little moderated.' Watts was a populariser and he understood his audience. He set *Devout Exercises* in a historical context to offset possible criticism, explaining that 'it was much the fashion in former years, even among some divines of eminence, to express the fervours of devout love to our Saviour in the style of the Song of Solomon'. This, he now thought, was not 'the happiest language' for Christians.

Isaac Watts distanced himself from old-fashioned unconscious sexual sublimation in religious writing but he was still keen to promote Elizabeth Singer Rowe as a sexually exciting woman author. Some souls, he wrote, were 'favoured with such beautifying visits from heaven, and raptured with such a flame of divine affection, as more powerfully engages all animal nature in their devotions, and constrains them to speak their purest and most spiritual exercises in such pathetic and tender expressions as may be perversely prophaned by unholy construction'. She was 'spiritual' and pure but readers were reading perverse and unholy meanings into her work. Watts went on to offer a defence of Mrs Rowe's tendency to be 'a little too rapturous, and too near akin to the language of the mystical writers' based on her proven sexual attractiveness. She was a sexually fulfilled woman, much desired by men, and her full experience of human love was evidence to counter any suspicion that her 'secret and intense breathings after God' were sexual in an earthly sense. This reasoning managed to preserve both the ardent earthly lover and the religious. It was a thoroughly successful combination: *Devout Exercises* was in its sixth edition by 1754 and public demand for it stayed high throughout the eighteenth century and well into the nineteenth. The British Library catalogue alone lists twenty-four separate editions.

When Elizabeth Rowe's family and friends gathered her manuscripts together to produce a fitting memorial to a superior woman, they distinguished between 'slothful' or 'monastic' kinds of devotion, 'unprofitable to the world' and *her* preference for the 'silence and quiet of solitude'. Her retirement was not self-centred in the way a 'monastic' retirement might be; it had a social dimension and was a means of doing good. She was able to support her charities as well as 'composing those works with which she has obliged the public, which, as they inspire the noblest sentiments of benevolence and piety, may be of the most lasting and extensive benefit to mankind'.

Writing was an activity which might oblige the public; monastic devotions were 'unprofitable'. That certain women might write books that were of 'benefit to mankind' had become a cultural commonplace by the end of the 1730s when the *Life of Mrs Rowe* was published. Rowe's biographers nostalgically and affectionately evoked the bright young poet at the same time as they put the wise moralist before the reader. The *Life of Mrs Rowe* presented her as an object of worship, the adored centre of a self-confident genteel network. The addition of some account of Thomas Rowe's life – 'Mr Rowe knew how to value that treasure of wit, softness and virtue, which the divine providence had given to his arms in the most lovely of women' – and a selection of his poems, helped the reader understand how to value the 'exalted' subject. The point of an exemplary memoir was to inspire emulation. As Mrs Rowe's biographer put it, praising those of 'extraordinary accomplishments' has a 'strangely animating' impact on those of like mind.

We cannot know what most eighteenth- and nineteenth-century readers took from Elizabeth Rowe, but we know that she was widely read, her books adopted as aids to devotion, part of the prayer and meditation regimes of individuals in congregations up and down the land. Elizabeth Carter was typical in this respect: she read her Bible every day and supplemented her personal study of religion by reading sermons and writings, like those of Mrs Rowe, which helped her 'acquire the temper and practise the duties of a Christian life'. We know, too, that the idea of duty and usefulness, of not only obliging the public but leading it, was a powerful justification for female authorship in the mid century, driving the production of didactic texts of every description and helping to construct the young – especially the female young – and the foolish – especially the female foolish – as needy reading publics. It may be that the glowing tributes to Rowe for being a writer and doing what writers do, which included knowing best about how she should spend her time, had a specially animating effect on readers who were neither foolish nor needy but keen to be writers themselves.

Chapter Seven

SUSANNAH CENTLIVRE
AND CATHARINE TROTTER

But do not imagine, that women are to be considered only as objects of your pleasure, as the fine gentlemen of the world seem, by their conduct, to do. There is nothing more unjust, more base, and barbarous, than is often practised towards them, under the specious names of love and gallantry; as if they had not an equal right, with those of the other sex, to be treated with justice and honour.

    Catharine Trotter Cockburn, 'Letter of Advice to her Son'[1]

Platonic ladies

In 1706, Susannah Centlivre dedicated her play *The Platonick Lady* 'To all the generous encouragers of female ingenuity', announcing that she hoped to find 'some souls great enough' to protect her against 'the carping malice of the vulgar world who think it a proof of sense to dislike everything that is writ by women'. She claimed she had met with prejudice on that account; people had said her plays were really written by a man. 'Nay, even my own sex, which should assert our prerogative against such detractors, are often backward to encourage a female pen.'[2]

How far this was true to experience and how far a rhetorical strategy (appealing to the 'natural' good sense of the great against the vulgar lower classes and women) is impossible to say. With the aid of an energetic literary coterie, Susannah Centlivre, orphaned daughter of a parliamentarian family that had suffered badly after the Restoration, had risen from almost nothing to become a well-received dramatist. For her, the 'encouragers of female ingenuity' in the immediate sense were her friends Anthony Hammond, Charles Gildon, George Farquhar, Samuel Garth, John Oldmixon and others with whom she published (using the pen name of Astraea) in *Familiar and Courtly Letters* (1700) and *Letters of Wit* (1701), collections that mixed wit and politics with gallantry, raillery with intimacy, and the posturing of lovers with the puncturing of romantic illusion. Like Katherine Philips's Society of Friendship, the members of the coterie all had pen names – Daphne, Chloë, Celadon, Damon – some of whom can be identified: 'Daphne' was the playwright Jane Wiseman, George Farquhar was 'Damon' and also 'Celadon'. Centlivre began corresponding with Farquhar after sending him a complimentary poem on *The Constant Couple*. In the second volume of *Familiar and Courtly Letters* there are seven 'familiar' letters between Celadon and Astraea, four by him and three by her, which may have drawn on this exchange, and which begin in courtly love mode and become explicitly sexual. The lady, seemingly angry, breaks off the correspondence. In real life, Centlivre and Farquhar remained friends and he wrote the prologue for *The Platonick Lady*.

Centlivre seems to have had some education during her Lincolnshire childhood, but she left home early and made her way to London, apparently with the intention of becoming a strolling actress. She was more or less destitute when she was picked up on the wayside by Anthony Hammond, then a poetry-writing student at Oxford. Hammond took her to Oxford with him and installed her in his rooms where she put her acting talents to use: they disguised her as a boy and pretended she was his 'cousin Jack'. She seems to have spent several months in residence there. John Mottley, who collaborated with Centlivre on *A Bold Stroke* and whose *A List of all the Dramatic Authors* provides contemporary biographical detail, explained that Hammond had been 'so much moved with her story and the simple and affecting manner in which she related it, and more especially with her lovely shape and features, that he found himself so attached to her person and interest, that he could not think of parting with her . . . he therefore entreated her to put herself under his protection, which after some modest and faint reluctance she consented to'. She blossomed, apparently, in the improving atmosphere of conversation, sex and books; and as an actress who had a masculine air and specialised in breeches parts, she carried off the disguise with ease. When she left

Oxford, Hammond gave her 'a handsome present of gold' and a letter of introduction to a woman friend.

'From her first coming to London,' Mottley tells us, 'she took care to improve both the charms of her person and her genius.'[3] It was probably through Hammond that Centlivre first became acquainted with her London literary friends. Her story was evidently no secret: it was told as an amusing theatrical anecdote, an 'adventure' of early life that demonstrated wit, talent and laudable self-improvement. As a lone female of 'lovely shape and features', the young actress/writer had been an object of benevolence capable of inspiring warm feelings in those who contemplated her. An actress who gave pleasure when she dressed as a man on stage gave no less pleasure when offered to the imagination performing in the character of an Oxford student.

By the end of 1700, when she was in her early thirties, Susannah Carroll (as she then was) was well established in London. Her first play was a moderate success and it was printed with her name on the title page. Between 1700 and 1707 she went on to write eight plays, a number of which entered the repertoire and went on being performed until well into the next century. Perhaps they failed to make much money, for she continued to take parts as a strolling actress. The influence of Jeremy Collier, whose *A Short View of the Immorality and Profanity of the Restoration Stage* (1698) attacked Dryden, Congreve, Wycherley and others for promoting vice, meant it was a difficult time to be a playwright. Tragedy was considered more morally uplifting than comedy, but Centlivre's gift was for comedy. She inherited a tradition established at the Restoration which depended heavily on audience recognition of familiar stereotypes: the cuckold and the coquette, the wit, the City merchant and (especially) his wife, the country wife, the country cousin come to town and revealing his boorish ignorance, the fop and the prude. Plot lines, too, were familiar and built around seductions, cuckoldry and machinations for money. In the prologue and epilogue to *The Perjur'd Husband* (1700), Centlivre mentioned Collier by name, aligning herself with the movement against immorality in stage representations, and claiming that the stage merely copied life: if people would reform, then the stage would be a reformed place also.[4]

The tone of Centlivre's dedications and prefaces was not unlike the tone of some of her dialogues in which the comic effect was achieved through parodic exaggeration of clichés, such as 'a female pen', our 'prerogative' and our 'detractors'. By 1706, when she wrote *The Platonick Lady*, the association of platonic love with intellectual women and the men friends who encouraged their ingenuity was one more cliché: the serious-minded woman had joined the ranks of stereotypes. We can read in the dedication a sardonic reference to men like John Norris, John Dunton and John Locke who publicly supported women's claims to sense and souls and whom Centlivre mocked when in *The Platonick Lady* she had a character like Belvil quote Cowley.

Credit for the post-Restoration introduction of the learned lady as a stage figure of fun might go to Aphra Behn whose Lady Knowell, in *Sir Patient Fancy* (1678), was drawn from Molière's *Les Femmes savantes* (1672). In Centlivre's *The Basset Table* (1705), a play which depicts a coffee house where gambling went on as well as discussion (and which features a female gamester), there is a modern young lady, Valeria, who is too much occupied with her scientific work to be available for love. Busy with experiments on frogs, fishes and flies, coolly dissecting her pet dove – 'what did you imagine I bred it up for? Can animals, insects or reptiles be put to a nobler use than to improve our knowledge?' – and glued to her microscope, she is not the wife for Hearty, the sea captain her father favours. Ensign Lovely, however, is willing to examine the tapeworm Valeria has taken from the inside of a dog and, because he wants to marry her, helps fish her eels out of the vinegar she uses to preserve them.

In this comedy of manners, the message is that love wins over science and this is a good thing, but our sympathies remain with Valeria. Mockingly advised, 'you should bestow your fortune in founding a college for the study of philosophy, where none but women should be admitted', Valeria simply replies, 'What you make a jest of, I'd execute, were fortune in my power.'[5]

The best-known caricature of a writing woman from this period, however, is Phoebe Clinket in Pope, Arbuthnot and Gay's very funny *Three Hours After a Marriage* (1717). Phoebe Clinket wears a writing desk strapped to her back so that her maid can write down her thoughts as they occur, wherever they occur. In a 'key' to the play, published a few months after it was performed, Anne Finch was named as the inspiration for Phoebe Clinket: this character 'is designed to ridicule the Countess of W—n—ea who, Pope says, is so much given to writing of verses that she keeps a standish in every room of the house, that she may immediately clap down her thoughts, whether upon pindaric, heroic, pastoral or dramatic subjects'.

Pope was, as we have seen, an admirer of Finch's verse, a personal friend and, by 1717, when he was lodging with the painter Charles Jervas in St James's (he was taking art lessons from Jervas), a neighbour and regular dining guest. The 'key' was part of a sustained pamphlet attack on Pope, probably instigated by Edmund Curll. Other attempts have been made to suggest originals for Phoebe Clinket in Susannah Centlivre, and, more tenuously, Lady Mary Wortley Montagu, but it is a futile exercise. The impetus of the farce in *Three Hours After a Marriage* is generalised rather than personal, and not specially gendered except in attributing negative feminine characteristics to writerly stereotypes. Phoebe Clinket is as much a satire on the writing self as on female writers, just as the play as a whole is a satire on writing as much as marriage. Indeed, it could be argued that the choice of a female in this role reflects the taken-for-granted presence of women in the literary world rather than an effort to warn them off. Meanwhile, the naming of the Countess of Winchilsea in the 'key' (a number of 'keys' were published) reflected political factionalism and her prominence as a writer. Pope had to do much smoothing in the months that followed, placating friends for what he referred to as not his but 'Gay's play' which cost him 'much time and long suffering to stem a tide of malice and party, that certain authors have raised against it'. Anne Finch did her best to keep aloof from the pamphlet wars of the time. She left no comment on this episode, but we can assume it did not damage her friendship with Pope: her commendatory poems were included by Pope in his *Works* published later that year, and there were other poems by her in *Poems on Several Occasions* which Pope edited.

Centlivre's *The Platonick Lady* made fun of cant of every kind – cant about country innocence, love, and about female philosophising – or 'platonic' talk. The play is about love and money: Sharper, who cannot pay his man Equipage's wages, comes to town chasing a Somersetshire widow, Mrs Dowdy, worth £50,000; Lucinda, meanwhile, in love with

Belvil, is the platonic lady. To win her, Belvil utters the platitudes of platonic love in a comic scene written in such a way that the actor could be enacting what he vows to renounce – he could be trying to 'kiss those rosy lips' while assuring Lucinda he will not; he could be pressing 'that soft white hand' and sighing his soul out on the actress's very 'bosom'. Centlivre's skilful use of dramatic irony turns a scene of virtue into a scene of seduction in which the woman is an eager participant. The exchange leads inexorably to the word 'yield':

> LUCINDA: I hate a false prude that won't know a gentleman in company, tho three hours before she had held private conference with him in her bedchamber; that solemnly declares she never writ or received a billet doux in her life, and knows at the same time she keeps a woman on purpose for the business.
>
> BELVIL: Like your reforming ladies, who all the while they are giving a young fellow advice against wenching, their looks insinuate a liking to his person.
>
> LUCINDA: Or Mrs Prim the poetical she-philosopher, whose discourse and writings are filled with honour and strict rules of virtue; that vows she could not sleep if she was guilty of one criminal thought . . .
>
> BELVIL: Oh! how I hate the noise of virtue in my ears from a woman – whom I know lives by vice; and 'tis a maxim with me – that she who rails most, yields soonest.[6]

The theatre was the most important source for the circulation of old and new female types. There was comedy to be drawn from bringing railing and yielding together, and false prudes, reforming ladies and poetical she-philosophers were offered up to town merriment along with tattling women, timid wives, gossips and platonics. The titles alone of Susannah Centlivre's three most acted comedies, *The Busie Body* (1709), *The Wonder! A Woman Keeps a Secret* (1714) and *A Bold Stroke for a Wife* (1718), not to mention *The Platonick Lady* itself, suggest how much of Centlivre's popularity rested on this comedy of female types.

Early plays like *The Perjur'd Husband*, *The Platonick Lady* and *The Gamester* were well received but *The Busie Body* was Centlivre's first major triumph. By then, having been married and widowed twice, she had married Joseph Centlivre, Yeoman of the Mouth (i.e. one of the cooks) in Queen Anne's household. Sociable, politically outspoken (a Whig and fierce anti-Jacobite), Centlivre kept up good relations with actors and audiences – she was careful never to criticise the players if her plays fell flat – retained her friendship with Hammond and other Whig writers, among them Richard Steele and the Poet Laureate, Nicholas Rowe (a distant relation of Elizabeth Rowe), to whom she addressed a delightful poem on his charms in 1718, congratulating his wife on her good fortune; and became a part of the coterie around Aaron Hill that included Ambrose Philips, Eliza Haywood and Martha Fowke Sansom.

A popular figure whose plays made people laugh, towards the end of her life Centlivre looked to the court and government for reward. Her support of the Hanoverians after 1714 led to command performances and considerable presents, but unlike a number of her male friends who were, like her, in the heart of Whigland and who were provided for under the new regime, she was rewarded with no institutional position and therefore had neither salary nor pension. (Joseph Addison, having been made Chief Secretary for Ireland and Lord Commissioner of Trade, retired in 1718 on a pension of £1,500.)

Accustomed to making her views known, in 1720 Susannah Centlivre published a long poem, *A Woman's Case*, in which she outlined her political services to the Whigs, a party famous for following Charles ii's maxim of advancing foes because friends would always be friends –

> But Whigs in place have still been known
> To help all parties but their own:
> To Charles the Second's maxim kind,
> Advance your foes, your friends ne'er mind

and made a plea for well-deserved provision. She depicted herself as a prominent Whig derided by the Tories for still being 'unprovided' for. Unlike the Whigs, she explained, who when in power 'want no scribblers on their side', the Tories 'kept their herd in constant pay' – including 'Some female wits of Tory strain'. Within the poem, which dramatised a matrimonial dispute on the subject, the complaint about the lack of provision was made by the husband. 'Spouse' is the one who is anxious about bills and disappointed by the rewards of his wife's literary endeavours:

> Deuce take your scribbling vein, quoth he,
> What did it ever get for me?
> Two years you take a play to write,
> And I scarce get my coffee by't.
> Such swingeing bills are still to pay
> For sugar, chocolate, and tea,
> I shall be forc'd to run away.
> You made me hope the Lord knows what,
> When Whigs should rule, of this, and that,
> But from your boasted friends I see
> Small benefit accrues to me:
> I hold my place indeed, 'tis true;
> But I well hop'd to rise by you.[7]

As a cook in the royal household, Joseph Centlivre's position was at risk if his wife caused royal offence. But she had never been in danger of doing that; after the Protestant succession in 1714, she was so well known for her eulogistic verses that she was congratulated in the press. The *Patriot* in January 1715 carried this commendation: 'upon the subject of female resolution and virtue, I cannot forbear mentioning the name of Mrs Susanna Centlivre, a woman, whose good sense and noble passion for the Protestant succession in the present illustrious family, make her an honour to her sex, and a credit to our country'. Joseph Centlivre's disappointed hope of rising by his wife is an index of what could reasonably be expected by one who was 'an honour to her sex, and a credit to our country'.[8]

A poetical she-philosopher

The mixed message put out by Susannah Centlivre was characteristic of the time: the use on the one hand of a proto-feminist rhetoric lamenting the lack of encouragement for 'a female pen' and blaming 'my own sex' for failing to come forward in support; and on the other, an unabashed resort to *ad feminam* attack. In *The Platonick Lady*, many would have recognised in 'Mrs Prim the poetical she-philosopher' Catharine Trotter (later Cockburn) whose book on John Locke, *A Defence of the Essay of Human Understanding*, had been published in 1702, and who was a sister playwright.

Churchmen like Thomas Birch and Thomas Sharp, the Archdeacon of Northumberland and Prebendary of Durham, who became interested in the philosopher Catharine Cockburn in the 1730s and 1740s and helped raise support for the edition of her *Works* which appeared in 1751, did not remind mid-century readers of Cockburn's earlier career as the dramatist Catharine Trotter nor mention that she had been reviled in print by both Susannah Centlivre and Delarivier Manley. It is possible that they didn't know, but more likely that they chose not to investigate on the grounds that philosophy was virtuous (it was an activity of the mind) and theatre not.

For the theatregoing public of the late 1690s and early 1700s, Catharine Trotter, Delarivier Manley and Susannah Centlivre, along with Mary Pix, were very much associated.[9] They were regarded as the successors to Aphra Behn. Catharine Trotter's *Agnes de Castro* (based on a novel by Aphra Behn) had been one of five new plays by three women dramatists in the 1695–6 season which had inspired a satire, *The Female Wits*, in which Trotter, as Calista, was depicted as a hypocritical prude. The other two 'wits' made fun of were Delarivier Manley and Mary Pix, respectively 'Marsilia', a kept woman, and 'Mrs Wellfed', fat, good-natured and fond of wine. Aggressively ambitious, all three were to go on to have successful careers which *The Female Wits* probably helped advance.[10] They were friends and mutually supportive in these early years, although Delarivier Manley's cruel satire of Katherine Philips in *The Lost Lover* (1696) as hypocritical, affected, shallow and self-important was a foretaste of what she would later do to Catharine Trotter. In 1695, Manley provided a sonnet preface to *Agnes de Castro*, 'To the author of *Agnes de Castro*', which situated Trotter as the successor to Katherine Philips and Aphra Behn:

Orinda and the fair Astrea gone,
No-one was found to fill the vacant throne;
Aspiring man had quite regained the sway,
Again had taught us humbly to obey;
Till you (Nature's third start, in favour of our kind)
With stronger arms, their empires have disjoined,
And snatched a laurel which they thought their prize,
Thus conqueror with your wit as with your eyes.

Fired by the bold example, I would try
To turn our sexes weaker destiny.
Oh how I long in the poetic race,
To loose the reins, and give their glory chase;
For thus encouraged, and thus led by you,
Methinks we might more crowns than theirs subdue.

Similarly, Trotter and Pix both wrote militantly feminist commendatory verses for Manley's *The Royal Mischief* (the play which was the provocation for *The Female Wits*). Trotter hailed Manley as the champion of 'our sex' who had 'maintained our equal right in fame / To which vain man had quite engrossed the claim'.

Catharine Trotter and Mary Pix were associated with William Congreve and the theatre at Lincoln's Inn Fields and were caught up with him in theatrical rivalries and politics. When Mary Pix's comedy *The Deceiver Deceived* was plagiarised by George Powell of Drury Lane, Congreve staged it with a prologue attacking Powell for the theft. This produced a vicious counter-attack in which Trotter and Pix – 'these presuming two' – were depicted as sexually incontinent (Trotter) and insufferably dull (Pix). Congreve was shown sitting in the audience 'among his chief actors and actresses, together with the two she-things, called poetesses, which write for his house'.

Mary Pix was a merchant's wife, and if her characterisation in *The Female Wits* as Mrs Wellfed is anything to go by, she was sociable and well liked. Between 1696 and 1706 she wrote thirteen plays – six comedies and seven tragedies – all of which were staged. She was friends with the actors and actresses for whom she wrote lively parts; and she was close friends, and possibly a collaborator, with the equally prolific Susannah Centlivre. In 1709, after Pix's death, Centlivre organised a production of her own play, *The Busie Body*, as a benefit for Pix's estate.

Women represented a sizeable portion of the audience in the theatre. One French observer of 1698 distinguished between three groups: there were plenty of 'damsels that haunt for prey' in the pit, but among them were 'ladies of reputation and virtue'; and in the amphitheatre opposite the stage, where 'persons of the best quality' sat, the audience was mostly female: there were 'very few men'.[11] Women seem to have had some power as a pressure group and perhaps used it to cry down immorality. George Farquhar certainly thought so and appealed to one of the well-received women authors to help him out. He sent Catharine Trotter his first comedy, *Love and a Bottle*, complaining that it had been 'scandalously aspersed for affronting the ladies' and so 'as an argument of its innocence, he sent it to stand its trial before one of the fairest of the sex, and the best judge'. And anyway, he added, it was his way of showing his gratitude that she had come to his third night even though she didn't know him personally. Farquhar then admitted that his true intention was simply to introduce himself; she was established, he was trying to make his name known.[12]

Charles Gildon, who in 1696 wrote his *Memoirs on the Life of Mrs Behn*, as the preface to the first edition of *The Histories and Novels of the Late Ingenious Mrs Behn*, went so far as to adopt a female persona. The title page claimed that the *Memoirs* had been written by 'One of the Fair Sex', who went on to explain:

> My intimate acquaintance with the admirable Astrea, gave me, naturally, a very great esteem for her; for it both freed me from that folly of my sex of envying or slighting excellencies I could not obtain; and inspired me with a noble fire to celebrate that woman, who was an honour and glory to our sex; and this re-printing her incomparable novels, presented me with a lucky occasion of exerting that desire into action.

Aphra Behn could be promoted as 'an honour and glory' for multiple purposes, as Gildon's ventriloquised 'female' author so alert to 'the folly of my sex' makes clear. In the 1699 *Lives and Characters of the English Dramatick Poets* (begun by Langbaine and completed by Gildon) Gildon produced some more platitudes. Behn was a 'lady [who] has very happily distinguished herself from the rest of her sex, and gives us a living proof of what we might reasonably expect from womankind, if they had the benefit of those artificial improvements of learning the men have'. The terms in which individual women were praised invariably incorporated blame of 'womankind' as a whole. For a woman to be distinguished was to be 'distinguished from the rest of her sex' among whom folly and envy and lack of learning prevailed. Meanwhile, wishing to be distinguished could always be represented as a (bad) 'womanly' wish that emanated from 'the folly of my sex'.

As Calista in the satire *The Female Wits*, Catharine Trotter was 'a lady that pretends to the learned languages, and assumes to herself the name of a critic'. In fact, the learned languages were not Trotter's particular concern, although she had been tutored in Latin; they served the satire as a shorthand for scholarship, and minus the denigratory modifiers – 'pretends to', 'assumes to herself' – they provide an accurate enough introduction: Trotter was a serious intellectual with a lifelong interest in religious and philosophical issues.[13] Philosophers and theologians took her very seriously indeed, not only, as we have seen, in the mid century when she was recuperated but also in her own time. Her major work of philosophy which established her reputation as a thinker was an intervention into an ongoing debate. John Locke's *Essay Concerning Human Understanding* of 1690 had involved him in an extensive pamphlet war with Bishop Stillingfleet. Stillingfleet published a series of *Remarks*, the last of which appeared in 1699. By 1701, Catharine Trotter had completed and published her *Defense of the Essay of Human Understanding*, a detailed philosophical rebuttal of these *Remarks*. Locke himself read and was pleased with the *Defense* and wrote to thank her for it, acknowledging at the same time that it was no shame to him to be linked with her in the public mind: 'as the world take notice of the strength and clearness of your reasoning, so I cannot but be extremely sensible that it was employed in my defence'.

The *Defense of the Essay of Human Understanding* had been published anonymously, but as was often the case the author's identity was quickly revealed. Trotter sent a copy to Elizabeth Burnet, wife of Gilbert Burnet, Bishop of Salisbury. Elizabeth Burnet's *Method of Devotion* had passed through a number of editions and she was well known as an intellectual woman in contact with intellectual men. From her hands the book passed to her husband, to John Norris, and to John Locke himself. All these men liked what they read, so Elizabeth Burnet told them who had written it, took due note of their responses and then reported back to Catharine Trotter. That the author was a woman was inevitably a matter for comment: 'it is not without difficulty some can believe, that anyone, not bred to science and logic in particular, could be capable of so close and clear reasoning'. Difficult or not, they did believe it (Elizabeth Burnet was herself an example, as was Elizabeth of Bohemia and Damaris Masham – though it could be argued that Masham, as the daughter of the Cambridge Platonist, Ralph Cudworth, *had* been 'bred to science and logic') and concurred with Burnet in her good wishes for the author's future writings: 'I heartily wish you may improve to the best uses such excellent talents, that nothing may obscure their lustre.' Burnet praised Trotter's style and tone in a comment that reflected her own reading and was implicitly critical of customary modes of philosophical disputation. She admired the way the *Defense* was 'written short and clear, without affectation of wit or eloquence, needless reflections on your adversary, or making him more in the wrong than he is'.[14]

The Bishop of Salisbury and his wife also praised Trotter's plays. They, unlike the general theatregoing population, admired her comic talents, which was a pleasant surprise. (Trotter crowed: 'I may prefer the judgement of two such persons to the rash censures of a giddy multitude.') But her correspondent Thomas Burnet of Kemnay (a distant cousin of the Bishop – there were many Burnets) thought all playwriting was beneath her. He was glad to hear that when she left town for the winter, she turned to more 'contemplative' studies. He wanted her to quit 'fictitious and poetical' writing, for 'the more serious and solid; especially knowing perfectly the strength of your genius that way; and that particular inclination and fame both together seem to invite you to raise your reputation by this new and untrodden path'. When she had discussed with him her plan to write the 'apology' for Locke, he advised that it needed careful consideration. It would be 'a nice and important subject'. There was the fact of her 'sex and years' to be taken into account; and that she would be writing

in defence of such an aged philosopher, and whose notions have not been thought by many to have done the best service to religion, I know not what to say, that may be cautiously enough contrived for taking off all suspicion of vanity, novelty, or too great curiosity of examining sacred things rather by the principles of philosophy than by the balance of the sanctuary.[15]

The principles of philosophy – as something available to the minds of all individuals, male and female, clerical and lay – were exactly what concerned Trotter. Burnet warned her that she should 'insert something of a strain of orthodox sentiments in theology' just in case people got the wrong idea about her own beliefs; and he suggested that if the main part of the text didn't make it clear that she (unlike Locke) was thoroughly committed to religious values – or, as Burnet put it, 'if there be little divinity sprinkled up and down the work itself' – she could probably do what was necessary by writing a long preface with sufficient divinity in it. If she still wasn't sure, he recommended she ask a Mr Cunningham of Salisbury who would be able to direct her. (In a later letter Burnet revised his opinion of Mr Cunningham's good sense, lamenting that Cunningham had 'too much of a metaphysical brain; his notions are so subtle, that they will spend his days like the silk-working in spinning them out. And his projecting is so vast and wide always, and his conversation and acquaintance so various and numerous, that it is no wonder that he hath never time for execution.')

The quality of thought revealed in Trotter's *Defense of the Essay of Human Understanding* brought widespread and lasting praise. A female dramatist like Susannah Centlivre might mock her as 'Mrs Prim the poetical she-philosopher' but men of philosophical mind were happy to introduce her into their circles. Evidently, her identity as a published woman of letters gave her a measure of autonomy, enabling her to choose to live alone in London for the sake of her work, or go to Salisbury or elsewhere when she liked; to engage in correspondence and receive visits from men, some of whom might have a sexual interest in her.

Trotter's 'sex and years' – being young and unmarried – were, as Burnet pointed out, facts that had to be taken into account. Marriage clearly represented some risk to intellectual development since a wife's duty was not to think but to obey. Friendship was more open, equal and inclusive; it allowed for the dignity of the female mind. There was a long tradition of well-born women engaging in correspondence networks with intellectual men, in which the 'monopolizing' tendencies of the heart (which led to marriage) were the negative that could be set against the more 'beneficent' effects of friendship. Catharine Trotter explained to Thomas Burnet that she had 'all the sense I ought of your concern to secure my friendship' and that there was 'a due esteem and gratitude for every degree of merit and kindness we observe in our friends'. Love was 'that niggard passion' that 'excludes all but one object from having a part of it, and is not satisfied without monopolizing the affections of the heart'. Marriage was an institution to approach with great caution: 'I have been always very fearful of putting my happiness entirely in the power of anyone.' Though she was young and unmarried, Catharine Trotter could offer friendship with easy freedom:

> You may depend upon finding me willing to contribute all I can to your satisfaction; and that I shall always use your confidence in me with the sincerity and faithfulness becoming a friend, and a Christian; nor will there be any difficulty for you to visit me, when you please. I know not of any occasion that will remove me soon from the lodgings I still have in Beaufort Buildings, where I am at present (as I shall be all the summer, and perhaps the winter) more alone than I have been of a long time; for my sister and I have not parted in a year and a half till last June she returned to Sarum [Salisbury], whither she would have had me with her; but I have so little time to myself, when I am in the family, that I found my writing go on very slowly; so resolved to stay till I have finished what I am about in a place where I am as solitary as I can wish; for most of my acquaintance are out of town.[16]

Trotter had been in correspondence with Thomas Burnet since at least 1701. As well as taking advice from him before publishing her *Defense*, she borrowed books and philosophical pamphlets from him. Burnet was an ardent Protestant and Trotter a Catholic convert whom he hoped to persuade back to Protestantism. He also seems to have been nursing some romantic hopes.

Thomas Burnet had left England for the Continent in the autumn of 1701 and he and Trotter exchanged letters at least until 1708 when Trotter married the Revd Patrick Cockburn. From their correspondence, we can piece together some glimpses of the scope of a woman of letters at the beginning of the eighteenth century, what she felt entitled to think and say to a man designated an intellectual friend. Many of their exchanges were about religion. Trotter approached the question of religious communion from the point of view of a philosopher, governed by the desire to make choices based on logical principles. She frequently reminded Thomas Burnet that his arguments were not consistent with themselves, or that the conclusions he drew did not correspond to the grounds he had laid out. Paragraphs of logical exposition might begin, 'I see not how upon your principles...' or, 'To be consistent with yourself, you must establish some surer rules of determining what are essential articles and what are not...' Religious controversy in itself did not interest her. She thought moral duty the important part of religion and that it should permeate daily life in an easy and natural way. She heartily disliked the rigidity of the Geneva Calvinists whom Burnet praised to her, suspecting they were 'precise in their forms and outward discipline' while being 'most negligent of the moral duties'. She explained, 'I have observed this so often both in private persons, and public societies, that I am apt to suspect it everywhere,' and went on: 'Certainly an easy turn of words, a free action, and cheerful countenance, are not inconsistent with religion; and, as far as that will allow, I think all pious Christians ought to conform themselves to the air of the world, as the good St Paul became all things to all.'

Some of Trotter's trust in her own observation of life, her respect for the airs of 'the world', came from her experience as a successful dramatist, and some from her financially straitened upbringing. A Londoner of Scottish parentage with high-ranking connections, she was the daughter of a naval officer in favour with Charles II. His death at sea during her childhood left her mother dependent on a royal pension that was never secure and often not paid. Furthermore, her father's effects and booty money were all lost to them. Much time and energy was spent in petitioning those whose interest might serve to restore or recompense. As a little girl whose genius was early apparent and whose 'forwardness of her wit' was encouraged – an uncle remarked 'what satisfaction it would have given her father, if he had been living, as he had a peculiar taste and love for poetry' – she would have had plenty of opportunity to observe the gap between precise outward forms and genuine morality.

Trotter's earliest known verses were sent in 1693 to the poet Bevil Higgons, who had recently recovered from smallpox. She went into print in the same year with an epistolary novella which took love and seduction as its theme and proposed platonic relationships as the ideal. *The Adventures of a Young Lady* appeared in a collection entitled *Letters of Love and Gallantry and Several Other Subjects. All Written by Ladies.* That they were on the subject of love and 'written by ladies' gave them commercial appeal while at the same time suggesting a female perspective on love and gallantry in which the men were likely to be dupes: the 'gallant' or rake with a high opinion of himself was a familiar type in Restoration comedy, as was the witty woman. Trotter's fiction offered a rational and prudent heroine, Olinda, a platonic male friend, Cleander, and a gallery of irrational, mercenary and generally unimpressive men. *Agnes de Castro* followed in 1695, and there were four more successfully staged and printed dramas between *Agnes de Castro* and Trotter's last play, *The Revolution of Sweden*, in 1706.

A discourse of friendship, which articulated the view that the proper conduct of a friendship required the control of the rational mind, served women well. Trotter's use of the word 'monopolizing' in describing 'that niggard passion', love, served to downgrade sexual love and the narrowness of marriage, in preference to the open arena of friendship. Clearly this was a strategy (conscious or unconscious) to make other freedoms available, not licentious freedoms but the freedom to be seen in ways other than sexual. Once it had been acknowledged that a woman was indeed in possession of a rational mind, she might command a freedom to conduct her friendships as she considered fit. This freedom might be jeopardised if she failed in the important task of ordering the relation of head and heart, using her reason to control her own 'monopolizing' feelings. (For Trotter, as for other intellectual women throughout the eighteenth century, the job of resistance was seen as an internal responsibility, psychic not social: it was not a risk of *being monopolised by* any single man but of being overcome by one's own feelings.)

As Thomas Burnet travelled about on the Continent, he reported back on his encounters with literary and philosophical thinkers. In Paris there was much new writing 'though never anything almost that deserves to be read', and plays and other entertainment at court which he enjoyed – the *Electra* of Sophocles, something by Euripides. On the subject of the ancient Greeks,

I must not omit, that the famous Madam Dacier is putting out a work that will eternise her memory, and enrich the stock of learning also exceedingly. It is a new edition of Homer, in Greek and French I think, with many learned and critical remarks, which will make the book of two volumes in folio. I had the account from herself, and have been obliged to her own and her husband's acquaintance for one of the best conversations I have had at Paris. It is but the least and shortest thing can be said of her, that she never had, nor has her match for a woman in true and useful learning, and that to the highest degree, and is a good reasoner to the boot.[17]

Madam Dacier apart, women's 'true and useful learning' could sometimes appear to be doubted by even such enthusiasts as Thomas Burnet. When he wrote in 1704, soon after the death of John Locke, to tell Trotter that Leibnitz, with whom Burnet had become friendly at the court of Hanover, had received philosophical letters – 'philosophical in reasoning' – from Lady Masham, he commented, 'It is like the hand of Joab was in all these: however, Mr Leibnitz has not spared to answer her very home in his last.' Trotter wanted more details. She understood Burnet to be implying that Damaris Masham had merely been reproducing somebody else's reasoning – presumably, mouthing what the ghost of Locke might have said – and she objected:

I wish to know on what particular subjects that lady wrote to Mr Leibnitz; but whatever they were, I wonder you should suspect any other hand than her own in it. It is not to be doubted that women are as capable of penetrating into the grounds of things, and reasoning justly, as men are, who certainly have no advantage of us but in their opportunities of knowledge. And as Lady Masham is allowed by everybody to have great natural endowments, she has taken pains to improve them; and no doubt profited much by a long intimate society with so extraordinary a man as Mr Locke. So that I see no reason to suspect a woman of her character would pretend to write anything that was not entirely her own. I pray be more equitable to her sex than the generality of yours are; who, when anything is written by a woman that they cannot deny their approbation to, are sure to rob us of the glory of it by concluding 'tis not her own; or at least that she had some assistance, which has been said in many instances to my knowledge unjustly.[18]

Both observation of things said 'in many instances to my knowledge unjustly' and reason could be mobilised against the usual tendency of men to refuse to give credit to women. Trotter's reasoning was grounded in knowledge of the world. Several decades later she was to mount a defence of Elizabeth Thomas (far more vulnerable than Lady Masham) against unthinking malice, drawing on a similar combination of weighty reasoning and assertions drawn from her own experience. Trotter's 'I see no reason to suspect a woman of her character...' carried all the gravitas of a philosopher whose reasoning on John Locke was admired by the reasoning males who unreasonably suspected her sister philosopher, while at the same time it incorporated a worldly knowledge of the characters of women and men that any successful dramatist might be expected to have.

Catharine Trotter was well supported in her dramatic and philosophical work. The tone of her prefaces and dedications – the public address system for a dramatist – was dignified and authoritative. In the preface to *The Unhappy Penitent* in 1701 she offered an essay on English writing for the theatre, assuming to herself the name of a critic and including herself in elevated company: Dryden was 'the most universal genius which this nation ever bred'; Shakespeare copied nature (this was already the standard line); and with references to Boileau, Cardinal Richelieu and others, which showed the range of her reading, she assessed more recent times – Otway, Lee – and explained that the drama existed to instruct as well as delight. The theatre was under severe attack by moralists at this time so insisting on its instructive capacities was pragmatic. In Trotter's case, an emphasis on morality and rational behaviour, and especially on women's capacity to act from reasoned principle rather than uncontrolled passion, was central to her work.

Also in the preface, Trotter posed the question whether love was a sufficient subject for tragedy. Love in this case meant sexual passion and its disruptive effects, but it also referred more broadly to private interest and impassioned belief. In arguing for something larger than love, Trotter reached out to public political issues: what was the moving principle in society, and how was the state to be governed – by principled morality or by private expediency driven by lust or greed? In her life, however, she found herself having to argue *for* rather than *against* amorous passion when her soon-to-be husband Patrick Cockburn was apparently drawn towards celibacy.[19] She explained to him that she could not accept that 'to resolve against pleasure, or taking delight in such persons as are worthy of our esteem, is any part of

Christian wisdom'. The Stoics might have taken that route, but they were pagans. God designed humans and gave them their nature, which included sexual pleasure, that pleasure 'which we find ourselves inclined to take in persons agreeable to us, for an incitement to the mutual duties of society'. This was 'friendship joined with tenderness'. To his anxiety about losing self-control she offered mature assurance: 'you should not absolutely resolve against pleasure . . . it is not impossible that you may some time or other meet with one to pass your life with, whose conversation would at once unbend, and strengthen your mind, and whose tenderness would endear the little services, and sweeten your cares, without any danger of transporting you from yourself'. He should not let his fears deprive him of a satisfaction that might be rare but not impossible.

To argue for reason did not mean giving up passion; it was not necessary to be cold to be a moralist. Catharine Trotter took the initiative in her relationship with Cockburn, first by proposing that they correspond and then by making her reasoned feelings plain as their 'rational and religious friendship' developed. She made sure he knew there was a rival lover, Mr Fenn:

> all here tell me I have made a conquest of the young divine and I cannot say there was no appearance of it, though he said not a word about it, only saw me as often as possible whilst he stayed, which was just a week, professed to have greater satisfaction in my conversation than he ever had in any before &c, and sent me two books, which, when I talked of returning, I found were designed for presents.

And, since Cockburn was a friend of Thomas Burnet and knew of her correspondence with him, she mischievously made plain their relative value in her eyes: 'by the way I hope Mr Burnet does not know the size of my letters to you'.[20]

Staying in Surrey – 'in as profound a solitude as even you could wish for; the place very agreeable, and nothing wanting but a tender companion of our unbended hours to make it perfectly so to me' – she sent him on many commissions for her, some to do with books, some on matters of family interest. For all of these tasks, he was given meticulous instructions. As someone who had spent her life on the fringes of court and government, Trotter knew whom to approach and where to find them. Cockburn was told to search out 'Mr Potter' and deliver a letter to him on her nephew's behalf. Mr Potter was the agent for the minister at the War Office: 'he lives in Bedford Court, just in the angle on the right hand, as one goes into it from Bedford street, Covent garden; but he dines every day very near it, at the Rummer tavern in Henrietta street, at which time he is more certain to be found there than in any hour at home, and a man may, without inconvenience, enquire for him there'. Cockburn seems to have acquitted himself well, for she explained that she usually had cause to complain that people did not do things properly; she would always rather do them herself.[21]

In the summer of 1707, when the question of marriage began to press, Catharine Trotter was in her thirties and a respected woman of letters. Her return to the Protestant communion was probably not unconnected to her interest in Patrick Cockburn, but it also marked her appearance in print as a philosopher again. She was glad that Thomas Burnet liked what she had to say about religious toleration in *A Discourse Concerning a Guide in Controversies*, though she didn't expect her 'Letters' to be 'as convincing to those who need them' – meaning religious dogmatists and theological controversialists – since she knew too well 'the power of strong prejudices to hope for much effect from them, or greatly to wonder that others do not see what seems sufficiently plain to me'. Seeing clearly and devising systems that allowed for a full and satisfying rational religious life, based on principles that incorporated true morality of whatever doctrinal persuasion, was her objective.

Some passages of *A Discourse Concerning a Guide in Controversies* had been garbled in the printing. She asked Burnet to take some copies when he went to visit some friends of hers, setting down exactly how the eight lines should have read. She told him: 'You may, if you please, write this on the margin, and strike out seven lines in the book betwixt line 12 and line 20, and it would not be amiss to give notice of this fault to all you know, who have the book, if it can be without too much trouble.' As a professional writer and thinker, it mattered to her that the words should be read in exactly the form she had intended.

Having been in the public eye since 1696, by 1707 Catharine Trotter's social world encompassed theatre and literary circles, highly placed political families (these overlapped: her friend Harriot Godolphin, one of the daughters of the Duke and Duchess of Marlborough, was the lover of William Congreve), professional men and senior clergy. Churchmen sought her out: Thomas Burnet showed her writings on Locke to Leibnitz; Dr Denton Nicholas said she wrote 'more clearly and more effectually in half a sheet than Grotius in a whole volume'. She lived an independent life, sometimes in London, sometimes with her sister in Salisbury. She might choose where she wanted to be according to the demands of her work. When she was with the family her study time was precious and she would not interrupt it to write letters: 'I have so few hours at my command, that I am unwilling to interrupt my constant employment in those I am sure of, which I wholly give to some solid study.' But she could take herself off and live alone in London, where in the off-season it was as solitary as the country, or go to Surrey where there was society without family obligation. Hearing that in Surrey 'the ladies were afraid of her' she became annoyed: 'Pray on what grounds is this?' If Mr Fenn had been spreading such rumours she instructed him to stop: 'for I am sure I passed for a very harmless animal among them before, as indeed I am, and much value that character; nor shall easily forgive you if you have robbed me of it, for I think everything impertinence in a woman that makes her unfit for the conversation of her own sex, whatever fine names may be given it.'

Financially, however, she was not secure enough to be sure she would always be able to be independent. She told Fenn that she had always supposed she would not marry, giving as her reason 'the irregularity of most men's lives, and the ill example they give their families'. She told Burnet the same thing, noting that Addison had been given Locke's place in reward for a poem he wrote to the Duke of Marlborough 'on his last glorious campaign'. She had written and printed such verses too, but no government place had been forthcoming. She needed to do something to make herself 'easier in my circumstances'. In 1704 she had been actively soliciting at court, writing letters, seeing people with influence; she was quite hopeful of arranging something 'in which all the satisfaction of my life and the establishment of my fortune depends'. Probably she was hoping for a pension. Thomas Burnet, far away in Europe, generously provided a legacy for her in his will, but as she pointed out to him he had failed to make it secure: whether she got anything or not would depend 'on the conscience of your executors'. She had more knowledge of such things than he, having lived in a world of hopeful promises and apparent goodwill but without being provided for.

Marriage was for life, and according to the husband's circumstances it established likely income for life. But not only was she 'very fearful of putting my happiness entirely in the power of anyone', she 'could never, on the account of fortune, think one moment on any man in whom I could not propose to find a useful friend and an agreeable companion'. Cockburn, not Fenn, met that criterion. For Cockburn she felt 'a well grounded esteem' joined with a 'foolish unaccountable tenderness' which added 'a great deal of agreeableness'. What she called 'that softer part' was every bit as important as esteem: 'I confess I am for a little of both, having no aversion for pleasure, and believing it may be had without danger in due circumstances.' Cockburn needed to be convinced. He was worried that pleasure might 'discompose'. She explained: 'I own your conclusion to be generally true, that out of that state, the pleasure flowing from love must discompose the mind more or less, because some of those transporting passions will, for the most part, accompany it.' Delicately, they discussed sex. Single people perhaps could manage without, but she did not think the celibate priests in the Catholic Church fared well and thought they would be better off with wives.

In spite of his doubts about pleasure, Patrick Cockburn was someone she decided she could be perfectly satisfied with. It was a surprise: 'I had never before known any man that I liked or liked not in whose manners or temper I did not find something that would have made me unhappy; and therefore I had long thought it would be best for me to continue as I am.'[22] Esteem, inclination and convenience met in a way she had given up expecting. Writing to him gave her pleasure and thoughts of him kept her awake at night.

Evidently she persuaded him. She 'bid adieu to the Muses', and they were married in 1708 with every prospect of living a modestly comfortable clerical life.

Chapter Eight

LIVED EXPERIENCE

I had a mind to make an experiment, whether it was not possible to divert the Town with real events just as they happened.

Mary Davys, *The Fugitive*[1]

Delarivier Manley's *Rivella*

Susannah Centlivre claimed that Whigs in power wanted 'no scribblers on their side', male or female, while the Tories 'kept their herd in constant pay'. Delarivier Manley was the most celebrated 'female wit of Tory strain', but it was not her good fortune to be kept 'in constant pay'. She petitioned and solicited, determined to be paid for services to Crown and party, but to no great effect.

Manley typified one kind of woman writer: shrewd and capable, party political, journalistic, sensationalist and outspoken, with a freewheeling firecracker of a voice that exploited female sexuality for overtly political ends. Swift compressed Manley's career into a quatrain. She was 'Corinna', and Cupid pronounced over her cradle that she would always speak and write of love, while a satyr vowed that the world would 'feel her scratch and bite':

> At twelve, a poet, and coquette,
> Marries for love, half whore, half wife;
> Cuckolds, elopes, and runs in debt;
> Turns authoress, and is Curll's for life.[2]

Like Aphra Behn claiming the same ground as men for her 'masculine part, the poet in me', Delarivier Manley opened her autobiographical *The History of Rivella* with the blunt observation that men could get away with things that in a woman were 'scandalous and unpardonable'. Rivella's 'virtues' were her own; her 'vices' were visited upon her, they were her 'misfortunes', and if she had been a man she would have been 'without fault'. Among Manley's virtues were the capacity to love and feel sexual desire; among her misfortunes, her 'ruin' at the hands of her cousin John Manley who bigamously married her and by whom she had a son.[3]

Manley's father, Sir Roger Manley, was a scholar and Cavalier, exiled like other leading royalists during the Commonwealth, given his knighthood for services to the Crown and appointed governor of the Channel Islands after the restoration of monarchy. It was probably during his time in Jersey, between 1667 and 1672, that Delarivier was born. A garrison child, she moved frequently with her father's postings, surrounded at all times by handsome soldiers. At Landguard Fort in Suffolk, when still very young, she became infatuated with a soldier, James Carlisle, who had been an actor in London and could sing the latest amorous songs in a charming voice. In *Rivella*, she described his effect on her as a 'disease' and a 'distemper'. She could neither eat nor sleep. She had read about love but had not felt it. Now she 'drank the poison both at her ears and eyes, and never took care to manage or conceal the passion'.[4]

Carlisle's regiment was ordered elsewhere and the distracted girl was sent to France, where she soon became fluent in the language. Her father died in 1687, leaving his children in the hands of their much older cousin, John Manley, a lawyer and politician who 'had always had an obliging fondness that was wonderfully taking with girls. We [she and her younger sister] loved him as much as it was possible.' They were sent to live in the country with 'an old out-of-fashion aunt' who 'read us books of chivalry and romances with her spectacles. This sort of conversation infected me and made me fancy every stranger that I saw, in what habit soever, some disguised prince or lover.'[5] When the aunt died soon after, John Manley took them to London and immediately began making protestations of love, a development Manley claimed she was not pleased by except that it 'answered something to the character I had found in those books that had poisoned and deluded my dawning reason'. Imagining himself a charmer, he was (in her later judgement) a vain, opinionated, talkative fool. Worse, he was 'so perfect a libertine that he never denied himself the gratifications of any of his passions'. A fellow MP described him as 'a silly hot fellow'. Jonathan Swift called him 'a beast' – no doubt reflecting Delarivier Manley's view.

In *Rivella*, Manley drily observes – by way of acquainting the reader 'that mine was not his first deceit' – that her cousin-guardian had a wife, for she was later to hear this first wife angrily recount the tricks he had used to persuade *her* into marriage. Manley herself, not yet fourteen by her own account, fell ill and was nursed by John Manley. In gratitude, she 'fatally' agreed to marry him. And thus, 'to sum it all in a little, I was married, possessed and ruined'.[6]

How far Delarivier Manley was complicit in the bigamy, how far she married for love and how far to further family interest – any or all of which are possibilities – is impossible to know. Manley used stories about her life for different purposes, and apart from her own versions of events little evidence remains. She stayed with John Manley for three years, after which she was taken in by the unloved and unlovely Lady Castlemaine. ('Querulous, fierce, loquacious, excessively fond or infamously rude ... The extremes of prodigality and covetousness, of love and hatred, of dotage and aversion were joined together in ... [her] soul.')[7] From 1696 to 1702 she was the lover of a lawyer, John Tilly, governor of the Fleet prison, and from 1709 to 1714 she lived with her printer, John Barber.

Manley admitted that lies would be deliberately disseminated if there were political or other interest involved: 'the prejudice of party runs so high in England that the best natured persons and those of the greatest integrity scruple not to say false and malicious things of those who differ from them in principles'.[8] Manley was a Tory party writer and her prejudices were anti-Whig. She was utterly scornful of the Whig narrative whereby 1688 was a 'Glorious Revolution' liberating the nation from tyranny. (John Manley threw his lot in with the Whigs.) Her scandal chronicles were political commentary which mingled affairs of state with gossip, innuendo and fiction. It is not known when or why hostilities began between herself and Catharine Trotter, nor is there any record of Trotter's response, but Trotter was a Whig; her loyalties (and hopes for reward) were with the Duke and Duchess of Marlborough. Trotter published two encomiastic poems celebrating Marlborough's military victories, first at the Battle of Blenheim in 1704, and then at Ramellies in 1706.

Manley's attacks on Catharine Trotter were obscenely sexual in nature. They did not appear until after Trotter had married the Revd Patrick Cockburn, moved to Suffolk, and temporarily withdrawn from professional authorship. In the *New Atalantis* and in *Rivella*, Manley took up from *The Female Wits* the name 'Calista' for Trotter, her 'sister-authoress'. Lovemore, the narrator of *Rivella*, mentions in an aside that he will entertain his companion with Calista's story along with the stories of 'the other writing ladies of our age', but the promise is not fulfilled. Manley also made use of 'Cleander', the name Trotter had given to Olinda's platonic lover in her *Adventures of a Young Lady*. These intertextual references were put to the service of biographical 'truth': drawing on the authority of personal acquaintance, Manley accused Trotter of hypocrisy and depravity.[9]

Delarivier Manley's *New Atalantis* wove scandalous stories around public figures, such as the Duke of Marlborough (Count Fortunatus), for political ends and in the hope of attaining a reward. In doing so, it drew on personal knowledge and experience which, as the full title shows, Manley deemed it wise to obscure. The text was cautiously introduced as a memoir several times removed from its 'real' English origins: *Secret Memoirs and Manners of several Persons of Quality of both Sexes. From the New Atalantis, an Island in the Mediterranean. Written originally in Italian, and translated from the third Edition of the French.* Geographically and linguistically distanced (the 'third edition' of the French version is a nice touch), it was located somewhere between the fictional 'Atalantis' and the real Mediterranean. So, too, the stories Manley told about these 'persons of quality of both sexes' occupied an ill-defined space where fictional selves – Olinda, Calista, Cleander – collide with living individuals. Symbolic identities – 'the female author', 'bright shes' or 'she-things' (Catharine Trotter and Mary Pix, those two 'she-things, called poetesses' sitting in the theatre with William Congreve) – were more potent in this realm than humdrum women, even writers like the many writers Manley knew, going about their everyday lives.

Manley's representations, full of the verve of contemporary pamphleteering, were complex and vivid responses both to lived experience (including her own) and literary conventions. Whatever personal malice or spite underlay her accounts, it is also true that she exposed and exploited the potential of printed text to invest symbolic selves with a power all their own. Poets who praised public figures, such as Trotter when she praised Marlborough, were buying into the power of the symbolic selves they helped create. Manley employed the same tactic but reversed the lie: instead of heaping false praises, she heaped slander. Writing about Catharine Trotter in the *New Atalantis*, the *Memoirs of Europe* and *Rivella*, Manley offered different versions of her erstwhile friend as a hypocrite masking sexual licence in piety. She depicted Trotter as a whore and a prude, describing her as one who had become 'the diversion of as many of the town as found her to their taste and would purchase. Yet she still assumed an air of virtue pretended and was ever eloquent (according to her stiff manner), upon the foible of others'.[10] Calista had 'little talent in poetry' but a 'larger one in amour'. The mixture of particularity, her 'stiff manner' and generality, a woman who was the 'diversion' of the town, is specially effective. Manley's 'truth' was the truth of insult not documentation. The point was to offend, and the offence was in the service of known political allegiance.

Manley's propagandist fiction, beginning with *The Secret History of Queen Zarah and the Zarazians* (1705) which attacked Sarah, Duchess of Marlborough, and the leading Whigs, and the *New Atalantis* made her famous. The *New Atalantis*, which went through six editions in its first ten years, caused Manley to be arrested, along with the printer and the publisher; its publication just before the opening of Parliament in 1709 had been carefully timed to do maximum damage. She was credited with bringing down the Whig government in 1710 and she certainly tried to ingratiate herself with the Tories, offering her services to Robert Harley. Jonathan Swift noted in his *Journal* that on going to Lord Peterborough's one morning he 'met Mrs Manley there, who was soliciting him to get some pension or reward for her service in the cause, by writing her *Atalantis*, and prosecution &c upon it. I seconded her, and hope they will do something for the poor woman.' All she ever got from the public purse for 'what some esteem good service to the cause' was £50, and in 1714 she was feeling the pinch, at least, if we are to believe what she told Harley which was that she had 'nothing but a starving scene before me'.[11] This is not the persona projected in *Rivella*.

The story of the writing of *Rivella* is important to the story told within its pages, though how 'true' it is can no more be established than the 'truth' of *Rivella* or of the *Atalantis*. According to Edmund Curll, Charles Gildon, who had so successfully ventriloquised the voice of a female author in his 1696 *Memoirs on the Life of Aphra Behn*, was in the process of completing a life of Delarivier Manley. Curll had probably commissioned it and had already begun printing. It was an attack, written 'upon a pique', and, as Curll admitted, promised to be 'a severe invective on some part of her conduct'. Hearing about this, and no doubt knowing perfectly well what Gildon would make of her, Manley intervened. She wrote to Curll asking him to halt production (two sheets had been printed off). She would come personally to speak to him. Her letter pointed out that it might be in his interest to 'oblige' her. Curll described what happened next as follows:

> I returned for answer to this letter, that I should be proud of such a visitant. Accordingly, Mrs Manley and her sister came to my house in Fleet-Street, whom, before that time, I had never seen, and requested a sight of Mr Gildon's papers. Such a request, I told her, I could not by any means grant without asking Mr Gildon's consent; but upon hearing her own story, which no pen but her own can relate in the agreeable manner wherein she delivered it, I promised to write to Mr Gildon the next day; and not only obtained his consent to let Mrs Manley see what sheets were printed, but also brought them to an interview, by which means all resentments between them were thoroughly reconciled. Mr Gildon was, likewise, so generous, as to order a total suppression of all his papers; and Mrs Manley, as generously resolved to write the history of her own life, and times, under the same title which Mr Gildon had made choice of.[12]

Such uniformly 'generous' behaviour might arouse our suspicions about this account and in fact Curll used the existence of Gildon's hostile manuscript in 1714 to fan publicity for the original publication. By 1725, when Curll included this account as a preface to the fourth edition of *Rivella* which he issued after Manley's death in 1724, there was commercial advantage in the genteel version offered here: morally upright publisher ('Such a request, I told her, I could not by any means grant without asking Mr Gildon's consent') divulging a secret history; celebrated female author with a story to tell, a charismatic presence, and compelling narrative skills ('upon hearing her own story, which no pen but her own can relate in the agreeable manner wherein she delivered it'); and a polite hack deferring at once to the polite request that he make himself scarce. Whether Gildon was in a position to object or not, Curll was more than happy to abort his project when Manley intervened. To have Delarivier Manley tell her own story was an enticing prospect, especially when she agreed to use Gildon's title which had already been advertised and undertook to meet the tight deadline already in place.

In divulging the secret history – the story behind the book – Curll printed what he claimed were genuine letters written to him by Delarivier Manley. These letters may indeed be genuine; it is also possible that he made them up. They are conveniently informative about such matters as Manley's high regard for Curll – 'your services are such to me, that can never be enough valued. My pen, my purse, my interest, are all at your service. I shall never be easy till I am grateful . . . How can I deserve all this friendship from you?' Perhaps she did look on him as a sincere friend. But 'genuine' letters that were made up and 'true' stories that had happened only to fictional characters were stock ingredients, and letters written by celebrated authors ('genuine' or not) were in vogue. It is as well to be cautious, especially since all three were proficient in the arts of self-promotion, and neither Manley nor Gildon, who also died in 1724 when the fourth edition with these letters appeared, were alive to tell a different tale even supposing they were minded to do so.

If Curll's preface to *Rivella* included fictional writing that claimed to be the truth about real people – himself, Manley, Gildon – this was in keeping with the pages that followed. The title itself, *The Adventures of Rivella; or, the History of the Author of the Atalantis, with Secret Memoirs and Characters of several considerable persons her contemporaries. Delivered in a conversation to the young Chevalier D'Aumont in Somerset House Garden, by Sir Charles Lovemore. Done into English from the French*, mixed the fictional with fact. 'Rivella' evoked 'Delarivier' who was 'the Author of the *Atalantis*', but was not avowedly Delarivier Manley. The secret memoirs and characters of several contemporaries indicated real and recognisable people who figured under such names as 'Lysander', 'Hilaria', 'Count Fortunatus' and 'Sir Peter Vainlove', and whose identities could be checked out by consulting the key which Curll provided. No author's name appeared on the title page: nobody claimed to have written the book, it was 'delivered' in a conversation between two fictional men. Furthermore, the text was supposedly a translation from the French and there was even a 'translator's preface' explaining how the French publisher (a fiction) came by the papers.

Rivella is an account of her life written by a woman with an established reputation as a successful writer. Rivella is presented throughout as the object of admiring males; she is the 'famous author of the *Atalantis*', loved by all who knew her, desired by many who might wish they knew her, witty, warm, talented and good. The narrative is structured as a conversation between two men, the one ardent to hear everything the other no less ardently speaks in Rivella's praise. (Having taken her story away from two men, Manley metaphorically wrote them back into it as her fictional admirers.) Instead of choosing to speak in her own voice as Delarivier Manley, she 'delivered' her autobiography through a staged conversation set in Somerset House gardens (illustrated in the frontispiece) between a cavalier, Sir Charles Lovemore, who has been from his youth in love with her, and a French nobleman, D'Aumont.

These men lock themselves in the gardens one fine summer's evening in order to satisfy the desire they both feel to converse about 'ingenious women' in general and the author of the *Atalantis* in particular. D'Aumont has a theory which he explains by making a parallel with Madam Dacier. Dacier, according to D'Aumont, though neither young nor beautiful, was sexually charming (she 'makes a thousand conquests') by virtue of her wit and sense. This was the appeal of clever women as Frenchmen understood it. Lovemore, admitting his admiration of Dacier's learning, cannot imagine how the intellectual pleasure of conversing with her – 'admirable scholar', 'judicious critic' as she was – could translate into sensuous or sexual pleasure. He supposes it would be like having a conversation with a very eminent intellectual man. 'You are, I find, a novice,' answers D'Aumont, 'in what relates to women; there is no being pleased in their conversation without a mixture of the sex which will still be mingling itself in all we say.' The delight of conversation with women of wit and sense was its capacity to produce the feelings associated with love. Even Madam Dacier, who was 'unhandsome' and did not write about love, gained hearts. How much more so did the 'famous author of the *Atalantis*', who made a point of writing about love, bringing its representation to a high degree of perfection in descriptions that were 'of the sort that inspire immediate delight, and warm the blood with pleasure', though she too, in 1714, was neither young (she was fifty) nor, by her own account, handsome.

Through D'Aumont, Manley then itemised some of her most famous scenes: Germanicus naked on the embroidered bed; Chevalier Tomaso 'possessing' Madam de Bedamore 'in that sylvan scene of pleasure the garden'. These 'enchanting descriptions' served as guides to the rapture every mortal was capable of feeling. Representing human nature in this way 'raises high ideas of the dignity of human kind, and informs us that we have in our composition wherewith to taste sublime and transporting joys'.

Madam Dacier is the touchstone for the story – a woman unequivocally admired and whose culture supported her. (Meanwhile, the French romances of Madame de Scudery were important models.) Rivella, with yet more talents than Madam Dacier, had not enjoyed similar tokens of support. Still, she was able to use her bookishness: going to meet Cleander (John Tilly) for the first time and knowing him to be 'a man of business', which meant she might have to wait, she took with her a book – apparently to help pass the time, but really to display her reading. Having chosen Rochefoucault's *Moral Reflections*, she casually put it on his table. Cleander absent-mindedly picked it up. The result was exactly what she wanted:

> He formed an idea from that book of the genius of the lady, who chose it for her entertainment, and tho he had but an indifferent opinion hitherto of woman's conversation, he believed Rivella must have a good taste from the company she kept. He found an opportunity of confirming himself, before he parted, in Rivella's sense and capacity for business as well as pleasure; which were agreeably mingled at supper, none but these two gentlemen and Rivella being present.[13]

A woman of the world, Rivella was good at business too. She showed Cleander that a woman could have these larger, more rounded capacities – could be more than he had previously thought a woman (i.e. his wife) could be. In encountering Rivella, Cleander was the one who experienced an illumination; his world was widened by the encounter:

> He was married young, but as yet knew not what it was to love. His studies and application to business, together with the desire of making himself great in the world, had employed all his hours . . . he was civil to his lady, meant very well for her children, and did not then dream there was anything in her person defective to his happiness, that was in the power of any other of that sex to bestow.

Cleander, a bit of a booby, falls in love – 'he was so awkward, and so unfashioned as to love'.[14] Rivella, the sophisticated woman of the world, revelling in the attentions her fame and success as an author have brought her, understands how to use her sexuality. Not an innocent abused nor a symbol of virtue in distress, she commanded both pleasure and business. In the story as a whole, these elements, the 'bright part of her adventures' – meaning the way others admired rather than calumniated – were, she announced, subordinated to 'that part of Rivella's history which has made the most noise against her'. The telling of the life was a defence. Manley had been ruined in the eyes of the world by her bigamous marriage at an age when, as she told it, she was too young to know any better, and further compromised by her affair with John Tilly. In *Rivella* she rewrote her story, leaving out the 'misfortunes' of her early years since interested readers could look that up in the *Atalantis* – as Charles Lovemore tells D'Aumont, 'I must refer you to her own story, under the name of Delia, in the *Atalantis* for the next four miserable years of her life' – but putting in the details of her relationship with John Tilly and her imprisonment after the *Atalantis*, by which time 'all the world was out of humour with her, and she with all the world'.

The two stories at the heart of *Rivella* – the relationship with John Tilly and Manley's arrest and imprisonment – are both given as accounts of heroism and as demonstrations of her exceptionality. When Cleander's wife dies, Rivella, the mistress, understands at once that everything is over: his debts mean that he must try to marry a fortune. There is 'a rich young widow' already in the frame. Rivella, being 'a woman of an exalted soul' – or, in Lovemore's ambiguous expression, displaying her 'romantick bravery of mind' – agrees to give Cleander up. Having experienced ruin herself she could not be the means of the ruin of another, even if her heroic self-sacrifice (Cleander would have married her) means emotional misery for both of them. Cleander is reported as saying that 'what ever happened he should never be acquainted with a woman of her worth, neither could anything but extreme necessity force him to abandon her innocence and tenderness'. Reluctantly they part. She, retiring to the country for a single life, 'seemed to bury all thoughts of gallantry in Cleander's tomb' while he, wooing and wedding the widow but not getting his hands on her money, sickens and within a few years dies.

Lovemore encounters similar romantic bravery when Rivella tells him there is a warrant for her arrest and that she proposes to surrender herself to save the printer and all his family from ruin. It lay in her power 'to discharge those honest people from their imprisonment'. Rivella, according to Lovemore, was 'in one of her heroic strains', insisting that

> she was proud of having more courage than had any of our sex, and of throwing the first stone, which might give a hint for other persons of more capacity to examine the defects and vices of some men who took a delight to impose upon the world, by the pretence of public good, whilst their true design was only to gratify and advance themselves.[15]

In a heated exchange Lovemore forces Rivella to think about the reality before her. 'I asked her how she would like going to Newgate? She answered me very well; since it was to discharge her conscience; I told her all this sounded great, and was very heroic, but there was a vast difference between real and imaginary sufferings.' When 'railing at her books' and her 'barbarous design of exposing people that had never done her any injury' fails to shift her, Lovemore reminds Rivella that the Tory Party was 'most supine, and forgetful of such who served them; that she would certainly be abandoned by them and left to perish and starve in prison'. He offers to help get her away to France where the exiled Queen would take her into protection. Rivella, a stout Protestant, refuses to countenance any connection with a Roman 'bigot'. Nor would she go to Switzerland, for if she did, what would become of 'the poor printer, and those two other persons concerned, the publishers, who with their families all would be undone by her flight?' It was true that theirs was the profit from the book but, nevertheless, hers was the responsibility. Rivella remained 'obstinate' and Lovemore is shown taking his leave, vowing that he will not visit her in prison.

Towards the end of October 1709, nine days after the publication of the second volume of the *New Atalantis*, Manley had been arrested for seditious libel, along with her publishers, John Morphew and J. Woodward, and her printer, John Barber. The men were released on 1 November. She managed eventually to talk her way out of trouble though she was kept in prison for perhaps two weeks, 'close shut up in the messenger's hands from seeing or speaking to any person, without being allowed pen, ink, and paper ... [and] ... tyrannically and barbarously insulted by the fellow and his wife'. (This treatment she considered too low to complain about when asked at the hearing if she had been 'civilly used', but it went into the book.) She was given bail on 5 November, and the change in the ministry which followed removed her difficulties.

In *Rivella*, Lovemore describes a later conversation in which Rivella recognised the evil consequences to her of her political writings, and agreed to give up writing about 'party' – the Whigs, now in power, would never promote her anyway because of her past allegiance to the Tories. Politics, she concurs, 'is not the business of a woman'. She would write of 'pleasure and entertainment only'. Pleasure and love were the business of a woman, something Rivella knew how to give and receive; although, since she was no longer young, praise and flattery were not her object. What she could look to give and receive was 'delicate, sensible, and agreeable' conversation.[16]

Manley ended this story about herself with an extraordinary set of images. Lovemore evokes the pleasures of being with Rivella, a woman who understands life, which includes the pleasures of the body as well as the mind, and the beauties of the external world. Lovemore explains how Rivella may best be enjoyed and appreciated: she must be experienced at her table, where her sparkling wit and gaiety is displayed; then in her bedroom, a love nest for the afternoon; and then she should be accompanied on to the water, or in the park in the evening. The images were drawn less from daily life in London where Rivella lived on Ludgate Hill, and more from romance tales set in hot climes; what they idealised was womanly sophistication. This womanly sophistication is what D'Aumont wants; the story rouses desire for her person. He urges Lovemore to take him to Rivella: 'let us not lose a moment before we are acquainted with the only person of her sex that knows how to live, and of whom we may say in relation to *love*, since she has so peculiar a genius for and has made such noble discoveries in that passion, that it would have been a *fault in her not to have been faulty*'.

That we receive her story through a conversation between two men who end by excitedly rushing off to find her might lead us to argue that the text reduces the woman who is its subject to a sexual object available for male possession. Clearly there is a deliberate erotic charge here and sex of some variety is on offer. Through the framing of a conversation between men – a narrative device chosen for the purpose – an accomplished, experienced and sophisticated woman author offers herself to the reader. The key question is where power lies in this arrangement. Does it lie with the men because patriarchy gives men power over women? Parts of *Rivella* can certainly be read that way, especially if we forget that Lovemore is the creation of his female author and not a male with power outside the text in which she allows him to speak the words she writes. It is a measure of Delarivier Manley's skill that Lovemore seems to have a 'real' existence. This is his function in a narrative that purports to tell a true history. Lovemore gives legitimacy to Rivella's story in two important ways. By having known Rivella since their youth, he is the witness to truths others cannot dispute; he contains her history, he is the witness who was there. (Occasionally in the text he pops up in the most unlikely scenes, reminding us of his status as eyewitness.) By loving Rivella he enacts the effects of her desirability. In this capacity he serves as an example to others. An unsatisfied but still eager lover, in him desire exists to be aroused and maintained; he is to be always ready to observe and report, to know and to tell. Lovemore, who tells Rivella's story, is her faithful reader.

Possession of the imagined female self, the self made available through words, is rendered in (male) sexual terms as possession of the

238

actual female body. Rivella is presented to us as a living being: she exists on the page and in the world. She can be talked about, written about, reflected upon and visited. She has a past existence about which stories can be circulated and a present one which can be experienced by personal contact. When the text arouses pleasurable desire it can be literalised by visiting, having dinner, enjoying her wit and easy gaiety, and (the ultimate fantasy) sharing her rose-strewn bed. *The Adventures of Rivella* gives us Rivella as a woman with a history and a present potency. Keeping this present potency alive in our minds is one means by which Manley gives prominence to the writing woman, the 'ingenious' woman whose history is told in *The Adventures of Rivella*, which, as the subtitle emphasises, is also the history of an author: *The History of the Author of the Atalantis*. As everybody who had read the *Atalantis* knew (and everybody *had* read the *Atalantis*), the author was female.

But there is more to it than that because *The Adventures of Rivella*, like the *Atalantis*, affirms the potency of female knowledge and experience, including sexual feeling. Rivella loves and understands Cleander and she knows the world so well that she understands the pressures bearing on him, hence her heroic decision to give him up. As society is constituted, heroic renunciation is the only heroism available to her in the public realm (she cannot rescue Cleander from his financial difficulties) but her integrity is rooted in a self-possession that derives from observation and experience. What the world calls her 'ruin' Rivella calls her worth, especially in a corrupt and ruined world such as that in which she finds herself, having been, as she put it in the story of Delia in the *Atalantis*, 'married, possessed, and ruined' before barely becoming adult. In giving up Cleander, Rivella asserts the power of love over interest, of agency over subjection. The episode amplifies an earlier debate dramatised in the *Atalantis* in a conversation between lovesick Charlot and her new friend, a young countess. The Countess, though 'full of air, life and fire', had been 'bred up in the fashionable way of making love, wherein the heart has little or no part' and her advice to Charlot was to resist sexual feeling since such feelings – 'love' – rendered women vulnerable: 'the first thing a woman ought to consult was her interest and establishment in the world . . . love should only be a handle towards it'; giving in to pleasure led inevitably to 'contempt and sorrow'.[17]

The Countess articulates a commonplace aristocratic view. It is about female behaviour but it does not only concern women (which is to say that it has general political implications as well as alerting us to a sexual politics). Love is the real threat to hierarchy and rank, the real disturber of arrangements made according to the larger interests of family, clan, party and nation. Manley signalled that her own life story was told in the story of Delia in the *Atalantis*, but it is also told in the story of Charlot who is seduced by her guardian as Manley herself was seduced by her cousin-guardian, John Manley. In being seduced, Charlot learned the pleasures of love. In espousing the virtues of love – its capacity to make one know as well as feel – Manley mounted an anti-aristocratic argument, exposing the manipulations at work in 'precepts of virtue' that had nothing to do with 'nature' or truth and everything to do with interest and gain. Rivella loses Cleander as Charlot fails to pursue worldly interest, but Rivella's survival as a desired woman registers the endurance of a political and philosophical vision. In this vision, mind and body, reason and passion, are integrated. As such, they threaten a social system which chooses to separate mind and body for worldly advantage.

Jane Barker's histories of 'Galesia'

In 1714, making books out of lived experience was still novel. A year earlier, Curll's list featured the first book by one of his authors to be described as 'a novel'. The book was *Love Intrigues; or, the History of the Amours of Bosvil and Galesia, as related to Lucasia in St Germain's Garden*, and its author was Jane Barker.

Love Intrigues was prefaced by some commendatory verses by George Sewell. Titled 'To Mrs Jane Barker', the poem addressed Barker in her fictional persona of 'Galesia'. Sewell's praises began with an apology: he had assumed, from its description as a novel, that the manuscript would be contrived and trifling, a fiction in the old sense full of nymphs and knights, 'Poor, dry Romances of a tortured brain'. Reading, however, he discovered his error. Barker's story was about 'real passions'. It was true to 'nature'. Moreover, it was *her* story, the story of a young woman badly treated by a capricious lover. As such, it offered pleasures the old dry romances did not give – the pleasures of empathy with the author: 'We mourn thy sorrows, and we feel thy pain.'[18]

Sewell's poem served the function of a publisher's blurb: partly puff and partly descriptive of what the reader might expect to find – or at least what the publisher and perhaps the writer thought would best catch the public eye. Drawing attention to the psychological realism of the narrative, Sewell guided the reader's sympathies. The lover in the story, Bosvil, the 'perjur'd swain', was a fool and a knave, meriting every punishment and at the same time barely worth attention; Galesia/ Barker, however, adored and spurned, trying to make sense of Bosvil's behaviour to her and of her own feelings for him, was an object of intense interest. She was a real person, she made the 'real' feelings of a young woman available. Perhaps it was the novelty and excitement of this that provoked the decision to declare on the title page that *Love Intrigues*, written by the sixty-year-old Jane Barker, was 'By a Young Lady'.

Barker had returned to England in 1704, probably already working on some version of this manuscript as well as the manuscript of a heroic romance, *Exilius*, which appeared in 1714. She went back to live on the family farm at Willsthorp in Lincolnshire, although as a Catholic she was subject to financial penalties, including double taxation. Life cannot have been easy, but Barker was both resourceful and resilient. We have seen how as a young woman and aspiring poet, she had responded to the enthusiasms of Benjamin Crayle and his Cambridge friends and become one of their coterie, circulating poems and enjoying the attention. *Poetical Recreations* was the result. Settled again in England, having continued to present poems on public themes at the exile court at St Germain, hoping perhaps for a royal gift or pension, she looked for other forms in which she could publish her verse. The genre she evolved, in *Love Intrigues*, *A Patch-Work Screen for the Ladies* (1723) and *The Lining of the Patch-Work Screen* (1725), had some of the characteristics of an album or compendium, a loosely structured but coherent assemblage of poems and stories arranged around a strong central character, Galesia. It was a form which other women were to adopt, most notably Laetitia Pilkington in her *Memoirs*, where the story of her life provided a frame for the publishing of her poems.

Nothing is known of Barker's negotiations with Edmund Curll, but her choice of him as the publisher for *Love Intrigues* makes plain her commercial ambition. Was it Curll or Barker who decided that the title page should carry the flagrant falsehood, 'written by a young lady'? Were there discussions about the format and subtitle which figured the story as a conversation in a garden – strangely foreshadowing the format of *Rivella* the following year? And who was responsible for dedicating the volume to the Countess of Exeter without first asking permission? When the novel was reprinted in 1719, Barker's dedication carried an apology for the earlier breach of decorum: she claimed to be 'extremely confused to find my little novel presenting itself to your Ladyship without your leave or knowledge', begged pardon, but claimed she was 'not guilty', and could not conceive 'by what concurrence of mistakes it so happened'.

Grovelling apologies of this sort were the inevitable consequence of print practices, and the publisher had less to lose than the author by taking the blame. The Countess of Exeter was Barker's local aristocrat (it was the Exeter family from whom her father had leased Willsthorp in 1662). Barker claimed that Burleigh House 'with its park, shades and walk' was her model for the country retreat she described in *Exilius* and that the noble ladies who lived there were the real (and vastly superior) originals of the 'bright heroines' she created in that romance. The compliment reveals that by 1719 at least the Countess of Exeter had acted as patron to Barker, raising her from 'obscurity' by her encouragement. It may be that the Countess was not specially troubled by the original unsolicited dedication: by apologising, nevertheless, Barker was able to exploit the high-ranking connection, presenting it in more detail (showing that it reached back to her childhood) and, going further still, elaborate an analogy – between herself and the Countess of Exeter, and Sir Philip Sidney and the Countess of Pembroke – that had obvious literary resonance.

Love Intrigues is a narrative about Barker's own early history, a troubled and troubling personal story about a failed romance set in the context of ruinous national events. The family history had been defined by loss of property and position. Supporters of Charles 1 (Barker's father had had a senior position at court), they lost everything in the political chaos of the 1640s and 1650s. Born in 1652 just three years after the execution of the king, Barker grew up on stories of suffering. The 'non-existence of riches' among her father's family was still a shocking fact, though easily explained: 'for some were in battle slain, and some in prison died; some ruined in their estates, some in their persons, and so (like most of the adherents to the royal cause) were unhappy'.[19] Unhappy in their fortunes, they were also, this account seems to suggest, unhappy in their psyches.

Born into adherence to the royalist cause, Barker made it the centre of her life, not only following James into exile in 1689 but remaining a loyal Jacobite up to and beyond the plots of 1715 during which she is known to have passed messages to the Duke of Ormond. The life she might have lived and the values associated with it – stability, respect and the rank of a gentlewoman; pride in material prosperity and the productive management of a comfortable estate, plus, in her case probably, admiration for her literary abilities – pressed against unhappy realities. Dislocated and impoverished, troubled but obstinately self-seeking, Barker was forced to make up a life and identity as she went along. Much of what she observed about herself and others is recorded in her poems, and it was as a poet, 'the Orinda or Sappho' of her time, that Barker first sought fame. The unusual psychological realism that marks her writing, poetry and prose alike, was a product of her attention to the psychic damage of the 'unhappiness' she was part of. She knew many who were ruined 'in their persons' as well as in their estates.

A woman in her sixties who had observed and experienced a great deal, Jane Barker's prose writings were much meditated distillations of experience. In *Love Intrigues* and in *A Patch-Work Screen for the Ladies* and *The Lining of the Patch-Work Screen*, she examined the forces that had shaped her, a woman born into political conflict and defeat. Her themes were love and loss, betrayal and rejection, exile and longing. The feelings associated with larger historical events – the decision to execute the King, for example – wash through what seem at first sight tales of an individual life and subjectivity. Barker was an overtly autobiographical writer but, like Delarivier Manley, the stories she told included the inner life of the nation.

Barker positioned herself within the *Patchwork* narratives as a writer at work within an admiring community, allegorising history (including personal history) and storytelling as the female work of putting together patches on a screen. Throughout her writings, from early poems to the prose fictions of her old age, she made use of the persona 'Galesia' to write about herself. Galesia's different identities reflect the varied activities in which we know Barker engaged: poet; medical student and practitioner (in 1685, 'Dr Barker's gout plaster was available for sale at Benjamin Crayle's bookshop'); estate manager (after her father's death, she managed the family farm until the pressures of 'debtors, creditors, and lawyers' became too much and she moved with her mother to London); Jacobite exile and Stuart loyalist. Always, and most importantly, Galesia is a thinking, speaking and writing woman; she looks both out and in and she writes what she sees and thinks and feels. It is no accident that she 'commonly' happens to carry in her pocket a 'little pen and ink'. She dreams of being a writer as Orinda was before her, though she mocks herself for thinking she could ever reach Orinda's heights. In *A Patch-Work Screen for the Ladies* she describes a country existence in which she passed her time 'in my shady walks, fields and rural affairs, the pleasure of which was greatly improved by reading Mrs Philips. I began to emulate her wit, and aspired to imitate her writings'. Such an aspiration was like the weaver Arachne in Ovid's *Metamorphosis* challenging the goddess Athena to a contest to see whose art was best: Athena turned Arachne into a spider. Compared to the goddess Philips, Galesia was a mere spinning spider:

> Her noble genius being inimitable, especially in praise of a country life and contempt of human greatness; all which I swallowed as draughts of rich cordial to enliven the understanding. Her poetry I found so interwoven with virtue and honour that each line was like a ladder to climb, not only to Parnassus but to Heaven: which I (poor puzzle as I was!) had the boldness to try to imitate, till I was dropped into a labyrinth of poetry, which has ever since interlaced all the actions of my life.[20]

In *Love Intrigues*, the location of the telling, St Germain's Garden, identifies Galesia/Barker as a supporter of the exiled Stuarts; and the name of the person to whom the story is told, Lucasia, signals its literary intent: 'Lucasia' was the literary name given to Katherine Philips's friend, Anne Owen, in the Society of Friendship. Galesia is manifestly self-enrolled in Philips's Society, a young woman 'resolved to espouse a book, and spend my days in study.' In her verses the muses encourage her:

> Methinks I hear the muses sing,
> And see 'em all dance in a ring,
> And call upon me to take wing.
>
> We will (say they) assist thy flight,
> Till thou reach fair Orinda's height,
> If thou canst this world's folly slight.

What is required to slight worldly folly is to cast off men and 'vow a virgin to remain'. As well as taking Orinda for her model, Galesia adds a fictional character, the faithful shepherdess in John Fletcher's play of that name: 'I resolved to imitate her, not only in perpetual chastity, but in learning the use of simples for the good of my country neighbours. Thus I thought to become Apollo's darling daughter, and maid of honour to the muses.'[21]

Walking in St Germain's Garden on a hot summer's day sometime in the 1690s, Lucasia and Galesia at first discuss current politics and then turn with relief to the more 'diverting' subject of Galesia's early years. Galesia describes a happy Lincolnshire childhood, in which education was considered the most important investment for future fortune. The family's difficulties do not prevent one brother going to school and later Oxford. She herself is sent away to school at Putney until she is ten or eleven when her mother withdrew her, 'finding those places the Academies of vanity and expense'. Back home, in training for a country gentlewoman, her brother's friend Brafort, a gentleman with an estate and 'not disagreeable' in looks, though considerably older than she, decides he will marry her when she has grown up. At fifteen, however, Galesia discovers love. At the first sight of Bosvil – who is eligible, without having anything extraordinary to recommend him – she experiences a passion she cannot control. Bosvil appears to return her affection. Sent to stay with an aunt in London, Galesia is able to see Bosvil and conduct a courtship of sorts, anxious to preserve her reputation – pretending to take his protestations as 'banter' and putting him off 'with one little shuffle or other' – while at the same time becoming more and more enamoured of him. When Brafort fortui-tously dies, there seems to be no reason why she should not marry Bosvil. Back home in the country, longing for him and expecting him to come to her as 'an overjoyed lover' or at least as 'a fond admirer', Galesia's 'tender' fantasies fill her thoughts. But when he arrives, he is cold towards her.

In Galesia's presence, Bosvil asks her father about another woman in the neighbourhood whom he might marry. Galesia forces herself to participate in this conversation 'with seeming tranquility' although she is inwardly tormented. Bosvil's motivation is and remains throughout a mystery. He blows hot and cold and Galesia alternates between hope and despair, all the time nursing and observing her 'interior' responses. The interest and focus of the narrative is less on Bosvil than on the twists and turns of Galesia's reactions. She notes that her anxieties lead her to seek solitude and then to want to write and be praised for her writing. Hurt pride leads her to be secretive: even her brother cannot be told of Bosvil's 'contempt of my youth and beauty'. She adopts a plain 'habit', giving up ribbons and lace and fine clothes, partly, as she explains, because having been sexually slighted she was too miserable to care for adornment, but also (and at the same time) anticipating praise for self-denial, 'vainly imagining that the world applauded me, and admired that a person in the bloom of youth should so perfectly abdicate the world'. With no diminution of her passion for Bosvil, she lives behind a mask of 'indifferency', behaving well in social situations but subject to sleepless nights, loss of appetite, tears, sighs, an obsessive self-scrutiny, and wild fantasies that 'made but harsh music to my interior'.

This heroism of self-denial turns into a violent longing for heroism of a different kind. As her suffering increases, so Galesia ceases to take satisfaction from being well behaved. Her fantasies become murderous. Full of 'rage and madness' she can think of nothing but 'revenge and malice'. The thought of killing Bosvil pleases her; she is 'delighted . . . to think I saw his blood pour out of his false heart'. Snatching up a sword, she goes towards his house, convinced that to kill him was a service to the female sex:

The false Bosvil shall disquiet me no more, nor any other of my sex; in him I will end his race; no more of them shall come to disturb or affront womankind. This only son shall die by the hands of me an only daughter; and however the world may call it cruelty, or barbarity, I am sure our sex will have reason to thank me, and keep an annual festival, in which a criminal so foul is taken out of their way.

By this act she would also secure her reputation to future times:

For it was for ridding the world of monsters that Hercules was made so great a hero, and George a saint; then sure I shall be ranked in the catalogue of heroines, for such a service done to my sex.

This part of the story can be read as a protest against male behaviour. It could also be considered a moral fable or psychological thriller, or as a reflection on Barker's own and the nation's history. Bosvil's arbitrary behaviour is like that of the Stuarts. Galesia's reactions when 'inspired by an evil genius, I resolved his death', reflect the psychology of those who killed the King. The comparison is not developed in any systematic way but this is one element in a larger study of the causes and effects of 'ruin' and 'confusion'. What Barker explores is the movement of emotion between those whose behaviour cannot be satisfactorily read or relied upon, and the feelings and fantasies in others to which such behaviour gives rise. However much Bosvil is to blame, he is not as much to blame as Galesia for failing to restrain violent passions, no matter how badly he treated her. Reason is seen not as a check on passion but as an accomplice: 'what sophisms one can find to justify any attempt, though never so mad or desperate', Galesia reflects, 'and even affront, if not quite reverse the laws of Nature'. Only weariness and the 'feebleness' of her hands prevents her putting Bosvil to the sword (a woman killing a man would certainly be considered an 'affront' to 'the laws of nature', almost as much as killing a divinely ordained ruler) and when she finally collapses in tears, all her anger is turned upon herself:

In these wild thoughts I wandered, till weariness made me know my own weakness and incapacity of performing what fury had inspired ... my flowing tears mitigated the heat of my rage, washing away those extravagant thoughts, and made me turn my anger against myself, my wretched self, that woeful and unworthy thing, the scorn of my kinsman, lover, friend; which thoughts I branched into many reflections against myself, and him, and hard fortune.

Self-hatred is produced by the scorn of others. Those who are outcast, no longer favoured, 'ruined' in their persons as well as their estates, have to do battle with their own feelings as well as material circumstances. Wanting to be forgiven for contemplating murder – 'to be delivered from blood-guiltiness' – Galesia seeks solace in practical activities. She takes up estate management, becoming 'as perfect in rural affairs as an Arcadian shepherdess'. Woods, fields and pastures become her study; she learns useful things such as when to sow and reap, what kind of pasture is best for beef and what for sheep, how to manage servants and labourers. The work is tiring, engrossing, creative, honourable. It is what 'the nobles in ancient times' took for granted they should do. And it is more effective than 'reason, devotion or philosophy' in dispelling the pain caused by Bosvil. There was

no space for love to agitate my interior. The labour of the day was recompensed with sound sleep at night; those silent hours being passed in sleep's restorative, the day provided new business for my waking thoughts, whilst health and wholesome food repaid this my industry. Thus, in a country life, we roll on in a circle, like the heavenly bodies, our happiness being seldom eclipsed, unless by the interposition of our own passion or follies. Now, finding myself daily to get ground of my sickly thoughts, I doubted not of a perfect recovery if I continued the constant application of this wholesome receipt of laborious industry.

Physical work, the regular life of attendance on the business of an estate, was a remedy for love. Passions – those destructive 'follies' – were best driven underground.[22]

The other remedy was study. Helped by her brother and able to make use of the books he brought back with him from his medical studies in Leyden, Galesia teaches herself anatomy, herbal medicine, Harvey's theories about the circulation of the blood and Richard Lower's ideas about blood transfusions. These activities are described in detail in *A Patch-Work Screen for the Ladies* which appeared ten years after *Love Intrigues*. In 'To the Reader', Barker imagined her readers impatiently waiting to hear more about her heroine Galesia. She apologised that it had taken her so long to come up with the sequel and explained why: 'I had lost my Galesia, she being gone from St Germains, and I retired into an obscure corner of the world.' But the author unexpectedly encountering her character in an open field, she was able to renew acquaintance, hear her story and continue telling it. Barker the author is also present in *A Patch-Work Screen for the Ladies*, no longer retired into an obscure corner but travelling about in stagecoaches, falling into rivers, being rescued by poor people with kind hearts and dirty chamber pots, and welcomed into the comfortable house of a fine lady busy at her patchwork screens to which Barker is able to contribute by 'pasting' her stories and poems.

The 'Continuation of the History of Galesia' which forms 'Leaf 1' of *A Patch-work Screen for the Ladies* is a history of Jane Barker the writer. (It could just as easily have been called, after *Rivella*, the *History of the Author of Love Intrigues*.) It contains many of her poems, including some from *Poetical Recreations*, and it revisits the episodes of her early youth to describe her intellectual and emotional formation. Galesia recalls the awkwardness of ceasing to be interested in girlish games that revolved around dreams of love – 'laying things under each other's heads to dream of our amours; counting specks on our nails, who should have the most presents from friends or lovers; tying knots in the grass; pinning flowers on our breasts, to know the constancy of our pretenders' – and wanting instead to study medicine: 'an amusement different from my sex and years'. Even without the crushing experience of Bosvil's rejections, these developments would not have been easy. Characteristically, Galesia/Barker examines them in terms of her own contribution to the social difficulty: her young friends 'began to look grave upon me' but it could also have been that 'I, perhaps, looked so upon them'. In the transitional stage, she was 'unfit company for everybody':

the unlearned feared, and the learned scorned my conversation; at least, I fancied so: a learned woman, being at best like a forced plant, that never has its due or proper relish, but is withered by the first blast that envy or tribulation blows over her endeavours. Whereas everything in its proper place and season is graceful, beneficial, and pleasant.

Looking in as well as out, the conservative vision (everything in its proper place) also looks forward as well as back. Growing out of childish things (including Bosvil), on her way to becoming a learned woman, Galesia develops a satisfying life, one that pleases her parents and new friends, none of whom seem to be troubled by her learning.

But this movement towards a life of graceful and pleasant learning depended to a large extent on Galesia/Barker's brother. His death shatters the idyll. The misery she had felt for Bosvil was as nothing to what she now experienced:

> this was grief in abstract, sorrow in pure element. I grieved without ceasing . . . I read those books he had most studied, where I often found his hand-writing, by way of remarks, which always caused a new flux of tears. I often called upon Death, but Death was deaf, or his malice otherwise employed on more worthy prey, leaving me a useless wretch, useless to the world, useless to my friends, and a burden to myself: whilst he that was necessary to his friends, an honour to his profession, and beneficial to mankind (but chiefly to me) the tyrant Death had seized and conveyed away for *ever*! – O that word *Ever*! that thought *Ever*! The reflection of *Ever* and *Never*, devoured all that could be agreeable or pleasing to me. *Ever* to want his wise instructions! *Never* to enjoy his flowing wit! *Ever* to regret this my irreparable loss! *Never* to have his dear company in my shady walks! Thio *Ever* and *Never* stared in my thoughts like things with saucer-eyes in the dark, serving to fright me from all hopes of happiness in this world.[23]

Time 'and the Muses' slowly took the edge off this grief. It was a comfort to think of him in heaven, knowing everything by divine vision:

> All learning and science, all arts and depths of philosophy, without search or study; whilst we in this world, with much labour are groping, as it were, in the dark, and make discoveries of our own ignorance.

She wrote poems to him – 'Thou know'st, my Dear, more than Art can! / Thou know'st the essence of the soul of man' – in which she tried to imagine what it was like to be 'converted to divinity' in a place where there was no winter and summer, no change and no end, and no limitations on knowledge or pleasure:

What joys, my dear, do thee surround,
As no where else are to be found?
Love, music, physic, poetry,
Mechanics, grave philosophy;
And in each art, each artist does abound . . .

And she combined her medical interests with poetry – emulating Ovid, who had put law into verse – attempting to write a poem explaining the principles of anatomy.[24]

In 'To the Reader' in *A Patch-Work Screen for the Ladies*, Barker drew attention to the new fashion for 'histories' by mentioning Defoe's *Robinson Crusoe* and *Moll Flanders* among others. Perhaps she was trying to show that she was up to date; not a leftover from a former era scraping what she herself called 'an old tune, in fashion about threescore and six years ago' but a voice of modernity producing fictions out of the facts of experience. Part of the fiction in 'To the Reader' was a fiction of a community of readers, a group by the fireside, perhaps, in a well-appointed country house, reading about Galesia as they might have read a letter from a friend while getting on with their needlework. As the title made clear, Barker conceived her readership as a female one. In offering such readers an 'old tune', she merged the pleasures of the old romances with a new kind of historical fiction, one full of nostalgia for a specific English past – pre-Hanoverian – and if not quite pro-Jacobite at least infused with some of the idealism of the cause.

Barker the author denied being 'much of an historian'. She represented herself in the address to the reader as a quirky and eccentric poet, her pockets stuffed with manuscript ballads and her head with metaphors that she was inclined to carry 'too high'. Metaphorical speech is cryptic and plural, meaningful without making its meaning unambiguous, and it served Barker well for political and social observations about 'this latter age' where women's 'sentiments' or political views were so mixed. Barker's 'latter age' was specifically the 1690s, as her characterisation of people's different sentiments, existing side by side like patches in a quilt or as close together as ladies round a tea table, reveals: 'Whigs and Tories, High-Church and Low-Church, Jacobites and Williamites, and many more distinctions, which they divide and sub-divide, till at last they make this dis-union meet in an harmonious tea-table entertainment'.

Competent to report women's discussions round the tea table, Barker declined to speak about men – 'I am out of my sphere, and so can say nothing of the male patch-workers' – but she could not ignore the fact that the world was composed of mixed sexes, generations and social classes. Borne on the metaphor of flight, she depicted herself as an Icarus aiming too high and falling to the ground among a company of happy people projecting some scheme – 'a wonderful piece of patch-work they had in hand' – that was to restore Paradise on earth. Her initial delight turns to misery when these people eject her: 'I was forced to get away, every one hunching and pushing me, with scorn and derision.' Why? Because she was a poet: 'they finding some manuscript ballads in my pocket, rejected me as one of that race of mortals who live on a certain barren mountain till they are turned into camelions'. But as it happens their scorn and derision is misplaced: it was the happy projectors who had carried their metaphor too far – the metaphor of the South Sea Bubble and financial corruption which in 1720 caused thousands of investors to lose large sums of money. (Among them was Elizabeth Carter's mother, who apparently never recovered from the catastrophe.)

The poet's mountain may be 'barren' in terms of financial reward, but it is not corrupt and its metaphors and stories remain close enough to the ground to be of use. 'To the Reader' ends with Barker's reunion with Galesia: leaving the throng whose financial schemes have 'blown up about their ears, and vanished into smoke and confusion, to the utter ruin of the many thousands of the unhappy creatures therein concerned', she meets her fictional alter ego out in the open fields where she has come to stretch her legs after a long time of sitting and working. The story that follows is the story Galesia has been working on, her 'patch-work', supposedly told to Barker and now offered for sale to the reader: 'be sure to buy these patches up quickly . . . thereby you'll greatly oblige the bookseller, and, in some degree, the Author. Who is, Your humble servant, Jane Barker.'[25]

This authorial self was one among Barker's many selves, coming and going as opportunity allowed. After a period in London having 'rubbed on in the midst of noise and bustle, which is everywhere to be found in

London, but quiet and retreat scarce anywhere', Barker's Galesia rediscovered her 'impertinent muse' in a garret in lodgings by Westminster Hall. She 'crept' into this room, 'as if it had been a cave on the top of Parnassus, the habitation of some unfortunate muse that had inspired Cowley, Butler, Otway or Orinda with notions different from the rest of mankind, and for that fault were there made prisoners'. Cave or cell, heaven or hell, it was the place for reading, writing and dreaming. Sometimes Galesia would 'repel' the 'insinuations' of her muse and sometimes 'accept her caresses' (but she 'tumbled over Harvey and Willis', her medical textbooks, 'at pleasure').[26]

Ambivalence about writing marked her thoughts. Did the muse 'infest' or 'console'? Did she have an 'unlucky genius'? Was it, as her mother good-naturedly agreed, a 'fatal necessity' that she should dwell with her 'fantastic companions, the muses'? Was poetry more or less harmful than the institutions of Church, state and law that she could see when she went out of her garret door and on to the leads of the roof: Westminster Abbey, Parliament and Westminster Hall? It was certainly inescapable, poetry being 'one of those subtle devils, that if driven out by never so many firm purposes, good resolutions, aversion to that poverty it entails upon its adherents, yet it will always return and find a passage to the heart, brain, and whole interior'.

In the midst of thoughts like these, Galesia is disturbed one day by an unexpected knocking at the door giving on to the leads. Opening it, she finds a gentlewoman who has escaped across the roof pursued by parish officers who have heard that she is pregnant, unmarried and at risk of giving birth to a baby that will be a charge upon the parish. Galesia, her mother and their landlady take the gentlewoman in and hear her story of how she had been impregnated by a married man. Not exactly a rape but rather more than a seduction, Belinda explains that she had been beguiled by his talk about platonic love,

> and the happy state any two might enjoy that lived together in such a chaste affection. In these kind of discourses we passed many hours, sometimes in walks, sometimes in arbours, and oftentimes in my chamber till very late hours. At last the mask of Platonic love was pulled off and a personal enjoyment concluded the farce, composed of many deceitful scenes and wicked contrivances.

Platonic love discourses were a 'mask'. Women, led into free association with men by their shared enjoyment of things of the mind, were at risk of being deceived and betrayed. The serious business of talk could turn at any moment into farce, and when 'personal enjoyment' (men's) broke through the controls of decorum or convenience, the farce became a tragedy.

However remote from actual life the cave on Parnassus might seem, the female who crept into it would never be able entirely to banish from consciousness the ruined woman who haunted its outer door. Like an early version of Charlotte Brontë's Bertha Mason, Barker's Belinda erupts into the writer's life as a reminder of the sexual vulnerability of women. Here, unlike Rochester's mad wife in *Jane Eyre*, the gentlewoman falls among friends: she is not only listened to but believed. The landlady cares for her and undertakes to deal with the parish officers. Galesia's mother, meanwhile, turns her protective instincts on Galesia and bans her from spending time in her garret 'lest I should encounter more adventures'.[27]

This story of the gentlewoman is related by Galesia to the lady in *A Patch-work Screen for the Ladies* into whose country house she has been welcomed. The lady and Galesia comment on the story not by discussing Belinda and her pregnancy but by reflecting on books, solitude and social expectations. They agree that women have duties in life. Their true end was to be mistress of a family, as Galesia's mother had impressed upon her: 'an obedient wife, a discreet governess of your children and servants, a friendly assistant to your neighbours, friends and acquaintance. This being the business for which you came into the world, and for the neglect of this you must give an account when you go out of it.' But they also agree that happiness depends on following inclination. Galesia deprived of her solitude was like Ovid banished from Rome: she was required to do without the thing she preferred above all others.

Galesia is more like Ovid than she is like other young women. She is like Cowley, Butler, Otway and Orinda: she has 'notions different from the rest of mankind'. The philosophical question is whether this is good or bad. In conversation with her mother, Galesia debates what is best for her to do: should she comply with her mother's desire to see her settled as the mistress of a family, living 'like others of my rank', even though there would be no prospect of happiness for her in such a life given her 'secret disgust against matrimony'? Or should she continue as she is? She agrees that books and learning are 'pernicious' because so much more pleasurable than other options: 'by their means we relish not the diversions or embellishments of our sex and station, which render us agreeable to the world and the world to us'. To be immersed in the pleasures of the mind is to become unfit for the world; mental pleasures threaten the social order of rank and gender. But she cannot resist them. Indeed, in a poem, 'The Necessity of Fate', Galesia points out that her mother had envisaged this very future for her when she had commanded that a picture of her as a child should show her holding a laurel bough, even though other people said an apple, a bird or a rose would have been more fitting objects. Convinced by the poem, Galesia's mother ceases to insist that marriage be the business of Galesia's life. She recalls 'one of the ancient poets' saying that nature would always take its course. For Galesia that course was poetry, an innocent enough 'diversion' after all.[28]

By means of a loosely connected sequence of scenes, images and conversations – a collage or a patchwork – Jane Barker unfolded the female author's dilemma. Was she to be considered gifted by fate, a chosen one holding the symbol in her hand, whose destiny was unlike that of other women? Or was she an oddity indulged in her fancies who would be better off if she could 'quench' them? Immured in her attic, alone with her books and papers, her situation sometimes pleased her – 'this hole was to me a kind of Paradise' – and sometimes not: it was 'a den of dullness'. These subjective responses, the movement of feeling in relation to event, were of interest in themselves. Through Galesia, Barker attempted to describe both a way of living and a way of being that were sufficiently novel to be worth exploring as a set of interior responses as well as requiring constant justification: for one of her 'sex and station', the choice of books over more customary female activities was 'uncouth'. It was also risky. The most obvious danger was to her own peace of mind when the cave became a den of dullness, or, to put that another way, when Galesia's desire failed her. But as the story of Belinda showed, there were outside dangers too. Neither her room nor her mind could protect Galesia from the incursion of social reality in the shape of the doubly wronged woman, seduced by a married man and pursued by the authorities.

Pope gave the name Belinda to the heroine of his mock epic ('an heroi-comical poem') *The Rape of the Lock* (1712). It was a conventional name for a romance heroine. Perhaps in using it in this instance, Barker was offering her own heroi-comical comment on the relation of reality and imagination, real women's lives and those to be found in books. It is tempting to think so because in many ways Barker's Belinda was premonitory. If we ask which of these heroines is replicated in prose fiction as it evolved and became the most significant literary genre by the end of the eighteenth century, the answer is Belinda the wronged woman, not Galesia the thoughtful, reflective, awkward and always interesting writer.

As for Jane Barker herself, she was not remembered. By the time of her death in 1732 she was almost eighty and had no loving family or genteel network of like-minded friends to produce a celebratory *Life* that would memorialise her and preserve her works for posterity in the way that Elizabeth Rowe's family and friends had done. Such family as she had she was at odds with: in 1717 she had been involved in a lawsuit with a niece. At that time (and probably for much of her adult life) Barker was 'in necessitous circumstances' and, judging by her niece's unfriendly account, could be experienced as manipulative, high-handed and unpleasant.[29] Marginalised by the turn of political events, loyal to the old cause, addicted to 'idle dreams on Parnassus and foolish romantic flights', Barker had spent a good deal of her time reading and writing and doing her best to leave her name in life's visit, as Matthew Prior put it, by her pen. She wanted to leave more than her name; she wanted to make sure that her story survived and that it was understood as part of the nation's story.

Mary Davys and real events

To some extent in the early days of print culture, reading and writing itself, the attraction to books and 'dear pen and ink', was understood to be about the desire to know and understand the world, and about the opportunity to enter it in one's own chosen shape, telling what had not been told (true or false, fact or fiction) in one's own chosen words.

In 1705, an Irish clergyman's widow, Mary Davys, published *The Fugitive*, an account of her experiences travelling alone, poor and unprotected except by her native wit, through the English countryside. She declared the autobiographical nature of the work: 'I had a mind to make an experiment, whether it was not possible to divert the Town with real events just as they happened.' The 'real events' included familiar travellers' experiences such as filthy beds, miserly landladies, scolds, prudes and fortune hunters. Fending for herself wherever she fetched up, Davys countered the standard prejudice against the Irish by making fun of English yokels whose notion of 'the wild Irish' was that they still had tails.[30]

Twenty years later, a modest success as a playwright enabled her to open a coffee house in Cambridge. As a coffee-house keeper, Mary Davys was in a position to issue her collected works in two volumes, supported by 169 subscribers, among whom were 107 students of the university – all gentlemen and including 'a good number of both the grave and the young clergy' – as well as three duchesses, Alexander Pope, Mrs Martha Blount and John Gay. By this time, Davys had developed ideas about literature as well as life. In her general preface, she outlined a theory of prose fiction which, in its emphasis on the 'real' as opposed to 'romance' seems to have been a self-conscious bid, directed at her mostly male audience, to distance herself from stereotypical assumptions about female authors.

Entertaining fiction, she announced, should draw upon real life, 'the commonest matters of fact, truly told'. This was what she had tried to do in *The Fugitive*, to explore 'real events, just as they happened, without running into romance'. Romance was identified with the French in the first instance and women in the second. Romance was likely to be 'flat or insipid or offensive'. Real life included 'true history'; one problem with the French was that when they 'pretend to write true history [they] give themselves the utmost liberty of feigning', as well as being 'tedious', 'dry in their matter' and 'so impertinent in their harangues that a reader can hardly keep themselves awake over them'. How much Mary Davys cared about French romances is unclear, but that she cared about politics and history, particularly Irish history and its many 'barbarities', is not in doubt.

There was nothing tedious or dry in Davys's unsparing account of one among many massacres in Irish memory – she does not specify which. In *Familiar Letters Betwixt a Gentleman and a Lady* it is given to the lady, Berina, to tell the gentleman in no uncertain terms things he might not wish to hear:

> more than three hundred thousand souls [were] murdered in cold blood, the clergy's mouths cut from ear to ear, their tongues pulled out and thrown to the dogs, then bid go preach up heresy; men's guts pulled out and tied to each other's waists, then whipped different ways; some stabbed, burnt, drowned, impaled and flayed alive; children ripped out of their mother's womb and thrown to the dogs, or dashed against the stones . . . with a thousand other barbarities too tedious as well as too dreadful to repeat.[31]

Her words are an unexpected explosion of outrage in what is for the most part a lively, sophisticated commentary on modern courtship. The familiar letters pass between Berina and Artander, a 'platonick' couple negotiating love and friendship, and discussing the pros and cons of marriage as they move inexorably towards it. To be married 'were to be blind indeed', according to Berina, but on the other hand there were 'the dismal effects of not loving' to be considered: 'to be called ill-natured and an old maid, who would not rather choose to be undone than lie under such scandalous epithets?' Politically, the two are on opposite sides: Berina is a Whig and Artander a Tory and their exchanges allegorise an end to factionalism. Berina, whose 'darling passion' is politics, speaks the language of constitutional liberty against the 'arbitrary power' of love and beauty and men's helplessness before a woman's 'killing eyes'. She has no interest in a man who, sexually enslaved, promises to be 'all obedience': 'I should despise a husband as much as a king who would give up his own prerogative, or unman himself to make his wife the head. We women are too weak to be trusted with power . . . The notion I have always had of happiness in marriage is where love causes obedience on one side, and compliance on the other, with a view to the duty incumbent on both.' The platonic relationship posed a common-sense balance of power, where women's inherent weakness and men's weakness in relation to women could both be corrected. Like the state, marriage suffered when tyranny was allowed to prevail.[32]

Mary Davys's writing made fun of women as well as men while at the same time using current forms – epistolary exchange, picaresque travel narrative, plays, novels, and at least one poem on what was becoming the definitive writerly subject: the impoverished poet in his squalid garret – with some subtlety. In all these genres the influence of her immersion in the dramas of Farquhar, Congreve and Centlivre was clear. Similarly, she opted for what was modish. Her novel *The Reformed Coquet* (1724), which blended comedy of manners and stock dramatic types with the new novel of sentiment, went on to be reissued at least seven times. *The Reformed Coquet* was dedicated 'To the ladies' with a rather gentlemanly flourish, one of its editions refining this still further: it was specially intended 'for the use of ancient ladies' and therefore 'printed in a large letter'. (Short-sighted 'ancient ladies' who had left their coquetting days behind them and were eager to relive it all in imagination were perhaps a promising market.) Davys's final novel, *The Accomplished Rake: Or, Modern Fine Gentleman* (1727), anticipated Hogarth and Richardson in its vivid detailing of the plain 'facts' of a country rake's progress in London. No doubt she drew for some of her material on the escapades of her coffee-house customers.

Presiding over her own version of the 'penny universities' (so-called because a penny dish of coffee bought hours of sociable improvement) in the shadows of the real university which did not admit women, making allies of the 'men of taste' who gathered there, Mary Davys was in a position to absorb a strong sense of audience for her speech which carried over into her writing. Though her subject matter was female experience – *The Lady's Tale*, *The Northern Heiress*, her own wanderings in *The Fugitive* – the assumed audience can often be felt to be male, a detail which perhaps accounts for a certain bluff and breezy handling of male and female stereotypes. In the general preface to her *Works* she described the way her clients entered into her writing and publication plans. It was two students who suggested she print *The Reformed Coquet* by subscription. She added that they were surely motivated by 'charity' rather than the 'novelty' of her novel: 'it was not to the book but the author they subscribed'. The author presented herself as an elderly clergyman's widow rather than a coffee-house keeper or a moderately successful playwright and novelist ('The two plays I leave to fight their own battles; and I shall say no more than that I was never so vain as to think they deserved a place in the first rank, or so humble as to resign them to the last'), though by 1724 her husband had been dead almost thirty years and she had shifted for herself, taking on a number of roles and identities. The cheerful worldliness of her comedies which traded in mockery of provincial types – Lady Greasy, the chandler's widow, Lady Swish, the brewer's wife, and Lady Cordivant, the glover's wife – and diverted London audiences, suggest a life in which she met people from many different social groups, and it is possible she had worked as a female companion. The Yorkshire merchant class were the butt of her jokes; and her settings, like those of Eliza Haywood's fiction, show much familiarity with the comings and goings of lodging-house interiors. Nevertheless, it was as the 'relict' of a clergyman that she came before the public:

> Perhaps it may be objected against me ... that as I am a relict of a clergyman, and in years, I ought not to publish plays, &c. But I beg of such to suspend their uncharitable opinions till they have read what I have writ, and if they find any there offensive either to God or man ... tis then time enough to blame. And let them further consider that a woman left to her own endeavours for twenty-seven years together, may well be allowed to catch at any opportunity for that bread which they that condemn her would very probably deny to give her.

The objection to imagined objections ('I beg of such to suspend their uncharitable opinions') carried more than a slight touch of aggression. Davys had honed a combative resourcefulness in the years of fending for herself, in writing for the theatre and latterly, no doubt, in coffee-house disputation. She was confident that her subject matter did not expose her to reproach: she did not deal in obscenity, her sexual reputation was unblemished. Was there a veiled allusion to Aphra Behn in the choice of words? Under the protection of a coffee-house coterie of clergymen and students, the widow of a clergyman and in her fifties, she wrote for bread and was not ashamed to own it. The clergymen who encouraged her might also take a pride in what had been achieved. Perhaps they shared her indignation that those who (putatively) condemned were likely to lack charity in the strictly financial sense.

Laetitia Pilkington's *Memoirs*

Mary Davys had known Jonathan Swift well enough to appeal to him for small sums of money when times were hard, and to dedicate *The Fugitive* to Esther Johnson, Swift's 'Stella', whom she barely knew. Laetitia Pilkington, who crossed to London from Dublin in the late 1730s had, along with her then husband, Matthew, been an intimate friend of the Dean of St Patrick's for nine or ten years. Pilkington was to exploit the public fascination with private life in a novel way. As well as writing about her own experiences as a poet for pay in her *Memoirs* of 1748, she was the first to provide anecdotes of the 'private' Jonathan Swift, a national hero in Ireland ever since the 1724 *Drapier's Letters* (fireworks were set off to celebrate his birthday) but whose death in 1745 had not been marked by any biographical memoir.

Like Elizabeth Thomas with her cache of letters from Pope and others, Laetitia Pilkington had a commodity to sell: not letters but private knowledge, and not papers for someone else to use but the wit and literary talent to turn her experiences – the experience of friendship with a famous writer – to advantage. Like Mary Davys she was needy; unlike Davys, she was no respectable widow, having been divorced in the Church courts. Supposedly (and probably in fact) she had been having an affair with a surgeon, Robin Adair, and been caught in the act. Pilkington claimed that her husband, a clergyman who was involved in an affair of his own, had ill-treated her, verbally and physically, and that he had 'an aversion' to her person that led him to prefer the arms of 'buxom Joan'. She did not press her own innocence – 'here, gentle Reader, give me leave to drop the curtain. To avouch mine own innocence in a point where appearances were strong against me, would perhaps little avail' – but she charmingly offered herself as a heroine of romance and literature, drawing on the gentle reader's pleasure in imaginative contemplation of women in a variety of textual and stage representations. For example, in describing Matthew's 'aversion' to her, she instanced a domestic exchange which took place after she had accidentally pricked her breast while putting on her gown. As nobody but her husband and children were present, she took the gown off and uncovered her breast to see what had happened, an action which provoked Matthew to leave the table in disgust saying that the sight of her breast turned his stomach. She, thinking he was joking, quoted Prior, who, in 'The Lover's Anger', forgets his anger when he sees his lover's breast – 'That seat of delight I with wonder survey'd / And forgot ev'ry word I design'd to have said'. The allusion and seven-line quotation from Prior served many purposes. It identified her as a woman of polite learning and her husband as a brute (he did not respond as a poet should); it licensed half-naked self-display (gown off and assuring the reader she had 'a fine skin'); and it suggested that she should have been treated, like any other heroine, as an object of adoration.[33]

The odious Matthew Pilkington's 'machinations' brought about the catastrophe. Robin Adair was found in her bedroom in the middle of the night. When she wrote about it, Pilkington rendered this moment as a scene from a farce, drawing the reader into a collusion with herself – the bemused, book-loving innocent – and against her husband – a posturing, cowardly fool:

I own myself very indiscreet in permitting any man to be at an unseasonable hour in my bed-chamber; but lovers of learning will, I am sure, pardon me, as I solemnly declare, it was the attractive charms of a new book, which the gentleman would not lend me, but consented to stay till I read it through, that was the sole motive of my detaining him. But the servants being bribed by their master, let in twelve watchmen at the kitchen window, who, though they might have opened the chamber door, chose rather to break it to pieces, and took the gentleman and myself prisoners.

For my own part, I thought they had been house-breakers, and would willingly have compounded for life, when entered Mr Pilkington, with a cambric handkerchief tied about his neck, after the fashion of Mr Fribble, and with the temper of a Stoic, bid the authorised ruffians not hurt me; but his Christian care came too late, for one of them had given me a violent blow on the temple, and another had dragged two of my fingers out of joint. The gentleman at the sight of Mr Pilkington, threw down his sword, which he observing made two of the watchmen hold him, while he most courageously broke his head.

After this heroic action, he told me, who stood quite stupefied between surprise and pain, that I must turn out of doors . . .[34]

The comic monologue is consummately done. By the time she wrote her story for publication, Pilkington had been dining out on it for years. Turned out of doors and divorced, she had refused to go quietly, lodging an appeal in order to get some maintenance. The appeal failed. Alone and cut off from respectable society, forced to make her own way in the world, she had been driven by 'want', like Mary Davys and numerous other Irishwomen before her, into a wandering life. She left Dublin for London, planning to publish a volume of her poetry by subscription. In the meantime, she was able to earn her keep by her witty banter, and by ghost-writing love poems for the noblemen and gamblers who hung out at White's, the fashionable club in St James's opposite which she took lodgings. Conveniently situated, she did good business. Was she a whore? She doesn't say so. What she says is that she was a poet and a wit and men came because of her skill with words.

Nor did she sit passively waiting for custom. She took herself off to likely subscribers and solicited their support. Getting patronage from the great could be time-consuming and expensive. Pilkington made an inventory of how much it cost, beginning with one penny for pen, ink and paper and a total of thirty-seven shillings and sixpence in bribes or tips: a shilling to the person who would find out when his Lordship would be at home, half a guinea to the porter, a guinea to the valet and a crown to the footman. All this went into the *Memoirs*, along with names and amounts given: when the Bishop of London gave her only half a crown she disdainfully handed it on to his porter – the Bishop might be mean but she knew what was owing to her, and once she published their encounter in a book the world knew it too.

Pilkington's talent was for conversation. Having known Swift so well, she had a fund of anecdotes about the famous Dean of St Patrick's. Colley Cibber was one of the regulars at White's who helped her by presenting her verses to those, like Henry Pelham, who might reward – Pelham gave her ten guineas for some fawning verses. Cibber had been 'determined to have my history from my own lips', and he invited her to his house to have breakfast. 'Accordingly I waited on him,' she wrote in her *Memoirs*, describing a scene reminiscent of Delarivier Manley going to visit Edmund Curll and telling her story in words 'no pen but her own can relate in the agreeable manner wherein she delivered it'. The part of Pilkington's history which most interested Cibber were her stories about Jonathan Swift: 'wonderfully was he delighted with my account of Doctor Swift. He had the patience to listen to me three hours, without ever once interrupting me, a most uncommon instance of good breeding, especially from a person of his years, who usually dictate to the company, and engross all the talk to themselves.'

The delighted Cibber, becoming more and more animated as he listened, 'at last, in flowing spirits, cried, "Zounds! Write it out, just as you relate it, and I'll engage it will sell." '[35]

Telling Cibber about Swift was part of Pilkington's own story. Though Swift wanted nothing to do with her after the scandal of divorce, referring to her as 'the most profligate whore in either kingdom', Pilkington's literary enthusiasm had made her company congenial to him and given her unusual access. She had been allowed to leaf through his letters from Pope and Bolingbroke, Addison and Congreve, Bishop Burnet, Arbuthnot and Gay – 'A noble and learned set! So my readers may judge what a banquet I had' – heard his versions of anecdotes concerning Pope and others, and had free run of his unpublished writings: 'The Dean running into the parlour, threw a whole packet of manuscript poems into my lap, and so he did for five or six times successively, till I had an apron full of wit and novelty, for they were all of his own writing, and such as had not then been made public.' Pilkington understood the value of what she had in her lap. The Dean's poems, the Dean's eagerness to share them with her, his eccentric behaviour, her account of her own writing and her husband's jealousy (one evening, she recalled, they both produced Horatian odes and hers was better: 'if a man cannot bear his friend should write, much less can he endure it in his wife') all combined in the *Memoirs* to produce a picture of a busy literary circle, distinguished because of Swift, full of energy and oddity and spite, in which the diminutive Laetitia Pilkington was authentically a poet, even if she claimed that everything she wrote was offhand: 'for I am too volatile to revise or correct any thing I write'. Being 'volatile' was another of the qualities by which a genius might be recognised.[36]

In building up this picture of herself in the *Memoirs*, Pilkington's description of her breakfast with Cibber and his appreciation of what she had to say were important details. Like Joseph Warton figuring himself breaking in upon Dr Young's retirement ('the residence of virtue and literature') to exchange ideas about Pope, what they helped create was an image of how literary work was conducted and what sort of people did it. If being remembered defined authorship, then being able to remember and tell stories about famous authors was another way of being an author at a time when biography, autobiography and literary criticism were emerging genres.

Cibber himself, the actor made fun of in *The Dunciad*, had turned notoriety into profitable celebrity when in 1740 he published a lively autobiography, *An Apology for the Life of Mr Colley Cibber, Comedian*, which sold well. (He was said to have received at least £1,500 for it.) There was a vogue for the self-told life which both factual and fictional prose writers sought to satisfy, often taking misfortune as the starting point (Cibber's misfortune was his passion for the stage, Lady Mary Wortley Montagu's 'unfortunate lady' had an unfortunate passion for knowledge) and drawing on romance elements such as the triumph over impossible odds or commitment to abstract ideals. The 'apology' format – or confessional – was a version of the familiar spiritual autobiography, although the salvation that women like Laetitia Pilkington sought was financial not spiritual. There was no suggestion that Pilkington might recoup her reputation; rather, she was seizing an opportunity to make a newly available one by drawing on unique knowledge and the observations of private friendship.

Cibber knew the trade. Fighting female speech had commercial potential. Whether Pilkington had *done* wrong was less important commercially than the fact that she had *been* wronged and was amusing on the subject. The courtesan Constantia Phillips set the example. She had used her wit as well as her beauty to present herself as an exceptional woman ill-treated by an unworthy man. The bookseller who bought Phillips's story for £1,000 (an offer which she was not minded to refuse, having spent 1745-7 in debtors' prison) responded to her much as the judges did on one of the many appearances in court that she managed to turn into much admired performances. Captivated by her 'lovely form', we are told, they 'rose from their seats to salute her the moment she appeared, and, after some trifling objections by her husband to the bail, in which he made a most contemptible figure, my Lord Chief Justice begged she would stay no longer in Court, for fear of catching cold.'[37]

Pilkington was working the same market for her goods: judges, bishops, men of letters, businessmen, politicians, lawyers, gamblers, rakes, artists, older sons, younger sons, anyone who would give her a guinea or two. Like Phillips she was a performer. Her *Memoirs* told her story. The daughter of a prominent Dublin physician, comfortably brought up in a family which had kinship ties to landed gentry and nobility, she married (slightly beneath her) a parson who shared her poetical ambitions but had less talent and less virtue. The couple became friends with Swift, were divorced, and she went to London and attempted to support herself by her pen. That the story was the story of *a writer* is made clear early on, as she describes her reputation as a child prodigy, able to recite Pope at the age of five: 'my performances had the good fortune to be looked on as extraordinary for my years; and the greatest and wisest men in the kingdom did not disdain to hear the prattle of the little muse, as they called me'.[38]

The *Memoirs* displayed Pilkington's 'scribbling and prattling vein'. They had the immediacy of rattling talk and the artfulness of a composed account. Aggressively satirical and with nothing to lose nor any reputation to protect, her virtue was in the eye of the beholder – that reader whom she constantly addressed. Sometimes she was sorrowful – 'alas! Poor I, have been for many years a noun substantive, obliged to stand alone' – sometimes vengeful, but always self-assertive and busy; perhaps at work accosting a named nobleman, perhaps talking to strangers on a park bench, perhaps browsing in a bookshop, perhaps in jail – 'Misery unspeakable, which not to tease my readers, I have slightly passed over; for what entertainment can it possibly give to the curious, learned, or polite reader to hear from me what every person who has ever been in jail can relate as well as I'; perhaps telling how she spent a night locked inside Westminster Abbey, or how her fifteen-year-old daughter unexpectedly turned up, pregnant, and the two of them were turned out of the lodging house; or how, after getting soaked to the skin walking to Chelsea to petition Sir Hans Sloane and finding him 'a conceited, ridiculous imperious old fool' who gave her only half a crown, she wanted to throw it back in his face but reflected like Falstaff 'that I had ne'er a shilling in my pocket, and . . . little as it was, I could eat for it', unlike the two guineas she had brought home from a more charitable character – 'Reader, give me leave to trespass a moment on your patience, to make one remark, which is that amongst all the persons who are celebrated for being charitable, I never met one really so' – and which she had thrown into the air with delight, thereby losing one of them between the floorboards: 'the board my landlady would never permit me to remove, lest, as she said, I would spoil her floor'.[39]

She herself, by her own account, was not scandalous; the scandal was in what had happened to her, her story or 'history', which had caused her to be obliged to live by her wits and which she would relate to any sympathetic ear, interspersing her conversation with apposite references from Shakespeare and Milton and Pope to show that she was a woman of gentry upbringing. Being treated politely by polite people was 'proof that I was not an imposter'. It was important to convince people that she had 'once been in esteem, even in my own country'. She was 'a worthy gentleman's daughter . . . nurtured in ease and plenty' and driven to distress by an unworthy husband.

Opening the pamphlet and print shop in St James's, close to her 'noble benefactors', was an improvement on 'the misery of extreme want', but she was nonetheless a little self-conscious: 'So, Reader, here was a new scene, and I, for the first of my family, took my place behind a counter.'[40] Installed in her shop, Pilkington went on writing, turning out anti-Walpole pamphlets as well as 'a flaming prologue' to a ballad opera adapted from *The Taming of the Shrew* 'in honour of my fair countrywomen'. Whatever loyalty she felt towards Irishwomen in general did not extend to 'our female writers', of whom she had little that was good to say and that little entirely conventional. Too many women, apparently, had 'the wicked art of painting up vice in attractive colours . . . amongst whom Mrs Manley and Mrs Haywood deserve the foremost rank':

But what extraordinary passions these ladies may have experienced I know not; far be such knowledge from a modest woman: indeed, Mrs Haywood seems to have dropped her former luscious style and, for variety, presents us with the insipid: her *Female Spectators* are a collection of trite stories, delivered to us in stale and worn out phrases, bless'd Revolution!
   Yet of the two, less dang'rous is the offence
   To tire the patience, than mislead the sense.
And here give me leave to observe, that amongst the ladies who have taken up the pen, I never met with but two who deserved the name of a writer; the

first is Madam Dacier ... the second is Mrs Catherine Philips, the matchless Orinda, celebrated by Mr Cowley, Lord Orrery, and all the men of genius who lived in her time.

Being celebrated by the men of genius was the mark of literary success. Pilkington also mentioned as a female who was worth reading her countrywoman Constantia Grierson, another prodigy and one of the few contemporaries to be included in George Ballard's *Memoirs of British Ladies* (she died young, in 1732), who, along with poet Mary Barber and critic Elizabeth Sican, formed Swift's 'Triumfeminate' of Dublin wit. But among the ladies who had taken up the pen, nobody else 'deserved the name of a writer'.[41] Like the tag from Pope − that it was less dangerous to bore the reader than to 'mislead the sense' − this sentiment had become so worn from overuse by the mid century that it was virtually meaningless except as one among the many ways a woman could assert her own claims to authorship.

Chapter Nine

READINGS AND REPRESENTATIONS

Virtue of all sorts is a mighty perishable commodity.
Charlotte Smith, letter to Dr Thomas Shirly[1]

Being remembered

Upon marriage to the Revd Patrick Cockburn in 1708, the philosopher
and dramatist Catharine Trotter had 'bid adieu to the muses' and taken
on the responsibilities of a curate's wife, first at Nayland in Suffolk, and
then, from 1713, at St Dunstan's in Fleet Street, where it is not unlikely
that they knew Parson Elstob and his scholarly sister who lived a little
further east at St Swithin's. Whatever comforts this security brought
were short-lived: in 1714 Patrick Cockburn's conscience prevented him
from taking the oath of abjuration on the accession of George 1 and he
lost his post. For twelve years after this, the family (there were two
daughters and one son) pieced together an income: he taught Latin at a
school, and they probably had some support from his father, an eminent
cleric, and from her sister; but interestingly there is no evidence that the
woman who for ten years had successfully written and made some sort
of income from her writing sought to do so at this stage. Delarivier
Manley's attacks on her in the *New Atalantis* and *Rivella* are likely to
have been a factor. As a writer, Catharine Trotter, now Cockburn,
became invisible, only to re-emerge in 1726 – the year her husband was
persuaded to take the oath – with another defence of John Locke: *A
Letter to Dr Holdsworth*. By then, Delarivier Manley had been safely
dead for two years.

A Letter to Dr Holdsworth, which defended Locke against Holdsworth's accusations of heresy, demonstrated that the former Catharine Trotter remained alert to current philosophical and theological concerns. It also indicated where her own preferred sense of herself as a writer lay. But by the late 1720s and early 1730s, theological controversy was not an obvious route to fame. When Cockburn tried to get a subsequent commentary on Locke, the *Vindication of Mr Locke's Christian Principles*, published, the booksellers were uninterested. She was despondent: 'all subjects of divinity are disregarded now'.[2]

The sense that it was not only 'all subjects of divinity' but that she too had been 'disregarded' came to dominate Catharine Cockburn's last decades. In 1732, she addressed a poem to Queen Caroline which, in the politest terms, expressed her discontent. Cockburn's 'Poem, occasioned by the busts set up in the Queen's Hermitage', was 'occasioned' by at least two envy-producing episodes: the Queen's patronage of the thresher poet, Stephen Duck; and her setting up of portrait busts in honour of philosophers Locke, Newton and Clarke in her hermitage at Richmond. Cockburn did not quite consider she should have been among the company of philosophers represented by a bust – she was, after all, a commentator, not a deviser of philosophical systems, which is perhaps why she figured herself as a cleaner brushing the dust and vermin from their features – but nevertheless she wanted her labour and worth recognised. In the poem, she made a claim for herself not on the basis of her individual achievements but on behalf of her sex, employing what was by then a familiar rhetoric of indignation at oppression and prejudice unworthy of an advanced civilisation. If Stephen Duck, a rural poet, was deserving of reward, how much more so were women whose progress to knowledge and achievement was systematically obstructed:

> Tho not the flail and sickle could retard,
> Or cares discourage more the rural bard
> Than those restraints which have our sex confin'd,
> By partial custom, check the soaring mind;
> Learning deny'd us, we at random tread
> Unbeaten paths, that late to knowledge lead;
> By secret steps break thro th'obstructed way,

Nor dare acquirements gain'd by stealth display.
If some advent'rous genius rare arise,
Who on exalted themes her talent tries,
She fears to give the work, tho praised, a name,
And flies not more from infamy than fame.

This version of female experience as one defined by obstruction, confinement, denial and restraint, was a commonplace in the discourse of and about clever women. Essentially sentimental, it depended on the idea of thwarted genius or 'injur'd merit'. Apparently speaking for women as a whole – 'our sex', 'we', 'us' – it actually concerned itself only with exceptional women, those whose soaring minds aspired to 'exalted themes'. Critical of social customs which denied women the opportunity for knowledge, it was at the same time critical of women who were uninterested in learning, those who preferred 'trifling pleasures' to reading books. Such women were incorporated into the 'us' and 'we' of the poem by a rhetoric which turned them into victims of social custom. Everything that lay outside the 'wide realms of science' and learning was corrupt: women who were denied knowledge were denied the opportunity to learn how not to be corrupted. Ruined by custom, they needed to 'reform their taste'. According to the poem, the Queen's commendation of Catharine Cockburn's writings – the productions of a woman who had refused to be refused knowledge and who was therefore a shining example of what women could be – would assist in this noble endeavour. It would help all women give up quadrille, go to bed earlier, and be better mothers, friends and wives:

Important is the boon! Nor I alone,
The female world its influence would own,
T'approve themselves to thee, reform their taste,
No more their time in trifling pleasures waste;
In search of truths sublime, undaunted soar,
And the wide realms of science deep explore.
Quadrille should then resign that tyrant sway,
Which rules despotic, blending night with day;
Usurps on all the offices of life,
The duties of the mother, friend, and wife.
Learning, with milder reign would more enlarge

Their powers, and aid those duties to discharge;
To nobler gain improve their vacant hours;
Be Newton, Clarke, and Locke their mattadores.

Then, as this happy isle already vies
In arms with foes, in arts with her allies;
No more excell'd in aught by Gallia's coast,
Our Albion too shall of her Daciers boast.[3]

Catharine Cockburn felt undervalued. France famously encouraged its intellectual women such as Madame Dacier; 'Albion' famously did not. France boasted of its Daciers while England leaned down to pluck an agricultural labourer from the soil but ignored a gentlewoman who had written philosophy and was considered by some a genius.

If we consider the poem as autobiography, we have to say it isn't true to what we know of Cockburn's experience as a writer and thinker. Her 'soaring mind' was not checked and she was not denied the opportunity to read and write philosophy. She put her 'vacant hours' to excellent use in studying Newton, Clarke and Locke. Thus the poem, though personal, was not autobiography. The 'I' represented an exemplary ideal in what was essentially a polemical petition. The poem urged Cockburn's superiority to the mass of women, and her usefulness as an example. As a call to arms, the argument – that constraining women's energies led to folly and vice – was a conventional one. Queen Caroline would have had no difficulty in seeing the point; quite a few women of high rank were saying the same things. To encourage female philosophy represented no threat since it was allied to the patriotic and loyal goal of national improvement, and sought to strengthen not undermine the hierarchy of rank.

Cockburn's daughter was given the task of trying to present the petition to the Queen. This required her presence in London on her mother's behalf, chasing up any contacts of high rank prepared to interest themselves in the matter. In February 1733, Cockburn reported that her daughter was still in London, 'detained by a new prospect of succeeding in my affairs; at least in the matter of the poem; and of being presented to some great ladies to whom I was formerly known'.[4] These efforts seem not to have been successful. Three years later, when the poem was published (in a slightly different version) in the *Gentleman's Magazine*, a 'great lady' materialised: Lady Betty Gordon requested a fair copy. This produced a flurry of activity and was so distracting that Catharine Cockburn forgot to send compliments to her niece, Anne Arbuthnot, who had recently married. In 'debt' to her niece, she would still not have written first to her when there was a Lady Betty Gordon to respond to. The excitement of having her work valued by such a reader animated the letter she eventually sent, which explained how much she had had to do as a result:

> There were several alterations in it, that I thought for the worse, which cost me some writing, both to my son and the publisher about it; besides another little thing I sent them with it. And Lady Betty Gordon having taken a copy from the print, hearing there were faults in it, was very pressing to have a correct one from me. This obliged me to write a fair copy (for I have none by me) and I have since received a very ingenious letter from her ladyship, that I must answer. I have before heard she was a great reader, and now find she has read Mr Locke's *Essay*, and the controversies he was engaged in, upon which she speaks very judiciously. She tells me she has seen some of my former performances (but does not say of what kind) which made her desirous to see my late poem, and wishes for an opportunity of subscribing to my *Vindication of Mr Locke*, if it were to be published in that way. All this I have told you, to make a merit to you (that may in some measure atone for past omissions) of deferring to answer the obliging expressions of so great a lady that I might first acquit myself of my debt to you.[5]

Through the 1730s and 1740s Catharine Cockburn enlisted the support of all her family in the cause of making her writings better known and doing justice to her achievements. She viewed herself not as one who had been deprived of opportunity because of her sex, but as an exception – an 'advent'rous genius rare' – who had arisen and made a mark and therefore deserved reward. All the family stood to benefit from attentions paid to her by those of high rank. Petitioning on these grounds in the 1730s and 1740s, they continued a family tradition the writer's mother had begun in the 1680s when she petitioned for compensation for her husband's booty money and effects lost when he died at sea, and that Cockburn herself had been doing when as Catharine Trotter in 1704 she was hopeful of getting a pension.

Cockburn's 'genius' was the equivalent of her father's exceptional qualities as a naval officer. Just as a well-regarded naval officer was lowered by being deprived of the emblems of his success, so too a well-regarded author was denied her appropriate place in the system without the 'boon' of a royal gift. And just as much of the nation's wealth and pride depended on its naval officers, so too in the culture wars it depended on its writers and thinkers.

Catharine Cockburn reads Pope

Having begun writing seriously again, Catharine Cockburn reflected on her situation. The writer who mattered most to her was Alexander Pope, both for his writings and for his 'moral character'. She often discussed Pope with her niece, explaining that she particularly admired his *Essay on Man* and the *Epistle to Dr Arbuthnot*, and spelling out for the younger woman the worldly fact that 'great merit', such as Pope obviously had, would always raise enemies. Reading his translation of Homer she had been 'charmed with the humanity of his remarks on some passages, which, though suitable to the manners of those times are very shocking to us; and he is always very gallant to the ladies. To say the truth, I am grown of late very fond of the man.' Many malicious things had been published about Pope and his friends, but as far as she was concerned 'his private letters show him to be in all respects the most amiable character I ever met with in so great a genius'.[6]

Many women, reading the published versions of Pope's letters in the 1730s, were moved to write to him personally. Pope's 'humanity' aroused a 'fondness' that contrasted with the apparent inhumanity of his 'enemies'. In 1738, Catharine Cockburn sat down in her house in Northumberland – far from literary London – and penned him a long letter which she did not send but carefully preserved. (Whether she ever intended to send it cannot be known, but it is likely that she always intended to publish it, probably in the edition of her works which she was already assembling at that time and where it duly appeared.) She introduced herself in the first instance as a member of the public, indignant at 'the vile faction set up against you', and with an appropriate interest in him: he was an honour to the country and the country owed him something in return, which in her case was 'friendship and best wishes'. But she was also a writer, one whose active publishing career had ended thirty years earlier, in 1708, the year before Pope's began with the publication of the *Pastorals*, followed by the *Essay on Criticism* in 1711 which made him famous. The letter addressed Pope as writer to writer. In doing so, it claimed equality with him and even, since she was of an older generation, some superiority. It is a rare example of a mature woman writer measuring herself against a man of acknowledged stature and thinking about her own life and career through the comparison. As a piece of writing, it was driven by much the same brooding discontent with the lack of reward her works had brought her as the 1732 poem addressed to the Queen.

I might lay some claim to you as a brother poet; but it would be a very empty one, since I can plead no affinity with your excellent talents that way; and an indifferent poet is a very scurvy character. However, I happen to be extremely pleased (though without much vanity) at my situation in my poetical capacity with respect to you. 'Twas my good fortune that most of my performances were as well received as I thought they deserved. They gained me some friends among the great and the good; and, what is perhaps a better proof of their merit, they even raised me some enemies. This raises me above envying the universal applause you have met with; and I am too far below you to repine at it, or hate you as a rival. So I find that, happily for me, by being in the middle class of writers, I can rejoice in your triumphs, and be fond of your virtues: in short there is nothing left for me, but to admire and love you. You need not be alarmed at the expression, though from a woman, when I tell you I am about the borders of threescore. I cannot indeed but regret that you did not come sooner into the world, or I later; for I flatter myself, I should then have had the pleasure of your acquaintance by the means of one or other who have had a share in your friendship, to whom I was not unknown, Mr Wycherly, Congreve etc. But they are all gone before me, though I was in a manner dead long before them. You had but just begun to dawn upon the world, when I retired from it. Being married in 1708, I bid adieu to the muses, and so wholly gave myself up to the cares of a family, and the education of my children, that I scarce knew there was any such thing as books, plays, or poems stirring in Great Britain. However after some years, your *Essay on Criticism*, and *Rape of the Lock*, broke in upon me. I rejoiced, that so bright a genius was rising on our isle; but thought no more about you, till my young family was grown up to have less need of my assistance; and beginning to have some taste for polite literature, my inclination revived with my leisure, to enquire after what had been most celebrated in that kind.

She explained that she had read his Homer and a number of his other works, but it was his letters most of all that made her think of him as a potential friend (though she found she had to defend this choice among her own friends) and encouraged her to approach him in epistolary fashion. Her expectations of the benefits of friendship extended from this world to the next: his friendship now would contribute to her happiness in the afterlife. This was because heightened love, admiration and delight when directed to God was the highest possible of its kind, so the most admired people were the closest to God. This led to 'the perfection of felicity'. As geniuses together, close to God, their souls would take pleasure in each other in the afterlife, a state that could only be enhanced by some preparatory exchanges beforehand.

From the perspective of the imagined felicity of the afterlife, Cockburn had a fault to find in Pope's letters, and that, she explained, was his disparagement of 'the finest performances of wit and genius'. He had allowed himself to speak of such efforts in general as 'mere trifles, of no service at all to a man's real happiness here or hereafter'. This she would not condone. She scolded him:

> I can by no means think that when you was writing the *Essay on Man* or even translating Homer, you was trifling all the while, and doing nothing towards your own future happiness. I am rather persuaded that God, in giving you a genius so peculiarly fitted to set the noblest things in the most beautiful light, has pointed out to you the way in which he would be served by you; and I wish you would consider it as the ten talents committed to your trust, which you are not at liberty to keep idly by you.[7]

God gave genius. The parable of the talents made the failure to use such God-given gifts a sin. The moral was obviously applicable to women in general and herself in particular.

One of the friends Cockburn had to defend Pope against was her own niece who had read more widely in periodicals and miscellanies that she herself had not been able to get hold of, and was familiar with Pope's 'Epistle to a Lady' ('Nothing so true as what you once let fall / Most women have no characters at all') which her aunt – who had to

admit, 'I know nothing more than you tell me of that satirical poem' –
was not. Cockburn insisted that Pope was the genius of the age and his
moral character was 'excellent': 'I do not remember any bitter things he
has said against our sex (perhaps some things of that kind that were
Dean Swift's may be taken for his) but if he had, his extraordinary
regard for his mother, and friendship for Mrs M. Blount would cancel
them all.' She dismissed criticism of him: 'The aspersions of him are by
no means to be credited; the best rule to judge of him is by his own and
his friends letters, which gained him my heart entirely. It is the fate of
all men of great merit to have many enemies.'[8]

Catharine Cockburn reads Elizabeth Thomas

The supply of books was not good in remote Northumberland. In the
summer of 1739, however, Cockburn was 'well entertained' by a two-
volume work which gave further cause for debate between herself and
her niece about Pope. The book was *Pylades and Corinna*, the full title
of which ran as follows: *Pylades and Corinna, Or, Memoirs of the lives,
amours and writings of Richard Gwinnet, Esq of Great Shurdington in
Gloucestershire and Mrs Elizabeth Thomas Jun of Great Russell St
Bloomsbury containing the letters and other miscellaneous pieces in prose and
verse which passed between them during a courtship of above sixteen years
faithfully published from their original manuscripts attested by Sir Edward
Northey, Knight. To which is prefixed, The Life of Corinna. Written by her
self.* As we have seen, it had been published by Edmund Curll in 1731
in a handsome edition at five shillings and it consisted, as Catharine
Cockburn explained, of

> some account of the life of Mrs Thomas (who is mentioned at the beginning
> of Pope's letters) and letters which passed betwixt her and Mr Gwinnet,
> under the names of Pylades and Corinna, during an honorable love for
> sixteen years. There appears a great deal of good sense, solid virtue, and
> sincere piety in all his writings; and as she was a lady of fine talents and true
> worth, it cannot but grieve one to find such persons so unfortunate. Her case
> is indeed extremely pitiable, and may afford matter of submission and even
> gratitude to providence, under many uneasy dispensations, when we reflect
> how unhappy some have been, who seem to have deserved much better than
> ourselves.[9]

Although Richard Gwinnet's name featured first on the title page, the volumes had been put together by Elizabeth Thomas and Edmund Curll. Gwinnet had been dead for ten years. Thomas was also dead by the time the books came out and it is impossible to say how much involvement she had in the final product. *Pylades and Corinna* was a compilation of her papers, mostly letters between herself and Gwinnet from the early part of the century which evoked the life of a learned but hard-up literary gentlewoman in London, along with poems, essays, literary commentary and gossip, and inset stories. The figure of Corinna was 'unfortunate' and 'extremely pitiable' in several respects. Her love was sexually unfulfilled since she was unable to marry Gwinnet, and she was unfortunate because his family refused to honour the legacy of £600 which he bequeathed her. Hence the significance of Sir Edward Northey, Knight, on the title page, attesting to the authenticity of the letters: letters to Thomas in Gwinnet's handwriting were the proof that he had intended to marry and provide for her. Thomas was unfortunate in a further sense. In 1711, she swallowed a chicken bone and for the rest of her life suffered from an obstruction which produced distressing symptoms: periodic episodes of water and stool retention had to be relieved by powerful purgatives. A full account of her condition and the interest taken in it by medical men was printed as an appendix to *Pylades and Corinna*, but her medical history was already well known and Pope may have been unpleasantly alluding to it in *The Dunciad* in his image of Curll sliding about in Thomas's piss and shit.

The volumes contained accounts of Elizabeth Thomas's life as well as a good deal of material relating to the financial difficulties which followed on her mother's death and the legal battle with Gwinnet's relations for the legacy he had left her. According to Curll, whose hand is very evident especially where occasion arises to add a footnote advertising his other wares, Thomas had been writing while confined to prison for debt. In 1730 her topical, sprightly poem *The Metamorphosis of the Town: Or, a View of the Present Fashions* appeared, and was well enough received to go into four editions by 1744. In the preface, Curll explained that Thomas had 'fully resolved upon publishing her own life, and often, in letters to her friends and by word of mouth, wished that she might only live to finish it'. Right up to her death she was apparently writing twelve hours a day in the hope of completing it. It is likely that she provided most of the autobiographical detail in *The Life of Corinna* but it is also likely that Curll heightened and shaped the raw materials for particular effects; by the time the volumes went to press he had, after all, complete freedom to use the manuscripts as he chose and he was a shrewd publisher. Catharine Cockburn's response, finding 'good sense, solid virtue, and sincere piety' in Gwinnet's writings, and 'a lady of fine talents and true worth' who was 'unfortunate' and 'pitiable' in Thomas, was surely what Curll aimed for. Far away in Northumberland, she was his ideal reader: removed from London's intense literary hostilities and inclined to identify with a woman who had struggled against financial and personal difficulties to realise her literary ambitions.

Catharine Cockburn's niece had not read *Pylades and Corinna*, but she seems to have known about Pope's depiction of Elizabeth Thomas as 'Curll's Corinna'. Evidently, Anne Arbuthnot made some reference to Thomas's less savoury reputation. She received an indignant response from her aunt which reproved her for 'conceiving an ill opinion of one you knew nothing of, upon very insufficient grounds'. Cockburn defended the impression she herself had formed of her fellow writer from reading Pope's letters and *Pylades and Corinna*:

Pope says nothing to her disadvantage in his letters. Cromwell indeed speaks slightingly of her, and calls a letter, which he publishes of hers, a romantic one: but as the letter was there for everybody to judge of, I could not but acquit it of that character; and though I had never heard of Mrs Thomas before (which, by the way, I wonder at) was much displeased to find a man speak so unhandsomely of a lady, whom it appeared he had once had some regard for, with a kind of insult on her unhappiness. And since I have read her life and seen the cause of her distresses, it gave me the more indignation against him, who had known her in better days, and was then a great admirer of her. Pope, in a pique for her having published his Letters, put the name of Corinna, which Mr Dryden had given to that lady, into his *Dunciad*; but in his notes afterwards made an apology for it. I think it is a piece of justice due even to strangers, not to conclude against them from any reproaches thrown at them without examining upon what grounds.[10]

With the clarity and discrimination she had brought to the defence of John Locke, Cockburn picked her way through some very murky waters to give the justice that was due to a stranger. There were a number of editions of Pope's letters – 'authentic', 'surreptitious', 'genuine', 'correct' and 'incorrect' – all prefaced by claims and counter-claims of provenance and reliability. Pope represented himself as having been 'obliged', much against his will, to publish an authentic edition of his letters because he had been so 'very disagreeably used' by those who had first acquired his early letters and published them without his consent, and by the publication of false letters attributed to him. The villain was Pope's antagonist Edmund Curll but the finger of blame was pointed firmly at Elizabeth Thomas.

Thomas was the 'woman' who had 'voluntarily' given the publisher Pope's 'whole correspondence' with Henry Cromwell, 'which letters being lent her by that gentleman, she took the liberty to print'. In Curll's edition of Pope's works, he included a preface which printed Elizabeth Thomas's letter to Henry Cromwell explaining why she had sold the letters, along with Cromwell's two grovelling letters to Pope exculpating himself. (The second edition in 1737 incorporated Pope's preface to his own 'first genuine edition' which also blamed Thomas for starting it all.)

Elizabeth Thomas's letter to Henry Cromwell was written in 1727 and it broke a silence of at least five years, since the publication of her poems in 1722. She explained that she had been struggling under 'many and great oppressions':

> But as it was always my resolution, if I must sink, to do it as decently (that is as silently) as I could, so when I found myself plunged into unforeseen and unavoidable ruin, I retreated from the world, and in a manner buried myself in a dismal place, where I knew none and none knew me. In this dull unthinking way I have protracted a lingering death (for life it cannot be called) ever since you saw me, sequestered from company, deprived of my books, and nothing left to converse with but the letters of my dead or absent friends.[11]

She admitted lending these letters to 'an ingenious person' who published them 'I must not say altogether with my consent, nor wholly without it'. She justified the action by the value the letters had to the public, adding that 'common modesty' would have forced Cromwell and

Pope to refuse, if asked, 'what you would not be displeased with if done without your knowledge'. In any case, Cromwell had given them to her as a free gift to do what she pleased with. She asked him to write her a line stating that she had indeed obtained them 'honestly' in the way she described. There was a postscript signed by Curll: 'A letter, directed to Mrs Thomas, to be left at my house, will be safely transmitted to her.'

Curll had been pursuing Cromwell, who anxiously assured Pope ('the last thing I should do would be to disoblige you') that he had not been near Curll's shop, and had forgotten all about giving any letters to 'this Sappho, alias E. T.' whom he hadn't seen for seven years. It was only when he noticed in the newspaper letters from Lady Packington, Lady Chudleigh and John Norris to 'the same Sappho or E. T.' that he had begun 'to fear that I was guilty'. Cromwell claimed that Thomas's account of how she came by the letters strained the truth, but he would not send Curll a note to that effect. His equivocation under pressure (he admitted 'indiscretion' in putting the letters 'into the hands of this precieuse', also that the story 'might be . . . as she writ') and refusal to write accounted for Curll's final thrust: the postscript addressed directly to Cromwell. Unable, out of the 'honour' that Thomas credited him with, to deny the obvious truth that he had given her the letters, Cromwell was reduced to rather desperate measures. As Catharine Cockburn observed, his description of Thomas's account as a 'long romantic letter', using the word 'romantic' to suggest distance from 'truth', could be tested against the letter itself by any impartial reader.

In a second letter to Pope, Cromwell admitted giving Thomas the letters because she wanted them so badly, though he was sure that at that time (twelve years earlier) she had no intention of printing them. 'But as people in great straits bring forth their hoards of old gold and most valued jewels, so Sappho had recourse to her hid treasure of letters.' The simple truth simply told (he had given her the letters, they had commercial value and she had sold them in a time of need), Cromwell appealed to Pope man to man. He had made a mistake, but it was a mistake men had made from time immemorial: 'As for me, I hope when you shall coolly consider the many thousand instances of our being deluded by the females since that great original of Adam by Eve, you will have a more favourable thought of the undesigning error of your faithful friend.'

Pope's concern for control over the uses to which his private writings might be put was not unreasonable, but Cromwell's language – the reference to Adam and Eve, the evocation of men being 'deluded by the females' – sexualised a matter that had nothing to do with sexual behaviour. Certainly there was honour and dignity at stake: hidden in some hole, faced with 'unforeseen and unavoidable ruin' and sinking silently, Thomas's cache of letters were all that remained of an honour and dignity she had once aspired to. As a woman without resources and in debt, who had been for years selling off her precious possessions, Elizabeth Thomas finally relinquished what had been among her dearest comforts, those vital testimonials to her status and identity as a woman of letters, 'the letters of my dead or absent friends'. The books had already gone and so, it seems, had the friends; although those who continued to support her included clergymen like the Bishop of Durham, which suggests that Thomas's sexual reputation at the time was untarnished or not considered of particular significance.

It may have been through her own contacts with northern clergymen like the Bishop of Durham that Catharine Cockburn acquired the volumes of *Pylades and Corinna*, in reading which she found herself 'well entertained' by a vivid representation of a female writer's life more or less contemporary with her own. Although she did not know Thomas, she was able to bring to her reading an empathetic understanding of the literary world she moved in. It was no surprise to Cockburn that a literary figure and man about town such as Henry Cromwell should have admired Thomas 'in her better days', nor that Dryden should have given her the name of 'Corinna' as testimony to his high opinion of her worth. Loyal to Pope, Cockburn shifted the blame for the negative portrayal on to Cromwell, and mounted a dignified defence of the importance of examining evidence over accepting hearsay. Whether she thought back to the attacks made upon herself in her own 'better days' by Delarivier Manley and other 'enemies' her writings were good enough to raise against her, we do not know. She made no reference to them. Nor do we know whether she knew that in Curll's *Compleat Key* to *The Dunciad*, which supplied names where Pope had left dashes and asterisks, the 'T— signifying Thomas was given as 'Trotter'.[12]

Though at first sight very different, one element at least in the structural model underlying *Pylades and Corinna* aligns it with Katherine Philips's *Poems*, Jane Barker's *Poetical Recreations*, John Dunton's promotion of Elizabeth Singer beginning with the *Athenian Mercury*, and Delarivier Manley's *Adventures of Rivella* – along with other female-authored publications. Its essential component was the woman writer *as writer* around whom one or more admiring males gathered and with whom conversation took place on the page.

The word 'conversation' could carry a sexual meaning: 'criminal conversation' was, after all, grounds for divorce. In the early eighteenth century, the word was also being put to use as a major carrier of the virtues of polite society. The arts of conversation were the arts of civility. Women, represented for these purposes as the 'politer' sex, helped spread civility through their skills in the conversational arts. Men's rougher natures were smoothed by social contact with women. The more well read and well bred women were, the more effective the smoothing process. The well-read woman might be constructed (or construct herself) as one who had chosen books in preference to men; or she might come before the public as unstoppably ardent – for literature, God, or the general good. Elizabeth Singer was clearly in the second category while Mary Astell was in the first. Either way, they could be textually admired. They served in the imaginations of readers as examples of femininity other women might try to emulate and as models of superior womanhood men might seek out in their own circles.

Elizabeth Thomas projected herself and was presented in *Pylades and Corinna* as a figure of some authority in a community of literary enthusiasts. Her persona owed more to Astell than Singer, both of whom have walk-on parts in *Pylades and Corinna*. Urban and sardonic, a browser in bookshops where she seems to have had no compunction about striking up conversations with literary men, visited by men like Cromwell and Pope as an ingenious woman whose opinions were worth hearing, perhaps we can also imagine her as one among the relatively few women who joined in the debates in coffee houses. An admirer of Lady Mary Chudleigh's poetry, Thomas wrote to her in the late 1690s and began an acquaintance. She also wrote to John Norris and to Dryden, delivering her letter of appreciation to him along with some copies of her own poems at the coffee house where it was well known he held court. All three established writers responded with warm encouragement and pleasure; they were pleased to receive her praises and declared themselves happy to be of service to one who showed such promise. Later, Thomas became one of the circle that formed around Aaron Hill which included Susannah Centlivre and Martha Fowke Sansom. Until the 1720s when her financial troubles began she published little, but lived a life of day-to-day contact with literary folk, reading, writing, circulating poems, having her books borrowed and her advice on matters poetic regularly sought.

Elizabeth Thomas was on friendly terms with her local bookseller and perhaps it was in his shop that she met Richard Gwinnet, a lawyer and aspiring author. There were many other such men in her life, for example the 'poetaster' described in letters to Gwinnet, an acquaintance whom she had not seen for two years but who turned up again 'according to custom, both pockets stuffed out with poetry like an attorney's term bag, and all for the unfortunate Corinna to correct, or at least to hear read'. It was in vain that she pleaded she had neither the ability nor the time. 'Bard was proof against all denials, and cried; he had experienced the first and as for the second he would take a more convenient opportunity.' The 'bard' left but returned in less than an hour 'with a fresh cargo'. Faced with an amateur poet determined to be heard, she, a woman whose judgement he had tried and tested, took as much control of the situation as she could. She submitted to 'destiny' – the destiny of having her abilities valued – and made the best of things 'by choosing my task and confining his desires to my choice'.

Other encounters of this sort, drawn for comic effect and shared with a correspondent who was also superior to the follies displayed are scattered throughout *Pylades and Corinna*. They contribute to the impression of a community in which Elizabeth Thomas was able to play the professional. Compared to the 'bard', hers was the better informed intelligence. She was able to point out that he had stolen twelve of his lines from Waller and should omit them. Turning to his paraphrase of Psalm 148, she noted that it was no different from Roscommon's. As Gwinnet commented in response to a satire she had been sent by an anonymous poet, it was 'poor Grubstreet stuff'. In relation to 'poor Grubstreet stuff', Thomas assumed the position habitually taken by Pope (created, one might say, by Pope) in which the 'real' 'authentic' 'true' poet, quietly going about his business at home – Great Russell Street lodgings in her case, Twickenham house with garden and grotto in Pope's – was besieged by second- and third-rate 'poetasters'.[13]

The Life of Corinna, Written by her self, which prefaced *Pylades and Corinna*, presented Corinna/Thomas as someone whose natural habitat was the realm of books. The daughter of a lawyer who died when she was two, she is depicted as a prodigy whose bookish desires were established in infancy. Offered 'playthings', she would not be diverted but 'always flung them away with a contempt uncommon to so tender an age; but give her a book, and she would sit poring over it from noon to night, without knowing one letter'. Her mother taught her to read and by the age of five she had read the Bible – 'the whole Bible three times over' – and for nine months had a tutor who taught her Latin, writing and arithmetic. This brief period of private education was, we are told, when she felt herself to be 'truly happy ... She transcribed chapters, compiled little common-place books, and was forever a scribbling. Covetous she was of learning to the last degree.'

The scribbling girl was self-taught from the age of six. Reading and writing went together: she wrote 'familiar letters' in prose and verse to her cousins, and was understood to be actively forming herself as a learned woman. She was given gifts of money by 'sponsors and other relations', all of which was spent on books: before she was twenty she had 'a small tho valuable collection of the best authors and editions, estimated by a bookseller at an hundred pounds'. As a learned woman she had, of course, no vanity about her body, 'having always affected solitude and a private life'. The body, we are told she would say, was 'only a case for the soul, like the wooden work of a clock, which, if kept but whole and clean dusted was sufficient'. And, it was claimed, she had 'but little, if any, of the amorous in her constitution', only 'a soul wonderfully turned for friendship, in its most exalted sense'. Friendship was 'a darling passion of her soul'. All this, along with the pointed reference to her reading of Descartes and application to Church history, a religious crisis, some routine condemnations of the present age for too much levity, and the observation that she took care to improve her handwriting because she had heard women's spelling 'generally ridiculed', suggest the self-conscious formation of a female literary persona.[14]

The concepts Thomas deployed and the vocabulary she used evoke both Mary Astell and Elizabeth Singer. She might claim (in the spirit of Jane Barker) to have 'nothing of the amorous' in her and make a point of refusing to write love poetry, but just as reading and writing went together, so did love and literary identity. The 'true nature of love' was the definitive subject for a writer: for Astell it was love of God and friends – the circle of aristocratic ladies who were her supporters; for Singer (after her husband's death) it was love of God and angels – friends in heaven. In *The Life of Corinna*, Thomas's writings were carefully positioned in the irreproachable traditions headed by Katherine Philips on the one hand (love of friends) and John Norris on the other (love of God). Love, for one who had 'but little, if any, of the amorous in her constitution', was produced by literature rather than life, and it expressed itself in the terms of exalted friendship not vulgar sexuality:

> She was without doubt inspired with this noble passion by reading the works of the justly admired Mrs Katherine Philips, and those of Mr Norris of Bemerton, the first of which she endeavoured to imitate, and the second she enjoyed a constant correspondence with during the last sixteen years of his life, tho they never once saw each other. This intercourse of letters was a great advantage to her in directing a course of her studies.[15]

As a correspondent, Norris's role was supposedly to help Thomas with 'such doubts as sometimes happened to arise' in her religious beliefs. His real importance was to signal her status, just as Dryden did when he gave her the pen name 'Corinna' in letters that she afterwards sold. Perhaps she hoped to publish her letters with Norris, as Astell had done. Early in the correspondence with Gwinnet, Thomas sent him Astell's *A Serious Proposal* (which he liked as an idea but didn't think could be carried out in practice) and in a letter dated October 1700 he remarked that he would 'love to know the substance of Mrs Astell's conversation with you'. Evidently, Edmund Curll, editing the letters for the press, thought readers of *Pylades and Corinna* would also like to know what Mary Astell had said in conversation, not, alas, reported by

Elizabeth Thomas. Curll provided a footnote, addressed to the reader, explaining that there were political differences between the women. Mrs Norris (wife of John Norris) is quoted: 'Mrs Norris, in a letter to Corinna, thus declares herself – "As far as I can perceive, your greatest crime with Mrs Astell is you are too much a Williamite; I know where she has slighted some of her best friends upon that account." '

The occasion upon which Elizabeth Thomas was 'slighted' by Mary Astell may have been the episode described later in *Pylades and Corinna* when Thomas paid a goodbye call on the Devon-based Lady Mary Chudleigh who had been in London. The room was crowded with people Thomas knew and she found herself embroiled in some awkward raillery which was brought to an end by Mary Astell's entry into the conversation. Astell did not, however, acknowledge Thomas's presence. Thomas was mortified and behaved in a way she was afterwards ashamed of. She explained to Gwinnet: 'You may, perhaps, expect something from Mrs Astell, but, I will assure you, she would not know me. However, I was even with her at my departure, and returned her as slighting a notice.' Confused and embarrassed, Thomas pushed her way out of the room without saying goodbye for fear that others might slight her too. 'Upon cooler thoughts, I am ashamed of the public incivility, which I should not have been guilty of, at another time, in respect to my lady; but I was so provoked with Mrs Astell's haughty carriage, that I knew not how to behave myself.'

Thomas attributed Astell's behaviour not to politics but to female vanity – in Astell's case, the vanity of celebrity: 'O, how hard it is, for one of our frail sex, to resist the vanity of public applause' – and explained that she had asked Lady Chudleigh to try to find out if there was any more personal reason for Astell's coldness towards her:

I have several times put my lady upon pumping her for a reason of this alteration, and she protests to me that Mrs Astell never gave her any; but her ladyship's own thoughts were, that she was so much solicited by women of the greatest quality and fortune, that she had not time enough to repay all their kindnesses with her conversation. This may be true for aught I know, and she who has no certain subsistence, may be allowed to improve a friendship with those that have; but methinks she might forbid the addresses of her insignificant admirer with a little more decency, in gratitude to her true friend Mr Norris who gave the acquaintance, but what she pleases; nothing against stomach.[16]

'Nothing against stomach.' High stomach was the consciousness of rank. By birth, Mary Astell was of no higher rank than Elizabeth Thomas; nor, as Thomas knew, was she any more secure financially. Lady Chudleigh's emollient explanation that Astell simply didn't have time to notice those at the bottom end of the hierarchical system since 'women of the greatest quality and fortune' required her conversation, did not impress. Though she characterised herself as 'an insignificant admirer', Thomas's anger stemmed from the feeling that within the world of literature she was quite as significant as Mary Astell, not least because both John Norris and Lady Chudleigh had treated her as such. John Norris, a man, and Lady Chudleigh, an aristocrat, ranked above Astell. The attentions they had paid Thomas were paid to her in her capacity as a promising literary woman and on that level she was equal to Astell who had herself, not so many years earlier, been a destitute and unknown supplicant.

Writing to Gwinnet, Thomas demoted Astell, whose writings she admired so much, to 'one of our frail sex' unable to resist 'the vanity of public applause'. Nevertheless, it was precisely that public applause that enabled Astell to carry off a social role displaying all the *hauteur* of ladies of 'the greatest quality and fortune'. None of those ladies seem to have found her manners objectionable: genius entitled Astell to adopt the manners of those in the highest social rank. In more adoring mode, Thomas compared Astell to St Teresa. In the poem 'To Almystrea, on her divine works', published in 1722 in her only collection, *Miscellany Poems* (but probably written much earlier), Thomas hailed Astell as the 'happy virgin' of a 'celestial race', the 'generous heroine' who 'stood forth, / And showed your sex's aptitude and worth'.[17] The invented pen name, 'Almystrea', is an anagram of Mary Astell which also manages to evoke the 'Astrea' of Aphra Behn – a composite female forerunner who in the shape of Aphra Behn could be accorded honorary virginity and in the shape of Mary Astell was a happy and generous leader.

The account of Elizabeth Thomas's life in *Pylades and Corinna* is in two overlapping versions. The first is told in the third person as if by a close friend, one who, like Sir Charles Lovemore in Delarivier Manley's *Rivella*, had lived 'in the strictest amity with her from earliest remembrance', and it concerns her early formation as a writer. It makes more obvious use of fictional devices than the second version, which is a letter of appeal written by Thomas, then in prison, to the Bishop of Durham begging his help. The letter explains her financial difficulties, and gives an account of the unjust treatment she had received from Gwinnet's family and the miseries of her legal struggles.

The title page assures us that the 'Life of Corinna' was 'written by her self', which may be true, but Curll edited and perhaps interpolated passages. He may have reworked a manuscript originally written by Thomas. As with the text of *Pylades and Corinna* as a whole, the origin and generic status of the essay is not clear. It incorporates biographical with recognisably mythical elements, drawing on prose narratives of various kinds including lives of authors, such as the *Life* of Abraham Cowley, which was frequently reprinted in the late seventeenth and early eighteenth centuries, and *The Adventures of Rivella*, which Curll reprinted in 1725 with a preface explaining his part in its genesis. (He also gave it a new title, *Mrs Manley's History of her own Life and Times*, exploiting the popularity of Gilbert Burnet's *The History of My Own Times* which had come out the previous year and similarly mixed autobiography, history and anecdote.) *The Life of Corinna* had ideological work to do. It put before the reader a powerful image of the deserving woman writer as unfortunate victim of a callous society, the publication of whose life and works was an act of restitution, and whose saviour was Edmund Curll.

If the persona Elizabeth Thomas projected in her letters owed something to Mary Astell and Elizabeth Singer, there are scenes in *The Life of Corinna* which could have been drawn directly from the writings of Delarivier Manley. For example, there is an oblique account of Thomas's mother's economic struggles as a young widow with a small daughter in the late 1680s which credits her with having been 'a very notable assistant' to the dukes of Devonshire, Buckingham and Dorset in the conspiracy leading up to the 1688 Revolution. Apparently, the Earl of Montagu established himself as a 'lodger' at her house in Russell Square, supposedly for the purpose of giving a dinner to some friends now and then. The house served as a safe house for the conspiracy. The newspapers would report that the dukes were at their country houses when in fact they were concealed at Mrs Thomas's from where they went on visits to The Hague or elsewhere without being missed. The arrangement came to an end when the number of foreign letters coming to the address aroused suspicion. The dukes continued to frequent the house, promising Mrs Thomas a pension or a large gift. Nothing came of it.

The exact nature of Mrs Thomas's relationship to these dukes is not specified, but an anecdote built on the account depicts the men as aristocratic rakes and aligns the mother with bawdy-house mores and morals. At one point the Earl of Montagu appeared to be offering £500 and a place for Richard Gwinnet, so long as 'Corinna' came to ask for it in person. This Elizabeth Thomas haughtily refused to do. The issue is presented as a dispute between mother and daughter over family 'interest', in which the daughter disobeyed her mother on the grounds of female dignity. What mother and Earl assumed Corinna would do in 'asking' the Earl the favour was in fact to give him her favour – to offer her body in exchange. Her mother wanted to prostitute her. In refusing to be used in this way, Thomas explained that the Earl had already tried to seduce her with promises of gifts. The description owes much to the *New Atalantis*:

> my Lord coming through out of the garden sat down on the couch by me, which was no ways surprising, he frequently using, as you know, when alone to divert himself with his little news-monger. But I was extremely shocked when I found he began a new discourse, telling me I was very pretty, how much he loved me, and if I would give myself to him he would settle an estate, should render me happy all my life.

In the *New Atalantis*, books furthered the purposes of seduction: the Duke introduced Charlot to amorous feelings by giving her sexually explicit books to read. In *The Life of Corinna* books work differently. The Earl of Montagu progressed from bribery to attempted rape, which the child resisted:

> I heard him without answer, when he perceiving I was putting up my work to be gone, caught me suddenly in his arms and attempted to throw me on

the couch, but as frighted as I was, I scratched and bruised his face, at the same time tearing off his fine wig which cost sixty guineas, flung it on the floor; this indeed moved him to let me go, and with a scornful sneer asked if I did not know what was due to his quality? I replied, Yes my Lord, I know what is owing to your title, but at the same time I must not forget what is due to my own honour.

Corinna's mother is not best pleased when told about the episode:

Get out of my sight, said her mother (who loved money, and had not all the fine taste her daughter afterwards discovered), it makes me sick to hear a girl of thirteen talk of womanhood; and since your books teach you disobedience, I'll take care you shall not have so much leisure to consult them. The poor girl suffered many a bitter frump, but having a long fit of illness she had more leisure than madam designed, and meeting with some better authors than Broome and Quarles, she began to brighten up, and on perusing the polite writings of Suckling, Waller, Denham and Dryden, she made a notable and sudden advance in letters.[18]

This 'sudden advance in letters' was the prelude to Thomas sending poems to Dryden and launching her literary career. Symbolically, as she moved from childhood to adult womanhood, literature (head) triumphed. Her options ('fine taste', intellectual and aesthetic 'honour') were larger than those of her mother's generation. Men of letters – the 'polite writings' of Suckling, Waller, Denham and Dryden – could give a girl more honourable means than aristocratic men with their promises and charm offensives that rapidly turned to real offence when they were rebuffed. 'I will not lessen the dignity of my sex by asking a favour of any man,' Thomas told her mother, though what she objected to was not being required to ask favours but to give them. The critique of her mother's behaviour was made possible by a new vision of womanly dignity, derived from a mixture of heady influences which, looking back from the 1720s when the account was written, might have included, to greater or lesser extent, the lives and writings of Delarivier Manley, Aphra Behn, Katherine Philips, Mary Astell, Susannah Centlivre, John Dryden, John Norris, Lady Mary Chudleigh, Elizabeth Singer Rowe and Anne Finch, Countess of Winchilsea, among others.

One function of *Pylades and Corinna* was to place Elizabeth Thomas in the tradition of female wit established in modern times. Thus she was linked with Katherine Philips, famously celebrated by Cowley as the solitary female poet among the larger company of men, alone 'on the female coasts of fame'. Dryden apparently found 'much of Orinda' in the verses Elizabeth Thomas had sent him; 'Pylades', too, happening to be reading Philips's poems while travelling, declares there is much in them to remind him of his own 'Corinna'. These associations with Philips were underlined by Curll: Philips's poem 'A Country Life' is inserted following Gwinnet's comment, with a footnote explaining that it was printed 'for the reader's entertainment and to confirm the just taste of Pylades'.

In giving Thomas the pseudonym Corinna, Dryden had stressed that he meant 'not the lady with whom Ovid was in love, but the famous Theban poetess, who overcame Pindar five times, as historians tell'. (He also added, 'I would have called you Sappho, but that I hear you are handsomer.') Like Orinda and like Corinna, Thomas was raised above her sex; but unlike Orinda, she was one among a number of female worthies who composed her mental and social world as it was represented in *Pylades and Corinna*. In one of Corinna's letters to Pylades, she tells him:

I have been shown a poem which is said to be written by one of the most ingenious ladies in the west of England. I pressed to know her name, to which my friend gave me such dubious answers that I concluded it was our good natured heroine Melissa [Lady Chudleigh]. But before I had read ten lines, I discovered such a genius, such learning, so much depth of thought, such harmony in the numbers, and such elegance in the expression, that I cried out, O! Sir, it is in vain you strive to deceive me, this can be no other than the charming Philomela that sings so sweetly.

Thomas knew that Gwinnet was among the enthusiasts who had contributed commendatory verses to Elizabeth Singer's 1696 *Poems*. At the prospect of more verses from Philomela's hand, she urged her lover:

Rejoice Pylades, rejoice; Philomela is preparing to bless the world with the beauteous images of her mind; Philomela is preparing to make her sex burst with envy, and what strikes me with greater terror, Philomela is preparing to make a second conquest on the heart of her affectionate Pylades.

With just a little 'malicious satisfaction' she informed him (wrongly) that Singer was married and become 'Mrs Copley at the Lord Weymouth's', a fact she knew would make him 'disconsolate'.[19]

These anecdotes and comments might all have been written by Elizabeth Thomas. It is equally possible that some were written by Edmund Curll who did more than any other bookseller of the time to promote female authorship, both by publishing women's writings and by putting into circulation valorising images of women authors. Curll, the businessman, was motivated by financial rather than sexual interest, seeking profit through the commodification of femininity. In place of the rake and the kept woman, Curll offered new stock figures: the entrepreneur and the paid writer. His protection was not inconsistent with a rhetoric of dignity and independence, unlike that of the libertine aristocrat whose worthless promises reduced women to dependency and ruin.

Pope might sneer at Elizabeth Thomas as 'Curll's Corinna' – in a formulation that gave power and possession to Curll and made an appendage of the woman – but Thomas's life story (whoever wrote it) and the miscellaneous writings that compose *Pylades and Corinna* contest that definition and put a new stereotype into circulation. What they display is 'an unfortunate author' at last receiving her due and being well treated: her manuscripts were saved, shaped, annotated and produced in a relatively expensive edition. The male editor found the female author worth his attention and protection. He deferred to her. What the volumes assert is her achievement against the odds in a social order designed to press her into servitude. Being a 'wit' was a defence against sexual enslavement. This was the 'nobler gain' that Catharine Cockburn's 'Poem, occasioned by the busts set up in the Queen's Hermitage' spoke up for. It offered a vision of a reformed femininity, defended against male libertinism by the passion for knowledge. The fact that one of the defenders was himself a noted rake (Curll enjoyed the company of high-class prostitutes) didn't necessarily compromise the message.[20]

Lady Mary Wortley Montagu and Pope

Of all Pope's enemies, one of the most strenuous, and a leading figure in the 'vile faction' set up against him that Catharine Cockburn deplored, was Lady Mary Wortley Montagu. In 1735, when Cockburn reported that she had read a 'very satirical poem on Pope by a lady', it was probably Lady Mary Wortley Montagu's *Verses addressed to the Imitator of Horace* which, though Lady Mary denied authorship, is generally considered to have been a collaboration between herself and her close friend Lord Hervey. Pope thought so: he called the verses a 'witty fornication' whose mother was Hervey and whose absconded father was Lady Mary. The *Verses addressed to the Imitator of Horace* accused Pope of being hard-hearted, of obscure birth, sexually impotent, and deformed in soul as well as body.[21]

Arguably Pope's equal in malice, quarrelsomeness and wit, when he included her among his satirical targets Lady Mary Wortley Montagu used her high birth and position at court to circulate counter-attacking verses and prose squibs. Until the early 1720s, they had been friends. In 1715, they met frequently and perhaps collaborated at a time when Lady Mary was writing poetry seriously. Her town 'eclogues', three of which were published as *Court Poems* in 1716 by Curll who came by them somehow, were probably read and first discussed in company with Pope and John Gay. (Pope used the excuse of his unauthorised publication of the *Court Poems* to poison Curll, slipping an emetic into his drink at a tavern meeting, and issuing an anonymous pamphlet a few days later: *A Full and True Account of a Horrid and Barbarous Revenge by Poison, on the Body of Mr Edmund Curll.*) When Lady Mary left England and went with her husband on a diplomatic mission to Turkey, Pope maintained an animated correspondence and, in the opinion of some commentators, fell in love at a distance. When she returned a few years later, she settled at Twickenham, near enough to Pope to ask to borrow his harpsichord for one of her concerts.

It is not known how or why the friendship turned to enmity, but open hostilities began with *The Dunciad* in 1728 and were consolidated with the Variorum edition of 1729 (a revised and expanded *Dunciad* complete with spoof footnotes) followed by the *First Satire of the Second Book of Horace* (1733) and the *Epistle to Dr Arbuthnot* (1735). By then,

Lady Mary was a courtier very close to the Prime Minister, Robert Walpole, and his leading adviser, Lord Hervey, and Pope was identified with the Tory opposition. Party spirit had a role in some of the viciousness of their attacks on each other's persons and works.

Throughout the 1720s and 1730s and until she left England for good in 1739, Lady Mary was a prominent figure, living in the limelight but unlike Pope not cultivating an identity as a writer in relation to a public of readers and critics: she had what she needed privately in terms of position, place and income. When not intriguing at court, she spent her days reading and writing, building up manuscript albums of her own and other people's work. She was a close friend of other high-born literary women, such as Lady De La Warr, the patron of Elizabeth Thomas. A reader and writer all her life, at the age of fourteen Lady Mary's ambition had been to be abbess of a Protestant nunnery of the sort that Mary Astell proposed in her *Serious Proposal*. In old age it was her habit to read and write for seven hours a day. Much of what she wrote has been lost. She destroyed a great deal herself and her relations destroyed still more (including the journal which she kept from the time of her return from Turkey until her death). Even so, when her published works appeared in 1803 they ran to five substantial volumes.

Ambivalent about print publication, Lady Mary Wortley Montagu had no ambivalence about the activities of reading and writing, nor about her reputation as a poet, a wit and a learned woman. She was 'the famed Lady Mary'. Unnamed topical poems which circulated were attributed to her. To be 'witty' was to be like Lady Mary. The Duke of Buckingham proposed her as successor to Nicholas Rowe as Poet Laureate. She was included in anthologies, such as Anthony Hammond's *A New Miscellany of Original Poems* in 1720, where Elizabeth Tollett read her with excitement, and she occasionally published individual poems, as when her (anonymous) answer to Jonathan Swift's excremental vision, *The Dean's Provocation for Writing the Lady's Dressing-Room. A Poem*, appeared in handsome slim folio. In *The Lady's Dressing-Room*, Swift had Strephon enter Celia's dressing room to find the squalor that lay beneath the surface of 'lillys and roses' which supposedly composed the ideal woman. He discovers not only sweat, snot and soiled garments but the chamber pot which stinks and informs him his beloved Celia shits. In *The Dean's Provocation*, Lady Mary pictured the Dean visiting a prostitute, failing at sex and, shamed by his impotence, writing the poem in revenge. Perhaps she was familiar with Aphra Behn's poem, *The Disappointment*.[22]

As well as poetry, Lady Mary wrote critical essays, translations and adaptations (in 1710, she translated the *Enchiridion* of Epictetus and sent the work to the Bishop of Salisbury for approval with a letter explaining that education would correct women's follies), lampoons, political journalism, including in 1737-8 the short-lived weekly periodical, *The Nonsense of Common-Sense*, designed to defend Walpole's ministry from Opposition attacks, and history. She told her daughter she was writing a 'History of My Own Time' and destroying it as she wrote it. She used her influence to help her cousin Henry Fielding get his plays staged and she acted as patron to Richard Savage who in 'The Wanderer' praised 'Fair Wortley's angel-accent, eyes, and mind'. Fielding collaborated with her in attacks on Pope.

Lasting fame came from the *Embassy Letters*, which seems to have been what she hoped and intended, although the circumstances of their publication and survival were as marked by ambivalence about print and the wider reading public as were her other writings. The *Embassy Letters* built on Lady Mary's experiences travelling as a diplomat's wife across Europe to Turkey. After her return, she used notes she had kept at the time to construct, in the form of letters, a fabricated compilation of her experiences and observations. The result was not a collection of 'real' letters that had been sent to the named individuals, but a travel treatise. In this treatise, she described her visits to the courts of Western Europe, her journeys across the vast expanses of troubled and often war-ravaged lands (going in convoy with an army of retainers, carrying her own bed and often dependent on the thuggery of their guards for food), and the beauties and civilised mode of life she found in the East. The gardens, the sunshine, the culture, the landscape, the history of Turkey all captivated her. She took issue with other travellers' accounts of the places she visited; and she exploited the opportunity being female and of high rank afforded, to go to places, such as the female Turkish baths, that male travellers could not enter.[23]

The manuscript of the *Embassy Letters* was completed by 1724 when it was loaned to Mary Astell, with whom Lady Mary had become friends. Astell urged publication and provided a signed preface which thereafter stayed with the manuscript as it passed from hand to hand and travelled about with Lady Mary in her wanderings on the Continent through the 1740s and 1750s. In style, Mary Astell's preface was part commendatory eulogy, part feminist polemic, and partly informative. It was framed by verses in which Astell presented herself as a rival for literary laurels who, having read the manuscript, was moved to overcome her natural enviousness of a 'genius so sublime and so complete' and 'gladly lay my laurels at her feet'. In doing so, she invited men – the 'male-authors' who 'with an envious eye / Praise coldly, that they may the more decry' – to learn from her. The question of envy – the dark side of commendation – is central to the preface. Astell explained that she wanted the credit of persuading Lady Mary to publish, but failing that ('alas! The most ingenious author has condemned it to obscurity during her life') she wanted it to be known that she as a woman had testified to another woman's merit, not only because of the intrinsic merits of the manuscript – 'I confess I am malicious enough to desire that the world should see to how much better purpose the Ladies travel than their Lords, and that whilst it is surfeited with male travels, all in the same tone and stuffed with the same trifles, a Lady has the skill to strike out a new path and to embellish a worn-out subject with variety of fresh and elegant entertainment' – but also to contradict stereotype:

In short, let her own sex at least do her justice. Lay aside diabolical envy and its brother malice with all their accursed company, sly whispering, cruel backbiting, spiteful detraction, and the rest of that hideous crew, which I hope are very falsely said to attend the tea-table, being more apt to think they haunt those public places where virtuous women never come. Let the men malign one another, if they think fit, and strive to pull down merit when they cannot equal it. Let us be better natured than to give way to any unkind or disrespectful thought of so bright an ornament of our sex, merely because she has better sense. For I doubt not but our hearts will tell us that this is the real and unpardonable offence, whatever may be pretended. Let us be better Christians than to look upon her with an evil eye, only because the giver of all good gifts has entrusted and adorned her with the most excellent talents. Rather let us freely own the superiority of this sublime genius as I do in the sincerity of my soul, pleased that a woman triumphs, and proud to follow in her train. Let us offer the palm which is justly her due, and if we pretend to any laurels, lay them willingly at her feet.

Astell urged women to be 'pleased that a woman triumphs' and do as she had done by being 'proud to follow in her train'.[24] Her homage to Lady Mary's 'merit' and 'sense' was unforced but at the same time (as Elizabeth Thomas had had cause to observe) was probably not unconnected to her rank.

Merit and rank came together to produce the 'superiority of this sublime genius', making Lady Mary and her manuscript an object of intense interest to men as well as women in the decades that followed. Readers, travellers, philosophers, poets, politicians, those who haunted public places and those whose lives passed in privacy at home or abroad, knew about the manuscript. Visitors were shown it. Like Lady Mary herself, it had iconic status. By 1761, Lady Mary was dying and had decided to return to England. She was going home to her daughter, who was now Lady Bute and married to the British Prime Minister. During a stopover in Rotterdam, Lady Mary made the acquaintance of a local Presbyterian minister, the Revd Benjamin Sowden. For reasons that cannot be known, she wrote on her manuscript that it was her 'will and design' that Sowden should dispose of it as he thought proper. That done, she consigned it to his care and continued on her journey. By this act she divested herself of writings which had been an important part of her entire adult life: they had gone with her everywhere, been constantly returned to and revised, and from them she had gained a deal of reputation. Though she gave away the well-known letters, Lady Mary retained her 'voluminous' journal. This she gave to Lady Bute, who in later life read it only when she was safely alone, kept it under lock and key, and ensured that it was burned before she herself died.

The Revd Benjamin Sowden very properly delivered the manuscript of the letters to Lady Bute when he returned to England. But before then he allowed two English travellers to borrow it. They transcribed the whole thing and it was their version which came out to widespread acclaim in 1763.

In the *First Satire of the Second Book of Horace*, Pope, following Horace, represented himself as a peace-loving satirist, friend to virtue, unafraid to speak the truth because he had neither place nor pension to protect ('all the distant din that world can keep / Rolls o'er my grotto, and but soothes my sleep'), and honoured with the friendship of the best, who came to his 'retreat' to share 'The feast of reason and the flow of soul'. Among those friends Lady Mary no longer featured. She was damned as 'Sappho', and associated in general terms (along with 'Delia') with slander, poison and rage. More pertinently, Pope's couplet about her, 'From furious Sappho scarce a milder fate, / Poxed by her love, or libeled by her hate', was a brilliant compression of the general into the particular. It unmistakably identified Lady Mary, who was well known for her support for inoculation against smallpox, but at the same time it reduced her to the generic woman writer of stereotype. Any woman writer could be 'Sappho'. Elizabeth Thomas was 'Sappho'. All women writers were promiscuous, dirty and vain (the terms in which Pope attacked Lady Mary). Public association of her name with a method of controlling the disease of smallpox was elided with public association of female writers with whores (the 'punk and poetess' equation, as in the formulation of Robert Gould from the 1690s: 'for punk and poetess agree so pat / You cannot well be this and not be that') and the diseases of sexual promiscuity.

Like Elizabeth Thomas, Lady Mary Wortley Montagu took on generic identity through the circumstances of her appearances in print. Also like Thomas, she had worked hard to control her public image. She had nurtured an ambiguous anonymity, making it well known that she preferred not to go into print, and gaining an unparalleled reputation as a wit for verses and bon mots which circulated freely within her own high-ranking milieux. Pope's attacks and her own responses drew her into pamphlet warfare involving different audiences, putting her in the tradition of 'Delia' – Delarivier Manley – and allowing the assumption that, like Manley, Lady Mary wrote scandalous histories which concerned themselves with sex, and told lies for party interest (some of which was certainly true). Much of the force of Pope's attacks on Lady Mary derived from the value she invested in secrecy which was at the same time part of the complex of values involved in rank. Secrecy was not the same as a desire for privacy and nor should it be taken to imply a shy or retiring disposition. Lady Mary Wortley Montagu was an energetic, aggressive, politically active public woman with a highly developed sense of caste. Born into one of the premier families in the land, her sense of herself in relation to writers like Pope and Swift included no assumption of inferiority based on gender: to be a woman within her world was to receive homage and deference. Pope and Swift, by contrast, were, as she put it, no more than a couple of 'linkboys'. In Venice, Lady Mary had a commode painted with the backs of books by Pope, Swift and Bolingbroke which she showed one of her visitors, explaining that though they were rascals, she had 'the satisfaction of shitting on them every day'.[25]

The private satisfaction of reducing public luminaries to squalor perhaps went some way to diminishing the 'distant din' of the world. Having fallen in love with the bisexual Francesco Algarotti (whose *Newtonianismo* was translated by Elizabeth Carter as *Sir Isaac Newton's Philosophy Explained for the Use of the Ladies*), Lady Mary followed him to Italy. But instead of joining her in Venice as she proposed, Algarotti took himself off on a tour of the royal courts of Europe, ending up at Rheinsburg where the future Frederick the Great was Crown Prince. Sharing sexual and artistic tastes, Frederick and Algarotti probably became lovers – Frederick's verses hailed Algarotti as the Swan of Padua. Lady Mary stayed in Venice where she 'wrapped' herself up in books; Algarotti never came. Cosmopolitan, and with a tradition of veneration for learned and literary ladies, Venice and later Florence, Rome, Naples and elsewhere provided literary society which honoured her. As in England, she mixed in the highest circles. Away from England, she was an item on the grand tour, 'Lady Mary Wortley Montagu, Mr Pope's friend, who is most exceedingly entertaining'.

Crammed into the last half-page of Volume Two of Elizabeth Thomas's *Pylades and Corinna* was an advertisement for another book available from the printer. The notice advertised one of those productions with which, according to Mary Astell, the press groaned – 'male travels', though whether this was quite the tone and subject matter Astell meant when she dismissed them as being 'all in the same tone and stuffed with the same trifles' we do not know. In tiny print, the following full details were given:

Letters which passed between two Persian noblemen residing at Paris and their friends in Persia, 1720. Giving an account, I. Of a new set of characters never before represented in Europe, wherein is opened a scene of action, which the curiosity of the most inquisitive travellers could never discover, and has given us so agreeable an idea of the seraglio, the thoughts and passions of a confined number of women, solely reserved for the pleasures of a single man, the notions of the eunuchs, whose lives are spent in watching these ladies, their complaints of the misery of their condition, and the troublesomeness of their employments. II. The liberties of the Italian women. III. An entertaining description of the city of Paris, of the French plays, operas, fops and actresses. IV. The modesty of the Persian women compared with the assurance of the European women. VI . . . of the desire of old women to be thought young. VII . . . of the best manner of pleasing the French women . . . IX. A description of some ladies brought up for the seraglio.

As a postscript to *Pylades and Corinna* it is both unsurprising and disheartening. When actresses appeared on the public stage after 1660, the number of scenes involving rape and sexual violence increased, a reflection of the range of pleasures that could be taken. Similarly, the woman who offered herself to the imaginations of readers on the pages of a book that told about herself – her childhood, her thoughts and feelings, her friendships – licensed male looking and male responses of a sexual kind, whether, like Delarivier Manley, she represented herself as supremely desirable, sexually and socially (Rivella was worth watching and being with), or, like Elizabeth Singer Rowe, she was exuberant and appetitive, or, like Elizabeth Thomas, Jane Barker and Mary Astell, she seemed to have little or no interest in men as sexual partners. The heat in books that could offer 'so agreeable an idea of the seraglio' was transferable to books like *Pylades and Corinna* which opened doors into women's private worlds and public hopes. The bedroom and the boudoir, the nun's cell – those places where the thoughts and passions of a confined number of women could be met with – were readily turned into objects of consumption for polite readers by writers of all kinds, inciting a range of sensations from amused condescension to lust and disgust. From the semi-pornographic agreeable ideas of the seraglio to Eloisa's thoughts and feelings in Pope's 'Eloisa to Abelard', Belinda's 'toilet' in Pope's *The Rape of the Lock* – with its perfumes, puffs and powders – and haughty Celia's close stool into which she shits in Swift's *The Lady's Dressing-Room* was but a short step.

These and other writings reflect the public fascination with private life and they have a bearing on how female authorship could be imagined and lived. Male authors did not find themselves occupying both subject and object position, the dual role that Delarivier Manley so brilliantly evoked in *The Adventures of Rivella*. Few women followed the example set by Manley and Jane Barker in writing directly about authorship, although by the 1720s there was an accepting climate for women and numbers of them were active as writers. Eliza Haywood, the most active by far, chose not to write about her life as an author – and went so far as to ensure that those who knew her history kept it secret. The autobiographical elements in Elizabeth Thomas's correspondence with Richard Gwinnet, the self-conscious display of herself as a literary woman in the early part of the century, was, by the time the material appeared in *Pylades and Corinna*, overwhelmed by Grub Street associations: debtors' prison, duncehood and shame. And in any case, what Thomas wrote about was less the construction of an authorial self than the display of authorial identity.

Writings that concerned themselves with the lived experiences of female authors – Jane Barker's *Love Intrigues* and the *Patch-Work* novels, Manley's *Rivella*, Thomas's *Pylades and Corinna*, Martha Fowke Sansom's *Clio* and the *Memoirs* of Laetitia Pilkington – were not recognised as such. All became 'lost', or obscure or shameful texts. None was recovered by later generations as an example of how female authorship was lived and imagined in the early part of the century. By the mid century, the mark of female authorship was invisibility. To accomplish a vanishing act in the process of conducting an active life as a woman of letters was the post-1740 ideal. Eliza Haywood achieved it and so did Charlotte Lennox.[26]

By the 1770s, the *idea* of obscurity was so embedded in myths of female authorship that Frances Burney performed her own hiddenness – disguising her handwriting and having her brother deliver the manuscript in a cloak and hood – when she submitted her first novel, *Evelina, or the History of a Young Lady's Entrance into the World*, in 1778. To some extent this was a way of imitating high-ranking authors such as Lady Mary Wortley Montagu who made so much of their disdain for the commercial world of print. Burney even adopted a mock-heroic tone for the diary entry that recorded this 'grand and most important event!' In the dedication (archly addressed to the reviewers) and preface, grand importance took second place to temerity. The 'trifling production of a few hours' was offered by the 'humble novelist' ('In the republic of letters, there is no member of such inferior rank, or who is so much disdained by his brethren of the quill, as the humble novelist') who came before the public as an 'editor', 'hopeless of fame', and anxious not to be associated with 'the vulgar herd of authors':

> The following letters are presented to the public . . . with a very singular mixture of timidity and confidence, resulting from the peculiar situation of the editor; who, though trembling for their success from a consciousness of their imperfections, yet fears not being involved in their disgrace, while happily wrapped up in a mantle of impenetrable obscurity.

Burney's prefatory remarks were a pastiche of authorial diffidence and ambition, a self-conscious fiction about fiction, and in the tradition of the first important English novel, *Robinson Crusoe*, which had artfully been put before the public as the work of an 'editor' who had merely organised 'found' materials. Whether editor or humble novelist, Burney's voice was implicitly male. She addressed the authors of the *Monthly* and *Critical Reviews* as a younger version of themselves: 'Remember, Gentlemen,' she abjured them when begging not to be treated with derision, 'you were all young writers once, and the most experienced veteran of your corps may, by recollecting his first publication, renovate his first terrors, and learn to allow for mine.' Allowing for a young man's terrors when he sought 'protection' was one thing; but Burney, as was soon revealed, was a young woman, and for women authors the rhetoric of timidity had a different meaning altogether.

Timidity and obscurity – those 'mantles of impenetrable obscurity' – were to be worked and reworked in the decades ahead. Ideas about authorship in the later eighteenth century incorporated increasingly rigid gendered distinctions. In the early days of print culture, when Elizabeth Thomas dropped her poems off at Will's Coffee-House so that Dryden could read them, when Elizabeth Singer sent her poems to the *Athenian Mercury*, when Catharine Trotter wrote about Locke and Delarivier Manley was a political journalist, the integration of women into the world of writing and publishing proceeded in tandem with that of men. Nobody expected genius – whether in male or female form – to display modesty and timidity; to do so would be at least a contradiction in terms, and even a denial of reality, for the whole point of genius and exceptionality was that it raised the few above the mass.

Nor was it considered peculiar to be female and an author, which Fanny Burney's words so mischievously suggested. Men of letters like Pope and Swift, Richardson, Fielding and Johnson took for granted the presence of women of letters. Women did not have to pretend to be men to find their way into print or to be taken seriously as authors. But Fanny Burney's high-spirited pantomime did reflect some important changes. Pope's life and writings had a profound impact on the social construction of authorship, putting into circulation highly polarised versions of what constituted desirable and undesirable authorial selves, giving mythical status to the distinction between 'low' and 'public' – Grub Street hacks – and 'high' and 'private' – small coteries of the chosen. Although this distinction was not in itself gendered and many women adopted the Popeian authorial mode, more was always at stake for women, as Elizabeth Thomas's experiences showed, when they were exposed to public view.

No less important, as we have already seen, was the impact of Richardson's *Clarissa*. Edmund Curll, a libertine in his private life, promoted Delarivier Manley, Elizabeth Thomas and other female authors, as women worthy of celebration for their love of books, knowledge and high-mindedness. They were not presented as objects of his libidinous interest. By contrast, the fictional Clarissa's doom was marked precisely by the fact that her respectable author made of her an object of libidinous interest. The message of *Clarissa* was that being a superior woman of literary talent, knowledge and high-mindedness was no protection against a determined libertine like the fictional Lovelace. The reader's pleasure in contemplating Clarissa in her room was more like the imagined pleasures of the seraglio, as advertised on the last leaf of *Pylades and Corinna*, than, for example, the pleasure of conversation at dinner with Rivella, 'the author of the *Atalantis*', who might indeed take her companion on the river with her, or even into her rose-strewn bed, but if she did so it would be by her own choice and not as a prisoner (one of the 'confined') but as a free woman.

Chapter Ten

USING THE PAST

I wish to see women neither heroines nor brutes; but reasonable creatures.

    Mary Wollstonecraft, *A Vindication of the Rights of Woman*[1]

Have you read that wonderful book, *The Rights of Woman?*

    Anna Seward[2]

The firmest champion, and . . . the greatest ornament her sex ever had to boast!

    William Godwin, *Memoirs of the Author of 'The Rights of Woman.'*[3]

The female author

Literary activity had high cultural status and women associated with it could be raised from the general 'low' rank of women to become objects of admiration. By being placed 'high' in the social order they took on honorary masculinity. (A 'masculine understanding' was a term of praise.) Genius, talent, learning and wit were not considered male prerogatives. Those recognised as exceptions were pushed up the hierarchy: women were allowed some of the freedoms of 'the lordly sex', while low-status men gained some of the privileges of higher-status men.

Like the aristocracy in society at large, the exceptional woman sat on top of the pile of ordinary women. Just as the aristocracy had an unshakeable belief in their right to be where they were, so exceptional women imitated that assumption of prerogative and took strength from it. Their abilities earned them privileges. Their writings brought them rewards. What they only rarely brought were the means of subsistence. Until the later eighteenth century (and arguably not even then), the capital-intensive publishing industry was not organised in a way that made it likely to sustain many writers without help from patrons, universities, the Church or the professions. Women were not eligible to join the universities, the Church or the professions, could not be given government places in acknowledgement of their contributions to literature, and were generally less successful than men in finding patrons.

Those who had a secure place and portion, like Anna Seward of Lichfield, were able to behave like aristocrats in the world of letters. Their model was the vanishing world of elite country-house coteries. Some of the literary forms and practices they took up, such as Seward's correspondence network, went to some lengths to display this because it was an important part of their identity; it was what separated them from the mass whose 'trash' was supposedly everywhere. Managing the contradictions that inevitably arose was not always easy. Charlotte Smith, for example, in the prefaces to her novels throughout the 1780s and 1790s, bemoaned the fact that she was forced to write in order to raise money to support herself and her nine children. A well-born woman, Smith depicted herself as a drudge, exposed to the impertinencies of lower-class booksellers because of her trade. Her writing self was presented to the reading public as a lowered self measured against an implied non-writing self. The higher ideal, had not patriarchy in the form of an inadequate husband failed her, would have been not merely not to write for pay but not to write at all.[4]

The impact of commercialisation and the expansion of the press hastened the decline of aristocratic modes while at the same time it constructed celebrated women for a new public, not a public of supposed lettered and social equals but an uncontrolled and ill-defined mass who might admire or disapprove but would do so according to laws of their own devising. Intense and far from respectful press scrutiny had a bearing on Hannah More's shift from literature to evangelical charity work in the late 1780s, and on the eclipse of Catherine Macaulay's reputation in the same period. Macaulay was fêted for her *History of England*, from the appearance of the first volume in 1763 until the late 1770s, her powers fully recognised and applauded. But to be a Republican and forthright in England in the 1780s was not the same as in the 1760s. Even more importantly, her insistence on her singularity as an exceptional woman lauded by admiring males – Thomas Wilson raised 'a superb white statue' to her in his London church, representing Macaulay as Clio, the Muse of history – provoked hostility.[5] A few decades earlier, this might not have been the case. The failure of her contemporaries in 1722 to raise a statue in Westminster Abbey to Susannah Centlivre was a source of indignation to her biographer in 1761.[6]

By the end of the eighteenth century, women writers may not have known much about their predecessors but, as always, some notion of a history or a tradition of female authorship was an important component of what men and women received from the past. Literary women reading books met versions of themselves; male readers and writers also encountered such women in the pages of books. Who they encountered and what uses they were able to make of predecessors is hard to establish: a discussion like that between Catharine Cockburn and her niece about Elizabeth Thomas and Pope's treatment of Thomas is rare. It also points to some of the problems. Cockburn's concern was to defend Thomas's reputation as a woman, that is, her 'fame' in its sexual meaning rather than her authorial fame, because that was what had been traduced. This common impulse moved the historical figure away from the everyday of a working writer's life where, like Thomas, Davys, Barker and others, she might be found rubbing along in the midst of ordinary concerns, and into a higher or more abstract realm. It wilfully obscured all the elements that composed the business of literature – the writing, rewriting, editing, production and distribution – and it moved her away from the literary tradition and her place in it. To be hidden rather than seen, unknown rather than known, silent rather than speaking and self-deprecating rather than self-assertive became key attributes of the laudable woman writer at the very time women were using their speaking, writing and self assertion to enter the literary world in ever greater numbers.

The expansion of the trade in books gave a peculiar intensity to these and other factors relating to female authorship. Femininity was a commodity to be sold like other commodities in a mixed and anonymous market, some at the luxury end for the few and some for the masses. Increasingly, in novels, sermons, conduct books, periodicals, poems, plays and prose writings of every kind, men and women addressed the subject of femininity: manners and conduct, the rights of women, the wrongs of women. Only rarely did anybody write explicitly about female authorship except for polemical purposes, and few showed interest in recovering any sort of female literary tradition. (Clara Reeve's *The Progress of Romance*, which clearly had this as part of its agenda, is a notable exception.)

It is hard to find a friendly representation of the woman writer later than Delarivier Manley's Rivella and Jane Barker's Galesia. Elizabeth Griffith presented herself as a writer in the very popular and much reprinted *Series of Genuine Letters Between Henry and Frances* (1757) which, like Elizabeth Thomas's *Pylades and Corinna*, used the genre of romance and the epistolary relationship to make a space for the female authorial self. Frances Brooke drew on her experiences as a woman coming to London to be an author in *The Excursion* (1777). There are certainly other examples, but it is striking how insistent the *not* writing about authorship was, given that for women writers questions about femininity frequently posed themselves as questions about the authorial life. Men were received as authors and might write about each other as such; women were received and written about as women. When women did represent female authorship it was likely to be in satirical vein: Frances Burney mocked Elizabeth Montagu and the bluestockings in *The Witlings* (1778) which featured a Lady Smatter, a Mrs Sapient and a Mrs Voluble; Elizabeth Hamilton's Bridgetina Botherim in *Memoirs of Modern Philosophers* (1800) satirised the supposed man-chasing feminism of Mary Hays and Mary Wollstonecraft; and Maria Edgeworth gave monstrous life to Harriet Freke in *Belinda* (1801).

Hackneyed forms

Chief among the polemical forms in which the concept of female authorship circulated in the late seventeenth and early eighteenth centuries was celebratory verse. Poetical paeans were given a boost by the mid-century recovery work of antiquarians like George Ballard and churchmen like Thomas Birch whose compilations were important sources of information about women writing in the earlier period, and by the example of poems like John Duncombe's *The Feminiad*, and Thomas Seward's *The Female Right to Literature*.

In 1774, Mary Scott made use of both of these to compose and publish a new poem celebrating learned women and protesting about 'tyrant' men's appropriation of the 'realms of knowledge'. *The Female Advocate* came right up to date, naming Anna Barbauld whose first publication, *Poems*, had appeared the previous year, as well as Elizabeth Montagu, Elizabeth Tollet (the friend of Isaac Newton), Charlotte Lennox and Catherine Macaulay among other living and dead eighteenth-century writers; and it repaired some of Ballard's omissions from the seventeenth century, putting in Margaret Cavendish, Anne Killigrew and Katherine Philips. Nevertheless, in selecting the form of the celebratory poem, Scott displayed a backward-reaching impulse, one which was driven less by the social realities of women's increasing opportunities in the 1770s and more by the lack of contemporary forms for her impassioned defence of women *as writers*. She included extracts from Thomas Seward's *The Female Right to Literature*, praising him along with Duncombe as among the exceptional men who did not have 'narrow views' on this matter. The poem was well received in the Bishop's Palace at Lichfield and Anna Seward kept up a correspondence with Mary Scott until the early 1790s.

Mary Scott lived in Somerset, apparently for some of her married life in what had been Elizabeth Singer Rowe's house at Frome. Perhaps we can trace the influence of Elizabeth Johnson's heated proto-feminist preface to Elizabeth Singer's *Poems* of 1696 in the tone of Mary Scott's dedication 'To a Lady' which prefaced *The Female Advocate*.[7] Scott attacked 'the illiberal sentiments of men in general in regard to our sex' in which so many of them 'glory' while at the same time acknowledging that much had improved since some vaguely indicated earlier time: 'the sentiments of all men of sense relative to female education are now more enlarged than they formerly were'. Indeed, there was a risk that it was no longer necessary to write in this vein at all on the subject. Still, 'fervent zeal' would out and, begging men 'of a more liberal turn of mind' to excuse her because she had suffered much illness, Mary Scott allowed her 'indignation' to flow along what by 1774 were some well-grooved lines:

If they have allowed us to study the imitative arts, have they not prohibited us from cultivating an acquaintance with the sciences? Do they not regard the woman who suffers her faculties to rust in a state of listless indolence with a more favourable eye than her who engages in a dispassionate search after truth? And is not an implicit acquiescence in the dictates of their understandings esteemed by them as the sole criterion of good sense in a woman?

Scott was 'zealous ... in the cause of my sex' but had to admit that not all women were formed for literature. 'All I contend for is that it is a duty absolutely incumbent on every woman whom nature hath blessed with talents ... to improve them.'

The uneasiness in Mary Scott's dedication to *The Female Advocate*, which while lamenting prohibition made much of women's successes in improving their talents – 'of late, female authors have appeared with honour in almost every walk of literature' – betrayed the mismatch between old rhetoric and new developments. Improved women were many, but the rhetoric still represented them as unique – as exceptions who had to woo the rest of the sex from 'pleasure's treach'rous charms' and 'the siren's fatal arms' and teach them to nobly scorn 'the little pride of man'.

Panegyric of this sort combined the old tradition of praise of famous men with the literature of female complaint popular since the late seventeenth-century translations of Ovid's *Epistles*. It worked with high abstractions and stock figures – tyrant man, vicious or foolish (listlessly indolent) lesser women, and liberal men – to produce profoundly fictional versions of the named and praised individuals. Nobody expected it to do anything else.

By 1774, it was as formulaic and backward-looking – while appearing to be modern – as, in a different sense, was Frances Burney's report in the same year upon meeting the author Frances Brooke. Though little known nowadays, Brooke was a woman of letters who had high visibility in the mid eighteenth century – as a periodical writer, novelist, translator, dramatist and theatre manager. She was one of many who composed the literary environment in which Burney grew up. Brooke had followed the example of Eliza Haywood, launching a weekly periodical, *The Old Maid*, in 1755 under the interesting pseudonym

'Mary Singleton, Spinster'. (She herself married in 1756.) She kept it going for twenty-two numbers and in 1764 reprinted the whole lot in a single volume. From 1773 to 1778 she was joint manager of the Haymarket Opera House with the actress Mary Ann Yates, and her own comic opera *Rosina*, put on at Covent Garden in 1782, was a resounding triumph, the second most popular afterpiece on the London stage for almost twenty years. (The most popular was Milton's *Comus*.) All this, combined with the success of her 1763 novel, *The History of Lady Julia Mandeville*, made her a substantial presence.[8]

When Frances Burney met Frances Brooke, the older woman had been actively writing for almost twenty years. Burney, young and ambitious (*Evelina* was still four years away) and understanding self-effacement as a key factor in managing her own authorial ambitions, had a talent for comic deflation of egotism. Of Mrs Brooke she wrote: 'Mrs Brooke is very short and fat, and squints; but has the art of showing agreeable ugliness. She is very well bred, and expresses herself with much modesty upon all subjects; which in an *authoress*, a woman of *known* understanding, is extremely pleasing.'[9]

It doesn't appear that Mrs Brooke needed cutting down to size but the idea that as an 'authoress' she would do so provided one element of comedy. Detraction, as Frances Burney practised it, combined the old misogynist tradition with a healthy alertness to what was passing in the literary world of her day, which in fact included acceptance of women writers on much the same terms as men.

Frances Burney drew on panegyrical assumptions about female superiority ('an *authoress*, a woman of *known* understanding') for comic effect. Hannah More adopted the panegyric to deliver spirited (and seriously intended) eulogies of her bluestocking friends in *Sensibility* (1782) and *The Bas Bleu* (1786). *Sensibility* rewrote the Popeian division between true and false writers as a division in the capacity for feeling, where those who could feel most were those with most mental endowments. The poems were addressed to the noble few: 'You who have melted in bright glory's flame / Or felt the spirit-stirring breath of fame; / Ye noble few . . .' These 'few' were those able to respond to the poets and really feel and understand as they did, who could 'divide the joys, and share the pains / Which merit feels, or Heav'n born Fancy feigns'. The 'vulgar' were not invited to the feast of reason and the flow of soul that was Hannah More's poem – 'Let not the vulgar read this pensive strain' – because their 'low enjoyments' were not of the mind.[10]

The problem as More expressed it in *Sensibility* was that far too many of the vulgar were learning the signs of feeling, and gaining credit for it, from literature (which was promiscuously available) rather than life (where rank and precedence still served to bar the door), from 'tender Otway's fires' and 'Clarissa's woes', and worse, from cheap 'counterfeit' versions. (More apologised to Richardson in the poem, assuring his shade she meant no 'cold contempt' of his 'peerless' writings.) Too many there were 'who fill with brilliant plaints the page'; too many 'well-sung sorrows every breast inflame'. Words were merely signs, 'And these fair marks, reluctant I relate, / These lovely symbols may be counterfeit.'

When she published *The Bas-bleu, or, Conversation. Addressed to Mrs Vesey*, More explained in the Advertisement that the 'trifle' had not been meant for publication, but that copies had been circulating in manuscript (not a few of them put out into the world by More herself, including the one in the possession of King George). Apparently driven to justifying print on the grounds that friends advised her to it to ensure an accurate version, the sophisticated Hannah More – worldly businesswoman and bookworm – confessed she was 'almost ashamed to take refuge in so hackneyed an apology'. To say that her friends had urged her writings into print was indeed a 'hackneyed' excuse by the 1780s. Ashamed or not, More used the 'apology' as a way of signalling the high-ranking social circles she had gained access to by her talents. Like Frances Burney, she identified with aristocratic ideology, having been welcomed by the highest on the grounds of exceptional literary merit. For young women from middling entrepreneurial backgrounds, not being judged 'low' or 'counterfeit' was vital. One of the ways More ensured her place among the bluestockings as a spokeswoman for elite literary values was to imitate one of the longest-standing traditions associated with high-ranking women writers. Her 'hackneyed' excuse put her in a line of development that stretched back to Katherine Philips, the 'matchless Orinda'.

Among the 'many' finding their way into print were some low-born children. In 1791, Elizabeth Ogilvy Benger of Portsmouth proudly put her name and age – thirteen – on the title page of a long poem, *The*

Female Geniad, which rendered into verse the celebratory message of Richard Samuel's painting, *The Nine Living Muses of Great Britain*. Aligning itself with the tradition in which 'high-born merit' was the pinnacle, Benger's poem, fifty-five pages of iambic pentameters divided into three cantos, praised meritorious women and was presented in a form which drew attention to its historicity: the printer used the old-fashioned long 'f' for 's'. In the preface, Benger made much of her youth, referring to 'the pen of a young author', to herself as 'yet in a state of childhood' and entreating pardon for 'a juvenile essay'.

That a child should pipe the merits of female genius, imitating the authoritative tones of the bluestockings, was not calculated to maintain a sense of the high status of the role. Making explicit the link with Thomas Seward's 1748 poem, Benger singled out Anna Seward, along with Anna Barbauld, as the key figures of her time. They were the two whose 'merits' claimed 'Of verse the homage, and a Muse's name'. The larger message conveyed by the poem as a whole was that Seward and Barbauld belonged to the past, in a world of ideal visions fit for children to consume.

Anna Barbauld

Anna Barbauld picked her way carefully through a changing realm of cultural and sexual politics. One of Barbauld's favourite forms was the verse epistle which Pope had made popular. In its naming and placing of a circumscribed group, the verse epistle offered a way of displaying belonging: 'To Dr Aikin, on his complaining that she neglected him, October 20th 1768'; 'To Miss Rigby, on her Attendance upon her Mother at Brixton'; or, in a title that harked back to Anne Finch, Countess of Winchilsea, and her evocations of the pleasures of matrimony: 'To Mr Barbauld, with a Map of the Land of Matrimony'.

Barbauld was a member of the nation's intellectual aristocracy, the Dissenters – by the 1770s the most important and progressive element in literary life. The daughter of a tutor at the leading Dissenting academy in Warrington, where Joseph Priestley, William Enfield and other Nonconformists taught, she grew up in an atmosphere of serious intellectual endeavour, one of the new generation of improved women. She did not allow her faculties to rust in listless indolence but was a dispassionate searcher after truth. Truth was not located in anything to do with women. There was no way to take authorial pride in specifically womanly qualities, though like any moralist she could point to what were good and bad ways of being female: good was to please men, bad was to claim special privileges for one's singularity. Singular Barbauld was, however, in her intellectual and literary abilities; and it was her acknowledged singularity that more or less guaranteed her early fame. Her poems circulated in manuscript and were discussed by the close-knit group in Warrington for many years before they appeared in print. With this support, they were an instant success in 1773.[11]

Barbauld came of the same stock that had nurtured Elizabeth Singer Rowe, produced the influential *Life of Mrs Rowe*, kept Rowe's works in print, and promoted her as a foremother worthy of emulation. That Barbauld was female and clever was not a novel or unwelcome idea to her male intellectual peers and mentors. As a writer and teacher she worked alongside her brother, John Aikin, and her husband, Rochemont Barbauld. Like Elizabeth Carter, she published a poem in praise of Mrs Rowe. Rowe's emphasis on earthly love in relation to divine was an important influence on Barbauld's thinking. However, while Rowe's male contemporaries had eagerly caught at the flames of enthusiasm issuing from her pen, the men of Barbauld's time were anxious to repudiate it. Joseph Priestley and Gilbert Wakefield were uncomfortable with arguments that assumed a resemblance between religious devotion and love, even 'that fanciful and elevated kind of love which depends not on the senses'. The word 'Platonic' in this context had become so debased they were reluctant even to use it.[12]

In tracts championing emotion in religion against what she called the mechanical 'systematic spirit' of Priestley and others, Barbauld faithfully reproduced the spirit of Elizabeth Rowe, though her version of the erotic in religious feeling was mild by comparison with her predecessor. Still, it upset the men. Priestley insisted in a letter to Barbauld that the language of 'profound adoration' addressed to humans was 'an abominable practice' and 'nothing less than a direct impiety'. The difference between them reaches back to the 1730s and Isaac Watts's discomfort with Elizabeth Rowe's fervour – his desire to tone down the *Devout Exercises of the Heart*.

Barbauld's political views were liberal, but on the question of female authorship and the related question of women's education, she was conservative. When Elizabeth Montagu asked her to consider becoming principal of a 'college for young ladies' so as to set new standards for a new era, she declined on the grounds that her own education had been 'peculiar'. Most women, she thought, were best educated by their fathers and brothers, and should be taught to be 'good wives and agreeable companions' not learned ladies. When Maria Edgeworth floated a proposal for a journal by and for women, Barbauld refused to be involved in that either. She acknowledged that 'the joint interests of their sex' might unite women in general, but 'there [was] no bond of union among literary women'. She saw herself as one who had 'stepped out of the bounds of female reserve in becoming an author'. She resisted incorporation into any 'bond of union' with other women authors and emphatically refused to demand women's rights.

Barbauld explained to Maria Edgeworth that in her view there was 'a great difference between a paper written by a lady, and as a lady', the latter suggesting 'a certain cast of sentiment' that would lead to writing 'in trammels'. To write 'as a lady' was to accept limitations such as those Barbauld herself urged on women in poems that encouraged them to behave in properly submissive feminine ways. For herself as an exceptional woman the terms were different: she could step 'out of the bounds of female reserve' because her intellect entitled her to some of the freedoms men had. Hence it was not in her interest to do anything which might – as she saw it – 'provoke a war with the other sex'.[13]

When Mary Wollstonecraft, also urging reason and mental freedom, attacked Barbauld in *A Vindication of the Rights of Woman* for her poem likening women to painted flowers ('sweet and gay, and delicate like you / Emblems of innocence, and beauty too . . . nor blush, my fair, to own you copy these; / Your best, your sweetest empire is – to please'), Barbauld responded with another poem, taking Wollstonecraft's title, 'The Rights of Woman', and reiterating her own view that reciprocal love and pleasing men were woman's sweetest empire.

In her critical work Barbauld wrote mostly about male authors, producing editions of Mark Akenside (1794), William Collins (1794), and six volumes of Samuel Richardson's correspondence (1806). She went on to edit and introduce the fifty-volume series *The British Novelists* (1810). Meanwhile, her tracts in support of the Dissenters' campaign against their legal disabilities were uncompromising. She used the 'masculine' freedoms she preserved for herself to address the nation at large on important political matters such as democratic government and popular education in *Civic Sermons to the People* (1792) – and against the war with France – in *Sins of the Government, Sins of the Nation* (1793). Like Hannah More she campaigned actively against the slave trade, putting her high reputation as poet and moralist to the service of the cause. Neither nation nor government objected in principle to being preached at by a woman, but Barbauld's vision of political and social corruption as expressed in her later Juvenalian satire, the powerful, bleak and controversial *Eighteen Hundred and Eleven*, was violently attacked by W. J. Croker in the *Quarterly Review* in 1812. It marked the end of her public career. Perhaps the poem would have produced much the same reaction had she been a man. (A cruel review by Croker was credited with 'killing' John Keats.) Nevertheless, one of the messages of this episode is that the masculine freedom of voice which gave Barbauld so much scope at the height of her fame and which allowed her to issue weighty sermons to the people could no longer be taken for granted, no matter how established and respected was the exceptional woman making use of it.

Exhibiting the soul of the author

Barbauld projected an authorial self that was politically informed, authoritative and assured. Implicitly, her public voice of critic and moralist was distinct from the feminine self which lived the life of Anna Barbauld and obeyed the dictates of 'female reserve'. During Barbauld's lifetime, the younger generation of women had begun to press on that distinction in ways that fatally weakened it by closing the gap between ordinary women whose sweetest empire was to please and exceptional women licensed to deliver unpleasing but necessary truths. Mary Wollstonecraft, Mary Hays and Charlotte Smith used their writing to present authorial selves that incorporated aspects of their womanly lives which did, indeed, tend to 'provoke a war with the other sex'.

The heroine of Mary Wollstonecraft's carefully titled first novel, *Mary, A Fiction* (1788), was one of the 'chosen few'. Her autobiographical or confessional origins were marked by the fact that she carried the author's name and by an explanation in the Advertisement that the best compositions were those in which 'the soul of the author is exhibited'.

Not the Julie of *La Nouvelle Héloïse* but the Rousseau of *The Confessions* (1781–8) and *The Reveries of a Solitary Walker* (1782) provided the model. Like Rousseau, whose *Confessions* began, 'I have resolved on an enterprise which has no precedent . . . My purpose is to display to my kind a portrait in every way true to nature, and the man I shall portray will be myself', Wollstonecraft declared the novelty of her enterprise. Her purpose was to display a portrait of herself as a new fictional heroine, one drawn neither from literary conventions nor social norms; who apparently could not be imagined in real life, but could be allowed as a possibility in fiction. This was 'a woman who has thinking powers'. Artfulness was disavowed: the tale was 'artless' and 'without episodes'. Its interest was in the originality of the figure portrayed, one whose 'grandeur' derived 'from the operation of its own faculties, not subjugated to opinion'.

What Wollstonecraft presented as a character, 'different from those generally portrayed' (she instanced Clarissa and Sophie), was in essentials a version of those high-minded women who in poems like *The Feminiad* had been praised for being superior to the follies of the sex. Hence, after introducing the tale as one in which 'the mind of a woman who has thinking powers is displayed', Wollstonecraft commented, 'The female organs have been thought too weak for this arduous employment; and experience seems to justify the assertion.' Wanting to speak for herself (the 'chosen few, wish to speak for themselves'), Wollstonecraft created a character who combined the exceptional woman from earlier in the century with the sentimental heroine of post-Richardsonian fiction. The radical element in this presentation, what made it new – the thing that could not be found in life but might be imagined in fiction – was the emphasis on female authorship: the exhibition of the 'soul' of the author. The philosophical heroine was to be received as both a 'real' person – Mary Wollstonecraft, the 'first of a new genus', a woman born not to 'tread in the beaten track', a busy professional writer – and a fictional character: Mary, in *Mary, A Fiction*, and Maria in the later *Maria, or The Wrongs of Woman* (1798).[14]

Wollstonecraft made plain that the reader of her fictions was to receive the living self through the fictional representation. In *Mary, A Fiction*, the heroine she displayed, whose mental, emotional and spiritual formation unfolded in a series of short and intense episodes, was a genius whose task in life was to discern 'what end her various faculties were destined to pursue'. As a child, of whom nobody took much notice, she read whatever she could get her hands on: 'Neglected in every respect, and left to the operations of her own mind, she considered everything that came under her inspection, and learned to think.' Self-discovery was a religious duty. Mary 'would sit up half the night, her favourite time for employing her mind', reading, composing verses and singing hymns.[15] Meanwhile, her feelings – religious, affectionate, benevolent and charitable – were as strong as her thoughts. From these auspicious beginnings, Mary's progress was obstructed by an enforced marriage into which her father pressed her (like some latter-day Harlowe *père* succeeding in marrying Clarissa off to Solmes) when she was distracted by her mother's death.

Having learned to think, this heroine needed to write. The text of *Mary, A Fiction* incorporated Mary's 'rhapsodies' and reflections much as the *Life of Mrs Rowe* – a book Wollstonecraft certainly knew through her connection with the Dissenters of Newington Green – included Rowe's prayers and religious reflections. Married but living without her husband – the groom having no interest in Mary and Wollstonecraft no interest in the groom, the author dispatched him to the Continent on the same page as the wedding ceremony – Mary's life by the end of the novel is modelled according to the type suggested by Mrs Rowe: economically independent, she does good and prays for some future state where her 'thirst of knowledge will be gratified and [her] ardent affections find an object'. This will be in the afterlife. Mary could only imagine happiness in heaven, or in prayer where 'enthusiastic devotion overcame the dictates of despair' and enabled her to achieve 'resignation'. Love and happiness in human form is impossible. 'Eternity, immateriality and happiness' go together and form what is to be yearned after: 'How shall I grasp the mighty and fleeting conceptions ye create?' Mary exclaims, like Rowe wanting to shape the 'mighty genius' that excited her breast with flames too great to manage or resist.[16]

Mary, A Fiction ends mournfully with the vision of Mary's frailty and likely early death. Thinking of death, 'a gleam of joy would dart across her mind'. The apparently morbid death wish reads less gloomily when understood in relation to the writings of Elizabeth Rowe, for in Rowe's work death meant removal to that Elysian world where sexual pleasure could be freely taken. Rowe depicted the afterlife, those 'mansions of life and bliss', as the place of erotic freedom. It was where superior women successfully combined head and heart. As a character in a novel, Mary was different to the heroines usually portrayed; for the unacknowledged model who sat for the picture was less the famous heroines of Richardson and Rousseau and more the famous woman writer from earlier in the century.

The confessional impulse in Wollstonecraft's work was an enterprise arrived at in the philosophic spirit of Rousseau: the soul of the (female) author was to be exhibited as an original but nonetheless natural object. The elevation of the singular woman rested on a depiction of the mass of women as low, for this was the logic of exhortation, developed more extensively in *A Vindication of the Rights of Woman* (improved women needed women to improve); however, Wollstonecraft used her fictions, as she used her polemical writings, to analyse the condition of all women. The singular woman, wronged by a society which supposedly did not allow a thinking woman to exist, emblematised the wrongs of women in a social order whose 'partial laws and customs' – especially marriage – gave men power over them. In *Maria, or the Wrongs of Woman*, Wollstonecraft placed two wronged women together in a lunatic asylum, the one imprisoned by a wicked husband (a man who spouted progressive rhetoric) and the other her wardress who in the end helps her escape. The novel forged a bond between the classes and it did so by means of the doctrine of exceptionality and the melodrama of miserable marriage.

The tragedy of *Maria, or the Wrongs of Woman* lay in the 'distressing' situation outlined in the preface. Wollstonecraft wrote, 'For my part, I cannot suppose any situation more distressing, than for a woman of sensibility, with an improving mind, to be bound to such a man as I have described for life.' The marriage of mental inequality required a wife to deny her desire for improvement. She had best 'avoid cultivating her taste' because otherwise she would cause herself pain – the pain of frustration. Any wife who did not suffer under these circumstances was 'ordinary'.[17]

By the end of the century it was a commonplace that clever women needed husbands of 'humour and spirit', as Sarah Fielding put it in her *Remarks on Clarissa*, a large part of the discussion in which concerns the deficiencies of husbands. This commonplace had been given a powerful contemporary twist in the 1790s by Charlotte Smith, who used the prefaces of her novels from *Desmond* (1792) onwards to tell the story of her married woes.

Smith took the rhetoric of superior womanhood and the cultural consensus that the true gruesomeness of the marriage laws was revealed when clever women found themselves chained for life to less clever men (or men who were less refined) and moulded it to protest about her circumstances, in the process offering a new version of the writing woman. Smith, a precocious child of the landed gentry whose father had squandered their wealth, had been married off ('sold, a legal prostitute') at not quite sixteen to the younger son of a wealthy merchant. Benjamin Smith was a wastrel and soon landed the pair of them in debtors' prison, from where Smith published her *Elegiac Sonnets and Other Essays* (1784) which were to produce a considerable income, going through ten editions in her lifetime alone.

Elegiac Sonnets expressed much unhappiness. Some of that unhappiness was attributed to the marriage of mental inequality in which Charlotte Smith found herself before she had barely become adult. Describing her dedication to self-education in these early years of marriage, having become 'mistress of her own time', putting it to good use in 'the cultivation of her mind', her sister and biographer, Catherine Dorset (also a published writer), explained the problems this gave rise to:

The result of her mental improvement was not favourable to her happiness. She began . . . to compare her own mind with those of the persons by whom she was surrounded.

The consciousness of her own superiority, the mortifying conviction that she was subjected to one so infinitely her inferior, presented itself every day more forcibly to her mind, and she justly considered herself 'as a pearl that had been basely thrown away'.[18]

Or, as Smith herself put it in a letter to a friend:

the more my mind expanded, the more I became sensible of personal slavery; the more I improved and cultivated my understanding, the farther I was removed from those with whom I was condemned to spend my life, and the more clearly I saw by those newly acquired lights the horror of the abyss into which I had unconsciously plunged.[19]

Smith made sure her readers connected her fictions with her own life. The *Elegiac Sonnets* were applicable to her personal history, and she knew (and remarked sardonically on the fact) that prison would make her literary persona all the more romantic. The 'abyss' into which she plunged had been none of her own making. In going to prison with a worthless husband, she displayed her own worth. In sending mournful sonnets out into the world from within prison walls, she gave a new twist to virtuous heroinism, recuperating even prison for new and sympathetic audiences. It was important, however, that the prison location was balanced by a more appropriate setting for a literary lady and perhaps that was why the title page described her as 'Charlotte Smith of Bignor Park, Sussex'. Smith had grown up at Bignor Park, and loved it, but the estate had descended to her brother. She exploited the location further: William Hayley, the most famous poet of the day, lived nearby. Having no acquaintance with 'the Bard of Sussex', Smith introduced herself in an unconventional way for the express purpose of getting his name on the pages of her first book. Pregnant, she seems to have ridden the five or six miles between Bignor Park and Eartham and then staged a stomach cramp in Hayley's garden so that the housekeeper invited her in. Hayley, who took a pride in his medical skills, 'played the physician with some success' as he told his cousin, and soon restored his 'tender sister of Parnassus' to health. They then had 'a poetical dinner' and he showed her round his house and garden. *Elegiac Sonnets* was dedicated to Hayley.[20]

Smith went on to be equally successful as a novelist. When *Emmeline, the Orphan of the Castle* was published in 1788, the first edition of 1,500 sold out at once. With a large family to support, ready money was vital, but Smith was 'humbled and hurt' when 'Mr Lane the bookseller' tried to give her twice as much money as Cadell if she would break her agreement for subsequent editions. Lane's visit left her 'all in a tremble'. She sent Hayley an amusing dialogue recounting it, staging the encounter as a play: 'Scene. The poor novelist at her desk . . . Enter her servant . . . Scene the Parlor. A consequential red-faced pert looking man. Enter to him the unfortunate novelist.' Congratulating herself on 'repulsing forever his pert advances', she lamented the circumstances that exposed her to them: 'Somebody I apprehend has told him how cruelly I want money.' Hayley, local squire and a man of means, was all sympathy. 'Alas!' she wrote, 'how unfit I am for the common intercourse of common life, and how very unfit for all I am forced to encounter.'[21]

Charlotte Smith's imagery of horror and abyss was echoed in the opening lines of Wollstonecraft's *Maria, or The Wrongs of Woman*, which began, 'Abodes of horror have frequently been described', and went on to claim that the abode of horror in which Maria found herself was both ordinary and unprecedented. Yoked to a man who was her inferior, morally, intellectually, emotionally, whose 'defects' of 'understanding' she had sadly observed and whose taste she had tried to improve so that his faculties might ripen along with hers, Maria had obeyed him even though it was impossible to love him. However, she could not act contrary to principle. When her husband tried to prostitute her to a friend to whom he owed money, she considered 'all obligation made void by his conduct'. The feelings that were 'the foundation of her principles' revolted.

According to the logic of improved womanhood, a superior woman 'must be allowed to consult her conscience', and choose how she lived her life – whether she stayed with a bad husband, whether she took a lover, or whether she established manufactories and threw her estate into small farms as Mary did at the end of *Mary, A Fiction* – for she not only knew better than men but was likely to *be* better. The woman who consulted her conscience was not a child. *Maria* (which was unfinished at Wollstonecraft's death) ends with a speech in which the heroine defends herself and her prison lover, Darnford, and claims a divorce from her husband, Venables. Darnford is accused of adultery and seduction. Crucially, Maria insists Darnford plead guilty to the charge of adultery but not guilty to the charge of seduction: she had not been seduced, she had given herself voluntarily to him on the grounds that her own 'sense of right' made her actions just under the circumstances:

> I was six-and-twenty when I left Mr Venables' roof; if ever I am to be supposed to arrive at an age to direct my own actions, I must by that time have arrived at it. – I acted with deliberation . . . Neglected by my husband, I never encouraged a lover; and preserved with scrupulous care, what is termed my honour, at the expence of my peace, till he, who should have been its guardian, laid traps to ensnare me. From that moment I believed myself, in the sight of heaven, free – and no power on earth shall force me to renounce my resolution.[22]

The *Clarissa*-like description of a virtuous woman at the mercy of a scheming man laying traps to ensnare her produces, in Wollstonecraft's sardonic ending, an equally *Clarissa*-like response from the judges. Maria's sense of what she owes herself is not endorsed. The judges disapprove of women pleading their feelings and did not want what they considered 'French principles' in public or private English life: 'What virtuous woman thought of her feelings? – It was her duty to love and obey the man chosen by her parents and relations, who were qualified by their experiences to judge better for her, than she could for herself.' Her conduct 'did not appear that of a person of sane mind'.

Lunacy, imprisonment and slavery ('poor Charlotte', as William Cowper sympathetically wrote of Charlotte Smith, 'chained to her desk like a slave to his oar') were the defining images for women's place in a social order in which men had power over and were supposed to protect them, but might instead lay traps.

The prison in which Maria was incarcerated symbolised a much larger prison: 'was not the world a vast prison and women merely slaves?' Women who entered the prison of marriage were 'bastilled for life'. The elaborate account of how things don't work for women in *Maria* served the vision of a future realm in which all women would be free – when the 'partial laws and customs of society' which oppressed women were altered. The female mind was unlikely to find sustenance in a female past since, in Mary Wollstonecraft's words, women had been 'degrade[d] . . . so far below their oppressors' by the evils they were 'subjected to endure', as 'almost to justify their tyranny'. The past was of

324

no help to a sex that had been systematically wronged. What mattered was the future, an imaginary place rather like the afterlife to which one knew one was going but about which one could form no sure conceptions. In the Author's Preface, Wollstonecraft appealed to those 'few' who were, like her, capable and daring enough to 'advance before the improvement of the age'.[23]

Through the figure of the wardress, Jemima, Wollstonecraft extended the social reach of the doctrine of exceptionality. Maria makes common cause with Jemima who, as the working woman in charge, was the 'true' inhabitant of the prison. Maria recognises something 'superior to her class' in Jemima. She is intelligent, but more than that she displays the autonomy of a thinking and experiencing self. Jemima's self and Jemima's story function in the novel as the real against which the tale of a prison romance, between Maria and Darnford, is played out. As split authorial projections, Jemima represents not just the working woman but the working woman writer, while Maria is the heroine of a fiction.

As paid writing could bring honourable independence to Wollstonecraft, so prison, by providing Jemima with the security of a steady income, was a place of freedom. It was better than brothels or casual prostitution, to which Jemima had been driven, and a great deal better than destitution and starvation. It allowed her the luxury of a moral self. She could deal decently with other people because the fact of having an income, no matter how small, raised her above the necessity to behave like a 'ravenous dog' or 'dumb brute'.

A key moment in Jemima's history was when she went into keeping with an elderly libertine intellectual. Born the unwanted illegitimate child of a servant, raped herself as soon as she was old enough, having been a thief, whore and laundrywoman, she was not one in whose company the writer and his literary friends thought to curb their conversation. The fictional Jemima thus found herself, much like those real-life exceptional women Mary Wollstonecraft and Anna Barbauld, Anna Seward and Catherine Macaulay, at table listening to discussions from which 'in the common course of life, women [were] excluded'. For five years, she benefited from immersion in literary society. She made use of her 'opportunities of improvement'. When her master shut himself up to write, Jemima spent the time reading. Reading led to thinking and thinking to speech: her 'untutored remarks' gave her master hints for his writing. By the end she was a colleague, editor and critic: 'he often led me to discuss the subjects he was treating, and would read to me his productions, previous to their publication, wishing to profit by the criticism of unsophisticated feeling'.[24]

This five years of mental improvement renders Jemima 'superior to her class' and fits her for the society of Maria and the gentleman prisoner, Darnford. The three compose a little literary coterie within the walls of the asylum, communicating via marginal notes in books (Dryden's *Fables*, Milton's *Paradise Lost*, Rousseau's *La Nouvelle Héloïse*) and by telling each other their life stories.

Mary Hays

A Vindication of the Rights of Woman had established Wollstonecraft's fame as a systematic philosopher. It was not considered odd that a philosopher should write fiction, though the form brought its own problems: the 'low' associations of the genre exist in tension with the autobiographical impulse (the desire to project a 'high' version of the literary woman) and visionary utopianism of *Mary, A Fiction*, and *Maria, or The Wrongs of Woman*. Still, the message of *Maria* was that literature and the exchange of ideas between men and women, and between the classes, was an index of civilisation; and that women were entitled to bring head and heart together in the search for love. Wollstonecraft's follower, Mary Hays, betrayed her own unease when she claimed philosophical licence to use fiction in a similar way. In the preface to *Memoirs of Emma Courtney* (1794), Hays apologised for addressing what she called 'a hackneyed sentiment in this species of composition' – love – but argued that 'free thinking, and free speaking [were] the virtue and characteristics of a rational being'.

Hays began as a philosopher. She launched her writing career by responding to Gilbert Wakefield's provocative suggestion that public worship should be abolished because it had become hypocritical. Hays's 1791 pamphlet, *Cursory remarks on an Enquiry into the Expediency and Propriety of Public or Social Worship: Inscribed to Gilbert Wakefield*, published under the name of 'Eusebia', introduced her to the public as 'a woman, young, unlearned, unacquainted with language but her own;

possessing no other merit than a love of truth and virtue, [and] an ardent desire of knowledge'. The self-description as 'unlearned' at the very moment of displaying her learning (for how else could she construct and publish philosophical objections?) echoed Mary Astell's courting truth 'with a kind of romantic passion' which had played so well with John Norris in the 1690s. By 1791 the persona of a 'woman, young, unlearned' was a cultural artefact. Frances Burney's *Evelina* had made her familiar as a heroine of fiction who could be found in the world of fact: the fictional Evelina and 'little' Fanny Burney timidly entering the world were happily linked in the public mind. Mary Hays was in fact considerably learned and, at thirty-one, hardly young (but younger than the sixty-year-old 'young' Jane Barker in 1713). As a formula, Hays's self-description was an invitation to intellectual men to make themselves known to her and this is exactly what happened.[25]

The direct outcome for Hays was a correspondence and friendship: her pamphlet inspired Cambridge mathematician William Frend to write to her in admiration. Frend's acknowledgement of Hays as a serious thinker and his network of male intellectuals extended her range. In 1793, she published a collection of pieces that displayed more of her learning: *Letters and Essays, Moral and Miscellaneous*. When Frend praised William Godwin's *An Enquiry Concerning Political Justice* (1794), Hays took the opportunity to write to Godwin. She told him that she had been excited by a long review of *Political Justice* in the *Analytical Review*, gave a précis of Frend's high opinion of it as communicated to her ('this book will in a few years operate as great a change in the political sentiments of our nation as Locke's famous treatise on government') and explained that she herself had been unable to obtain the book from the circulating libraries and couldn't afford to buy it, so would Mr Godwin please lend her a copy. She assured him she would take good care of it and as she had made similar requests to other people in the past ('I have been obliged to incur various obligations of this nature') he could find out that she was trustworthy. Some compliments about Godwin's novel *Caleb Williams*, and the presentation of herself as 'a disciple of truth' with 'a thirst after books', concluded a long letter to a famous philosopher from 'a stranger' (but a published author and one whose name he might have known) who 'from the first dawnings of reason, amid all the disadvantages of worse than neglected, perverted, female education . . . [had] an ardent love of literature and an unbounded reverence for truth and genius'.[26]

Through Godwin, Mary Hays was admitted to the most important literary circle of the time, the radical intellectuals who gathered round the publisher Joseph Johnson. Here she met the leading women writers, becoming friends with Mary Wollstonecraft and Charlotte Smith (Hays introduced Wollstonecraft to Godwin and she collaborated with Smith) as well as Elizabeth Inchbald, Amelia Opie, Anna Barbauld and others. Like the bluestockings of the earlier generation, these women shared a sense that they were in the vanguard. Convinced that progress lay in the emancipation of the female mind, it was their constant endeavour to show themselves as superior to ordinary women by virtue of their intelligence. They could 'write, reason, converse with men and scholars', in Hays's words, because they 'despise[d] many petty, feminine prejudices'. These constructions were much the same as earlier in the century but by the 1790s there was a further refinement: it was not just other women they measured themselves against but, as Wollstonecraft put it, the 'herd' of other lady writers, especially novelists such as those Wollstonecraft was reviewing in the *Analytic Review*. There were too many, they were too young, and they were ignorant. They were like 'timid sheep'. They copied each other, producing 'trash'. 'Without a knowledge of life, or the human heart, why will young misses presume to write?' How could they 'publish their foolish fancies'? A 'truly feminine novel' as far as Wollstonecraft was concerned, was one which had 'no marked features to characterise it'. In other words, it demonstrated Pope's dictum that most women had no characters at all.[27]

Even so, readers seemed to like the stuff. The press teemed with new publications. According to Samuel Johnson in 1773, 'all our ladies read now'. The question profitably posed by the *Athenian Mercury* in 1691, whether it was 'proper' for women to be learned, had by no means gone away; rather, it had branched out into a number of fruitful themes including the notion that the mass production of 'trash' was somehow the result of women's writing and reading. Women in general could be attacked on that score or they could be taken up as in need of rescue – this was a game all writers could play. The rhetoric that had developed earlier in the century protested about the lack of education available to women. By the century's end, the charge had altered. In a climate in which it was perceived that 'all our ladies read', the problem was not that they had no education, but that they had been subjected to a bad one. They had listened to men like John Gregory who, in his *Father's Legacy to his Daughters* (1774), had been one of the many men who undertook to improve women.

The burden of Mary Wollstonecraft's attack on 'female manners' in *A Vindication of the Rights of Woman* was that women as a class had been rendered weak and childlike by a 'false system of education'. Rescued from it, they would display the virtues of modesty, temperance and self-denial. Through the fiction of characterless, weak and childlike women, exceptional women like Wollstonecraft and Hays conducted conversations, in person or in print, with men like Gregory and Fordyce and Rousseau and others, which gave all of them ample scope. The role of the moralist as it had developed through the eighteenth century was available to men and women alike. The area of tension lay in the space between women in general and the superior or exceptional woman. Codes of conduct which were applicable to ordinary women – modesty, temperance and self-denial – were not formed for genius. Being superior, as Mary Hays put it, to 'the vain pleasures of the unthinking multitude', might also suggest the need for superior moral codes, individually arrived at by the singular thinking mind.

Mary Hays conducted a number of epistolary friendships in which her 'ardent desire for knowledge' and the men's presumed possession of it provided a workable structure for relationships, and which also offered a forum for ardent feelings. As well as William Frend and William Godwin, there was Robert Robinson, George Dyer, Henry Crabb Robinson and Robert Southey. (Godwin insisted on special terms: she could write to him as often as she liked but was not to expect written answers. Their 'contract' was: 'you shall communicate your sentiments by letter, and I will answer you in person'.) Hays was familiar with the genre of male–female correspondence in its early eighteenth-century mode as a vehicle for the representation of the budding woman of letters. She is likely to have known about Mary Astell and John Norris, if not from George Ballard then from Ffloyd's 1760 *Bibliotheca Biographica*, or Chambers' 1767 supplement to the *New and General Biographical Dictionary*, or the *Biographium Femineum* of

1766, or later recyclings of the information. She might have known Elizabeth Thomas's *Pylades and Corinna* (and could have read about Thomas in the biographical dictionaries), and she would certainly have known the *Series of Genuine Letters Between Henry and Frances* by Elizabeth Griffith and her husband Richard which detailed their romantic and literary travails. (Griffith tried to persuade Anna Seward into a romantic/literary correspondence with him. Seward thought him odious and obvious.)

Hays seems to have considered publishing a similar compilation: her 'genuine' epistolary exchanges with John Eccles, a young man she had hoped to marry and whose early death was a profound loss. Parental disapproval had made the correspondence necessary: it began when they were forbidden to consider marriage since neither of them had any money and he had no profession, though they met anyway and eventually both sets of parents came round. Hays assembled and ordered the correspondence in two large volumes, annotating it and providing an introduction as if for publication. Whether she ever sent them out to a publisher is not known. They were discovered in a cupboard by her great-great-niece and pruned and published as *The Love Letters of Mary Hays (1779-1780)* in 1925 – a time when compilations of letters from the courtships of famous authors had become popular, and the title 'The Love Letters of ...' was being applied to some unexpected couples.[28]

The shame of being singular: *The Memoirs of Emma Courtney*

Characteristically, female authorship was represented not as a bond of union between women but as a relationship with male authors; either internalised as identification or externalised as a friendship that was developed and displayed in epistolary exchanges, or as a rivalry which needed vindicating. The epistolary was popular with women not least because it was the most literal way of turning the desire to be noticed, recognised and distinguished in literature into literature.

Samuel Richardson's practices as a novelist helped mythicise the epistolary as a female mode, though in fact it was used by men and women alike. The epistolary was one way of ordering the relationship between authors and new reading publics, a fiction of intimacy between

330

writers and readers who were strangers. It served political polemic quite as much as imaginative fiction. All kinds of writing in the epistolary mode encouraged readers to take up their pens, sometimes to address themselves to the author, sometimes to be like the author or character they had read about. All authors were expected to write letters; the writing of letters virtually defined authorship, and after Pope an author's letters became valuable commodities.

Mary Hays incorporated the relation of correspondence in its Rousseauistic mode – whereby the men play tutor and have knowledge and the women strive to order head and heart so as to achieve intellectual and emotional satisfaction – into her novel *The Memoirs of Emma Courtney* (1794). Having studied Helvetius as well as Rousseau and Godwin, Hays understood from these writers how genius was to be identified and recognised: in a genius, 'strong mental powers appear to be connected with acute and lively sensation, or the capacity of receiving forcible impressions'. Addressing herself to the 'feeling and the thinking few', Hays created a sentimental heroine whose passions were as powerful as her mind: a type of the woman of genius, part Prior's Emma and part Rousseau's Julie. In the preface she explained how her heroine was to be received: readers were directed to find a representation of 'a human being', one liable to mistakes and weakness, not the usual novelistic character drawn according to what 'ought to be' rather than what was. Hays's Emma did not embody 'ideal perfection'. She was to serve 'as a warning rather than as an example'. Readers were invited to read and refuse rather than read and seek to emulate.[29]

The Memoirs of Emma Courtney is a fiction about a fantasy romance between Emma, a philosophical woman ardent for an intellectual life that includes sexual passion, and Augustus Harley, a man whom she casts as her ideal lover. Conceptually, it incorporates the fantasied other of epistolary exchange. The focus is on Emma's attempts to understand her feelings through the act of writing – 'I, once more, take up my pen with a mind so full of thought' – to male correspondents who, in imagination, understand more than she does. Augustus Harley, the object of her passionate desires, is known to her mostly through a picture and through his mother's adoring accounts of him. He is never represented as a likely lover for the simple reason that he is not the answer to the problems posed in the novel, though as a story of a woman's love it appears to move in that direction. The message of *Emma Courtney*, in which the heroine pursues a man who does not love her, offering herself to him and openly expressing her desire, is, like the message of Martha Fowke Sansom's *Clio*, as much about the desire to be free to think and feel and write and command one's own experience, including imagined and erotic experience, and to be received as a woman of letters, as it is about wanting to attain the living or fictional man who is the object of the pursuit.

However, while Clio struts and swaggers around town fending off advances and striving to avoid boredom, Emma struggles with her inner life. The more she is 'improved' the more unhappy she becomes: 'Philosophy, it is said, should regulate the feelings, but it has added fervor to mine!' Pride in exceptionality has turned into the 'shame of being singular'. The active mind is prey to doubts – Emma is caught in 'an incessant conflict between truth and error'. She is disappointed: intellect and virtue have not conferred happiness. Since, as a woman, she has come late to 'intellect and virtue' which traditionally belonged to men, it is a man, Mr Francis the philosopher (based on William Godwin: letters Hays had received from Godwin were copied verbatim into the novel), to whom she appeals for guidance: 'Assist me, in disentangling my bewildered ideas – write to me – reprove me – spare me not!'[30]

Mary Hays's use of letters from Godwin in her fiction about a painful imagined romance is in the tradition of Sarah Fielding writing to Richardson about *Clarissa*. It was a way of entering the realm of the literary, annexing resources and laying claim to ground. Hays wrote to Godwin and received an answer which she published as a letter written by a fictional character, Mr Francis, to a fictional Emma. As Emma Courtney, Hays adopted the posture of the confused child, drawing on the century-long myth that women, having been denied education, could not possibly know as much as men. (Sarah Fielding did not present herself as a confused child in her *Remarks on Clarissa* but as an authoritative witness.) The sentimental heroine was a simpler and cruder creature than her creator: the Mary Hays of everyday life, writing to Godwin or Frend, discussing philosophy and literary projects with Wollstonecraft and Smith, reading extensively and with an interest in the history of learned women that was to take shape in her compendium, *Female Biography* (1803), connected to the ideas and experiences of other thinkers in many more ways than the story of Emma Courtney allowed Emma to know.

Hays's representation of the conflict in Emma exhibited the soul of a child rather than the soul of an author. Emma failed to order head and heart to regulate her feelings because her feelings were impossible to regulate. It was necessary for Emma to fail in a tale designed – modishly – to operate as a warning. In the 1790s, anxiety and confusion, mixed emotions and intellectual uncertainty – states of mind that invited moralistic guidance – were the modern mode, just as conviction and celebration had been the mode of the mid century. By creating a heroine who combined intellectual aspiration with childish yearning, Hays attempted to escape some of the opprobrium that had begun to be directed at the figure of the female philosopher in the wake of the French Revolution.

Emma's story served as a sign of women's unfitness for philosophy. Mary Wollstonecraft, disliking what she considered Hays's textual obsequiousness towards men, had already had cause to reprimand her. Wollstonecraft reacted sharply to a draft preface to Hays's *Letters and Essays*, commenting that the authorial persona projected there was far too falsely deferential. There was no need to apologise so much, nor load her paragraphs with the names of learned men. Hays's 'vain humility' was hypocritical: anyone who really felt themselves inadequate to 'the task of instructing others' should not be writing books. As for 'the *honour* of publishing' as Hays had put it, that was merely 'the cant of both trade and sex': 'For if really equality should ever take place in society the man who is employed and gives a just equivalent for the money he receives will not behave with the obsequiousness of a servant.'[31]

If an employed man who gave value for money need not be subservient, nor, by the same token, need a woman. Through a vision of equality in society where labour (including intellectual labour) was given in exchange for appropriate pay, the old order with its stifling forms of thought and behaviour, its obsequiousness and deference, its 'cant' about honour to which women in general and writers in particular were subjected, could be dispatched, and the reality – that women were as fit for philosophy as men – put before the world in stories, letters, essays and poems.

Wollstonecraft's *Letters Written During a Short Residence in Sweden* (1796) projected an authorial persona illustrating her views. Here, the literary woman as philosopher, actively thinking, suffering and reflecting, alive to all the varieties of feeling and imagination, was fully projected and enthusiastically received. Wollstonecraft offered herself to her readers as a traveller in unknown lands – the icy north – who took with her a head keen to know what new there was to learn and a heart broken by love but capable of repair. She travelled with a child – her illegitimate daughter Fanny – and a maid. She displayed herself going from place to place, admiring and disapproving in equal measure, but always being welcomed as a professional woman, one with whom men expected to have interesting conversations. Her purpose was to make intellectual sense of what she observed in Sweden and Norway and discover the meanings of what she felt inside herself. Though unhappy in life and love, there was no shame in being singular and she was no mere victim: for her, as for other eighteenth-century writers like Rousseau in his *Promenades*, Sterne in *Sentimental Journey*, William Cowper, Goethe, Thomas Gray, the Edward Young of *Night Thoughts* and others, solitude and the lack of society was presented as a choice and an opportunity. A self-consciously literary text, *Letters Written During a Short Residence in Sweden* was hugely popular. The reviews were favourable, it was rapidly translated into several European languages, and an edition appeared in America.

Letters for Literary Ladies

The established world of letters fractured and began to come apart in the 1790s. Jon Klancher describes the five years between 1793 and 1798 as 'ruinous to the British republic of letters and to its central category, the larger Enlightenment classification of "literature"'.[32] The atrocities of the Reign of Terror in France meant that those who had supported the revolution became extremely unpopular. The progressives in English literature, the Dissenters – who edited the four leading literary reviews, and whose model of the republic of letters underlay the ideal political republics of William Godwin and Tom Paine – were in disarray by the century's end. A new breed of intellectual and new periodicals took their place: in the early nineteenth century the *Edinburgh Review*, *The Quarterly* and *Blackwood's* were all founded. The mode was sophisticated and the mood conservative. Literature was imagined not as a republic but as a club of men.

Literature was 'the great engine by which all civilized states must ultimately be supported or overthrown' T. J. Mathias explained in *The Pursuits of Literature* (1796), a conservative manual that was widely read, going through sixteen editions by 1812.[33] The politically instrumental view of literature it espoused had profound implications for women at a time when one of the markers of 'civilized states' was judged to be the behaviour of women. Wollstonecraft's *A Vindication of the Rights of Woman* had argued that the differences between men and women were largely 'factitious', an 'artificial distinction' imposed by society, not originating in the 'nature' of men or women; her claim for 'rights' was grounded in a vision of natural equality. This 'spirited support of the just and natural rights of her sex', her insistence that women should be considered 'in the grand light of human creatures who, in common with men, are placed on this earth to unfold their faculties', made her the symbol of all that had come to be feared. She was the 'champion' of her sex.

As one writer put it in 1795, 'the word *liberty*, applied to the female sex, conveys alarming ideas to our minds'. The 'we' in this case, anxious not to be called 'a champion for the rights of woman' on the grounds that he was 'too much their friend to be their partisan, and . . . more anxious for their happiness than intent upon a metaphysical discussion of their rights', was the unnamed gentleman who, in Maria Edgeworth's *Letters for Literary Ladies*, replied to a letter from his friend which he had supposedly received upon the birth of his daughter. This letter had advised him in no uncertain terms not to wish for her to have wit, and not to educate her for a superior woman.[34]

Letters for Literary Ladies was Maria Edgeworth's first publication, though she had been in training for a literary woman and had written a novel by the age of fifteen. Edgeworth's stepmother was that Honora Sneyd who had grown up as a foster-child in the Bishop's Palace, Lichfield, and been educated by Anna Seward before going on to become Richard Edgeworth's second wife. Full of energy and progressive ideas, Richard Edgeworth encouraged his clever daughter in literary tasks much as Thomas Seward had encouraged Anna and Honora. Edgeworth *père* co-authored a number of works with Maria, including the influential *Parent's Assistant* (1796–1800) and *Practical Education* (1798), both of which were projects originally conceived as collaborations with Honora.

In *Letters for Literary Ladies*, Maria Edgeworth introduced herself as an author through the debate about her future that had gone on between her father and Thomas Day when she was a schoolgirl. The two letters are *for* literary ladies and *by* a literary lady but they express the views and are in the voice of two literary gentlemen. These gentlemen canvass the problems, apparently taking different views: the answer to the first letter being in favour of female improvement of the sort Richard Edgeworth had urged on Maria when she was ten and he looked forward to her becoming 'a very excellent and an highly improved woman'. Both letters are full of the sense of danger and offence. Both convey very powerfully the assumption that there is much to be guarded against, summed up by the repetition of 'follies', 'faults' and 'evils' as characteristic of literary women unless prevented. Indeed, many readers were not clear that the second letter *was* in favour of female cultivation; in the second edition in 1798, Maria Edgeworth rewrote it, adding a note: 'In the first edition, the Second Letter upon the advantages of cultivating the female understanding, was thought to weaken the cause it was intended to support. That letter has been written over again; no pains have been spared to improve it, and to assert more strongly the female right to literature.'

The female right to literature was a much more muddled affair in the minds of men and women alike by the 1790s than it was in the 1740s when Thomas Seward wrote the poem of that name. As the men in *Letters for Literary Ladies* acknowledge, women writers were now numerous and vociferous. Many were famous. They had taken to heart the message that they were superior and had followed advice to improve their talents. But far from earning praise, the evidence of the gentleman's letter in *Letters for Literary Ladies* was that this brought 'evil' in its wake. Female vanity produced 'ostentation': 'To obtain public applause', women were 'betrayed too often into a miserable ostentation of their learning'. The deference paid to genius made them forget 'discretion': 'Those who have acquired fame fancy that they can afford to sacrifice reputation.' They opposed 'the common opinions of society' and revealed 'in their manners and conversation that contempt of inferior minds, and that neglect of common forms and customs, which . . . provoke[d] the indignation of fools, and which cannot escape the censure of the wise'.[35]

The letter ended with the observation that learned men preferred to choose for their wives 'women who were rather below than above the standard of mediocrity' and that literary ladies would be losers in love: 'Cupid is a timid, playful child, and is frightened at the helmet of Minerva.' In *Letters for Literary Ladies*, Maria Edgeworth gave expression to the reactionary cultural turn in its particular application to the woman of letters. This miscellany of misogyny marked the beginning of the new wave much as Mary Wollstonecraft's *A Vindication of the Rights of Woman* – 'that wonderful book' in Anna Seward's words – was the final polemical product of a long eighteenth-century celebration of improved womanhood.

Conclusion

Authorship attracted large numbers of women in the late eighteenth and early nineteenth centuries. This is one reason why writers as diverse as Mary Wollstonecraft, Mary Hays, Charlotte Smith, Hannah More, Maria Edgeworth, Frances Burney and Jane Austen among many others have been seen as the beginnings of a movement representing, in the words of Virginia Woolf, the middle-class woman who began, at that point, to write. But paradoxically, as more and more women took up their pens and wrote books that were published, the definition of 'real' or 'serious' authorship rapidly narrowed to exclude all but the male of the species, and what had been a relatively secure participation in high status lettered activity in the early eighteenth century became insecure as prescriptive models of femininity hardened, as professional organisation took hold, and as the class assumptions of literature and society changed.

Women writing in the late eighteenth century emerged out of a history of women's relationship to the development of a national literary canon which is both longer and more complex than is generally understood. There is much work still to be done before we can fully appreciate how little we have known and how much is yet to know. What came to an end by the 1790s was a social consensus that women and men might play an equal part in the authoritative shaping of culture, depending on the qualities of the individual concerned. The mainstream of English literature had been regarded as the proper province of all those entitled by ability to be in it – whether as readers or as writers, as the producers of original literature or as commentators on it. The desire to do so and the ability to convince others of one's entitlement by writing words they wanted to read was the only qualification for acceptance into the ranks of authors, and there were very few practices and certainly no policies that excluded women. The change at the end of the eighteenth century was in the direction of specific exclusion, through cultural definition and through institutions such as clubs and societies.

Insofar as it existed at all, the idea of exclusion from *English literature* on the grounds of gender was a late eighteenth-century invention, though it is possible to mark some earlier formative developments such as the new emphasis in the mid century on the fictionality of the writing woman and her historicity (the celebration of learned and literary women as figures from the past). As literary activity proliferated, divided and subdivided, as forms evolved, were imitated and reproduced, ways of working womanhood for commerce or esteem, especially in prose fiction, also proliferated. The elevated model of female authorship became increasingly tenuous and by the early 1800s it had more or less disappeared. High achievers from the mid century were viewed as relics from a former era, not quite openly mocked but certainly not promoted as examples for the younger generation. Clever women, or ambitious writing women, did not on the whole want to be associated with the word 'bluestocking'. A bluestocking, it was assumed, was a pedantic, self-important, dull and really rather ignorant woman. Jane Austen's characterisation of Mary, the bookish one of the five sisters in *Pride and Prejudice* (written 1797, published 1813), is drawn along these lines and shows how early the stereotype took hold.

These general developments could be illustrated in numerous ways and by means of many examples. But there is one book, about one writer, which in itself captured the values of the mid century and in its reception signalled the end of the era: William Godwin's life of Mary Wollstonecraft, the revealingly titled, *Memoirs of the Author of a Vindication of the Rights of Woman* (1798).

Mary Wollstonecraft died in 1797, a few months after marrying

Godwin and after giving birth to a second daughter, the future Mary Shelley. She was at the height of her powers and her fame, especially for the recent *Letters Written during a Short Residence in Sweden* which fascinated the younger generation of writers. (Coleridge, Wordsworth and Southey all made reference to it.) A grief-stricken Godwin immersed himself in his dead wife's papers in the autumn of that year and began ordering them for what was to be a four-volume edition of her posthumous works with an introductory memoir.[1] Whatever personal consolation this task brought, it was also one that Godwin viewed as a duty. His wife had been 'a person of eminent merit'. As her lover and husband he had privileged knowledge, and 'to give the public some account of a person of eminent merit deceased', as he was later to write in the preface to the memoir, was 'a duty incumbent on survivors'. With this in mind, Godwin had in fact begun assembling the materials for Wollstonecraft's life well before her death. He had encouraged her to relate the key biographical facts; he had repeatedly led their conversations to incidents in her life which had helped to form what he called her 'understandings and character'. He had made notes. Wollstonecraft's free-thinking and free-speaking, the philosophical system to which they both adhered, was a subject worthy of minute attention. But more than that, it was her fame as an author that called forth his exertions.

Godwin's memoir of his wife was conceived in the tradition of the pious family memoir, of which the *Life of Mrs Rowe* was the significant exemplar. (Godwin's grandfather had been a friend of Isaac Watts.) In honouring Wollstonecraft he was honouring one of 'the illustrious dead', a 'benefactor' to mankind, who, like many such, was always at risk of 'calumny' and 'misrepresentation'. Candid and sincere, Godwin ordered the evidence and pursued the logic of the facts available. Truth not piety was his guiding principle. He wanted to be true to Wollstonecraft's vision of a fully integrated intellectual, emotional and sexual life for women and men. He made no distinction between 'proper' and 'improper' episodes but brought everything to the bar of justice and truth: Wollstonecraft's parents' unhappy marriage, her love for Fanny Blood, her passion for the painter Fuseli, her affair with Gilbert Imlay, her illegitimate child, her two suicide attempts, her affair with Godwin himself and their decision to marry after she became pregnant by him, and then, in graphic and gruesome detail, the horrors of her death from puerperal fever ten days after giving birth.

Godwin's biography was a homage to Wollstonecraft's life, her courage and originality, her intellectual and imaginative vigour, and her commitment to truth. It was a homage, too, to the traditions that had formed them both and the values of eighteenth-century Enlightenment. Godwin offered the public the Life of an author who happened to be a woman. He explained how her unusual mind had developed and how she had reached the 'eminence of her genius', especially in the major work of her life, 'her most celebrated production', the *Vindication*, which set out to be the best book of its kind and, in Godwin's view, succeeded so emphatically that it would survive into an eternal posterity: it was 'not very improbable that it will be read as long as the English language endures'.[2]

The traditional justification for a memoir, which Godwin drew on in his preface, was that the illustrious were by definition virtuous and the more that was known about their virtues, the easier it would be to emulate them. But Godwin had written about his wife's miseries, attempted suicides and former lovers. Most readers, including those of his own radical circle, were appalled by his frankness. Emulating his subject – or, in Godwin's words, aiming to 'follow [her] in the same career' – seemed an inducement not to virtue but to vice. Far from receiving grateful thanks for a duty done to an illustrious figure, Godwin was subjected to a storm of criticism. He was blamed for exposing the 'frailties' of an unhappy woman – frailties which should have been 'buried in oblivion'. He was 'stripping his dead wife naked' and displaying his own 'want of all feeling'. Those who wanted to go on admiring Wollstonecraft as an exceptional woman and esteemed writer blamed Godwin, while those already hostile to Wollstonecraft's ideas seized the opportunity to damn her as a whore. Either way, Wollstonecraft's became a name that was best unmentioned.

The Revd Richard Polwhele was not unusual in his response. Reading the memoir confirmed his view that Wollstonecraft represented the same danger that the French Revolution was considered to demonstrate: that philosophy and reason led to a rejection of 'Nature'. Reason in France had led to the overturning of the 'natural' hierarchies of rank and 'natural' submission to God and His ministers. Reason among English women writers led to 'Gallic frenzy': 'the woman who has no regard to nature, either in the decoration of her person, or the culture of her mind, will soon "walk after the flesh, in the lust of uncleanness, and despise government" '[3].

Showing oneself willing to be governed by men – fathers, brothers, ministers like Polwhele, older writers – became the sign of the 'natural' woman, and that woman should be 'natural' was the sign of civilisation. To be exceptional was no longer to anyone's credit. No amount of reason, no acknowledged culture of the mind, compensated for the supposed lack of femininity.

Polwhele put his views into a poem, *The Unsex'd Females*, which attacked Wollstonecraft at great length – 'See Wollstonecraft, whom no decorum checks' etc. – along with Mary Hays, Charlotte Smith, Anna Barbauld and others. In form and style (and in the poor quality of the verse), the poem echoed John Duncombe's *The Feminiad*. Though weighted more to accusation than celebration, Polwhele's poem followed Duncombe in forcing phantom distinctions between 'good' female writers and 'bad'. A ventriloquised Hannah More – 'a voice seraphic' – laments a past in which 'the sex have oft, in ancient days, / To modest virtue, claimed a nation's praise', and lauds female genius in the shape of Carter, Montagu, Chapone, Seward, Burney and others.

Nothing could more clearly demonstrate the continuing usefulness of polemics for and against women. Polwhele himself had made his debut as a writer by penning a birthday ode for Catherine Macaulay when, in 1777, his mother (a friend of Macaulay and More) took him with her to Bristol and Bath for the celebrations that were held to honour 'the English Thucydides' and which culminated with the presentation to Macaulay of the statue that represented her as Clio.[4]

The nineteenth century reacted powerfully against what it saw as eighteenth-century laxity in morals and mores. Victorian emphasis on 'the proper woman' was a key element in its notion of reform. As codes of propriety which located women inside the home were vociferously sounded, so the notion of any kind of public life came to be defined rhetorically in opposition to them. The contradictions were no less apparent in the Victorian era than in the eighteenth century, for women continued to engage in public activity, and most women's lives, as ever, included paid work. The ethereal goddess presiding over hearth and home was a fiction; still, she served to make the past seem deeply improper.

Men set the pace in societies where women are subordinated. Male paradigms drove literary practice just as they have driven literary history. Men's writings, men's sociable interaction and rivalries, their cultural and political disputes as well as their ventures in publishing led the way. Though there were many women writers, men had social, political, economic and literary power. Literary recognition could only be fully provided by men. Few (perhaps no) women were able to succeed as writers without the support of men.

As we learn more about the individuals who made up the literary environment in Britain between 1660 and 1800, so our picture of women's place in literary history as a whole will shift. New chronologies will be shaped according to new knowledge and perspectives. The part the woman of letters played in eighteenth-century literary life will be better known. Neither a heroine nor a brute, neither specially brave nor particularly timid, but born with the capacity to think and a love of 'dear pen and ink', her contribution to the development of forms and genres, her impact on the categories of English literature, her aspirations and expectations as well as her fears and disavowals, will be more fully contextualised and some of the gross simplifications by which she has been dismissed will lose their power.

Notes

Introduction

1. In chapter 5 of *Northanger Abbey*, Catherine and Isabella read novels together. Austen defiantly comments: 'Yes, novels; for I will not adopt that ungenerous and impolitic custom, so common with novel writers, of degrading, by their contemptuous censure, the very performances to the number of which they are themselves adding.' In a wonderfully trenchant passage she goes on to lament the higher status of 'the nine-hundredth abridger of the "History of England", or of the man who collects and publishes in a volume some dozen lines of Milton, Pope and Prior, with a paper from the "Spectator", and a chapter from Sterne [which] are eulogised by a thousand pens'; concluding that 'there seems almost a general wish of decrying the capacity and undervaluing the labour of the novelist, and of slighting the performances which have only genius, wit, and taste to recommend them'.

2. Woolf, 'Aphra Behn', in *Women & Writing*, p. 91.

3. Woolf's essay on Eliza Haywood, 'A Scribbling Dame', a review of a 1916 biography, *The Life and Romances of Mrs Eliza Haywood* by George Whicher, is arrestingly uncharitable. It begins with an image of insects pinned to cardboard in the Natural History Museum. Haywood is 'this faded and antique specimen of the domestic house fly with all her seventy volumes in orderly array around her'. *Women & Writing* pp. 92–5.

4. Elizabeth Montagu to Elizabeth Carter, quoted in Eger, 'The Nine Living

Muses of Great Britain – Women, Reason and Literary Community in Eighteenth-Century Britain', p. 123.

5. John Brewer, in *The Pleasures of the Imagination*, conveys it very well. His chapter on Anna Seward provides a useful introduction.

6. The letters covered the years 1784–1807 and they were published in six volumes in 1811.

7. Ashmun, *The Singing Swan*, chapter 4, '1781–1783, The Bard of Eartham', pp. 90–109.

Chapter One

1. *Bluestocking Feminism, Writings of the Bluestocking Circle, 1738–1785*, vol. 4, *Anna Seward*, p. 221.

2. Ashmun, *The Singing Swan*, p. 130.

3. Ibid., p. 272. Constable prefaced the letters with a lukewarm 'Advertisement' in which he warned the reader that the 'merit' of the letters was too often obscured by 'affectations of style'. He praised her 'independent and vigorous mind', her 'warmth' of character and 'enthusiastic admiration of everything which seemed to her to bear the stamp of genius', but suggested that the anecdotes about the 'illustrious literary characters who adorned the latter half of the last century' and whose friendship she gained because of her celebrity, were the most attractive aspect of the volumes. Scott played some part in editing the letters. Constable lent him the transcripts and he marked passages to be omitted – mostly those concerning himself. The bulk of the editing was done by Revd Robert Morehead. See letter of 26 April 1975 from James Corson, Librarian of Abbotsford, regarding the 'common error' of supposing Scott edited the letters, Johnson Birthplace Museum, Lichfield.

4. Seward, *Poetical Works*, vol. 1, 'Biographical Preface', p. xxxvii.

5. Ashmun, *The Singing Swan*, p. 255. For Scott's responses, see pp. 250–5.

6. Ibid., pp. 259–63.

7. Seward, *Poetical Works*, vol. 1, 'Biographical Preface', p xiii.

8. Ibid.

9. Seward, *Letters*, vol. 1, p. 64.

10. Harriet Guest, in *Small Change, Women, Learning, Patriotism, 1750–1810*, is particularly interesting on the way Seward was 'attributed an extraordinary ability to speak for and to the nation'. See chapter 10, 'Britain Mourn'd: Anna Seward's Patriotic Elegies', pp. 252–67.

11. Seward, *Letters*, vol. 1, p. 191; vol. 5, p. 89. Criticism of Johnson, on these and similar grounds, is a recurring theme throughout the Letters.

12. These poems are all reprinted in *Bluestocking Feminism*, vol. 4.

13. Philip Laithwaite, Johnson Society Transactions, 1952. Johnson Birthplace Museum, Lichfield.

14. *Gentleman's Magazine*, February 1786, April 1786, January 1787, August 1787, November 1793, January 1794, December 1794. See also Ashmun, pp. 139–43, 204–8.

15. 'Protogenes and Apelles', *The Literary Works of Matthew Prior*, vol 1, p. 465.

16. *Memoirs of Richard Lovell Edgeworth*, vol. 1, p. 106.

17. Chadwyck-Healey English Poetry Database, disk 3.

18. *Bluestocking Feminism*, vol. 4, pp. 220–2.

19. 'Miss Seward's Literary Correspondence', *Poetical Works*, vol. 1, pp. lxxxiv–lxxxv.

20. National Library of Scotland, Seward manuscripts. Perhaps surprisingly, not being able to command resentments frequently figures in the self-descriptions of female authors of the period. It was one of the signs of genius.

21. Ibid.

22. *Bluestocking Feminism*, vol. 4, p. 215.

23. Lady Mary Wortley Montagu could recite the whole of 'Henry and Emma' at the age of fourteen and claimed in 1754 that she could still 'say it by heart to this day' though her view of it had changed. What she once adored she had become convinced was not only a 'senseless tale' but one which had 'hurt more girls than ever were injured by the lewdest poems extant'. *Letters*, p. 464.

24. National Library Of Scotland, Seward manuscripts; and 'Miss Seward's Literary Correspondence', *Poetical Works*, vol. 1.

25. Ibid., pp. cxxii–cxviii.

26. *Bluestocking Feminism*, vol. 4, pp. 1–22. For Pope's 'Eloisa to Abelard', see *Alexander Pope*, Oxford Authors, pp. 137–47.

27. 'Henry and Emma, a Poem, Upon the Model of The Nut-brown Maid', *The Literary Works of Matthew Prior*, vol. 1, pp. 278–300.

28. Anna Seward's own evocation of these years is in her *Memoirs of Dr Darwin* which offers vivid characterisations of Edgeworth, Day and Darwin. See also Hopkins, *Dr Johnson's Lichfield*.

29. Hopkins, p. 112.

30. Seward, *Poetical Works*, vol. 3, pp. 133–5.

31. Ibid., pp. 68–73, 65.

32. Ashmun, p. 62.

33. Hopkins, pp. 115–17.

34. Ashmun, p. 242.
35. Ibid., p. 187.
36. Hopkins, pp. 100, 118–19.
37. Achmun, pp 183–5
38. Seward, *Letters*, vol. 2, p. 83.
39. *Journals and Correspondence of Thomas Sedgewick Whalley*, vol. 1, pp. 12–15. Seward had written a great many letters to Thomas Whalley. Wickham published a generous selection of those which had not already appeared in Seward's *Letters*, though, like Scott, he seems to have found the task wearisome. He commented on Seward's 'abuse' of Mr Pitt (the letters to Whalley, who supported Pitt's government, contain the most explicit statements of her political views); her 'platonic affection' for Saville and the fact that she gave him money ('Her devotion was more valuable to him than that of Queen Bess to her "gentle Robin" for it conferred substantial benefits during her "Giovanni's life"'); the 'odium' she heaped on Johnson; her 'censures' of Richard Edgeworth; and her hostility towards 'a certain Mr Pratt', bookseller and publisher. Wickham viewed Seward's letter-writing as pathological: 'Her great object in life,' he wrote, 'seems to have been literary fame, and no sacrifice to ease or even health was deemed too great to offer at the shrine of this goddess. In the midst of pain, unable to rise from her chair without help, suffering from vertigo in consequence of the overtaxed powers of the brain, she still continued in her old age to indite those interminable letters.' Thomas Whalley's letters were no less long, and as he often made several drafts before sending them they probably involved more work.

Chapter Two

1. Sonnet XL, 'December Morning'. Seward, *Poetical Works*, vol. 3, p. 161.
2. 'The Sixth Satire of Juvenal', Dryden, *A Critical Edition of the Major Works*, p. 351.
3. Ibid. pp. 336–7.
4. English Poetry Database, disk 3.
5. Lonsdale, *Eighteenth-Century Women Poets*, p. 2.
6. Ballard Collection, Bodleian Library, Oxford. All quotations from the letters of Elizabeth Elstob unless otherwise indicated are from the Ballard Collection in the Bodleian, GB 0161 MSS Ballard, 1–46, 47–74.
7. Perry, Introduction to Ballard's *Memoirs of British Ladies*, p. 18.
8. *The Diary of Ralph Thoresby*, vol. 2, p. 131.
9. See the dedication of Hickes's *Sermons on Several Subjects*.

10. The short memoir is among the Elstob papers in the Ballard Collection.
11. Perry, Introduction to Ballard's *Memoirs of British Ladies*, pp. 22–3. 'Mrs' was a courtesy title.
12. Elstob, *An English-Saxon Homily*, Preface, p. iii.
13. Ibid., p. lvii.
14. Although the word would not then have been used, Astell is often described as the 'first' English feminist. Ruth Perry includes Elizabeth Elstob, along with Aphra Behn, Delarivier Manley and Lady Mary Wortley Montagu, as one of the contemporaries whose stories 'form an important context for understanding a woman like Mary Astell'. See Perry, *The Celebrated Mary Astell*, p. 2. This biography is still one of the best introductions to the period, offering a broad cultural and historical context for Astell herself, and thoughtful discussion of many themes relevant to the study of women writers in any era. For details about Elstob in Chelsea, see pp. 289, 528.
15. Ballard, Preface to *Memoirs of British Ladies*.
16. Perry, Introduction to Ballard's *Memoirs of British Ladies*, p. 24.
17. Elstob had misremembered the poet's name. In Winstanley, it is Thomas Tusser who shifts from job to job and place to place, unable to get any butter to stick on his bread. Although Elstob recalls reading Winstanley in her childhood, Tusser's wandering life, hard work and obdurate poverty clearly resonated with her own adult experiences. See Winstanley, *Lives of the Poets*, pp. 69–72.
18. George Ballard, who had been given a small stipend and a place at Magdalen College with free room and board, acquired one interesting subscriber among the college students: the future historian Edward Gibbon, then aged fifteen and, by his own account, wasting his time. In his *Autobiography*, in which he lashed the supine indolence of Oxford fellows – 'From the toil of reading, or thinking, or writing, they had absolved their conscience' – Gibbon mentioned Ballard as 'the only author' to be found there: 'a half-starved chaplain – Ballard was his name – who begged subscriptions for some memoirs concerning the learned ladies of Great Britain'. *Autobiography*, p. 77.

Chapter Three

1. *The Life and Works of Mrs Rowe*, vol. 1, p. 2.
2. Perry, 'George Ballard's Biographies of Learned Ladies', in *Biography in the Eighteenth Century*, p. 92.
3. Duncombe, *The Feminiad*, lines 143–4.

4. Birch, *The Life of Catharine Cockburn*, p. 2.

5. This point is more fully developed in Jane Rendall's introduction to the 1994 Thoemmes Press reprint of William Alexander's *History of Women*, 1781.

6. Anonymous biographical preface to *The Works of Susannah Centlivre*, 1761.

7. This theme is explored in Jennifer Summit's fascinating study, *Lost Property: the Woman Writer and English Literary History*, 1380–1589.

8. Catherine Talbot, Journals, 1751. See Myers, *The Bluestocking Circle*, p. 164.

9. *A Series of Letters Between Mrs Elizabeth Carter and Miss Catherine Talbot, from the year 1741 to 1770*, vol. 1, pp. 342–50. The Countess of Hertford was a noted literary patron and aspiring writer. When Richard Savage was tried and condemned for murder she helped get him a royal pardon. See Hughes, *The Gentle Hertford, Her Life and Letters*, for a general if rather obsequious account; and Holmes, *Dr Johnson & Mr Savage*, p. 130, for her intervention with Queen Caroline.

10. Lonsdale, *Eighteenth-Century Women Poets*, p. 167.

11. Reeve, *The Progress of Romance*, in *Bluestocking Feminism*, vol. 6, pp. 160–275, 251.

12. *The Life and Works of Mrs Rowe*, vol. 1, pp. xliv–xlvi.

13. Ibid., vol. 2, p. 34.

14. Duncombe, *The Feminiad*, l. 153–66. Jocelyn Harris's 'Sappho, Souls and the Salic Law of Wit' is a good introduction to the poem and its mid-century context.

15. Ibid., l. 147–50: 'Nor genuine wit nor harmony excuse / The dang'rous sallies of a wanton Muse: / Nor can such tuneful, but immoral lays, / Expect the tribute of impartial praise.'

16. Ibid., l. 141–2.

17. *Memoirs of Laetitia Pilkington*, p. xlvii.

18. Ibid., vol. 1, p. 207.

19. *The Life and Works of Mrs Rowe*, vol. 1, p. ii.

20. It is only very recently that Eliza Haywood has begun to receive significant scholarly attention. The six-volume Pickering & Chatto edition, which includes a generous sample of her non-fiction and, in the words of Ros Ballaster, corrects the image of Haywood as 'the Jackie Collins of her generation', is very welcome.

21. They were all childless (Montagu had one son who died in infancy) but they had willing nephews and nieces.

22. *The Progress of Romance* in *Bluestocking Feminism*, vol. 6, p. 214.

23. Biographical introduction by Christine Blouch to *Selected Works of Eliza*

Haywood. Subsequent biographical and other details are taken from this introduction.

24. Woolf's essay on Haywood is an unsympathetic piece of writing, beginning, as has already been noted, by comparing Haywood to the domestic house fly; but her real object of attack was the American academy. Woolf used her 1916 review of George Whicher's biography of Haywood to complain that academics were trawling the past to write unnecessary books: 'It does not matter, presumably, that she was a writer of no importance, that no one read her for pleasure, and that nothing is known of her life. She is dead, she is old, she wrote books, and nobody has yet written a book about her.' 'A Scribbling Dame', in *Women & Writing*, pp. 92-5.

25. Reeve, *The Progress of Romance*, p. 214.

26. Ibid., p. 215.

27. Ibid., p. 214. Of Aphra Behn, Reeve wrote: 'Let us do justice to her merits, and cast the veil of compassion over her faults.' She blamed the times: 'an age and ... a court of licentious manners'. p. 213.

28. Reeve devoted three pages of *The Progress of Romance* to the *Argenis* and her grievances, pp. 199-201.

29. Clara Reeve, 'Address to the Reader', *Original Poems on Several Occasions*.

30. Reeve, Preface to *The Phoenix*.

31. Reeve, *Memoirs of Sir Roger de Clarendon*, vol. 3, pp. 228-30. Gary Kelly describes Reeve's politics as 'old Whig' or classical republicanism learned as a child and 'intrinsic to her provincial situation, society and culture'. See Kelly, 'Clara Reeve, Provincial Bluestocking' in Pohl and Schellenberg (eds), *Reconsidering the Bluestockings*.

32. Catherine Macaulay, *History of England*, vol. 1, p. vii.

33. Reeve, Preface to *The Phoenix*.

34. For Elizabeth Carter's views on translating Epictetus and her discussions with scholarly men, see Clarke, *Dr Johnson's Women*, chapter 2.

35. Lonsdale, *Eighteenth-Century Women Poets*, p. 248.

36. Elstob, Preface to *The Rudiments of Grammar*.

37. Perry, Introduction to Ballard's *Memoirs of British Ladies*, p. 22.

38. 'Clara Reeve, Provincial Bluestocking', in *Reconsidering the Bluestockings*, p. 107.

Chapter Four

1. Woolf, *A Room of One's Own*, p. 69.

2. Jane Spencer, in *Aphra Behn's Afterlife*, explores this aspect of the

development of English literary history in fascinating detail. See especially chapter 3.

3. Woolf, *A Room of One's Own*, p. 70.

4. In the nineteenth century, there were three Acts of Parliament which gradually gave voting rights to all men: 1832, 1867 and 1884. It was not until 1918 and then finally in 1928 that the same rights were extended to women.

5. Woolf, *A Room of One's Own*, p. 40.

6. Ibid., p. 4.

7. Ibid., p. 21.

8. Ibid., p. 45.

9. 'Professions for Women', in *Women & Writing*, pp. 57–63.

10. See the essays in *Women & Writing*.

11. See especially pp. 75–6: 'almost without exception [women in fiction] are shown in their relation to men ... literature is impoverished beyond our counting by the doors that have been shut upon women. Married against their will, kept in one room ...' Woolf made use of the name Clarissa in her first novel, *The Voyage Out*, giving it to Clarissa Dalloway, the character who reappears as the eponymous heroine of *Mrs Dalloway*, a novel set very much on the streets.

12. S. Fielding, *Remarks on Clarissa*, p. 12.

13. H. Fielding, *Joseph Andrews*, pp. 203–6.

14. *Remarks on Clarissa*, p. 4.

15. Ibid., p. 14.

16. Johnson, *A Critical Edition of the Major Works*, pp. 660–1.

17. *Remarks on Clarissa*, pp. 19–21.

18. Zelinsky, Introduction to Manley's *The Adventures of Rivella*, p. 12.

19. Manley, *The Adventures of Rivella*, pp. 47–50.

20. See Appendix C in *The Adventures of Rivella*, 'Delarivier Manley and Richard Steele', pp. 127–37.

21. Roger Lonsdale offers a good sample of Thomas's poems in *Eighteenth-Century Women Poets*, pp. 32–44.

22. Ibid., see pp. 155–65.

23. Thomas, 'The Life of Corinna', in *Pylades and Corinna*, pp. lxx–lxxi. See also Thomas's 1727 letter to Henry Cromwell published by Edmund Curll in the preface to Curll's edition of *The Works of Alexander Pope*, vol. 5, 'Containing an Authentic Edition of His Letters'.

24. Thomas, *Pylades and Corinna*, p. lxxiv.

25. Ibid., pp. lxxiv–lxxvi.

26. Pope, *The Dunciad*, Book the Second, l. 69–76 and n. 70, 75.

27. Fowke, *Clio*, p. 58.

28. Woolf, *A Room of One's Own*, p. 4.

29. Guskin, Introduction to *Clio*.

30. *Clio*, p. 62.

31. Ibid. See Appendix A, 'Letters and Poems of Aaron Hill to Martha Fowke Sansom', pp. 168–90.

32. Her enemies also feature. In describing her father's death, 'the most terrible misfortune of my whole life' (he was fatally stabbed), Fowke devoted several paragraphs to 'the scorpion Haywood' whose 'mind is as harsh and unlucky as her features'. Haywood was a 'female fiend', a 'devil', a 'tigress' and the 'poison of her pen' was even worse than the blade that 'stabbed my father's bosom', pp. 81–2. Haywood had accused Fowke of incest with her father. In *Memoirs of a Certain Island* (1725) Haywood wrote: 'Some say it was from him she learned those deluding arts she has since practised to the ruin of as many women as she could get acquainted with their lovers or husbands. Whether this report be true, I will not pretend to determine, for my pure and hallowed fires would sicken at a sight so horrible, so shocking as an act of incest; but this is certain, that they scrupled not to be seen in the same bed together, and the old goat would run into luscious encomiums on the beauties of her limbs to all the young chevaliers who came to his levee.' Quoted in *Clio*, Introduction, p. 28.

33. Ibid., pp. 100–1: 'I had at this time very little passion, but for divine Shakespeare, who used to pass whole nights with me.'

34. Ibid., pp. 133–48.

35. Ibid., p. 65.

36. Lady Mary Wortley Montagu, *The Nonsense of Common-Sense*, in *Essays and Poems and Simplicity, A Comedy*, pp. 109.

37. Ibid., pp. 77–81.

38. Perry, *The Celebrated Mary Astell*, p. 99.

39. The observation is from Perry, referring to a suggestion by Terry Eagleton in *The Rape of Clarissa*.

Chapter Five

1. Woolf, *A Room of One's Own*, p. 42.

2. *Athenian Mercury*, vol. 1, no. 18. A full account of the *Athenian Mercury* is in McEwen, *The Oracle of the Coffee House*.

3. McDowell, *The Women of Grub Street*, chapter 1.

4. John Dunton, *The Life and Errors of John Dunton Late Citizen of London*, vol. 1, p. 189.

5. McEwen, *The Oracle of the Coffee House*, pp. 90–1, 105–10; Stecher, *Elizabeth Singer Rowe, the Poetess of Frome*, pp. 37–57; Prescott, *Women, Authorship and Literary Culture, 1690–1740*, pp. 142–66.

6. *Philomela: or, Poems by Mrs Elizabeth Singer [now Rowe] of Frome in Somersetshire*, 2nd ed, pp. 19, 51–2, 122–3, 128–33.

7. McEwen, *The Oracle of the Coffee House*, pp. 67–76. In his *Life and Errors*, Dunton includes the Spira episode as one of his 'errors'. See vol. 1, pp. 154–9.

8. Dunton, *Life and Errors*, vol. 1, pp. 183–4.

9. Prefatory verses by Cowley and the Earl of Orrery in *Poems by ... Katherine Philips, the matchless Orinda*, 1667. For a detailed account of Philips in the political context of her time, see Barash, *English Women's Poetry, 1649–1714*, pp. 55–100. See also Prescott, *Women, Authorship and Literary Culture*, pp. 4–7.

10. It is an interesting exercise to read this first with empathy, as a sincere expression of a wronged woman's feelings, and then as a conscious contrivance – a desperate attempt to repair damage. The passage is, perhaps, the *locus classicus* for what was to become very well-trodden ground. Whether Philips 'really' wanted her poems to be printed or not is a separate question: she undoubtedly wanted to be received as a poet, not a balladeer or scribbler.

11. Barash points out that the 'pirated' edition of 1664 was in fact 'very accurate' and not remarkably different from Cotterell's authorised version of 1667. Barash, p. 62. Sir Charles Cotterell was 'Poliarchus', a name taken from John Barclay's political romance, the *Argenis*, in which the character represents Henry IV of France.

12. For Aphra Behn, see Todd, *The Secret Life of Aphra Behn*, and Spencer, *Aphra Behn's Afterlife*. Battigelli, *Margaret Cavendish and the Exiles of the Mind*, is one of the most thoughtful recent studies of Margaret Cavendish.

13. Cavendish, *New Blazing World*, p. 124.

14. Turner, *Living By the Pen*, p. 136.

15. Spencer, *Aphra Behn's Afterlife*, p. 25.

16. Behn, *The Rover and Other Plays*, p. 191.

17. See Hansen, 'The Pious Mrs Rowe', in *English Studies*, 76, pp. 34–51, where this is reprinted.

18. Perry, *The Celebrated Mary Astell*, p. 81.

19. King, *Jane Barker, Exile*, p. 35.

20. Ibid., p. 32.

21. Ibid., p. 55–6.

22. Ibid., p. 55n.

23. *The Life and Works of Mrs Rowe*, p. xv.
24. Stecher, *Elizabeth Singer Rowe, the Poetess of Frome*, p. 25. Biographical details are mostly taken from Stecher.
25. Ibid., p. 30.
26. Ibid., pp. 27–8.
27. When Edmund Curll reprinted the 1696 poems in 1737 he included a short note from Elizabeth Rowe giving permission which pointed out that she had had no personal acquaintance with Richard Gwinnet. 'Verses to the Author, known only by report, and by her poems', Rowe, *Poems*, pp. x–xiv. Stecher, pp. 88–105, gives the story of Rowe's friendship with Watts.
28. Stecher, p. 54; Dunton, *Life and Errors*, vol. 1, p. 197.
29. Philips, *Letters from Orinda to Poliarchus*, prefatory note.
30. *The Platonick Lady*, Act Two, in *The Plays of Susannah Centlivre*, vol. 2, p. 203.

Chapter Six

1. 'Paraphrase on the Canticles', *Philomela: or, Poems by Mrs Elizabeth Singer [now Rowe] of Frome in Somersetshire*, Edmund Curll's 1737 reprinting of Rowe's early poems opens with this paraphrase from the Song of Solomon.
2. This correspondence is explored in Wright, 'Matthew Prior and Elizabeth Singer', from which the extracts are taken.
3. Spence's *Anecdotes* were a major source of information about Pope. Though not published until 1820, the manuscript was well circulated and the anecdotes were often quoted. Hester Thrale had access to it in 1780.
4. For Finch, see Barash, *English Women's Poetry*. I have also drawn on the fine introduction to the collection of Finch's poems edited by Myra Reynolds, *Poems of Anne, Countess of Winchilsea* (1903), which was for most of the twentieth century the only detailed scholarly consideration of her work.
5. Preface to *Poems of Anne, Countess of Winchilsea*, p. 10.
6. The whole poem is in *Salt and Bitter and Good*, ed. Cora Kaplan, pp. 65–70, still one of the best introductions to women's poetry; Lonsdale includes an extract, pp. 15–17.
7. *Poems of Anne, Countess of Winchilsea*, pp. 20–3.
8. Wright, *The Life of Isaac Watts*, p. 104.
9. Thomas Rowe's poems are printed at the end of vol. 2 of the *Miscellaneous Works of Mrs Rowe*, from which all extracts are taken. Biographical details are from *The Life of Mrs Rowe* which prefaces the *Miscellaneous Works*, and from Stecher, *Elizabeth Singer Rowe, the Poetess of Frome*.

10. Lonsdale, *Eighteenth-Century Women Poets*, pp. 49–51.

11. Rowe, *Miscellaneous Works*, vol. 2, p. 199.

12. Ibid., p. 28.

13. Maren-Sofie Rostvig's *The Happy Man* is a fascinating exploration of the subject of Horatian retreat in the eighteenth century.

14. Rowe, *Friendship in Death*, Letter 2, pp. 6–8.

Chapter Seven

1. *The Works of Mrs Catharine Cockburn*, vol. 2, p. 119. The letter runs from p. 111–21 and this comment is from the sub-section headed 'Women' which forms a substantial part of the whole.

2. Dedication to *The Platonick Lady*, in *The Plays of Susannah Centlivre*, vol. 2. Biographical details are from Bowyer, *The Celebrated Mrs Centlivre*, unless otherwise indicated.

3. Quoted in Bowyer, p. 7.

4. Collier's *Short View of the Immorality and Profanity of the Restoration Stage* had a mixed impact. It is credited with helping to produce a 'reformed' drama and may in fact have made openings for female dramatists.

5. *The Basset Table*, Act Two, in *The Plays of Susannah Centlivre*, vol. 1, p. 218.

6. Ibid. *The Platonick Lady*, vol. 2, p. 204.

7. Bowyer, pp. 226–9.

8. Ibid., p. 158. Centlivre's plays became staples of the repertoire and went on being performed – often as Royal Command performances – into the later nineteenth century, and were occasionally revived in the twentieth. In the forward to his 1952 biography – still the only full-length study – Bowyer observes, rightly, that she was 'a person of some importance in the literary life of the first quarter of the eighteenth century'.

9. Clark, *Three Augustan Women Playwrights*, has detailed discussion of Pix, Trotter and Manley. Kelley, *Catharine Trotter, an Early Modern Writer in the Vanguard of Feminism*, is a welcome recent study.

10. Performed in 1696, the satire of *The Female Wits; or, The Triumvirate of Poets at Rehearsal* ('Acted some years since') was still current enough to be published in 1704.

11. Henri Misson, 1698. Quoted in Clark, p. 8.

12. Kelley, p. 82.

13. For an assessment of Trotter as a philosopher, see especially Hutton, *The Cambridge Dictionary of Philosophy* (1995), and *The Routledge Encyclopaedia of Philosophy* (1998).

14. Letter from Elizabeth Burnet, quoted in the introduction by Thomas Birch to the *Works of Catharine Cockburn*, pp. xvii–xviii.

15. Trotter's correspondence with Thomas Burnet is in the *Works of Catharine Cockburn* from which all the extracts are taken. He is there named 'George'. Anne Kelley convincingly argues that Birch was mistaken and that the Burnet with whom Trotter (Cockburn) corresponded was named Thomas. See Kelley, p. 4.

16. Ibid., vol. 2, pp. 174–5.

17. Ibid., p. 175.

18. Ibid., pp. 189–90. Trotter's response offers an interesting early example of what was later to become a commonplace of feminist literary criticism: that if women did anything well, the work was assumed not to have been their own.

19. This is implicit in the exchanges between the two in the published correspondence but there are no further details. See vol. 2, pp. 217–22.

20. Ibid., pp. 228–40 for comments about Fenn; pp. 246–54 for letters to Fenn.

21. Ibid., pp. 225–6.

22. Ibid., p. 237.

Chapter Eight

1. Preface to *The Fugitive*, 1705, later reissued as *The Merry Wanderer*, in the *Works of Mary Davys*.

2. Swift, *The Complete Poems*, p. 120.

3. Manley, *The Adventures of Rivella*, p. 47.

4. Ibid., pp. 54–6.

5. Manley's description here of Rivella's state of mind prefigures Charlotte Lennox's *The Female Quixote* (1752) in which the heroine, Arabella, having read nothing but romances, thinks every man she meets is a prince in disguise. Criticism of romance literature on these grounds had become a commonplace by the mid century, but it is also likely that Lennox had read *Rivella*.

6. Morgan, *A Woman of No Character*, pp. 39–48.

7. Manley, *The Adventures of Rivella*, p. 64.

8. Ibid., p. 113.

9. Kelley, *Catharine Trotter*, pp. 19–24.

10. Manley, *New Atalantis*, p. 160.

11. McDowell, *The Women of Grub Street*, p. 243

12. Edmund Curll's preface and key to the fourth edition of *Rivella* (1725) is

printed in full as Appendix A in *The Adventures of Rivella*, ed. Katherine Zelinsky, pp. 115–120.

13. Manley, *The Adventures of Rivella*, p. 84.

14. Ibid., p. 86.

15. Ibid., p. 108.

16. Ibid., pp. 108–12.

17. Manley, *New Atalantis*, p. 40.

18. Barker, *Love Intrigues*, pp. 5–6.

19. Ibid., p. 8.

20. Ibid., p. 76.

21. Ibid., pp. 14–15.

22. Ibid., pp. 29–36 for the story of her violent feelings and recovery.

23. Barker, *A Patch-Work Screen for the Ladies*, pp. 82–4.

24. Ibid., p. 91.

25. Barker, 'To the Reader', *A Patch-Work Screen*, pp. 51–4.

26. Ibid., pp. 122–3.

27. Ibid., pp. 130–2.

28. Ibid., pp. 141–3.

29. King, *Jane Barker, Exile*, pp. 13–15.

30. *Works of Mary Davys*, vol. 1, pp. 162–3.

31. Ibid., vol. 2, pp. 272–3.

32. Ibid., p. 303.

33. *Memoirs of Laetitia Pilkington*, ed. A. C. Elias, vol. 1, p. 85.

34. Ibid., p. 88.

35. Ibid., vol. 2, pp. 159–60.

36. Ibid., p. 48.

37. Thompson, *The 'Scandalous Memoirists'*, p. 40.

38. *Memoirs of Laetitia Pilkington*, vol. 1, pp. 13–14.

39. Ibid. pp. 196–7.

40. Ibid., p. 210.

41. Ibid., pp. 227–8. The rhyming couplet is from Pope's *Essay on Criticism*.

Chapter Nine

1. Fletcher, *Charlotte Smith: A Critical Biography*, p. 126.

2. *Works of Catharine Cockburn*, vol. 2, p. 271.

3. Kelley, *Catharine Trotter*, pp. 213–15.

4. *Works of Catharine Cockburn*, vol. 2, p. 272.

5. Ibid., pp. 290–1.

6. Ibid., p. 278.

7. Ibid., vol. 1, pp. xxxix–xliv.

8. Ibid., vol. 2, pp. 320–1.

9. Ibid., p. 298.

10. Ibid., p. 299.

11. *The Works of Alexander Pope*, vol. 5, 'Containing an Authentic Edition of his Letters', Preface. Thomas's reputation was thoroughly destroyed. It was not until 1983 that the misrepresentation of Thomas, in the *DNB* and elsewhere, was addressed when T. R. Steiner challenged the view of Thomas as 'trollop-general to fashionable London' and pointed out that there wasn't a scrap of reliable eighteenth-century evidence to support it: 'On the contrary, Mrs Thomas's public character appears to have been exemplary: bishops testified to it.' See 'Young Pope in the Correspondence of Henry Cromwell and Elizabeth Thomas ("Curll's Corinna")', *Notes and Queries*, December 1983, pp. 495–7; and 'The Misrepresentation of Elizabeth Thomas ("Curll's Corinna")', ibid. pp. 506–8.

12. Guerinot, *Pamphlet Attacks on Alexander Pope, 1711–1744, A Descriptive Bibliography*, p. 111.

13. *Pylades and Corinna*, vol. 1, pp. 53–6. For the way women poets took up from Pope this model of the 'authentic' poet besieged by second-rate poetasters, see *Pope, Swift and Women Writers*, ed. Mell, especially Caryn Chaden, 'Mentored from the Page: Mary Leapor's Relationship with Alexander Pope'. Leapor's 'The Libyan Hunter, A Fable' was inscribed to Pope and paid homage to his *Epistle to Dr Arbuthnot*. As 'Mira', Leapor represented herself as a true poet withstanding assaults from the self-absorbed and superficial. Her 'Epistle to Artemisia' echoed both the cadence and sentiments of Pope's *Epistle to Dr Arbuthnot*. In place of Pope's Sporus, Leapor offered a weak-minded woman – brainless Cressida, 'blest with idle time' – one of thousands who, in need of something to do, might make up rhymes and waste the time of those for whom poetry was a serious vocation. There is a good selection of Leapor in Lonsdale, *Eighteenth-Century Women Poets*, pp. 194–217.

14. 'The Life of Corinna', *Pylades and Corinna*, vol. 1, pp. vii–xi.

15. Ibid., pp. xii–xiii.

16. *Pylades and Corinna*, vol. 1, pp. 80–1.

17. The poem is in Lonsdale, *Eighteenth-Century Women Poets*, p. 43.

18. 'The Life of Corinna', *Pylades and Corinna*, vol. 1, pp. lvi–lxiii.

19. Ibid., vol. 1, pp. 190–1

20. We have only to think about the Revd Nicholas Carter whose patron, Sir

George Oxenden, was denounced for his libertinism by Lady Mary Wortley Montagu. Revd Carter was quite happy for Sir George to concern himself with Elizabeth Carter's literary future. When 'Miss Carter' contemplated entering into the controversy over Pope's *Essay on Man* by translating Crousaz's *Examination of Mr Pope's Essay on Man*, a literary project that might have brought her into personal contact with Pope had she so desired, Sir George advised against. He warned that any literary woman who associated herself with Pope was liable to suffer for it in print afterwards. She went ahead with the translation but established no correspondence with Pope. See Clarke, *Dr Johnson's Women*, pp. 39–40.

21. Isobel Grundy's *Lady Mary Wortley Montagu, Comet of the Enlightenment* is a wonderfully detailed biography which deals especially well with Lady Mary's relations with Pope. I have made extensive use of it. For the *Verses addressed to the Imitator of Horace*, see pp. 309 and 338–42.

22. Ibid., pp. 342–4.

23. Clare Brant in the introduction to the Everyman edition of the *Letters* gives a finely nuanced account, pp. vii–xxiv.

24. The preface is published as Appendix 3 in (ed) Halsband, *Complete Letters of Lady Mary Wortley Montagu*, vol. 1, pp. 466–8.

25. Mack, *Alexander Pope, a Life*, p. 155.

26. The title of Catherine Gallagher's important book, *Nobody's Story: the Vanishing Acts of Women Writers in the Marketplace, 1670–1820*, captures this perfectly.

Chapter Ten

1. Wollstonecraft, *A Vindication of the Rights of Woman*, p. 83. The comment is in a footnote which instances as heroines Eloisa, Sappho and Catherine Macaulay ('The woman of the greatest abilities, undoubtedly, that this country has ever produced') and adds: 'These, and many more, may be reckoned exceptions; and, are not all heroes, as well as heroines, exceptions to general rules?' Macaulay died before Wollstonecraft finished the *Vindication* and she included a tribute to her in its pages, observing that 'this woman has been suffered to die without sufficient respect being paid to her memory' and trusting posterity to be 'more just'. *Vindication*, p. 113.

2. Seward, letter to Thomas Whalley, 26 February 1792. Seward had wasted no time getting hold of the *Vindication* which had only gone to the printer in January.

3. Godwin, *Memoirs of the Author of 'The Rights of Woman'*, p. 261.

4. When Smith began her writing career, with *Elegiac Sonnets* in 1784, she did not suggest that publishing poetry was in any way lowering.

5. For Hannah More, see the biography by Anne Stott. Given the significance of Catherine Macaulay's work, it is surprising that she has still received relatively little attention. Bridget Hill's biography is the best source for her life, but see also Susan Wiseman, 'Catherine Macaulay: history, republicanism and the public sphere', in Eger *et al.* (eds), *Women, Writing and the Public Sphere*.

6. Preface to *The Plays of Susannah Centlivre*, 1761. The preface was addressed 'To the World' and declared itself in its opening sentence to be by a woman, 'piqued to find that neither the nobility nor commonalty of the year 1722 had spirit enough to erect in Westminster Abbey a monument justly due to the Manes of the never to be forgotten Mrs Centlivre whose works are full of lively incidents, genteel language and humorous descriptions of real life, and deserved to have been recorded by a pen equal to that which celebrated the Life of Pythagorus'. A note informed the reader that the writer of the *Life of Pythagorus* was Madame Dacier. See also Bowyer, *The Celebrated Mrs Centlivre*.

7. Curll reprinted Johnson's preface in his 1737 edition of Rowe's 1696 poems, pp. vi–x. Anna Seward congratulated Scott (now Mrs Taylor) on living in 'the mansion that dear fascinating enthusiastic saint, Mrs Rowe, once inhabited', and told her how 'from twelve years old to twenty, not a year elapsed in which I did not rush to a reperusal of her letters, nor have they yet ceased to thrill my imagination, and to soothe my heart'. Seward, *Letters*, vol. 2, p. 229.

8. Todd, *The Sign of Angellica*, pp. 133, 176–7; Spencer, *The Rise of the Woman Novelist*, pp. 18–22.

9. Spencer, p. 96.

10. Lonsdale, *Eighteenth-Century Women Poets*, pp. 328–30.

11. An excellent brief introduction to Barbauld is in Lucy Newlyn's *Reading, Writing, and Romanticism*, pp. 134–69. See also Rodgers, *Georgian Chronicle*.

12. For a more detailed discussion of this in its wider context, see Taylor, *Mary Wollstonecraft and the Feminist Imagination*, chapter 3, 'For the love of God', pp. 95–142.

13. Lonsdale, *Eighteenth-Century Women Poets*, p. 230.

14. Wollstonecraft, preface to *Mary, A Fiction*. For biographical details about Wollstonecraft, see Todd, *Mary Wollstonecraft, A Revolutionary Life*.

15. *Mary, A Fiction*, pp. 4–5.

16. Ibid., p. 47.

17. The 'ordinary' were of no interest to fiction, nor had they any place in the values of literary life. These values were coming under attack by others besides Wollstonecraft (some of the objections to Frances Burney's *Evelina* concerned her inclusion of low vulgar characters insufficiently despised), but the heroine – and especially the philosophical heroine – was formed according to the old upwardly aspiring model: meant for elevation and doomed to disappointment.

18. Fletcher, *Charlotte Smith*, p. 37, quoting the memoir by Catherine Dorset which was included in Walter Scott's *Lives of the Novelists*, 1821.

19. Ibid., p. 38.

20. Ibid., p. 69.

21. Ibid., pp. 104–5.

22. Wollstonecraft, *Maria, or the Wrongs of Woman*, pp. 197–8.

23. Ibid., p. 73.

24. Ibid., pp. 110–13.

25. See Taylor, *Mary Wollstonecraft and the Feminist Imagination*, pp. 186–92.

26. The letters to Godwin are included in *The Love Letters of Mary Hays*, pp. 227-42.

27. Taylor, *Mary Wollstonecraft*, pp. 36–7.

28. It has often been remarked, for example, that *The Love Letters of Thomas Carlyle and Jane Welsh* contain little that is amorous in the generally accepted meaning of the term. See Clarke, *Ambitious Heights, Writing Friendship, Love. The Jewsbury Sisters, Felicia Hemans and Jane Welsh Carlyle*.

29. Hays, preface to *The Memoirs of Emma Courtney*.

30. *The Memoirs of Emma Courtney*, pp. 46–48, 85–87.

31. Quoted in Taylor, *Mary Wollstonecraft*, p. 39. Taylor's opening chapter, 'The female philosopher', takes up these and related issues of female authorship at the end of the eighteenth century in more detail than is possible here.

32. Klancher, 'Godwin and the Republican Romance', in *Eighteenth Century Literary History*, ed. Brown, p. 68.

33. Ibid., pp. 75–6.

34. Edgeworth, *Letters for Literary Ladies*, 'Letter from a Gentleman to his friend, upon the birth of a daughter', pp. 1–14. This letter puts the misogynist case, and the second letter, 'Answer to the preceding letter', which begins by disavowing any 'taste for Mad. Dacier's ragout' [i.e. her learning], supposedly defends learning in women.

35. Ibid., pp. 8–9.

1. The best account is in the introduction by Richard Holmes to his Penguin Classics edition of the *Short Residence in Sweden* and the *Memoirs*, a volume which, in his words, 'brings together two forgotten classics of English eighteenth-century non-fiction'. Pp. 43–55.
2. Ibid., pp. 223, 232.
3. Polwhele, *The Unsex'd Females*.
4. Introduction to *The Unsex'd Females*.

Bibliography

Alexander, William, *History of Women, from the Earliest Antiquity to the Present Time*, 2 vols, 1781, introduction by Jane Rendall, Thoemmes Press, Bristol, 1994.

Ashmun, Margaret, *The Singing Swan, an Account of Anna Seward and her Acquaintance with Dr Johnson, Boswell & Others of their Time*, Greenwood Press, New York, 1931.

The Cambridge Dictionary of Philosophy, Robert Audi (ed.), CUP, Cambridge, 1995.

Austen, Jane, *Northanger Abbey*, Oxford World's Classics, 1971.

Ballard, George, *Memoirs of British Ladies*, Ruth Perry (ed.), Wayne State University Press, Detroit, MI., 1985.

Ballaster, Rosalind, *Seductive Forms, Women's Amatory Fiction from 1684 to 1740*, Clarendon Press, Oxford, 1992.

Barash, Carol, *English Women's Poetry, 1649–1714, Politics, Community, and Linguistic Authority*, Clarendon Press, Oxford, 1996.

Barker, Jane, *The Galesia Trilogy and Selected Manuscript Poems*, Carol Shiner Wilson (ed.), Oxford University Press, 1997.

Barker-Benfield, G. J., *The Culture of Sensibility: sex and society in eighteenth-century Britain*, University of Chicago Press, 1992.

Battigelli, Anna, *Margaret Cavendish and the Exiles of the Mind*, University Press of Kentucky, 1998.

Behn, Aphra, *The Rover and Other Plays*, Jane Spencer (ed.), Oxford World's Classics, 1995.

Benger, Elizabeth, *The Female Geniad*, London, 1791.

Bowyer, John Wilson, *The Celebrated Mrs Centlivre*, Duke University Press, Durham, NC, 1952.

Brewer, John, *The Pleasures of the Imagination: English Culture in the Eighteenth Century*, HarperCollins, London, 1997.

Brown, Marshall (ed.), *Eighteenth Century Literary History*, Duke University Press, Durham, NC, 1999.

Browne, Alice, *The Eighteenth-Century Feminist Mind*, Harvester, Brighton, 1987.

Burney, Fanny, *Evelina*, Edward A. Bloom (ed.), Oxford University Press, 1982.

Carlyle, Alexander (ed.), *The Love Letters of Thomas Carlyle and Jane Welsh*, Bodley Head, London, 1909.

Cavendish, Margaret, *New Blazing World*, Pickering & Chatto, London, 1992.

Centlivre, Susannah, *The Works of Susannah Centlivre*, 1761.

Clark, Constance, *Three Augustan Women Playwrights* Peter Lang, 1986.

Clarke, Norma, *Ambitious Heights: Writing, Friendship, Love. The Jewsbury Sisters, Felicia Hemans and Jane Welsh Carlyle*, Routledge, London, 1990.

Clarke, Norma, *Dr Johnson's Women*, Hambledon and London, 2000.

Clarke, Norma, 'Soft Passions and Darling Themes: from Elizabeth Singer Rowe (1674–1737) to Elizabeth Carter (1717–1806)', *Women's Writing*, vol. 7, no. 3, 2000.

Cleland, John, *Fanny Hill, or, Memoirs of a Woman of Pleasure*, Penguin Classics, London, 1985.

Clingham, Greg, *Johnson, Writing and Memory*, (Cambridge University Press, 2002)

Cockburn, Catharine, *Works of Catharine Cockburn*, 2 vols, Thomas Birch (ed.), 1752.

The Routledge Encyclopaedia of Philosophy, Edward Craig (ed.), Routledge, London, 1998.

Darton, J. Harvey, *The Life and Times of Mrs Sherwood*, London, 1910.

Davys, Mary, *Works of Mary Davys*, 1725.

D'Monte, Rebecca, and Pohl, Nicole (eds), *Female Communities, 1600–1800: Literary Visions and Cultural Realities*, Macmillan, London, 2000.

Dowling, William, *The Epistolary Moment: the Poetics of the Eighteenth-Century Verse Epistle*, Princeton University Press, Princeton, 1991.

Dryden, John, *A Critical Edition of the Major Works*, Keith Walker (ed.), Oxford Authors, 1987.

Duff, Dolores Diane Clarke, 'Materials toward a Biography of Mary Delariviere Manley', unpublished Phd thesis, University of Indiana, 1965.

Duncombe, John, *The Feminiad*, Augustan Society Reprint, no. 207, Jocelyn Harris (ed.), 1981.

Dunton, John *The Life and Errors of John Dunton Late Citizen of London; Written by Himself*, 2 vols, 1818.

Eagleton, Terry, *The Rape of Clarissa, Writing, Sexuality and Class Struggle in Samuel Richardson*, Blackwell, Oxford, 1982.

Edgeworth, Richard Lovell, *Memoirs*, 2 vols, 1820.

Eger, Elizabeth, 'The Nine Living Muses of Great Britain – Women, Reason and Literary Community in Eighteenth-Century Britain', unpublished Phd thesis, Cambridge University, 1998.

Eger, Elizabeth *et al.* (eds), *Women, Writing and the Public Sphere, 1700–1830*, Cambridge University Press, 2001.

Elias, A. C., *Memoirs of Laetitia Pilkington*, University of Georgia Press, 1997.

Elstob, Elizabeth, *An English-Saxon Homily on the Birthday of St Gregory*, London, 1709.

Elstob, Elizabeth, *The Rudiments of Grammar for the English-Saxon Tongue*, London, 1715.

Eves, Charles, *Matthew Prior, Poet and Diplomatist*, Columbia, NY., 1939.

Ezell, Margaret, *Writing Women's Literary History*, Johns Hopkins University Press, Baltimore, MD, 1993.

Ezell, Margaret, *Social Authorship and the Advent of Print*, Johns Hopkins University Press, 1999.

Favret, Mary, *Romantic Correspondence: Women, Politics, and the Fiction of Letters*, Cambridge University Press, 1993.

Fielding, Henry, *Joseph Andrews*, Everyman paperback, London, 1962.

Fielding, Sarah, *Remarks on Clarissa*, London, 1749.

Finch, Anne, Countess of Winchilsea, *Miscellany Poems on Several Occasions: Written by a Lady*, London, 1713.

Finch, Anne, Countess of Winchilsea, *The Poems of Anne, Countess of Winchilsea*, Myra Reynolds (ed.), University of Chicago Press, 1903.

Firminger, Gabrielle (ed.), *Eliza Haywood, The Female Spectator*, Bristol Classical Press, 1993.

Fletcher, Loraine, *Charlotte Smith: A Critical Biography*, Macmillan, Basingstoke, 1998.

Folger Collective on Early Women Critics: *Women Critics, 1660–1820*, Indiana University Press, 1995.

Fowke, Martha Sansom, *Clio, the Autobiography of Martha Fowke Sansom*

(1689–1736), Phyllis J. Guskin (ed.), University of Delaware Press, Newark, 1997.

Gale, Maggie, and Gardner, Viv (eds), *Women, Theatre and Performance, New Histories, New Historiographies*, Manchester University Press, 2000.

Gallagher, Catherine, *Nobody's Story: the Vanishing Acts of Women Writers in the Marketplace, 1670-1820*, California University Press, 1994.

Gibbon, Edward, *Autobiography*, Meridian Books, New York, 1961.

Godwin, William, *Memoirs of the Author of 'The Rights of Woman'*, Richard Holmes (ed.), Penguin Classics, London, 1987.

Greer, Germaine, *et al.* (eds), *Kissing the Rod: an anthology of seventeenth century women's verse*, Virago, London, 1988.

Grundy, Isobel, *Lady Mary Wortley Montagu, Comet of the Enlightenment*, OUP, Oxford, 1999.

Guerinot, J. V., *Pamphlet Attacks on Alexander Pope, 1711–1744*, Methuen, London, 1969.

Guest, Harriet, *Small Change, Women, Learning, Patriotism, 1750–1810*, University of Chicago Press, 2000.

Hammond, Brean, *Professional Imaginative Writing in England, 1670-1740: 'hackney for bread'*, Clarendon Press, Oxford, 1997.

Hansen, Marlene, 'The Pious Mrs Rowe', *English Studies*, 76 (1995), pp. 34–51.

Hays, Mary, *The Memoirs of Emma Courtney*, Eleanor Ty (ed.), Oxford World's Classics, 1996.

Hays, Mary, *The Love Letters of Mary Hays* (1779–1780), A. F. Wedd (ed.), Methuen, London, 1925.

Hays, Mary, *Female Biography, or Memoirs of illustrious and celebrated women of all ages and countries*, 6 vols, R. Phillips, London, 1803.

Haywood, Eliza, *The Female Spectator*, Gabriel M. Firmanger (ed.), Bristol Classical Press, 1993.

Haywood, Eliza, *Selected Works of Eliza Haywood*, Alex Pettit, Margo Collins, Jerry Beasley, Christine Blouch and Kathryn King (eds), 6 vols, Pickering & Chatto, London, 2001.

Hickes, George, *Sermons on Several Subjects*, London, 1713.

Hill, Bridget, *The Republican Virago: the Life and Times of Catherine Macaulay, Historian*, Clarendon Press, Oxford, 1992.

Hobby, Elaine, *Virtue of Necessity, English Women's Writing 1649–88*, Virago, London, 1988.

Holmes, Richard, *Dr Johnson & Mr Savage*, Flamingo, London, 1994.

Holmes, Richard (ed.), Mary Wollstonecraft and William Godwin, *A Short*

Residence in Sweden and *Memoirs of the Author of the Rights of Woman*, Penguin Classics, London, 1987.

Hopkins, Mary Alden, *Dr Johnson's Lichfield*, Peter Owen, London, 1957.

Hughes, Helen Sard, *The Gentle Hertford, Her Life and Letters*, Macmillan, London, 1940.

Hunter, Revd Joseph (ed.), *The Diary of Ralph Thoresby*, 2 vols, London, 1830.

Johnson, Samuel, *A Critical Edition of the Major Works*, Donald Greene (ed.), Oxford Authors, 1984.

Johnson, Samuel, *Lives of the English Poets*, George Birkbeck Hill (ed.), OUP, Oxford, 1905.

Jones, Vivien (ed.), *Women in the Eighteenth Century: constructions of femininity*, Routledge, London, 1990.

Jones, Vivien (ed.), *Women and Literature in Britain, 1700–1800*, Cambridge University Press, 2000.

Kaplan, Cora (ed.), *Salt and Bitter and Good, Three Centuries of English and American Women Poets*, Paddington Press, 1975.

Kelley, Anne, *Catharine Trotter, an Early Modern Writer in the Vanguard of Feminism*, Ashgate, Hants, 2002.

Kelly, Gary (gen. ed.), *Bluestocking Feminism, Writings of the Bluestocking Circle, 1738-1785*, 6 vols, Pickering & Chatto, London, 1999.

Kelly, Sophia (ed.), *The Life of Mrs Sherwood*, London, 1887.

King, Kathryn, *Jane Barker, Exile: a Literary Career, 1675-1725*, Clarendon Press, Oxford, 2000.

Kramnick, Jonathan Brody, *Making the English Canon, Print-Capitalism and the Cultural Past, 1700-1770*, Cambridge University Press, 1998.

Langford, Paul, *A Polite and Commercial People, England 1727–1783*, OUP, Oxford, 1989.

Lennox, Charlotte, *The Female Quixote*, Margaret Dalziel (ed.), Oxford, 1970.

Lipking, Joanna, 'Fair Originals: Women Poets in Male Commendatory Poems', *Eighteenth Century Life*, 12 May 1988.

Lonsdale, Roger, (ed.), *Eighteenth-Century Women Poets*, OUP, Oxford, 1989.

Mack, Maynard, *Alexander Pope, a Life*, Norton, New York, 1986.

McBurney, William, 'Mrs Mary Davys: Forerunner of Fielding,' PMLA, 74 (1959), pp. 348-55.

Macaulay, Catherine, *History of England*, 8 vols, London, 1763-83.

McDowell, Paula, *The Women of Grub Street, Press, Politics, and Gender in the London Literary Marketplace, 1678–1750*, Clarendon Press, Oxford, 1998.

McEwen, Gilbert D., *The Oracle of the Coffee House. John Dunton's Athenian Mercury*, Huntington Library, CA, 1972.

McLaverty, James, *Pope, Print and Meaning*, OUP, Oxford, 2001.

Manley, Delarivier, *New Atalantis*, Rosalind Ballaster (ed.), Pickering & Chatto, London, 1991.

Manley, Delarivier, *The Adventures of Rivella*, Katherine Zelinsky (ed.), Broadview Press, Ontario, 1999.

Mell, Donald C. (ed.), *Pope, Swift, and Women Writers*, University of Delaware Press, Newark and London, 1996.

Montagu, Lady Mary Wortley, *Complete Letters*, Robert Halsband (ed.), OUP, Oxford, 1965–7.

Montagu, Lady Mary Wortley, *Letters*, Clare Brant (ed.), Everyman's Library, London, 1992.

Montagu, Lady Mary Wortley, *Essays and Poems and Simplicity, A Comedy*, Isobel Grundy and Robert Halsband (eds), Clarendon Press, Oxford.

Montefiore, Jan, *Feminism and Poetry, Language, Experience, Identity in Women's Writing*, Pandora, London, 1987.

Morgan, Fidelis, *A Woman of No Character, an Autobiography of Mrs Manley*, Faber & Faber, London, 1986.

Myers, Robert Manson, *Anna Seward, an Eighteenth Century Handelian*, privately printed, 1947.

Myers, Sylvia Harcstark, *The Bluestocking Circle*, Oxford, 1990.

Newlyn, Lucy, *Reading, Writing, and Romanticism: the Anxiety of Reception*, Oxford University Press, 2000.

Nussbaum, Felicity, *The Brink of All We Hate: English Satires on Women, 1660–1750*, University Press of Kentucky, 1984.

Pearson, Hesketh, *The Swan of Lichfield, being a Selection from the Correspondence of Anna Seward*, Hamish Hamilton, London, 1936.

Pearson, Jacqueline, *Women's Reading in Britain, 1750–1835*, Cambridge University Press, 1999.

Pennington, Montagu (ed.), *A Series of Letters Between Mrs Elizabeth Carter and Miss Catherine Talbot, from the year 1741 to 1770*, London, 1808.

Perry, Ruth, *The Celebrated Mary Astell, an Early English Feminist*, University of Chicago Press, 1986.

Perry, Ruth (ed.) George Ballard, *Memoirs of British Ladies*, Wayne State University Press, Detroit, MI., 1985.

Perry, Ruth, 'George Ballard's Biographies of Learned Ladies', in J. D. Browning (ed.), *Biography in the Eighteenth Century*, Garland Press, New York, 1980.

Philips, Katherine, *Poems by . . . Katherine Philips, the matchless Orinda*, 1667.

Philips, Katherine, *Letters from Orinda to Poliarchus*, London, 1705.

Pohl, Nicole, and Schellenberg, Betty (eds), *Reconsidering the Bluestockings*, Huntington Library, CA, 2003.

Polwhele, Richard, *The Unsex'd Females*, Cadell and Davies, London, 1798, and University of Virginia Library Electronic Text Center.

Pope, Alexander, *A Critical Edition of the Major Works*, Pat Rogers (ed.), Oxford University Press, 1993.

Pope, Alexander, *The Works of Alexander Pope*, Edmund Curll, London, 1737.

Prescott, Sarah, *Women, Authorship and Literary Culture, 1690-1740*, Palgrave Macmillan, Basingstoke, 2003.

Prior, Matthew, *The Literary Works of Matthew Prior*, H. Bunker Wright and Monroe K. Spears (eds), Oxford, OUP, 1971.

Rabb, Melinda Alliker, 'The Manl(e)y Style: Delarivier Manley and Jonathan Swift', in Donald C. Mell (ed.), *Pope, Swift, and Women Writers*, University of Delaware Press, Newark and London, 1996.

Reeve, Clara, *Memoirs of Sir Roger de Clarendon*, 3 vols, London, 1793.

Reeve, Clara, *Original Poems*, 1769.

Reeve, Clara, *The Phoenix; or, The History of Polyarchus and Argenis. Translated from the Latin, by a Lady*, 4 vols, London, 1772.

Reeve, Clara, *The Old English Baron: A Gothic Story*, London, 1778.

Reeve, Clara, *The Progress of Romance*, 1784.

Reeve, Clara, *Bluestocking Feminism, Writings of the Bluestocking Circle, 1738–1785*, vol. 6, *Sarah Scott & Clara Reeve*, (ed.), Pickering & Chatto, London, 1999.

Reynolds, Myra, *The Learned Lady in England, 1650–1750*, Houghton Mifflin, Boston, 1920.

Richardson, Samuel, *Clarissa, or, The History of a Young Lady*, Penguin Classics, London, 1985.

Rodgers, Betsy, *Georgian Chronicle: Mrs Barbauld and her Family*, Methuen, London, 1958.

Rostvig, Maren-Sofie, *The Happy Man: Studies in the Metamorphosis of a Classical Ideal*, 2 vols, Oslo and Oxford, 1955–8.

Rowe, Elizabeth, *Friendship in Death, or, Letters from the Dead to the Living*, London, 1728.

Rowe, Elizabeth, *Devout Exercises of the Heart*, London, 1737.

Rowe, Elizabeth, *Letters Moral and Entertaining*, London, 1729–32.

Rowe, Elizabeth Singer, *Poems of Philomela*, 1696, 1737.

Rowe, Elizabeth Singer, *The Life and Works of Mrs Rowe*, Theophilus Rowe, (ed.), 1739.

Rumbold, Valerie, *Women's Place in Pope's World*, Cambridge University Press, 1989.

Runge, Laura, *Gender and Language in British Literary Criticism, 1660–1790*, Cambridge University Press, 1997.

Scott, Mary, *The Female Advocate: a poem occasioned by reading Mr Duncombe's Feminead*, Joseph Johnson, London, 1774.

Seward, Anna, *Memoirs of the Life of Dr Darwin*, Joseph Johnson, London, 1804.

Seward, Anna, *Letters of Anna Seward, written between the years 1784 and 1807*, 6 vols, Edinburgh, 1811.

Seward, Anna, *Poetical Works of Anna Seward*, 3 vols, Walter Scott (ed.), Edinburgh, 1810.

Seward, Anna, *Bluestocking Feminism, Writings of the Bluestocking Circle, 1738–1785*, vol. 4, *Anna Seward*, Jennifer Kelly (ed.), Pickering & Chatto, London, 1999.

Spence, Joseph, *Anecdotes, Observations and Characters of Books and Men*, London, 1820.

Spencer, Jane, *The Rise of the Woman Novelist, from Aphra Behn to Jane Austen*, Blackwell, OUP, Oxford, 1986.

Spencer, Jane, *Aphra Behn's Afterlife*, Oxford, 2000.

Stanton, Judith Phillips, 'Charlotte Smith's "Literary Business": Income, Patronage, and Indigence', *The Age of Johnson*, vol. 1 (1987) pp. 375–401.

Steiner, T. R., 'Young Pope in the Correspondence of Henry Cromwell and Elizabeth Thomas ("Curll's Corinna")', *Notes and Queries*, December 1983, pp. 495–7.

Steiner, T. R., 'The Misrepresentation of Elizabeth Thomas ("Curll's Corinna")', *Notes and Queries*, December 1983, pp. 506–8.

Stecher, Henry, *Elizabeth Singer Rowe, the Poetess of Frome. A Study in Eighteenth-Century English Pietism*, European University Papers 14, Herbert Lang, Berne, 1973.

Stott, Anne, *Hannah More, the First Victorian*, OUP, Oxford, 2003.

Summit, Jennifer, *Lost Property, the Woman Writer and English Literary History, 1380–1589*, University of Chicago Press, 2000.

Swift, Jonathan, *The Complete Poems*, Pat Rogers (ed.), Penguin Books, London 1983.

Talbot, Catherine, *Selected Works* in *Bluestocking Feminism, Writings of the Bluestocking Circle, 1738–1785*, vol. 3, *Catherine Talbot & Hester Chapone*, Rhoda Zuk (ed.), Pickering & Chatto, London, 1999.

Taylor, Barbara, *Mary Wollstonecraft and the Feminist Imagination*, Cambridge University Press, 2003.

Terry, Richard, *Poetry and the Making of the English Literary Past, 1660–1781*, Oxford University Press, 2001.

Thomas, Claudia, *Alexander Pope and his Eighteenth-Century Women Readers*, Southern Illinois University Press, 1994.

Thomas, Elizabeth, *Miscellaneous Poems on Several Subjects*, London, 1722.

Thomas, Elizabeth, and Gwinnet, Richard, *Pylades and Corinna; or, Memoirs of the Lives, Amours and Writings of Richard Gwinnet Esq ... and Elizabeth Thomas ... To which is prefixed, The Life of Corinna. Written by Herself*, London, 1731–2.

Thompson, Lynda M., *The 'Scandalous Memoirists': Constantia Phillips, Laetitia Pilkington and the shame of 'publick fame'*, Manchester University Press, 2000.

Todd, Janet, *Feminist Literary History*, Blackwell, Oxford, 1988.

Todd, Janet, *The Sign of Angellica, Women, Writing and Fiction 1660–1800*, Virago, London, 1989.

Todd, Janet, *The Secret Life of Aphra Behn*, André Deutsch, London, 1996.

Todd, Janet, *Mary Wollstonecraft, A Revolutionary Life*, Columbia University Press, New York, 2000.

Turner, Cheryl, *Living By the Pen: Women Writers in the Eighteenth Century*, Routledge, London, 1992.

Varney, Andrew, *Eighteenth-Century Writers in their World*, Macmillan, London, 1999.

Warner, William B., *Licensing Entertainment: the Elevation of Novel Reading in Britain, 1684–1750*, University of California Press, 1998.

Whicher, George, *The Life and Romances of Mrs Eliza Haywood*, Columbia University Press, New York, 1915.

Wickham, Revd Hill (ed.), *Journals and Correspondence of Thomas Sedgewick Whalley*, Bentley, 1863.

Winstanley, William, *Lives of the Most Famous English Poets*, London, 1687.

Wiseman, Susan, 'Catherine Macaulay: history, republicanism and the public sphere', in Eger *et al.*, *Women, Writing and the Public Sphere, 1700–1830*, Cambridge University Press, 2001.

Wollstonecraft, Mary, *Mary, a fiction*, and *Maria, or the Wrongs of Woman* Gary Kelly (ed.), Oxford World's Classics, 1976.

Wollstonecraft, Mary, *A Vindication of the Rights of Woman*, Barbara Taylor (ed.), Everyman's Library, London, 1992.

Wollstonecraft, Mary, *A Short Residence in Sweden*, Richard Holmes (ed.), Penguin, London, 1987.

Woolf, Virginia, *A Room of One's Own and Three Guineas*, Michele Barrett (ed.), Penguin, London, 1993.

Woolf, Virginia, *Women & Writing*, Michele Barrett (ed.), The Women's Press, London, 1979.

Woolf, Virginia, *Books and Portraits*, Triad/Grafton Books, London, 1979.

Wright, H. Bunker, 'Matthew Prior and Elizabeth Singer', *Philological Quarterly*, 24.1 (1945), pp. 71–82.

Wright, H. Bunker, and Spears, Monroe K. (eds), *The Literary Works of Matthew Prior*, Oxford, 1971.

Wright, Thomas, *The Life of Isaac Watts*, London, 1914.

Index

Bowyer, Lady 127, 128–9
Brant, Clare 359
The British Novelists (ed. Barbauld) 99, 316
Brome, William 61
Brooke, Frances 102, 309, 311–12
Browne, Daniel Jr 96
Burke, Edmund 50
Burnet, Elizabeth 214–15
Burnet, Bishop Gilbert 214, 215, 264, 289
Burnet, Thomas 215–18, 219–20, 222, 223, 224–5
Burney, Fanny
  and Brooke 311–12
  Evelina 1, 302–3, 327, 361
  influence 7
  Polwhele on 342
  The Witlings 309
The Busie Body (Centlivre) 208, 212
Bute, Lady 298

Caleb Williams (Godwin) 327
'Canticle of Canticles' (Rowe) 151
Carlisle, James 227
Carlyle, Thomas 361
Caroline, queen of Great Britain and Ireland 270–2
Carroll, Susannah *see* Centlivre, Susannah Carroll
Carter, Elizabeth
  and Cockburn 79
  finances 128
  on Jones 127–8
  life 93–4
  Polwhele on 342
  portraits of 9
  presentation of works 84
  and religion 201
  and Rowe 82–3, 84
  and South Sea Bubble 252
  translations by 4–5, 104–5, 300, 359

  Woolf on 7
Carter, Revd Nicholas 358–9
Castlemaine, Lady 228
Cave, Edward 128
Cavendish, Margaret, Duchess of Newcastle 114, 148, 159–60, 310
Centlivre, Joseph 208, 210
Centlivre, Susannah Carroll 203–10
  and Ballard 78
  Duncombe on 8, 88, 89
  influence 259
  life and works 81, 203–6, 207–10
  literary portraits of 207
  memorials 308
  and Pix 212
  on platonic love and gender war 180–1
  reputation 120
  on Whigs and Tories 226
Chambers' *New and General Biographical Dictionary* 329
Chapman, Samuel 96
Chapone, Hester Mulso 9, 84, 93–4, 119
Chapone, Sarah
  and Elstob 58–9, 60, 75
  Polwhele on 342
  reputation 76
  works 30
Chaucer, Geoffrey 106
Chesterfield, Lord 140
Chetwood, William Rufus 96
Christianity, England's conversion to 65–70
Chudleigh, Lady Mary
  poetry 56–7, 58, 292
  and Thomas 125, 130, 281, 283–4, 287–8
Cibber, Colley 91, 92, 263–5
Civic Sermons to the People (Barbauld) 317
Clarissa (Richardson)

on work 53
Seward, Elizabeth Hunter 25, 28, 41, 44, 45
Seward, Sarah 27, 28, 35–7, 41
Seward, Thomas 10, 25, 27–8, 41, 43–4
  'The Female Right to Literature' 26–7, 53–5, 56, 57, 310
Sewell, George 240–1
Seymour, Lady Arabella 75
Shakespeare, Judith, Woolf's myth of 113
Shakespeare, William
  Cockburn on 221
  Montagu's essay on 5, 23, 77
Sharp, Thomas 211
Shelley, Mary 340
Sheridan, Frances 1, 6, 102
Sherwood, Mary Martha 45
Shirly, Dr Thomas 269
A Short View of the Immorality and Profanity of the Restoration Stage (Collier) 205
Sican, Elizabeth 268
Sidney, Sir Philip 185
Singer, Elizabeth *see* Rowe, Elizabeth Singer
Singer, Walter 174, 175
Sins of the Government, Sins of the Nation (Barbauld) 317
Sir Charles Grandison (Richardson) 83, 145
Sir Isaac Newton's Philosophy Explained for the Use of Ladies (Algarotti; trans. Carter) 300
Sir Patient Fancy (Behn) 161–2, 206
Sir Roger de Clarendon (Reeve) 103
slave trade, campaigns against 317
Sloane, Sir Hans 266
Smith, Benjamin 321
Smith, Charlotte
  authorial persona 307

Cowper on 324
and Hays 328
Polwhele on 342
on virtue 269
works 321–3
Sneyd, Honora 27–8, 41–2, 335–6
Society for the Propagation of Christian Knowledge (SPCK) 72
Society of Friendship 155, 244
Somerset, Countess of 195–6
South Sea Bubble 252
Southey, Robert 14, 16–17, 329, 340
Sowden, Revd Benjamin 298
SPCK 72
Spectator 7, 120, 139–40
Spence, Joseph 182
Spencer, Jane 350–1
Spenser, Edmund 106, 185
Spira, Francis 152–3
The Spleen (Finch) 184, 186, 187
Steele, Richard
  and Centlivre 209
  and Haywood 96
  and Manley 125
  and plagiarism 144
  on Sansom 132
  subject matter 139–40
  and Thomas Rowe 193
Steiner, T. R. 358
Sterne, Laurence 334
Stillingfleet, Bishop 214
Stow, John 73
Stuart court in exile 168–9, 170
Suckling, Sir John 291
Surrey, Henry Howard, Earl of 106
Swift, Jonathan
  on Anglo-Saxonists 107
  and Finch 185
  Gulliver's Travels 96
  on Haywood 95